Gramsci, Language, and Translation

Cultural Studies/Pedagogy/Activism

Series Editors

Rachel Riedner, The George Washington University
Randi Kristensen, The George Washington University
Kevin Mahoney, Kutztown University

Advisory Board

Paul Apostolidis, Whitman College;
Byron Hawk, George Mason University;
Susan Jarratt, University of California, Irvine;
Robert McRuer, The George Washington University;
Dan Moshenberg, The George Washington University;
Pegeen Reichert Powell, Columbia College;
Dan Smith, University of South Carolina;
Susan Wells, Temple University

The Lexington Press book series Cultural Studies/Pedagogy/Activism offers books that engage questions in contemporary cultural studies, critical pedagogy, and activism. Books in the series will be of interest to interdisciplinary audiences in cultural studies, feminism, political theory, political economy, rhetoric and composition, postcolonial theory, transnational studies, literature, philosophy, sociology, Latino studies, and many more.

Titles in Series:

Cultural Studies and the Corporate University, by Rachel Riedner and Kevin Mahoney

Democracies to Come: Rhetorical Action, Neoliberalism, and Communities of Resistance, by Rachel Riedner and Kevin Mahoney

Gramsci, Language, and Translation, edited by Peter Ives and Rocco Lacorte

Gramsci, Language, and Translation

Edited by
Peter Ives and Rocco Lacorte

LEXINGTON BOOKS
A division of
ROWMAN & LITTLEFIELD PUBLISHERS, INC.
Lanham • Boulder • New York • Toronto • Plymouth, UK

Published by Lexington Books
A division of Rowman & Littlefield Publishers, Inc.
A wholly owned subsidiary of The Rowman & Littlefield Publishing Group, Inc.
4501 Forbes Boulevard, Suite 200, Lanham, Maryland 20706
http://www.lexingtonbooks.com

Estover Road, Plymouth PL6 7PY, United Kingdom

British Library Cataloguing in Publication Information Available

Library of Congress Cataloging-in-Publication Data
Gramsci, language, and translation / edited by Peter Ives and Rocco Lacorte.
    p. cm.
  Includes bibliographical references and index.
  ISBN 978-0-7391-1859-7 (cloth : alk. paper) — ISBN 978-0-7391-1860-3 (pbk. :
alk. paper) — ISBN 978-0-7391-4785-6 (electronic)
  1. Gramsci, Antonio, 1891–1937—Criticism and interpretation. 2. Gramsci,
Antonio, 1891–1937—Political and social views. 3. Language and languages—
Political aspects. 4. Sociolinguistics. 5. Critical theory. 6. Marxist criticism.
7. Historical materialism. 8. Political science—Philosophy. I. Ives, Peter, 1968–
II. Lacorte, Rocco, 1969–
  P85.G72G73 2010
  335.43092—dc22   2010003948

Printed in the United States of America

We would like to dedicate this volume to the memory of Giorgio Baratta, whose intelligence, humanity, energy and enthusiasm will always be with us.

Contents

Abbreviations of Works by Antonio Gramsci   ix

Acknowledgments   xi

Introduction: Translating Gramsci on Language, Translation
   and Politics   1
   Peter Ives and Rocco Lacorte

Part I: Gramsci's Linguistics and Gramsci's Marxism

1   The Linguistic Roots of Gramsci's Non-Marxism   19
   Franco Lo Piparo

2   Linguistics and Marxism in the Thought of
   Antonio Gramsci   29
   Luigi Rosiello

3   Language from Nature to History: More on Gramsci
   the Linguist   51
   Tullio De Mauro

4   Linguistics and the Political Question of Language   63
   Stefano Gensini

5   Gramsci the Linguist   81
   Utz Maas

6   Gramsci from One Century to Another   101
   Interview with Edoardo Sanguineti by Giorgio Baratta

Contents

Part II: Language, Translation, Politics and Culture

7   Translation and Translatability: Renewal of the
     Marxist Paradigm   107
     Derek Boothman

8   Aunt Alene on Her Bicycle: Antonio Gramsci as Translator
     from German and as Translation Theorist   135
     Lucia Borghese

9   On "Translatability" in Gramsci's *Prison Notebooks*   171
     Fabio Frosini

10   Translations and Metaphors in Gramsci   187
     Maurizio Lichtner

11   Translatability, Language and Freedom in Gramsci's
     Prison Notebooks   213
     Rocco Lacorte

Part III: Politics, Theory and Method

12   Language and Politics in Gramsci   227
     Francisco F. Buey

13   Gramsci's Subversion of the Language of Politics   243
     Anne Showstack Sassoon

14   Some Notes on Gramsci the Linguist   255
     Tullio De Mauro

15   The Lexicon of Gramsci's Philosophy of Praxis   267
     André Tosel

16   Subalternity and Language: Overcoming the Fragmentation
     of Common Sense   289
     Marcus E. Green and Peter Ives

Index   313

About the Contributors   323

Abbreviations of Works by Antonio Gramsci

FSPN   *Further Selections from the Prison Notebooks.* Edited and translated by Derek Boothman. Minneapolis: University of Minnesota Press, 1995.

LP1   *Letters from Prison*, vol. 1. Edited by Frank Rosengarten. Translated by Raymond Rosenthal. New York: Columbia University Press, 1994.

LP2   *Letters from Prison*, vol. 2. Edited by Frank Rosengarten. Translated by Raymond Rosenthal. New York: Columbia University Press, 1994.

PN1   *Prison Notebooks*, vol. 1. Edited by Joseph Buttigieg. Translated by Joseph Buttigieg and Antonio Callari. New York: Columbia University Press, 1992.

PN2   *Prison Notebooks*, vol. 2. Edited and translated by Joseph Buttigieg. New York: Columbia University Press, 1996.

PN3   *Prison Notebooks*, vol. 3. Edited and translated by Joseph Buttigieg. New York: Columbia University Press, 2007.

QC   *Quaderni del carcere.* 4 volumes. Edited by Valentino Gerratana. Turin: Einaudi, 1975.

SCW   *Selections from Cultural Writings.* Edited by David Forgacs and Geoffrey Nowell-Smith. Translated by William Boelhower. Boston: Harvard University Press, 1985.

SPN   *Selections from Prison Notebooks.* Edited and translated by Quintin Hoare and Geoffrey Nowell Smith. New York: International Publishers, 1971.

SPW1   *Selections from Political Writings, 1910–1920.* Edited by Quintin Hoare. Translated by John Matthews. London: Lawrence & Wishart, 1977.

SPW2   *Selections from Political Writings, 1921–1926.* Edited and translated by Quintin Hoare. London: Lawrence & Wishart, 1978.

Acknowledgments

Edited collections are by definition collective projects, as are translations. Fortunately and appropriately, so too is Gramscian scholarship. It is the wide community of Gramscian scholars, in Italy and throughout the world, who made this volume possible. Most immediately, of course, we thank the fifteen contributors not only for allowing us to include their work, but also because that work has inspired both of our own scholarship. Making the issues and debates over Gramsci, language and translation available to a wider audience will hopefully reciprocate the generosity and commitment of this community of intellectuals working with Gramsci's ideas and writings. We would specifically like to thank Joseph Buttigieg for his kind advice and encouragement and for his own efforts in translating Gramsci's prison writings, which are essential to the broader project. Bob Jessop and Daniel Moshenberg also provided valuable suggestions. We would like to thank the Instituto Italiano for Philosophical Studies in Naples and its president, Gerardo Marotta, for their support. Silvio Pons and Fondazione Instituto Gramsci kindly provided images for the cover. Peter Ives would like to acknowledge the support of Adele Perry, Nell Perry and Theo Perry, who always provide the perspective on the smaller and richest moments of life. Rocco Lacorte would like to thank his mother, Sara Lacorte, for her support, and his father, Carmelo Lacorte, whose memory, energy and vitality also live on through this work. And thank you also to Joseph Parry and Lexington Press for their patience, enthusiasm and understanding of the particular requirements, delays and obstacles of such a project.

Introduction

Translating Gramsci on Language, Translation and Politics

Peter Ives and Rocco Lacorte

There is a fascinating silence concerning Antonio Gramsci's writings on language and translation despite his wide ranging and profound influence, particularly in fields and debates in which language features prominently such as poststructuralism and cultural studies. For example, Stuart Hall, Ernesto Laclau, Chantal Mouffe and Gayatri Spivak all draw on Gramsci in different and significant ways and have also been influenced by linguistically informed poststructuralism. Yet neither they, nor the important work that has followed in their paths, ever address Gramsci's own writings on language. It is as if the linguistic roots of poststructuralism, through structualism, block out or obscure Gramsci's studies in linguistics at the University of Turin, his lifelong interest in the "standardization" of the Italian language, and his extensive discussions and practices of language and translation throughout his famous *Prison Notebooks*. This is symptomatic of a more general reluctance within scholarship on Gramsci's political and cultural theory to fully integrate his approach to language and translation. From neo-Gramscian international political economy to social history, literary studies and political theory, Gramsci's wide influence remains constrained due to the neglect of many of his specific arguments especially concerning language and translation. This volume is, in part, an attempt to remedy this both through the act of translation but also by presenting a collection of diverse essays addressing this reluctance to recognize the significance and centrality of Gramsci's writings on language and translation to his entire social, political and cultural theory. After discussing the background and the organization of this volume, we will introduce several themes and examples to illustrate the potential significance of Gramsci's

1

writings on language and translation for an array of debates across many fields and disciplines.

In 1979, Franco Lo Piparo's *Lingua, Intellettuali e Egemonia in Gramsci* [Language, Intellectuals and Hegemony in Gramsci] added the first, thorough, book-length analysis to the small but significant Italian literature concerning Gramsci and language making it incontrovertible that his linguistic studies were central to his well known conception of hegemony and his entire approach to political analysis.[1] While Lo Piparo's book became *the* work cited on Gramsci and language, no part of it has ever been translated. Moreover, outside the Italian literature, there has been very little engagement with Lo Piparo's specific and rather polemical assertion. Lo Piparo went well beyond just revealing how Gramsci's key ideas were foreshadowed by the linguistic milieu he encountered through his linguistics professor, Matteo Bartoli, at the University of Turin, who was engaged in debates with the neo-grammarian school from which Ferdinand de Saussure and structuralism emerged. In an article in 1987, translated for the first time in this volume (chapter 1), Lo Piparo summarized his polemical thesis, "The primitive matrix of [Gramsci's] philosophy should not be searched for in Marx or in Lenin or in any other Marxist, but in the science of language."[2]

By pitting Gramsci's linguistics against, and in exclusion of, Marxist influences, Lo Piparo raises many fundamental questions concerning the role of language in social and political theory that are at the center of pivotal debates about cultural studies, poststructuralism, post-Marxism, discourse analysis and also a whole range of fields in which Gramsci's influential concept of "hegemony" is often utilized. These include multiculturalism, identity politics, feminism, cultural studies, critical education studies and, perhaps most important, postcolonialism. But it is only recently within Italian and German scholarship that the adequate basis for such implications has been provided. This book aims at bringing such research to the wider, English-reading audience, including specialists but also those with more pragmatic and empirical interests in Gramsci's ideas. Part I of this book begins with this 1987 article in which Lo Piparo summarizes the most polemical aspect of his earlier book-length study. We are pleased to be able to include an explanatory note at the beginning written by Lo Piparo and published here for the first time. The rest of part I contains various responses to Lo Piparo, all of which focus on the importance of seeing language as central to Gramsci's entire legacy. Part II contains five chapters dealing with how Gramsci writes about translation and develops it as a key concept clearly connected with his focus on language. Part III includes five chapters that elucidate various implications and methodological considerations stemming from the thesis that language and translation are central motifs of Gramsci's writings.

Most Italian Gramsci scholars regarded Lo Piparo's book primarily as a major contribution to a line of scholarship that had emphasized the importance of Gramsci's concern with language. This theme reaches back at least to Luigi Ambrosoli's brief article from 1960, "Nuovi contributi agli 'Scritti giovanili' di Gramsci" ["New Contributions to the 'Early Writings' of Gramsci"],[3] and earlier—for example, Pier Paolo Pasolini's 1953 article,[4] and others discussed by Tullio De Mauro (see chapter 14 of this volume). Lo Piparo's more ardent contentions about Gramsci's "non-Marxist roots" were taken up by scholars such as Rosiello, De Mauro, Gensini and Passaponti.[5] Chapters 2, 3 and 4 all represent such critiques, challenging Lo Piparo's framing of Gramsci's linguistics against his other influences while welcoming his accomplishment placing Gramsci's considerations of language at the center of his thought. Rosiello directly challenges Lo Piparo's argument that Gramsci derived the "theoretical instruments" to link his concerns with the politics of language with larger questions of culture and society from his studies in linguistics. Rosiello argues that Gramsci looked to the theoretical approach of Marxism's historical materialist method in order to correct for the inadequacies in the linguistics he was studying. De Mauro (chapter 3) notes that in order to understand Gramsci's varied approaches to "linguistic facts" we should see the many experiences of his life as activities of translation, a concept that Gramsci himself developed as the chapters in part II demonstrate. Maurizio Lichtner (chapter 10), while citing Lo Piparo favorably, proceeds immediately to challenge his general position, concluding that Gramsci's "Marxism seems to fully coincide with the historicist view of language."[6]

While there has been some notable scholarship in English engaging with Lo Piparo's general point about the importance of Gramsci's studies in linguistics,[7] none has addressed the specifics of the debate concerning the relationship—antagonistic or complementary—between Gramsci's linguistics and his Marxism (and Leninism). In Germany with Wolfgang Fritz Haug's important comparisons especially with Bertolt Brecht,[8] the work of Frank Jablonka[9] and Utz Maas' contribution (chapter 5), Gramsci's focus on language gained some recognition. However, as De Mauro wrote in 1991, "Everything considered, either one deals with language and linguistics, and therefore not with Gramsci, or one deals with Gramsci the politician and, again, not with Gramsci the linguist" (this volume, chapter 14). This statement has great resonance with the myriad of poststructualist-inspired work claiming to go beyond Gramsci, including Laclau and Mouffe.[10] The contributions to this volume show an alternative; various ways (and the debates they raise) to fully integrate Gramsci's political theory and his linguistic concerns. This collection is far from exhaustive in terms of important current work being carried out in these areas. There is also significant scholarship addressing the significance of language

to Gramsci's legacy that we were unable to include for reasons of space
and coherency. To give a few examples, Stefano Selenu's excellent essay,
"Alcuni aspetti della questione della lingua sarda attraverso la diade storia-grammatica: un'impostazione di tipo gramsciano" ["Some Aspects of
the Sardinian Language Question through the History-Grammar Dyad: A
Gramscian Formulation"], both interprets and uses Gramsci within the
specific context of Sardinian.[11] Alessandro Carlucci has recently stressed
the impact of Gramsci's receptivity to linguistic and cultural diversity to
his overall political theory.[12] Giancarlo Schirru has traced out the more
intimate relations between Gramsci's linguistics and linguistic development in the United States in the twentieth century.[13] Benedetto Fontana's
work does not focus specifically on Gramsci's writings on language, but
by taking Gramsci's ideas back to their Greek roots in questions of rhetoric, *logos*, reason and democracy, he touches on several of the main themes
raised in this volume concerning the importance of Gramsci's interest in
language and reason in relation to democracy.[14] And no other than the
Nobel Prize winner Amartya Sen has traced out the significant influence
of Gramsci and Wittgenstein on the economist Piero Sraffa, a friend and
key correspondent of Gramsci while in prison. As Sen writes, "It is useful to see how Gramsci's [prison] notes relate to the subject matter of
Sraffa's conversations with Wittgenstein, including the part played by
rules and conventions and the reach of what became known as 'ordinary
language philosophy.'" He argues that key parts of what Wittgenstein famously called language games "seem to figure quite prominently in the
Prison Notebooks."[15] And, according to Sen, these ideas are at the core to
Sraffa's contributions in economics. We hope this volume will highlight
and contribute to such diverse considerations of Gramsci's influence and
importance.

Perhaps out of respect for Lo Piparo's painstaking and vital research,
the Italian responses did not take an overly polemical form. But especially
throughout the 1990s as questions of language and communication grew
in importance throughout Italian society due to increasing globalization,
technological change and academic trends, the significance of Gramsci's
approach to language became increasingly apparent. This is one of the
points that Edoardo Sanguineti, a leading Italian intellectual, poet, writer
and translator, makes in an interview which we are delighted to have as
chapter 6. It is in this context that earlier debates on Lo Piparo's work
open onto a richer groundwork that pays much closer attention to his
prison writings as a site of his intellectual development and transformation, synthesizing the multiple sources of "hegemony."[16] Thus, our project
here is to go well beyond presenting Lo Piparo's most contentious thesis
and the Italian retorts. As Sanguineti notes, from the broader perspective,
and especially considering Gramsci's conception of "translation," the nar-

row debate that Lo Piparo kicked off becomes superfluous at the level of the desire for a single answer. The various contributions to this volume highlight crucial work carried out mostly in Italian, but also German and English, focusing on how Gramsci utilized linguistic concepts, concerns over language politics and translation, and how these link and build on connections among the many themes of Gramsci's entire thought. Thus, Francisco F. Buey (chapter 12) explains how "the fight to give meaning to the words of one's own tradition and the fight to name things is probably the first autonomous act of the fight among ideas during the end of the twentieth century," emphasizing Gramsci's importance in helping us increase communication among generations. Similarly, Anne Showstack Sassoon (chapter 13), focusing not on what Gramsci writes about language and translation, but how he uses language, highlights the subversive method by which Gramsci approaches the concepts and positions of others.[17]

Many of the analyses presented here follow a very philological and close textual reading of Gramsci's writings. They utilize the provisional, unfinished nature of Gramsci's notes to delve into the processes of Gramsci's thinking, his way of approaching analysis. Chapters 7, 10 and 15 draw on the specific distinction between Gramsci's passages that, following the Gerratana edition, scholars label as A-texts, B-texts and C-texts. The former are passages that are like first drafts, which Gramsci returned to and rewrote with minor or major revisions in later notebooks. Gerratana labeled these rewritten passages C-texts. B-texts are passages that Gramsci wrote originally and never revised.[18] The method of tracing out the differences in Gramsci's writings as they develop and the general focus on the minutia of Gramsci's writings may initially *seem* arcane and give the impression that the goal is solely the reconstruction of Gramsci's thought for a specialist audience. However, there are two things to keep in mind concerning this method. One, as described above, is the obstinacy that has faced the thesis that language is at the heart of Gramsci's thought, both within Gramscian scholarship and the larger fields in which Gramsci has been very influential. Especially within Gramscian scholarship, this close textual method is quite important in thoroughly establishing the centrality of language and translation to his entire thought. The other more important point to keep in mind is that this method, far from just taking Gramsci's word as gospel, should be seen as the opposite—as a window into *how* Gramsci approached and developed historical analysis rather than just *what* he wrote or thought. As Stuart Hall has famously argued, Gramsci's fragmentary writings are a positive feature that resist the "seamless garment of Orthodoxy."[19] By highlighting that Gramsci was continually revising and, indeed, "translating" his own writings, we can better understand Gramsci's way of thinking, his method.

ENGAGING LANGUAGE IN SOCIAL,
CULTURAL AND POLITICAL THEORY

Our hope is that this collection will speak to a broad range of issues and disciplines by opening up Gramsci's focus on language and translation. In the realm of social theory, for example, comparisons between Gramsci and other theorists for whom language is central—Foucault, Habermas, Chomsky, Bakhtin, Bourdieu—are common, but without an understanding of the role of language in Gramsci's approach, such comparisons remain shallow. Similarly, feminist analyses of production, reproduction and the role of ideology and identity that usefully draw on Gramsci[20] could be expanded and broadened through a thorough engagement with his views of the transformation of "common sense," connections between thought and action, and the intricacies of consensual power relationships all provided by Gramsci's discussions of language.[21] These issues could also be fruitfully related to the rich and varying feminist approaches to language from Julia Kristeva to Dale Spender and Deborah Cameron.[22]

Many of the chapters in this volume show how attention to Gramsci's writings on language and translation enables engagements with major thinkers of the twentieth century concerning language. Gensini (chapter 4) does not mention Gramsci until almost the halfway mark. Rather he starts with a critique of Chomskian linguistics by going back to Ferdinand de Saussure, and a particular reading of Saussure as providing a more dialectical, social framework that does not bracket out spoken language, or *parole*, in the manner that standard interpretations often describe. Gensini mobilizes a host of linguists against Chomsky, including ex-Chomskians, Wittgenstein and William Labov, all of which crucially lead him to Gramsci and the central theme of all the articles in part I of this volume, the relationships between language and society. Summarizing Lo Piparo's contribution and noting its positive value, Gensini proceeds to critique Lo Piparo for "flattening" Gramsci to a "liberal-linguistic" version that does not do justice to the diversity of his life experiences and his contributions to the line of thinking about language (contra Chomsky) *within* social and political relations of speakers from Saussure and Wittgenstein to Labov and the post-Chomskians. One could extend this notion of a flattened Gramsci to the way Laclau and Mouffe interpret and critique him.[23] Gensini's use of Gramsci to illustrate a Marxist approach to language resonates with other Marxist theories of language such the important work of Jean-Jacques Lecercle, Jean Louis Houdebine and Marnie Holborow.[24] However, it is Gramsci's specific perspective that enables Gensini, Buey and other contributors to this volume to raise questions of ideology and culture in a Gramscian way that other Marxist considerations of language never quite reach.

Postcolonial scholars, and especially the subaltern studies group, draw on certain themes within Gramsci's notion of "hegemony" and "subalternity," finding similarities with Gramsci's analysis of Italy but also emphasizing the very different dynamics of colonial and neocolonial power dynamics. However, their important attention to the role of languages in this process has never been connected substantially to Gramsci's own writings on language politics. Gayatri Spivak's influential essay "Can the Subaltern Speak?" grapples with the subaltern studies utilization of Gramsci's conception of the "subaltern" but totally ignores Gramsci's own concentration on this very question of subaltern speech.[25] Ranajit Guha captures succinctly in the very title of his book, *Dominance without Hegemony*, the distinction between European capitalist state dominance and the colonial type of domination. Drawing on some standard interpretations of Gramsci, Guha views hegemony as the construction of consent and persuasion. Because in colonial India, Guha argues, consent was "outweighed" by coercion, "hegemony" is inadequate to describe the dominance at hand. This is why he is constantly on guard against "spurious" notions of hegemony.[26] And yet, as Maas, Borghese, Frosini and Buey suggest, Gramsci's writings on language and translation provide a much richer and intricate analysis of state coercion and persuasion that does not *weigh* the two as if they were separate notions. The analyses of these chapters here could open new spaces to investigate Guha's analysis of the prestige that Gandhi fought for in 1920–1922, with the dynamics of hegemony, and especially the linguistic aspects of colonial power and domination of which Guha and others are so acutely aware. Gramsci's insight into language, politics and translation can also potentially shed light on how this rich historical analysis can be brought to bare on the changing situation in India today.[27]

NATION, LANGUAGE, PEOPLE

Turning to another example of how this volume may intervene in current debates, several scholars have put forth the vague notion that Gramsci was somehow locked by his historical period in a narrow conception of the nation-state, or addressed it in a manner that makes his concerns anachronistic and limited for us today. For instance, Susan Buck-Morss writes, "Whereas Gramsci's discussion concerns hegemony within the nation-state (the process whereby a nation assimilates all of society to itself), political hegemony is described today as extending globally."[28] Due to this perceived shortcoming, Buck-Morss finds it necessary to leave Gramsci in favor of Carl Schmidt and his conception of sovereignty. This notion that Gramsci's hegemony is confined to the nation-state is indeed supported by Richard Bellamy's emphasis on Gramsci as a national thinker who must be

understood within the confines of his historical context.[29] Even those advocating the use of Gramsci's concepts to analyze late twentieth- and twenty-
first-century processes of "globalization," such as Robert Cox and Stephen
Gill, reinforce this notion by describing the "neo-Gramscian" international
political economy (IPE) project as "internationalizing" his concepts, translating them not from the historical context of the 1920s and 1930s to the
1980s and the twenty-first century, but from the domestic or national level
to the international or global level.[30] Their critics frame their opposition
to neo-Gramscian IPE in terms of whether or not Gramsci's concepts from
civil society to hegemony *can be* "internationalized" and made relevant on
a global scale.[31]

Yet, as Adam Morton has astutely argued, this entire debate can only take
place by ignoring Gramsci's insistence that state formation and the nation
be put in the ("international") context of European and world history and
the development of interstate systems. In supporting his argument, it is
not just coincidental that some of Morton's key references are passages in
which Gramsci is discussing language.[32] Many of the chapters here, including Buey, Maas, Borghese and Lacorte's attention to the international or
non-national dimensions of Gramsci's reflections on language and translation, highlight such points. This does not mean Gramsci's relevance to our
contemporary world should not be challenged. Rather it insists that such
challenges cannot hinge upon ignoring the places where we find his considerations of what we now call the "global" level. We hope that this volume
can push such debates in neo-Gramscian IPE onto richer terrain.

TRANSLATION, TRANSLATABILITY

Gramsci's understanding of translation—both as an actual practice and
a metaphor for political and cultural analysis—shares several important
themes with recent perspectives in translation studies which include a particularly linguistically influenced analysis of nationalism. André Lefevere
and Lawrence Venuti, inspired by Jacques Derrida, highlight the active role
translators play in the political choices they make that is tied to the national
identities and relations to "foreignness" of the presumed readers. Thus,
Gramsci's position in the southern question against biologically defined
conceptions of "races" and his critique of the naturalization of the notion
of a "nation" raises similar issues as Venuti's critique of the role of translation in the construction of nationalism.[33] Venuti writes, "Translation can
be described as an act of violence against a nation only because nationalist
thinking tends to be premised on a metaphysical concept of identity as a
homogenous essence, usually given a biological grounding in an ethnic-
ity or race and seen as manifested in a particular language and culture."[34]

While it may be too hasty to draw any tighter connection here, and perhaps there are crucial differences which should not be overlooked, Gramsci's writings on translation and translatability enable engagements between Gramscian scholarship and what Edwin Gentzler has called the "power turn" in translation studies.[35]

Gramsci scholars, especially in Italy, have increasingly come to understand translation as a fundamental concept for Gramsci. Domenico Jervolino has argued that Gramsci's conception of translation is a successful response to the aporias of how Benedetto Croce and Giovanni Gentile deal with translation. Where Croce argues that translation in aesthetic realms (i.e., poetry) is impossible, it is a constant and necessary condition for everything in prose: philosophy, science and technology. Jervolino traces out Gentile's critique of such a stark delimitation of translation, but argues persuasively that Gentile's solution "ends up dissolving more than resolving this problem [of translation]." He argues that in his writings on translation, "Gramsci goes beyond Croce and Gentile and gets close to that rediscovery of hermeneutics realized in the 1920's in the arena of existentialist philosophies."[36] And, as Jervolino emphasizes, it is because Gramsci approaches translation as a practical activity, as the philosophy of praxis, that he rethinks translation in a manner that does not confine it as Croce does, nor expand it in a manner that leads to the spiritual idealism of Gentile.

As the four essays that make up part II of this volume demonstrate, Gramsci is concerned about the actual politics of translation, but also uses the linguistic concept to its full metaphorically analytical power in order to push socio-cultural-political analysis beyond a mere comparative structure acknowledging the profound and historical interactions across time and space, but also intricate relations of how Gramsci conceives of "common sense" and "philosophy" interacting with concrete politics, class relations and power.

Lucia Borghese's article (chapter 8), originally published in 1981, illustrates significant frustration with the state of Gramsci studies when it comes to language and translation.[37] She criticizes Valentino Gerratana, who is usually applauded for his meticulous attention to detail in his editing of the "complete," chronologically ordered, 1975, Italian edition of Gramsci's *Prison Notebooks*. She is also very critical of the publication of an edition that included Gramsci's translations of the Brothers Grimm's fairy tales. While her responses may read as uncompromising and harsh, they are a sign of dissatisfaction caused by the silence concerning the importance of language and translation in Gramsci's work. Her contribution must be taken within its context of the early 1980s, but her rich analysis of Gramsci's own translations of the Brothers Grimm is as fresh and evocative today as it was when originally published. Borghese's general points concerning the role of translation as a metaphor for politics but also a specific practice have, to a significant degree, been accepted, as Frosini, Lichtner and Lacorte's articles here (chapters 9, 10 and 11) demonstrate. It is only near the end of Borghese's chapter that you will discover how this all relates to the metaphor in her title about Gramsci's aunt riding her bicycle.

In 2004, Derek Boothman, a practicing translator, translation professor and meticulous scholar of Gramsci, published a book-length study detailing the many layers of Gramsci's approach to translation and translatability, *Traducibilità e Processi Traduttivi: Un caso, A. Gramsci linguista* [Translatability and the processes of translation: The Case of A. Gramsci, the linguist]. Chapter 7 draws significantly from that longer study, showing, as Frosini and Lacorte do in different ways (see chapters 9 and 11), that Gramsci goes well beyond the base/superstructure debates transforming the key components of those discussions into a richer dynamic of translation and translatability. Due to such detailed examinations like these, there is a growing awareness and acceptance of the notion that translation, as Prestipino writes, is a "cardinal element in Gramsci's conceptual dictionary."[38] This concurs with Borghese's argument in chapter 8 that "translation allows us to prevent contingent truths from being considered absolute and becoming fossilized as ideologies."[39]

These essays not only contribute to understanding of Gramsci's thought, but also provide a crucial platform from which to approach Gramsci's continued (perhaps increased) relevance for the twenty-first century. As Michael Cronin has shown in great detail, translation as a practical activity and a powerful metaphor is at the heart of any thorough understanding of the unwieldy set of phenomena often grouped together under the label of "globalization."[40] Fabio Frosini's contribution (chapter 9) makes a parallel argument that Gramsci's writings on translation get to the root of the philosophical status of Marxism and the integral connection between culture, philosophy and politics. It is also this conception of translation that Frosini and Lacorte use to show how, unlike many other Marxists, Gramsci's notion of politics is not about "unveiling ideology," simply showing that it does not correspond to "reality." Frosini comes quite close to Slavoj Žižek's contention that to view ideology as false consciousness that can be unveiled through recourse to "reality" is to misunderstand that ideology is real—"it consists in overlooking the illusion which is structuring our real, effective relationship to reality."[41] Of course, Gramsci's awareness of this dynamic does not lead to anything like the psychoanalytic perspectives of Žižek, but to more institutional and materialist analyses of these operations.

Translation has also become a key metaphor, often unexamined, in such a wide variety of discussions of "globalization" in all the different ways that term is used. Advocates of cosmopolitanism, multiculturalism, identity politics and global governance are quick to grasp at "translation" as a metaphor but they rarely offer much theoretical underpinning for it.[42] All too often, the concept of translation (not unlike language) is stripped of its political content and used to cast a vaguely positive glow of acceptance, accessibility, and interest in things "other." For Gramsci, in contrast, translation is always political and frequently related to questions of revolution. Just as Gramsci connects his use of linguistic metaphors for political relations to the actual power relationship involved in language use and language policy, so too is he at once aware of the critical and political nature of actual translation at the same time as using translation and translatability to articulate his political, cultural and social theory. In a letter to his wife on September 5, 1932, Gramsci recommends that she become "an increasingly qualified translator" which he goes on to explain would involve much more than just literal translation but would require "a critical knowledge" of the cultures involved.[43] Even in this practical advice, Gramsci concurs with the recent trends in translation studies insisting that it goes well beyond technical matters of transferring meaning between two languages. As the work of Susan Bassnet, André Lefevere, Edwin Gentzler and Michael Cronin has insisted, the economic, political and social contexts in which translation takes place are crucially important and inseparable from the methods and techniques of translation itself, including the minutia of specific word choices in specific translations, be they of literature, movies, product packaging, discussion of so-called global civil society or political treaties and agreements (such as those that form the European Union).

On a more philosophical level, Sanguineti may be alone in this volume arguing that Gramsci was in favor of a "universal language," looking to mathematics as a model, although Derek Boothman makes a nod in that direction balancing it with more historical particularity while Frosini and, to an even greater degree, Lichtner emphasize Gramsci's historicism as drawing away from any such "universalist" dimension. This parallels recent debates in social theory concerning "universalism" and "particularism." Our hope is that the readers of this volume will find in it various ways of rereading Gramsci, of seeing how his writings relate in new and different ways to other debates and discussions and ultimately that this work will help enable in our day what Gramsci was aiming for in his: a furthering of the struggle to understand and transform the exploitation, alienation and domination that characterizes the lives of so many of us today.

THE TEXTS AND TRANSLATION

Translating these texts presented various challenges and decisions as did the questions of how to present the very different citations styles and methods. We have converted all the various citations to a standard endnote Chicago-style system, with full citations for each work the first time it is cited within a chapter, so that the chapters stand on their own in terms of reference material. In the case of Gramsci's works, we have included a list of abbreviations on pages ix–x.

We have tried to use existing English translations for the authors' quotations and citations of Gramsci and all other material. All of the chapters that were originally in Italian use the 1975 critical edition of Gramsci's *Prison Notebooks*, which is taken as the definitive source due to its chronological ordering and comprehensiveness.[44] We have noted the several places where we found it necessary to alter the existing English translations. All other translations are done by the translator of that chapter unless indicated. The English translation of the critical edition of Gramsci's *Prison Notebooks* by Joseph Buttigieg based on Gerratana edition is still under way. Volumes 1–3 have been published, which include Notebooks 1–8, but much material from later notebooks has been translated in various anthologies. We have adopted the now-standard citation method of giving both the translation, if available, but also the notebook number preceded by a Q (for *Quaderno*, "notebook" in Italian) and then a § followed by the section number. This should make it easy to locate the passage across several editions. There is an excellent set of concordance tables compiled by Marcus E. Green available on the International Gramsci Society website: www.internationalgramscisociety.org/resources/concordance_table/.

All of the translators' or editors' additions are in square brackets: [ ]. This includes places where we felt it best to supply the original term—for example, when Gramsci uses the terms *lingua* and *linguaggio*. In Italian, specific languages are referred to with the term *lingua* (and *lingue* in plural), whereas *linguaggio* is more general, denoting the human capability to use language in speech or writing. It would be a mistake to conflate this distinction between the French *langue* and *parole* or its utilization by Saussure, although there is a slight overlap. As Rosiello notes (chapter 2), Gramsci never provides a theoretical distinction between *lingua* and *linguaggio*. Thus, we have included the term in brackets to allow the reader to see for himself or herself how the distinction is utilized both by Gramsci and by the authors.

NOTES

1. Franco Lo Piparo, *Lingua, Intellettuali e Egemonia in Gramsci* (Bari: Laterza, 1979). See chapters 3 and especially 15 of this volume for discussions of the early works on Gramsci and language. Lo Piparo is currently working on an updated and revised edition of this book.

2. See this volume, page 21.

3. Luigi Ambrosoli, "Nuovi contributi agli 'Scritti giovanili' di Gramsci," *Rivista Storica del Socialismo* 3 (1960): 545–50.

4. Pier Paolo Pasoini, "Laboratorio," *Nuovi Argomenti* 1, an abstract of which was published as "Gramsci's Language," in *Approaches to Gramsci*, ed. Anne Showstack Sassoon (London: Writers and Readers, 1982), 180–87.

5. See chapters 2, 3 and 4, respectively, and M. Emilia Passaponti, "Gramsci e le questioni linguistiche," in *Lingua, Linguaggi e Società*, second edition, ed. Sefano Gensini and Massimo Vedovelli (Florence: Tipolitografia F.lli Linari, 1981), 119–28.

6. See chapter 10, page 198.

7. See Niels Helsloot, "Linguistics of All Countries . . . ! On Gramsci's Premise of Coherence," *Journal of Pragmatics* 13 (1989): 547–66; Leonardo Salamini, *The Sociology of Political Praxis: An Introduction to Gramsci's Theory* (London: Routledge, 1981), esp. 181–96; and Fabiana Woodfin, "Lost in Translation: The Distortion of *Egemonia*," in *Marxism and Cultural Studies*, ed. Lee Artz, Steve Macek and Dana L. Cloud (New York: Peter Lang: 2006), 133–56. Nevertheless, none of these grapple with what is at stake in Lo Piparo's position as noted above. For example, Fabiana Woodfin seems to adopt Lo Piparo's emphasis on the roots of Gramsci's "hegemony" being "primarily" in historical linguistics, but she then emphasizes the Marxist context in which Gramsci utilized it precisely to critique Stuart Hall. Thus, ironically, she oversteps Lo Piparo's separation of Gramsci's "hegemony" from its Marxist roots.

8. Wolfgang Fritz Haug, *Philosophieren mit Brecht und Gramsci* (Hamburg: Argument Verlag, 1996). See also Wolfgang Fritz Haug, "Philosophizing with Marx, Gramsci, and Brecht," *Boundary 2*, 34, 3 (Fall 2007): 143–60.

9. Frank Jablonka, "War Gramsci ein Poststrukturalist 'avant la lettre'? Zum *linguistic turn* bei Gramsci," in *Gramsci-Perspektiven*, ed. Uwe Hirschfeld (Berlin: Argument-Verlag, 1998), 23–36.

10. See, for example, Peter Ives, "Language, Agency and Hegemony: A Gramscian Response to Post-Marxism," *Critical Review of International Social and Political Philosophy* 8, 4 (2005): 455–68. There I argue that Laclau and Mouffe's seminal work, *Hegemony and Socialist Strategy*, requires that they ignore Gramsci's writings on language in order to narrate a post-Marxist trajectory from an economically confined Marxism to a linguistically influenced post-Marxism.

11. Stefano Selenu, "Alcuni aspetti della questione della lingua sarda attraverso la diade storia-grammatica: un'impostazione di tipo gramsciano," *Antologia Premio Gramsci* IX (January 2005): 223–358.

12. Alessandro Carlucci, "The Political Implications of Antonio Gramsci's Journey through Languages, Language Issues and Linguistic Disciplines," *Journal of Romance Studies* 9, 2 (Summer 2009): 27–46.

13. Giancarlo Schirru, "La Diffusione del Pensiero di Gramsci nella Linguistica Americana," paper presented at the conference "Le Culture e il Mondo," organized by the Fondazione Istituto Gramsci and the International Gramsci Society, Rome, April 27–28, 2007.

14. See especially his article "The Democratic Philosopher: Rhetoric as Hegemony in Gramsci," *Italian Culture* 23 (2005): 97–123.

15. Amartya Sen, "Sraffa, Wittgenstein, and Gramsci," *Journal of Economic Literature* 41 (December 2003): 1240–55, here 1244–45.

16. For a succinct summary of the other sources of hegemony, see Derek Booth-man, "The Sources for Gramsci's Concept of Hegemony," *Rethinking Marxism* 20, 2 (April 2008): 201–16.

17. An interesting comparison and contrast could be made between Sassoon's discussion of Gramsci's "subversive use of language" and the "subversive" transla-tion strategy of Suzanne Jill Levine that Edwin Gentzler uses to highlight different ways in which poststructuralism has been used in translation studies, to be dis-cussed below. See Edwin Gentzler, "Translation, Poststructuralism and Power," in *Translation and Power*, ed. Maria Tymoczko and Edwin Gentzler (Amherst: Univer-sity of Massachusetts Press, 2002), 203–6.

18. For a full description, see Joseph Buttigieg, "Preface" to Antonio Gramsci, *Prison Notebooks*, vol. 1 (New York: Columbia University Press, 1992), xiv.

19. Stuart Hall, "Introductory Essay" in Roger Simon, *Gramsci's Political Thought: An Introduction*, revised edition (London: Lawrence & Wishart, 1991), 8. See also Buttigieg, 42–64, on the connections between philological approaches to Gramsci's writings and Gramsci's own method and the fragmentary nature of his writings.

20. See for example, Anne Showstack Sassoon, ed., *Women and the State* (Bos-ton: Unwin Hyman, 1987); Michele Barrett, *Women's Oppression Today: The Marx-ist/Feminist Encounter*, revised edition (London: Verso, 1988); Gundula Ludwig, "Governing Gender: The Integral State and Gendered Subjection," in *Gramsci and Global Politics*, ed. Mark McNally and John Schwartzmentel (London: Routledge, 2009), 93–106.

21. For example, see Renate Holub, *Antonio Gramsci: Beyond Marxism and Post-modernism* (London: Routledge, 1992), for feminist considerations of Gramsci that show extensive awareness of Gramsci's writings and the Italian literature.

22. For example, see Julia Kristeva, *Language: The Unknown*, trans. Anne M. Menke (New York: Columbia University Press, 1989); Dale Spender, *Man Made Lan-guage* (London: Routledge, 1980); and Deborah Cameron, *Feminism and Linguistic Theory* (London: Macmillan, 1992).

23. See note 10.

24. Jean-Jacques Lecercle, *A Marxist Philosophy of Language*, trans. Gregory Elliott (Leiden: Brill, 2006); Jean Louis Houdebine, *Langage et Marxisme* (Paris: Klincks-ieck, 1977); and Marnie Holborow, *The Politics of English: A Marxist View of Language* (London: Sage, 1999).

25. Gayatri Chakrovorty Spivak, "Can the Subaltern Speak?" *Marxism and the In-terpretation of Culture*, ed. Cary Nelson and Lawrence Grossberg (Urbana: University of Illinois Press, 1988), 271–313. For a critical discussion of Spivak and Ranajit's different uses of Gramsci, see Marcus Green, "Gramsci Cannot Speak: Presentation and Interpretation of Gramsci's Concept of the Subaltern," *Rethinking Marxism* 14, 3 (Fall 2002): 1–24; and chapter 16 of this volume.

26. Ranajit Guha, *Dominance without Hegemony* (Cambridge, Mass.: Harvard University Press, 1997).

27. See, for example, Selma Sonntag, *The Local Politics of Global English* (Lanham, Md.: Lexington, 2003), 59–78. Another example of an analysis of colonialism that uses Gramsci's writings on language explicitly is Epifanio San Juan Jr., "Sneaking into the Philippines, Along the Rivers of Babylon: An Intervention into the Lan-guage Question," *Kolum Kritika* 11 (August 2008): 78–88.

28. Susan Buck-Morss, "Sovereign Right and the Global Left," *Rethinking Marxism* 19, 4 (October 2007): 440.

29. Richard Bellamy, "Gramsci, Croce, and the Italian Historical Tradition," *History of Political Thought* 11, 2 (1990): 313–17; and Richard Bellamy and Darrow Schecter, *Gramsci and the Italian State* (Manchester: Manchester University Press, 1993). See Adam Morton's discussion of this approach as "austere historicism" in *Unravelling Gramsci* (London: Pluto, 2007), 24–29.

30. Robert Cox, "Gramsci, Hegemony and International Relations," *Millenium* 12, 2 (1983): 162–75; and Stephen Gill, ed., *Gramsci, Historical Materialism and International Relations* (Cambridge: Cambridge University Press, 1993).

31. See Randall Germain and Michael Kenny, "Engaging Gramsci: International Relations Theory and the New Gramscians," *Review of International Studies* 24, 1 (1998): 3–21.

32. Morton, *Unravelling Gramsci*, 56–59.

33. Antonio Gramsci, "Some Aspects of the Southern Question," in Antonio Gramsci, *Selections from Political Writings 1921–1926*, ed. and trans. Quintin Hoare (Minneapolis: University of Minnesota Press, 1978), 441–62.

34. Lawrence Venuti, "Local Contingencies: Translation and National Identity," in *Nation, Language and the Ethics of Translation*, ed. Sandra Bermann and Michael Wood (Princeton, N.J.: Princeton University Press, 2005), 177–202, 177.

35. Edwin Gentzler, "Translation, Poststructuralism and Power," in *Translation and Power*, ed. Maria Tymoczko and Edwin Gentzler (Amherst: University of Massachusetts Press, 2002), 195–218. See also Barbara Godard, "Writing Between Cultures" and "Relational Logics: Of Linguistic and Other Transactions in the Americas," in *Canadian Literature at the Crossroads of Language and Culture*, ed. Smaro Kamboureli (Edmonton: NeWest Press, 2008), 201–34 and 315–58.

36. Domenico Jervolino, "Croce, Gentile e Gramsci sulla traduzione," in *Croce Filosofo*, two volumes, ed. Giuseppe Cacciatore, Girolamo Cotroneo and Renata Viti Cavaliere (Soveria Mannelli: Rubbettino Editore, 2003), 431–41, here 36 and 39.

37. Borghese has follwed this work up in various articles—most recently, Lucia Borghese, "Gramsci, Goethe, Grimm o L'Archeologia dei Desideri," *Belfagor* 63 (2008): 121–47.

38. Giuseppe Prestipino, *Tradire Gramsci* (Milan: Teti, 2000), 6.

39. See chapter 8, page 135.

40. Michael Cronin, *Translation and Globalization* (New York: Routledge, 2003).

41. Slavoj Žižek, *The Sublime Object of Ideology* (London: Verso 1989), 33.

42. For a nice overview, see Michael Cronin, *Translation and Identity* (London: Routledge, 2006), 6–42. See also Peter Ives, "Cosmopolitanism and Global English: Language Politics in Globalisation Debates," *Political Studies* 58, 3 (2010): 516–35.

43. Antonio Gramsci, *Letters from Prison*, vol. 2, ed. Frank Rosengarten, trans. Raymond Rosenthal (New York: Columbia University Press, 1994), 207.

44. Antonio Gramsci, *Quaderno del Carcere*, four volumes, ed. and trans. Valentino Gerratana (Turin: Einaudi, 1975).

I

GRAMSCI'S LINGUISTICS AND GRAMSCI'S MARXISM

1

The Linguistic Roots of Gramsci's Non-Marxism

Franco Lo Piparo *

PREFACE AND GUIDE TO READING
"THE LINGUISTIC ROOTS OF GRAMSCI'S NON-MARXISM" **

In my book, *Lingua, Intellettuali, Egemonia in Gramsci* [Language, Intellectuals, Hegemony in Gramsci],[1] I provided broad documentation of the pervasive reflection on language [*linguaggio*] in Gramsci's work. In that book, I intentionally did not deal with the political implications of my research. Yet the following fundamental question is unavoidable: are the hidden sources of the cultural originality of Italian communism in the second half of the twentieth century to be found in the linguistic imprint that the young Gramsci received at the University of Turin in the school of Matteo Bartoli? The sociology of culture connected to the formation of the national states is not debated within Marxism during the 1920s and 1930s. But it does constitute a central subject in the Italian debates around the question of the [Italian] language [*lingua*]. Graziadio Isaia Ascoli's *Proemio* [Preface] to the *Archivio Glottologico Italiano* [Italian Glottological Archive] (1873), which both the young Gramsci and the Gramsci secluded in the fascist prison cite continuously, looks like a delightfully Gramscian essay if read with hindsight. Unlike his other works, in this essay inspired by a particular interpretation of liberalism, Ascoli grasped the theoretical knots starting from the question of language [*lingua*] which Gramsci's reflections never abandoned: the nexus

---

* Translation of "Studio del linguaggio e teoria gramsciana," *Critica Marxista* 2/3 (1987): 167–75. See preface for explanation about the title change.
** Translated by Rocco Lacorte with assistance by Peter Ives. This is a previously unpublished note that Franco Lo Piparo asked us to use to introduce his previously published essay.

between the organization of culture and the formation of the state; the civil role of intellectuals; and languages as places from which one can read their speakers' social relationships.

The essay published here was meant to be an attempt to open a debate on these themes. Written in 1987, just two years before the Berlin Wall fell, times were ripe for a serene reflection on the non-Marxist origin of Gramsci's thought. The article was sent to *Critica Marxista*, the periodical of the Italian Communist Party in those days,[2] in order to facilitate the start of a debate on these matters. The title originally proposed was "The Linguistic Roots of Gramsci's Non-Marxism," but the editors changed it to "The Study of Language and Gramscian Theory" [Studio del Linguaggio e Teoria Gramsciana].

The article published in *Critica Marxista* [reproduced below in translation] ended with a short paragraph entitled *A Doubt and a Question*. I am not going to include it in the body of the article printed here because it only has archeological and not current value. Yet I would like to quote it in this brief note. I am also going to include a clause, emphasized with italics, which was incomprehensibly censored by the editors of *Critica Marxista*.

A Doubt and a Question

In a historical period in which the question on orthodoxy (whatever it be) is pressing and urgent within the ideological debates of the PCI [the Italian Communist Party]—and the entire Left is preoccupied with searching for new cultural identities—is it possible *in the ideological periodical of the PCI*[3] to raise a doubt in the form of a question without being excessively scandalous? What if the Marxism of Gramsci (above all the Gramsci of the *Notebooks*) were only a very superficial exterior crust? Even if the PCI should be the first to respond to this question, it is obviously not the only one: Gramsci's heritage, as Togliatti loved to say, belongs to Italian culture as a whole.

THE LINGUISTIC ROOTS OF GRAMSCI'S NON-MARXISM

The Silences in the Literature on Gramsci

After more than half a century of debate about Gramsci and almost thirty years after the *Prison Notebooks*' critical edition, a philological question has still to be answered by Gramsci scholars—mainly from those scholars who study Gramsci as an original theorist of politics and intellectual work. The question is simple: a multiplicity of convergent indications (autobiographical testimonies, annotations of contemporaries, organization of the arguments in the *Prison Notebooks*, etc.) compels the formulation of the hypothesis that Gramsci had fully developed his theory of intellectuals, civil society, etc., while he was professionally interested in language [*linguaggio*]. The primitive matrix of his philosophy should not be searched for in Marx or in Lenin or in any other Marxist, but in the science of language [*linguaggio*]. We will cite only three among the many possible texts. Two of them are very well known and habitually cited but, notwithstanding their notoriety, the scholars of Gramsci's political thought seem to have difficulty transforming the unequivocal information contained in them into organic parts of their interpretations.

A

Let's begin with the very famous letter to Tania [Schucht] of November 17, 1930. We shall quote almost all of it because it is this entire context that throws into relief the autobiographical information unequivocally furnished by Gramsci which the Gramscian literature leaves absent:

> I've focused on three or four principle subjects, one of them being the cosmopolitan role played by Italian intellectuals until the eighteenth century, which in turn is split into several sections: the Renaissance and Machiavelli, etc. If I had the possibility of consulting the necessary material I believe that there is a really interesting book to be written that does not yet exist; . . . Meanwhile I write notes, also because reading the relatively little that I have brings back to mind my old readings of the past. Besides, this is not a completely new thing for me, because ten years ago I wrote an essay on the [Italian] language [*lingua*] question according to Manzoni, and that required a certain research into the organization of Italian culture, from the time when the written language (the so-called medieval Latin, that is, that Latin written from 400 AD until 1300) became completely detached from the language spoken by the people, which, Roman centralization having come to an end, was fragmented into infinite dialects. This medieval Latin was followed by vulgar languages, which were again submerged by humanistic Latin, giving rise to an erudite language, vulgar in lexicon but not in its phonology and even less in its syntax, which was reproduced from Latin: thus there continued to exist a double language, the popular or dialectical one and the erudite, that is, the language of intellectuals and the cultivated classes. Manzoni himself, in rewriting *The Betrothed* and in his treatises on the Italian language, actually only took into account a single aspect of the language, the lexicon, and not the syntax that is in fact the essential part of any language, so much so that English, though it contains more than 60 percent of Latin or neo-Latin words, is a Germanic language, whereas Roumanian [*sic*], though it contains more than 60 percent of [*sic*] Slavic words, is a neo-Latin language. As you see, this subject interests me so much that I've let it carry me away.[4]

This text is important, not only because it explicitly declares that his first systematic reflections on the "organization of Italian culture" arose while

Gramsci was writing "an essay on the question of the language in Manzoni," but also for the way in which the topic is being developed. The
theme is "the cosmopolitan function that the Italian intellectuals have had
until the end of the eighteenth century," but in the whole letter Gramsci is
dealing with only one aspect of the problem, the language, so that he "let it
carry me away." He does not say a word about the other aspects.

B

The next text is quoted even more often and is more famous than the
first. On March 19, 1927, Gramsci tells Tania he is "tormented . . . by this
idea: that I should do something *für ewig.*" The subjects he aims at to study
are four:

> (1) a study on the formation of the public spirit in Italy during the past cen-
> tury; in other words a study of Italian intellectuals, their origins, their group-
> ings in accordance with cultural currents, and their various ways of thinking.
> . . . (2) A study of comparative linguistics! Nothing less; but what could be
> more "disinterested" and *für ewig* than this? It would of course be a matter
> of dealing only with the methodological and purely theoretical part of the
> subject, which has never been dealt with completely and systematically from
> the new point of view of the neolinguists as opposed to the neogrammar-
> ians (this letter of mine, dear Tania, will horrify you!) A major intellectual
> "remorse" of my life is the deep sorrow that I caused my good professor
> Bartoli at the University of Turin, who was convinced that I was the archan-
> gel destined to put to definitive rout [*profligare*] the neogrammarians, since
> he, belonging to the same generation and bound by a million academic ties
> to this mob of most infamous men, did not wish, in his pronouncements,
> to go beyond a certain limit set by convention and by deference to the old
> funerary monuments of erudition. (3) A study of Pirandello's theatre and
> of the transformation of Italian theatrical taste that Pirandello represented
> and helped form. . . . (4) An essay on the serial novel and popular taste in
> literature. . . . *What do you say about all of this? At bottom, if you examine them
> thoroughly, there is a certain homogeneity among these four subjects:* the creative
> spirit of the people in its diverse stages and degrees of development is in
> equal measure at their base.[5]

Here too linguistics, even viewed from its strictly methodological aspects, is
fundamental, and is judged to be a subject of study that has affinities with
topics concerning intellectuals, Pirandello and the serial novel, "at bottom,
if you examine them thoroughly, there is a certain homogeneity among
these four subjects." I tried to provide an explanation for this proclaimed
homogeneity in *Lingua, Intellettuali, Egemonia in Gramsci.* Perhaps other
explanations are possible; but those who study Gramsci as a theoretician of
intellectuals have yet to provide one.

C

On November 19, 1933, Gramsci was transferred from the prison of Turi to the infirmary of the prison of Civitavecchia and, on December 7, to a clinic in Formia. From this moment onwards, the censors decreased their control and the *Notebooks* do not bear the preventative stamp of the prison authorities anymore.[6] On October 25 of the subsequent year, Gramsci obtained conditional freedom. In these conditions of semi-freedom he compiles what will be his last Notebook, dated 1935. He devotes it not to immediately political subjects, but to the concept of grammar.

Language [*linguaggio*] continues to be at the center of his intellectual activity until the end of his life. Is this a sign that the key to his political philosophy is to be found in language? This question demands an answer, whatever the answer, from the scholars of Gramsci's political theory. However, what remains is the fact that the founder of the Italian Communist Party,[7] and the theoretician of the cultural apparatuses and of the concept of hegemony, debuts intellectually as a linguist ("pupil of the good professor Bartoli," as a university student, and still called, in the *Avanti!* of January 26 and February 7, 1918, "emeritus scholar of glottology" and "young comrade, philosopher and glottologist") and concludes his theoretical activity as author of a short but dense tract on language [*lingua*]. This biographical information is waiting to become part of the reconstructions and theoretical treatises on Gramsci.

These and other philological indications (which I dealt with in my book quoted above) lead us to deem Gramsci's linguistics to be of interest not only to linguists and philosophers of language [*linguaggio*], but also to those political theorists who are, or have been, inspired by Gramsci's writings and those who are interested in giving an account of the non-Leninist, maybe not even Marxist, specificity of Gramsci's philosophical proposal.

Gramsci is not like one of the many Marxist philosophers from whom one can deduce a philosophy of language along with any number of other theories. Gramsci's case is radically different. His reflections on language [*linguaggio*] and his linguistic culture were the generative mechanism of his originality and what renders him radically different from other Marxists. This, obviously, does not mean that other experiences have not converged in the formation of his thought, Soviet Marxism included. The question at stake is different. Did those experiences have the original theoretical results that they did because they were grafted on to a branch predisposed to grow towards the theory of intellectuals and of hegemony? Or would their author's genius have caused them to reach the same theoretical results, regardless? The question could be reformulated in another way. If the theory of intellectuals and hegemony had Leninist or generically Soviet or Marxist origins, why did Togliatti not produce anything similar, considering that he went through a longer and more absorbent immersion in Soviet and non-Soviet Marxism? Is the recourse to Gramsci's greater geniality and inventiveness a satisfying explanation?

The People-Nation[8] and Language [*Lingua*]

In the *Notebooks* one can find several books: on the theory and history of intellectuals, on the "Party-Prince" as agent of transformation, on the Risorgimento, on folklore, on the philosophy of Benedetto Croce, on American industrial democracy, on the sociology and history of literature, on language [*lingua*] and maybe more. Togliatti divided them, and probably no one could do better. Gramsci argued on various occasions that the subjects he treated were deeply homogeneous. Scholars have often forgotten this indication of Gramsci. Each of the scholars has singled out their own Gramsci: a Gramsci fitting with their own discipline, without worrying excessively about the coherence between their Gramsci and the Gramsci singled out by their colleagues.

What ties the more than two thousand pages of the *Notebooks* together? One and only one question: the theoretical and historical study of the conditions "that enable action on a dispersed and shattered people to arouse and organise its collective will,"[9] in particular that collective will which Gramsci calls the people-nation. The socialist revolution is only one of the ways (although certainly for Gramsci the most important) in which the problem of the formation of cohesive national-popular organisms may present themselves in history. Starting from the notion of a people-nation, all the theoretical concepts and the historical analyses can be easily related back to an ordered and coherent system: hegemony, civil society, "Party-Prince," folklore, Italian intellectuals' cosmopolitanism, city-country, the failure of the Risorgimento, Jacobinism, intellectual and moral reform, grammar and so on.

With respect to the formation of unitary and cohesive national-popular wills, language [*linguaggio*] works simultaneously as: (A) a microcosm and laboratory in which one can find mechanisms and procedures that operate in a more complex way on the macro-social scale; and (B) an indispensable constitutive factor of complex collective wills such as the people-nations. Let's now examine these two points separately.

A

Gramsci studied the mechanisms that preside over the formation of a language [*lingua*] common to an entire people-nation since the very first years of his university apprenticeship in Matteo Bartoli's approach to glottology. It was in this context of specialized studies that he precociously came in touch with the nineteenth century's most penetrating analysis of the role of the intellectuals and of the cultural apparatuses with respect to the formation of a national language: the *Proemio* [Preface] that Graziadio Isaia Ascoli wrote for the first issue of the *Archivio Glottologico Italiano* [Italian Glottological Archive] (1873). Here the lack of popularity of the Italian language was related both to the "scarce density of culture" or the "concentration of knowledge in a handful of persons" in modern Italy, and to the cosmopolitanism of the Italian intellectuals. Ascoli's essay is continually absent in the library of Gramsci's scholars, yet its affinity with many of Gramsci's analyses is simply surprising.

The study of language [*linguaggio*] compels the young Gramsci to go back to the history and sociology of intellectuals because of an even more theoretical aspect. In the years in which he was preparing for his career as a glottologist, some European linguists (Gilliéron, Meillet, "the good professor Bartoli") were attempting to explain the diffusion of a language [*lingua*] beyond its original geographic and social confines by recourse to *geographic centers and social groups capable of irradiating cultural prestige*. A language is diffused neither by the force of armies nor by state coercion—this is the sociocultural thesis of the Italian neo-linguistics and of French sociological school—but because the ones who speak a different language spontaneously consent to the speech of the groups with cultural prestige. We cite here only one article that Meillet published in 1911 in the magazine *Scientia*:

> It is inevitable that among the actual ways of speaking some are used by more powerful groups or groups with superior civilization, which for some reason are given a greater prestige. Such ways of speaking function as models for the other ones. With respect to relationships among groups, if it is not possible to speak exactly the same way, the goal is to approximate the models. This is the beginning of the evolution through which the creation of a common language gets its start on the basis of one of the group's way of speaking and through which strictly local linguistic innovations are partly or entirely eliminated.[10]

I have tried to document the similarities between the concept of hegemony and the linguistic concept of prestige. In the years in which the term "hegemony" either does not emerge or emerges according to the banal meaning of "supremacy," Gramsci refers to the "spiritual government that knows how to produce spontaneous consensus" by using the term learnt from Matteo Bartoli's school: "irradiation of prestige." I will cite one suitable example from an article that appeared on December 27, 1919:

> With its revolutionary programme, the Socialist Party pulls out from under the bourgeois State apparatus its democratic basis in the consent of the governed. . . . And so that the Party comes to be identified with the historical consciousness of the mass of the people, and it governs their spontaneous, irresistible

movement. This is an incorporeal government that is transmitted through millions and millions of spiritual links; it is a irradiation of prestige, that can become a truly effective government only in climactic moments. . . . The Party . . . exercises the most effective of the dictatorships, a dictatorship based on prestige, on the conscious and spontaneous acceptance of authority that workers see as indispensable if their mission is to be accomplished.[11]

If it is true that the concept of hegemony was first forged in the theoretical laboratory of linguistics, the role of Leninism and/or Marxism within Gramsci's philosophy will have to be radically rediscussed.

B

A collective will is held together also by a common language. Gramsci insists on this aspect of the problem with obsessive frequency. We quote only a long methodological note from Notebook 10 and a quick annotation from Notebook 13:

> Language, languages and common sense. If philosophy is conceived as a conception of the world—and philosophical activity is not to be conceived [solely] as the "individual" elaboration of systematically coherent concepts, but also and above all as a cultural battle to transform the popular "mentality" and to diffuse the philosophical innovations which will demonstrate themselves to be "historically true" to the extent that they become concretely—i.e. historically and socially universal—then the question of language [*linguaggio*] and languages [*lingua*] must be "technically" put at the forefront of our enquiry. . . . It seems that one can say that "language" [*linguaggio*] is essentially a collective term which does not presuppose any single thing existing in either time or space.
>
> Language [*linguaggio*] also means culture and philosophy (if only at the level of common sense) and therefore, the fact of "language" [*linguaggio*] is in reality a multiplicity of facts more or less organically coherent and coordinated. At the limit, it may be said that every speaking being has her own personal language [*linguaggio*], i.e., her own way of thinking and feeling. Culture, in its various levels, unifies a larger or smaller number of individuals into many strata which come into greater or lesser expressive relations and understand each other to varying degrees, etc. . . . From this one can deduce the importance of the "cultural aspect," even in practical (collective) activity. Every historical act can only be performed by "collective man," and this presupposes the attainment of a "cultural-social" unity through which a multiplicity of dispersed wills, with heterogeneous aims, are welded together with a single aim, on the basis of an (equal) and common conception of the world. . . . Since this is the way things happen, the importance of the general question of language comes to light, that is, the question of collectively attaining a single cultural "climate."[12]

When can one say that there exist the conditions in order a collective national-popular will may be given rise and develop? . . . Why in Italy was not there the absolute monarchy at Machiavelli's times? One must go back until the Roman Empire (question of language, of intellectuals etc.).[13]

Due to its natural predisposition to form from "a multiplicity of fragmented wills" "a cultural-social unity" (i.e., a "national-popular collective will"), language [*lingua*] is the place in which one can read successes and failures of hegemonies and of processes of formation of the people-nations. This is the theme to which the last *Notebook* is devoted (bearing an only apparently odd title, *National Language and Grammar* [*Lingua Nazionale e Grammatical*]), and that must, instead, be read for what it is: a small and dense tract on the processes of the formation and on the conditions of success of the hegemonies capable of unifying and aggregating complex organisms such as the people-nation. Some of the passages from this notebook are very well known to the Italian linguists. We now call them to the attention of the nonlinguist readers. Yet the entire ntebook must be read as the central nucleus of Gramsci's theory of power:

> One could sketch a picture of the "normative grammar" that operates spontaneously in every given society, in that this society tends to become unified both as a territory and as a culture, in other words it has a governing class whose function is recognized and followed. The number of "immanent or spontaneous grammars" is incalculable and, theoretically, one may say that each person has a grammar of her own. Yet, alongside this actual "disaggregation," one has to consider the movements of unification, of greater or lesser amplitude both as territorial area and as "linguistic volume." Written "normative grammars" tend to embrace an entire national territory and the entire "linguistic volume," to create a unitary national linguistic conformism, that, under another respect, places expressive "individualism" at a higher level, because it creates a more robust and homogeneous skeleton for the national linguistic organism of which every individual is the reflection and the interpreter.[14]

> Every time that the question of the language [*lingua*] surfaces, in one way or another, it means that a series of problems are coming to the fore: the formation and enlargement of the governing class, the need to establish more intimate and secure relationships between the governing groups and the national-popular mass, in other words to reorganize the cultural hegemony.[15]

The failure of the Risorgimento and the incapacity of the nineteenth-century bourgeois at exercising hegemony (diffusive cultural direction) on the entire nation-people are historical processes isomorphic to the nonpopularity of the Italian language, to the vitality of folkloric cultures and of the idioms of dialects: "The question of the language posed by Manzoni also reflects this problem, that of the moral and intellectual unity of the nation and the state, sought in the unity of the language."[16]

NOTES

1. Franco Lo Piparo, *Lingua, Intellettuali, Egemonia in Gramsci* (Bari: Laterza, 1979).

2. [We should note that *Critica Marxista* was (and remains) *officially* an independent journal, although Lo Piparo is highlighting the overlap in specific people and interests between the two in 1987.]

3. [This phrase in italics was edited out of the original publication as noted above. See note 2.]

4. Antonio Gramsci, *Letters from Prison*, vol. 1, ed. Frank Rosengarten, trans. Raymond Rosenthal (New York: Columbia University Press, 1994), 360–61, hereafter LP1. See pages ix–x for a list of abbreviations.

5. LP1, 83–84. Italics Lo Piparo's.

6. See Valentino Gerratana's notes in Antonio Gramsci, *Quaderni del Carcere* (Turin: Einaudi, 1975), 2369–2442, hereafter QC.

7. [Many people were involved in founding the Partito Communista d'Italia (which became the Partito Communista Italiano) and Gramsci's prominance is still a subject of debate.]

8. [Lo Piparo uses *nazione-popolo*, which is a concept Gramsci uses a few times in the *Prison Notebooks*. But Gramsci uses *popolo-nazione* much more frequently. Given this situation and that in Italian modifying adjectives often follow the nouns they modify, we have translated *nazione-popolo* as people-nation.]

9. Q13§1, QC, 1556. [To facilitate locating passages in various translations and anthologies, we use the standard method of providing the notebook [*Quaderno*] number—in this case 13—followed by the section number, §. See the introduction, page 12, for discussion. We will indicate the English translation, if used.]

10. Antoine Meillet, *Différentiation et Unification Dans les Langues*, in *Scientia*, vol. IX, V (1911): n.9, and *Linguistique Historique et Linguistique Générale*, vol. 1 (Paris: E. Champion, 1921), 122.

11. Antonio Gramsci, *Selections from Political Writings, 1910–1920*, ed. Quintin Hoare and trans. John Matthews (London: Lawrence & Wishart, 1977), 143–44. Italics Lo Piparo's.

12. Q10§44, QC, 1330–31. We have altered the translation to better convey Gramsci's style and meaning but also to exploit grammatical ambiguities of Italian to introduce feminine pronouns. See Antonio Gramsci, *Selections from Prison Notebooks*, ed. and trans. Quintin Hoare and Geoffrey Nowell Smith (New York: International Publishers, 1971), 348–49, hereafter cited as SPN.

13. Q13§1; SPN, 130.

14. Q29§2, QC, 2343. English translation, modified slightly, in Antonio Gramsci, *Selections from Cultural Writings*, ed. D. Forgacs and G. Nowell-Smith, trans. W. Boelhower (Cambridge, Mass.: Harvard University Press, 1985), 181, hereafter SCW.

15. Q29§3, SCW, 183–84.

16. Q21§5, SCW, 210.

2

Linguistics and Marxism in the Thought of Antonio Gramsci

Luigi Rosiello *

The centrality of linguistic questions, both genetic and synchronic, to the political and sociological thought of Antonio Gramsci (1891–1937) has been demonstrated by Franco Lo Piparo.[1] Rejecting previous assumptions, he argues that Gramsci's linguistic interests—which matured during his years at university independently of Marxism—in large part influenced his future theoretical elaborations regarding the relationships between intellectuals and society and also the originality of his position in the arena of Italian Marxism. One of the theses sustained by Lo Piparo "is that Gramsci looked for those theoretical instruments which would allow understanding the question of language [*lingua*] in its exact terms and the problem related to it regarding the relationship between linguistic history, cultural apparatuses and society, inside the debate between neo-grammarians and neo-linguists."[2] I cannot completely agree with this position since Gramsci did not look for "theoretical instruments" within the neo-linguistic view of Bartoli against the neo-grammarians' positivism. Gramsci, rather, simply looked for methodological canons that would fit into the frame of a materialistic theory of history better than the ones of the neo-grammarians. This is the case provided that what he wrote in *Avanti!* on January 29, 1918, is true: "I am preparing my thesis for graduation on the history of language [*linguaggio*], trying to apply the critical methods of historical materialism even to this research."[3] For the young student, the methodological instrument to apply was Bartoli's neo-linguistics, which seemed to offer the possibility to

* Translation of "Linguistica e Marxismo nel Pensiero di Antonio Gramsci," in *The History of Linguistics in Italy*, ed. Paolo Ramat, Hans-J. Niederehe and Konrad Koerner (Amsterdam: John Benjamins, 1986), 237–57. Translated by Rocco Lacorte with assistance by Peter Ives.

highlight the sociocultural conflicts constituting linguistic changes rather than their linearity.

During his years at the University of Turin, Gramsci attended Matteo Bartoli's classes on glottology diligently and with interest. Gramsci collaborated with Bartoli both with his class in 1912–1913, editing the notes Bartoli wrote to be distributed to his students,[4] and in making available his proficiency as a speaker of Sardinian. Sardinian dialects always attracted Bartoli's interest since they tend to preserve their Latin features. He dealt with this topic in an early essay[5] and also in his exposition of the spatial theory of linguistic areas in order to document the norm of the isolated area ("the most isolated area usually preserves its anterior phase"). It may be that Bartoli was first interested in Gramsci as a Sardinian speaker—namely, as a possible direct source of information regarding words and Sardinian syntactical constructions—before discovering and appreciating his pupil's intellect. Gramsci did in fact write home in 1912 and 1913, including lists of Sardinian words and constructions, and asking his father or sister to carry out actual small investigations to check for their existence in the spoken language or to verify their phonetic and semantic exactness. Gramsci wrote the following to his father in January 1913:

> I am sending a list of words: have somebody translate them into Sardinian, yet into the dialect of Fonni (asking around will let you be more precise). Indicate clearly, for example, which S must be pronounced softly, as in *rosa* and which muted as in *sordo*. I beg you not to make mistakes, since this is an assignment that I was given by a professor with whom I must take an exam this year. I would not like to jeopardize myself by something foolish. As soon as you write it down, send it to me immediately, because my professor needs it for a work of linguistics he is carrying out.[6]

It does not seem that Bartoli used the materials with which Gramsci provided him in any way. Yet it is clear that Gramsci (and therefore Bartoli) was interested in the dialectal variety of "logudorese" [Logudoro's dialect], which is the most conservative among the various Sardinian dialects, if one considers, first of all, where the inquiry would have been carried out (in Fonni, a town in the Nuoro area) and the lists of words and constructions Gramsci sent to his sister Teresina (letter of November 1912: *pamentile, omine de pore, su pirone, accupintu, pingula,* etc.; letter of March 1913: *pus* for "poi," *puschena, portigale, poiu* and *poiolu*).[7] Probably, Bartoli wanted to further document this "logudorese" variety of Sardinian through Gramsci's help, because, as he would write later in 1925, "Central Sardinia is a more isolated area than Northern or Southern Sardinia."[8]

There is a trace of these inquiries on Sardinian dialects conducted through Bartoli's advising, in Gramsci's famous letter from prison (March 26, 1927), in which he recommends to his sister Teresina to let her son, Franco, speak in Sardinian. In this way, she would have facilitated his free spontaneity of linguistic expression during the first stage of his learning, without making the mistake of constraining his child's fantasy in the "straitjacket" of an inadequate Italian, made out of few sentences and words: "For one thing Sardinian is not a dialect, but a language in itself, even if it does not have a great literature, and it is a good thing for children to learn several languages, if it is possible."[9]

The contraposition language [*lingua*]/dialect is affected by certain abstract schematization at this stage (as we will see, Gramsci will deal with the language/dialect relationship in the *Prison Notebooks* in a different way): on the one hand, he speaks like a specialist used to thinking of Sardinian dialects as an autonomous variety of Romance languages, without any sociolinguistic consideration of their communicative function. On the other hand, he shows that he is aware that the free formation of a complete linguistic proficiency cannot but favor languages' learning.

In his first years in prison, Gramsci feels the urgent need to devote himself to work on topics that have broad theoretical dimension and are destined to last beyond what is contingent (*für ewig*). What appears in the outline for his research sent to his sister-in-law, Tatiana, in the letter of March 19, 1927, is "a study of comparative linguistics" (perhaps he meant "general"), where he would deal with the methodological aspect of the neo-linguistic theory against the naturalistic positivism (that is how at least it was understood) of the neo-grammarians' method. Moreover, this project had, for Gramsci, also an emotional value: it was meant to solve the old debt to his teacher. As Gramsci writes, "A major intellectual 'remorse' of my life is the deep sorrow that I caused my good professor Bartoli at the University of Turin, who was convinced that I was the archangel [*arcangelo*] destined to put to definitive rout [*profligare*] the 'neo-grammarians.'"[10] Gramsci's ironic use of words such as *arcangelo* and *profligare* is meant to temper the emotions due to his memory "of private conversations he had with his professor when he was a student."[11]

As we have seen, Gramsci feels the need to apply "the critical methods of historical materialism" to his linguistic research since his first years at the university. The method of neo-linguistics, which Bartoli was forging in Italy as a proliferation of Gilliéron's geographic method, was, in Gramsci's eyes, the most appropriate to be utilized according to a sociological approach that, while developing the history of languages, would tend to explain the facts concerning linguistic innovations through objective criteria inherent in the history of people and social class. The research Gramsci probably carried out for his graduation thesis convinced him to consider the formation of a national language as an historical and cultural fact strictly linked to the formation of the dominant intellectual stratum. Still, this will be one of the themes that Gramsci will meditate on incessantly, during his solitary elaboration in the *Prison Notebooks*. This conception of language [*lingua*] as cultural and social historicity is, however, already operating while he was a political militant of the Italian Socialist Party. He will indeed use it to fight and correct those ideological utopic-humanitarian and cosmopolitan tendencies which were still operating in the socialist movement. In the polemic against supporters of Esperanto, Gramsci unfolds in three pieces—two in the *Avanti!* (*Contro un pregiudizio* [Against One Prejudice], January 24, 1918; *Teoria e pratica* [Theory and Practice][12]) and one in "The Grido del Popolo" (*La lingua unica e l'esperanto* [A Single Language and Esperanto], February 16, 1918)[13]—he uses his scientific capabilities to assert the historicity of languages in opposition to the illusory utopia of a language created artificially without any ground or cultural participation, like Esperanto. Such an opposition results from the comparison between the history of the formation of a national language (like Italian, with a history in both productive activities and the intellectual strata) and the history of the attempts to form artificial languages, born because of the "impetus of seventeenth-century dogmatism and the eighteenth-century French Enlightenment," and whose task was to "give rise to the language of the bourgeois cosmopolis, the unity of bourgeois thought created by the propaganda of the Encyclopaedists."[14]

The historiographic discourse on international languages is complex because it should imply a more subtle periodization, where one would at least distinguish among the following: an hypothesis about an artificial language created for scientific communication (sixteenth-century empiricism); the research for logico-linguistic universals (sixteenth- and seventeenth-century general grammar); and, finally, the proposal of an international language of communication like Volapük or Esperanto (eighteenth-century humanitarianism). But what Gramsci is interested in is grasping the ideological aspect of the problem, namely, the bourgeois matrix of thought that constitutes the origin of the ideals of a linguistic unification artificially created. Gramsci opposes to such linguistic ideology the arguments of the science that is grounded on an empiricist conception of the historicity of languages: "*An international language* is, scientifically speaking, inappropriate. Languages are very complex and subtle organisms and cannot be artificially created."[15] This is what Gramsci firmly states against the ideological abstractionism of those who pretend to unite the people on the ground of a communicative instrument that does not correspond to the real cultural condition of the people themselves: "This is a *cosmopolitan*, not international, preoccupation, of those bourgeois who travel for business or leisure, namely, of nomads, rather than of steadily productive citizens."[16] Every process of national and international linguistic unification is based on existing politico-cultural realities, as Graziadio Isaia Ascoli argued against the Manzonians. Gramsci uses and quotes Ascoli's theses[17] in order to demonstrate the groundlessness of any artificially created solution and how the formation of a linguistic (national or international) unity is nothing other than the result of the convergent action of real intellectual and productive forces.

Gramsci, however, is capable of going beyond his adhesion to Ascoli's position, by defining the relationship language[*lingua*]-nation in correct materialistic terms:

> [Languages] have never determined national formations. Nations were formed because of the economic and political necessities of one class: the language [*lingua*] has only been one of the visible documents needed for propaganda, which bourgeois writers used to promote consensus among sentimental people and the ideologues. On the contrary, it is the national unification that has always and everywhere determined the diffusion of the traditional literary language among the learned strata belonging to a certain region.[18]

The correct setting of the historical problem of national language formation, its correspondence to hegemonic class needs, and its function as an instrument of organization of consensus provides the idea of how Gramsci proceeded in utilizing the results of the science of linguistics connecting them with "the critical methods of historical materialism." Gramsci reverses the relationship language-nation established by romantic idealism thanks to this type of critical analysis. He thinks that the relationship language-nation is based on determined historical conditions that have permitted a determined social class to become hegemonic within the arena of a national unity.

On a more general level, Gramsci demonstrates that he knows how to correctly posit the problem about the relationship that must exist between linguistic science and the way Marxist theory is to be applied and specified. Gramsci posits the problem mentioned above the same way as Friedrich Engels does in his essay on *The Franconian Dialect* [*Il dialetto francone*] (1881–1882). In this work, Engels showed how it is possible to correctly integrate the methods elaborated and the results achieved by linguistics in his times in a global materialistic theory of history and society.[19] In other words, Gramsci—and before him Engels—starts forging not so much an illusory pretense for grounding a Marxist theory of language [*linguaggio*], but rather an epistemologically correct proposal aimed at utilizing linguistic science within the framework of a more powerful theory, which should be capable of instituting the nexuses necessary for explaining interactive relationships between linguistic systems and the historically determined structure of social relationships.

Gramsci's reflection on linguistic themes becomes deeper and more articulated during his years in prison. Yet he could not realize his project of theoretically dealing with the neo-linguistic method, which he planned as one of the works *für ewig*. On many occasions, however, he deals with linguistics

in connection with a whole series of other problems regarding the nature of
Italian culture and the organization of intellectuals, the folklore and the culture of subaltern classes, the politics of education and teaching methods, etc.
Today, since the critical edition of the *Prison Notebooks* is available to us, we
can grasp better than before Gramsci's theoretical depth and follow the unfolding of the linguistic problem throughout the reading of the writings that
go from 1929 to 1935. Gramsci opens the *"First Notebook* (February 8, 1929)"
with a list of topics to treat and expand. *"The question of the language in Italy*:
Manzoni and G. I. Ascoli"; *"Neo-grammarians and neo-linguists* ('this round
table is square')"[20] appear among these topics. Notebook 29 (1935) is the last
one (except for the four devoted to translations) and is entitled "Notes for an
Introduction to the Study of Grammar." It closes with the annotation, *"The
title* of this study could be: 'national language and grammar.'"[21] It represents
another among the projects Gramsci was forced not to realize.

In the first letter he wrote, after his arrest, in the jail of Regina Coeli,
Gramsci asks his landlord, Mrs. Passarge, to have some of his books sent
to him, among which was the *"Breviario di [neo]linguistica* by Bertoni and
Bartoli." The letter, however, never reached its destination since the police
seized it. In a letter to Tatiana written in October 1927, Gramsci asks again
to have this book sent, which he will henceforth recall, even in the *Prison
Notebooks*, with the title *Manualetto di linguistica*. Still in December 1927
he says he never received this book from a librarian he ordered it from. As
a matter of fact, the latter does not appear in the list of books he had in
prison.[22] Gramsci also says that he will have to renounce dealing with the
theme: "This round table is square," even though he regrets it, because "it
is not a small question, if you consider that it means: 'What is grammar?'
and that every year, in all the countries in the world, millions upon millions
of textbooks on the subject are devoured by specimens of the human race,
without those unfortunates having a precise awareness of the object they are
devouring."[23] This theme, as we have seen, goes back to his plan of work
from 1929 and will constitute the subject matter of the notes written in the
last notebook (1935) positioned within his project of organic examination.
In the outline of 1929, Gramsci relates his treatment of the theoretical aspects of the neo-linguistic method to his other theme concerning the definition of grammar. Gramsci was inspired by reading an essay by Benedetto
Croce, "This round table is square," where the Neapolitan philosopher
wants to demonstrate the theoretical and scientific groundlessness of grammars, using a sentence by Steinthal to highlight the difference between
logic and grammar. Thus, the definition of grammar becomes a topic on
which Gramsci constantly meditates. He becomes aware of the theoretical
importance and sociological relevance concerning the use of grammar or
grammars in relation to a different series of cultural and social questions:
the definition of the concept of language, formation of literary-linguistic

norms, relationship of language/dialects, cultural function of scholastic teaching and so forth.

In attempting an organic reconstruction of Gramsci's thought on linguistics, one must first notice, in order to place it exactly historically and theoretically, the anti-idealistic and in particular anti-Crocean position characterizing the numerous pages of the *Prison Notebooks* devoted to linguistic problems. Lo Piparo focuses on the influence that Crocean philosophy exercised on the intellectual formation of the young linguist, Gramsci, documenting and insisting in terms of linguistic theory, what was already understood on a more general level by Gramsci's own statement, "I tended to be rather Crocean."[24] This does not rule out the hypothesis that the development of Gramsci's linguistic thought during the prison years leads him to a consciously anti-idealistic and anti-Crocean position. On the contrary, we can maintain that in Italy in those years Gramsci's neglected voice was the only one that was objectively anti-idealistic. Many linguists, indeed, were declaring in various ways their agreement with the reigning idealism, whereas others went on with their linguistic work, isolating themselves, using the traditional method of the neo-grammarians without intervening on theoretical questions.[25]

Instead, Gramsci intervenes, stressing and developing, in a Marxist sense, the sociological implications of Bartoli's linguistic method, taking almost for granted his overcoming of the polemic against the positivism of the neo-grammarians. The controversy Gramsci engages with Bertoni regarding the *Breviario di Neolinguistica* is indicative of the extent to which he unveils the fundamental misunderstanding encompassing the Italian culture of those times—namely, the bad consciousness of those intellectuals who, although scientifically formed in the positivist school, were repeating the formulas of idealistic philosophy on the level of the declarations of general principles without any critical attitude. One of these intellectuals was Giulio Bertoni, who wrote the "Principi generali" ["General Principles," part I] of the *Breviario di Linguistica*, whereas Bartoli composed the "Criteri tecnici" ["Technical Criteria," part II]. Gramsci criticizes Bartoli for having accepted to collaborate with Bertoni: "Bartoli is esteemed for his concrete works: letting Bertoni write the theoretical part [of the *Breviario*] induce students to make mistakes, pushing them onto the false path. In this case modesty and disinterest become guilt." There is indeed a sharp difference between the "General Principles" and the "Technical Criteria." In the former, Bertoni reduces linguistics to an aesthetics of words, assuming language [*lingua*] and its innovations as spiritually and individually created facts; in the latter, Bartoli sets out heuristic methods and criteria that postulate and study language in its objectively definable historical and geographical organization. Gramsci rightly observes that "Bertoni has failed both to provide a general theory of Bartoli's innovations in linguistics and to understand the

substance as well as the practical and theoretical importance of these innovations."[26] Eighteen years later, Giuseppe Vidossi (1948:209), a friend
and collaborator of Bartoli, will confirm Gramsci's statement about Bertoni
and Gramsci's criticisms of the misunderstanding characterizing idealistic
and Crocean linguistics. Yet Gramsci continues noting that Bertoni misun-
derstood not only the innovations brought forth by Bartoli, but also the
aesthetics of Croce in the sense that he has been unable to derive from
Crocean aesthetics a coherent research method: "He [Bertoni] did nothing
but paraphrase, exalt, and wax eloquent about certain impressions: he is essentially a positivist who swoons at the sight of idealism because it is more
fashionable and provides the occasion for flights of rhetoric."[27]

The contradiction Gramsci grasps acutely in Bertoni's theorizations is
typical of the cultural situation of Italian linguistics in those years. The un-
problematized trust in a factual legitimization of the science of linguistics
disarmed Italian linguists theoretically in the face of idealistic intrusiveness.
Italian linguists, since they were lacking the capability and habit of theorizing, happened to accept ideas and theories placing linguistics out of their
scientific field. The negative influence Croce's theories had does not consist so much in that they have divulged a conception of linguistic activity
as aesthetical individual activity, but rather its isolation as a consequence
of Croce's dialectic of distincts because Crocean theories have produced a
fracture between empirical method and scientific theory, technical research
and methodological discourse, and between the study of language and that
of style. This is precisely what Gramsci infers when reproaching Bartoli for
collaborating with Bertoni. Bertoni did not even know how to re-elaborate
Croce's theses in a linguistic and stylistic way (as Vossler did) and made
recourse to certain empirical categories, such as "language" [*lingua*] and
"speech" [*linguaggio*] (absolutely not comparable with the Saussurian concepts of *langue* and *parole*) in order to justify linguistics, on the one hand, as
aesthetics and, on the other hand, as cultural instrumentality.[28]

Certainly, the aesthetic dimension of a linguistic act is completely extraneous with respect to the way Bartoli practices the conception of language
[*lingua*]. Gramsci rightly affirms:

> I do not perceive any direct relationship of dependence between Bartoli's
> method and Croce's theories; Bartoli's relationship is with historicism in
> general, not with a particular form of historicism. Bartoli's originality consists
> precisely in this: that he took linguistics, narrowly conceived as a natural sci-
> ence, and transformed it into a historical science rooted in "space and time"
> and not in the physiology of the vocal apparatus.[29]

Evidently, Gramsci did not know about the theoretical formulations of the
neo-grammarian method contained, for example, in Herman Paul's *Prinzip-
ien der Sprachgeschichte* [Principles of the History of Language] (1880)[30]: he

does nothing but report the rather narrow terms and expressions of Bartoli's polemic against the Italian neo-grammarians. What concerns Gramsci the most, however, is to place Bartoli's neo-linguistic method in the realm of historicism. Historicism itself is not here to understand in the speculative sense idealistic philosophies assigned to it. Such philosophies would consider historical (linguistic) facts as events that are individual, unrepeatable and revealing spiritual and universal values. On the contrary, I think that historicism must be here understood in a more general, I would say methodological, sense: designating the time-space dimension of as a criterion for understanding and explaining the historicity of linguistic events and structures. Gramsci makes explicit the precise meaning of this "historicism" when he affirms:

> The history of the languages [*lingue*] is history of linguistic innovations, but these innovations are not individual (as in art); they are innovations of an entire social community that has renewed its culture and "progressed" historically. To be sure, they, too become individual, not as the individual-artist but in the *complete*, determinate individual qua [cultural]-historical element.

Gramsci goes on clarifying that linguistic innovations occur:

> by interference of different cultures, etc., and this takes place in very different ways, it still occurs for whole masses of linguistic elements, and it takes place molecularly. (For example: Latin, as a "mass," transformed the Celtic of the Gauls, but it influenced the Germanic language "molecularly," that is, by lending it individual words and forms.)[31]

The tradition of sociologically oriented historical linguistics, which Gramsci directly or indirectly experienced during his university years—Ascoli, Gilliéron, Bartoli and certainly Meillet, as Lo Piparo has demonstrated[32]—is mirrored in those pages of the *Prison Notebooks* mentioned above, where the concept of linguistic and cultural "interference" emerges, which remains one of the privileged themes of modern sociolinguistics. Yet Gramsci regards the phenomenon of molecular interference and influence, not only with respect to relationships between languages, but also within the same linguistic community: "There can be interference and a 'molecular' influence within a the same nation, between diverse strata etc.; a new class that becomes the ruling class brings about changes 'on mass' but the jargon of various professions, that is, of particular societies, changes in a molecular way." Gramsci defines the same relationship between speech and dialect under a sociocultural and not merely linguistic respect: "Even dialect is language[*lingua*]-art. Between dialect and national-literary language, however, something—precisely the cultural and politico-moral-sentimental environment—has changed."[33] This would amount to saying more explicitly that it is not possible to define the distinction between the concept of "language" [*lingua*] and that of "dialect" in linguistic terms. These concepts must refer to the different cultural, social, political and economic conditions that constitute the cause of the hegemony of one dialect or language over other languages and dialects related to the hegemony of one social class and intellectual stratum over an entire community. The dynamics of social relations are implied in the complex network of relationships established when the linguistic system is modified and when the linguistic norm (literary, national language) imposes itself as an element that unifies and organizes the diversity of the uses characterizing social stratifications or diversities.

Yet, as Lo Piparo rightly says, "The great novelty to stress is that, with respect to Ascoli, Gilliéron, Meillet and Bartoli, Gramsci introduces the concept of hegemony,"[34] which synthesizes the understanding of historico-geographical linguistics with militant Marxism: "Language [*linguaggio*] is transformed with the transformation of the whole of civilisation, through the acquisition of culture by new classes and through the hegemony exercised by one national language [*lingua*] over others, etc."[35] As Lo Piparo has widely demonstrated, the antecedent of the concept of hegemony is the one of linguistic and cultural *prestigio* [prestige] that can be found in Meillet and Bartoli's pages[36] ("One can say that *the causes of linguistic innovations are, in ultimate analysis, resolved by imitating other languages having greater prestige*. When we say: imitating *other languages*, we mean all languages, without distinguishing 'languages' and 'dialects' . . . and provided that they have *greater prestige*").[37] Bartoli further clarifies the concept of prestige in terms of relationship between the linguistic varieties of the dominant and dominated class. Yet the term "hegemony," which appears the first time in an article devoted to Lenin in *Ordine Nuovo* (March 1, 1924), offers to Gramsci the possibility to use a wider and more comprehensive concept used by Soviet militant Marxism and that can therefore be referred not only to the linguistic field. Indeed, as Perry Anderson states, "Gramsci's own treatment of the idea of hegemony descends directly from the definitions of the Third International" and from Lenin as Buci-Glucksmann and Gruppi have demonstrated, and as Gramsci himself has acknowledged.[38] At some point, Gramsci inserts the concept of "prestige" into the "theoretico-practical principle of hegemony,"[39] partly modifying its content, thus making the sphere of its applicability larger. Gramsci's trajectory—from the use of *prestigio* to that of "hegemony"—shows (also on a terminological level) that he continues to realize his scientific plan ("to apply even to this research the critical methods of Historical Materialism") by inserting the concepts and methods of historico-geographical linguistics in the theoretical sphere of a wider Marxist theory of history.

The basic points of the sociological conception of language [*linguaggio*] that neatly emerge from Gramsci's pages are the meaning of language [*lingua*] as a cultural product and his acknowledgment of the social conflicts intervening in the establishment of linguistic norms. Gramsci's sociological conception of language presupposes the encounter between the historico-geographic linguistics of his time and the materialist theory of history. Gramsci's conception retains its theoretical efficacy for contemporary sociolinguistics, even without the mediation of Saussure, of whom, it seems, Gramsci did not know. It must be clarified, however, what Gramsci means when he says, for example, that linguists "study languages in so far as cultural expression of a given people."[40] These statements should not make us think about Gramsci's conception of language [*lingua*] as the kind of generic cultural-linguistic relativism, on the grounds of which language [*lingua*] would be understood as subjective expression of an undifferentiated cultural community. On the contrary, Gramsci conceives language [*lingua*] as really produced by the convergence of the social and historical interests of a determined human group that both collectively reaches a common way of expressing and also expresses social and cultural differentiations and conflicts.

> It seems that one can say "language" [*linguaggio*] is essentially a collective term which does not presuppose any "unique" thing neither in time nor in space. Language [*linguaggio*] also means (even though at the level of common sense) culture and philosophy. Therefore, the fact "language" [*linguaggio*] is in reality a multiplicity of facts more or less organically coherent and coordinated: it may be said that every speaking being has her own personal language [*linguaggio*], at the least, i.e., her own way to think and feel. Culture in its various degrees unifies a majority or minority of individuals in numerous strata, more or less in expressive contact, and that understand each other in diverse degrees etc. It is these differences and historico-cultural distinctions that are reflected into common language [*linguaggio*].[41]

And that one must explain and interpret on the grounds of analyses conducted on the entire communicative context. Thus, *language* [*lingua*] expresses the culture of a given people, even if each culture contains some differences and diversities that are determined by historico-social conditions, which are expressed in various types of socially connoted *language* [*linguaggio*]. The existing relationships between these cultural and linguistic strata are not seen in terms of static opposition, but of reciprocal dialectical influence: "Although one may say that each social group has its own 'language' [*lingua*] yet it must be noticed (with a few exceptions) that there is a continuous adherence and exchange between the popular language [*lingua*] and that of the learned classes."[42]

Perhaps, in Gramsci, there is no full theoretical awareness of how to use the two terms: "language" [*lingua*] and "speech" [*linguaggio*] (Saussure's definitions were not operating). However, I believe that we can still interpret Gramsci's thought by saying that if, on the one hand, language [*lingua*] can express one culture in its whole entirety and concrete realizations, on the other hand, single "languages" [*linguaggio*] can be analyzed only in relation to concrete and differentiated communicative situations on the ground of the real sociocultural conditions.

The fact that Gramsci takes into account the sociocultural conditions of the speakers explains his position in relation to the problem concerning the relationship between national language and dialects, which, as it seems to me, expresses the same attitude he had toward the relationship between dominant and folkloric culture.[43] As we have seen, the distinction between speech and dialect must be referred to the cultural conditions and not to the linguistic quality of language systems. Yet a dialectal linguistic system linked to a narrow and subaltern cultural environment will have more limited and sectarian communicative potentials than those offered by the national language that, despite its internal differentiations, expresses a hegemonic culture:

> Someone who only speaks dialect, or understands the standard language incompletely, necessarily has an intuition of the world which is more or less limited and provincial, which is fossilised and anachronistic in relation to the other major currents of thought which dominate world history. His interests will be limited, more or less corporate or economistic, not universal. While it is not always possible to learn a number of foreign languages in order to put oneself in contact with other cultural lives, it is at the least necessary to learn the national language properly. A great culture can be translated into the language of another great culture, that is to say a great national language with historic richness and complexity, and it can translate any other great culture and can be a world-wide means of expression. But a dialect cannot do this.[44]

The fact that Gramsci's sociolinguistic approach is organic makes it possible to posit the problem of the relationship between language [*lingua*] and dialects in the programmatic terms of politics of language: As a matter of fact, Gramsci rejects the conception of dialect as expression of uncontaminated popular genuineness that is typical of romantic and populist ideology. He thinks that popular masses—to the extent that they organize themselves to become hegemonic class—must overcome every sectarianism of dialects in order to gain a more powerful communicative instrument, capable of expressing the new culture and of exercising new hegemony. For Gramsci, this does not mean that one has to negate the realities of dialects: he has never argued that dialects must disappear; he only affirmed that it is necessary to set in motion a determined cultural and political situation in order for popular classes to overcome every cultural and linguistic sectarianism[45] and to get the kind of linguistic system capable of guaranteeing the communication of universal cultural content, which characterize the new hegemonic function exercised by the proletariat.

When Gramsci talks about national language, however, he is well aware of using a compromised concept that, in order for it to be freed from every romantic and idealistic ideological implication, must be redefined in sociological terms and verified in the light of historical and social determinations. Therefore, Gramsci explains the formation of national languages directly relating it to the modalities in which intellectual strata are formed, to the latter political and social function and to the traits of the hegemonic culture they represent. This particular way of positing the problem of the formation of national languages constitutes one of the most original contributions that Gramsci's linguistic thought adding to the progress of knowledge in studies of history and sociology of language. His contribution is still productive if one connects it to the strong expansion of the modern sociology of language, which is attentively looking, for example, at linguistic policies in the developing countries. Gramsci complains about the lack of works of history of the Italian language carried out using the sociological method, such as F. Brunot's *Histoire de la Langue Française* [History of the French Language], which constituted the ground for Balibar and Laporte's study of the formation of the concept of the national language in France as a product of the politics of language actuated by the bourgeois class ruling after the revolution in 1789.[46]

Paragraph 76 of Prison Notebook 3 is entitled "The Question of the Language and the Italian Intellectual Classes."[47] In a few pages, Gramsci outlines the history of the Italian language as the history of those intellectual strata that have practiced this language for centuries. He shows how the basic character of the literary, written language, not the spoken or popular language, depends on the cosmopolitan function exercised by the intellectual caste since the times when it was the language through which the Catholic and universalistic culture of the dominant class used to express itself.

> The growth of the communes propelled the development of the vernaculars, and the intellectual hegemony of Florence consolidated it; that is, it created an illustrious vernacular. But what is this illustrious vernacular? It is the Florentine [dialect] developed by the intellectuals of the old tradition: the *vocabulary* as well as the *phonetics* are Florentine, but the syntax is Latin. The victory of the vernacular over the Latin was not easy, however: with the exception of poets and artists in general, learned Italians wrote for Christian Europe not for Italy; they were a compact group of cosmopolitan and not national intellectuals. The fall of the communes and the advent of the principality, the creation of a governing caste detached from the people, crystallized this vernacular in the same way literary Latin had been crystallized. Italian became, once again, a written and not a spoken language, belonging to the learned, not to the nation.[48]

Perhaps, a specialist of the history of the Italian language will be able to find some schematic simplifications, some lacunae in Gramsci, but such a specialist certainly cannot do so without grasping the originality of the sociological method applied by Gramsci, who, for the first time, established an explicative relationship between the history of language and the history of the organization of the Italian culture:

> After a brief interval (the freedom of the communes) during which intellectuals of popular (bourgeois) class origins flourished, the intellectual function was reabsorbed into the traditional caste where the individual members came from the people but where the character of the caste prevailed over their origins. In other words, it is not the case that an entire stratum of the population creates its own intellectuals when it attains power (which is what happened in the fourteenth century); rather, a traditionally selected body assimilates single individuals into its cadres (the typical example of this is the ecclesiastical structure).[49]

This explains the absence of a popular literature, the permanent fragmentation into dialects, the perpetuation of the question of language conceived as an "aspect of the political fight" or as

> a reaction of the intellectuals to the fragmentation of the political unity that existed in Italy under the name: "equilibrium of the Italian States" and to the fragmentation of the economic and political classes that came to gain shape after the year one thousand with the communes and it represents the attempt, which one can say in great part succeeded, to preserve and even empower a unified intellectual stratum, whose existence had to have not little significance in the eighteenth and nineteenth century (in the Risorgimento).[50]

The linguistic history of a society is the history of its own culture viewed with respect to the formation and organization of the dominant classes, of the intellectual strata and of the relationships the latter have with the popular classes, but it is also a key for the interpretation of the conditions in which popular classes participate in the life of an entire society. Gramsci became aware of the centrality of the linguistic thematic by dealing with a series of historical problems: this is also quantitatively measurable taking into account Gramsci's insistence in repeating the references to the linguistic thematic in an endless number of prison notes, which here I cannot examine thoroughly and in detail. But the *Noterelle sulla cultura cinese* [Little Notes on Chinese Culture] deserve to be mentioned to show the enormity of Gramsci's sociolinguistic interests. In these "little notes," Gramsci takes into account, first of all, the ideographic writing system as a way of organizing (and transmitting) the culture characteristic to an intellectual caste of the "cosmopolitan" kind, completely detached from the popular base, which does not have instruments other than the oral ones ("oratory, conversation") to transmit its own culture:

In certain respects, the Chinese situation can be compared to that of western and central Europe during the Middle Ages; in other words, it can be compared to "Catholic cosmopolitanism," when "Middle Latin" was the language of the ruling classes and their intellectuals.[51]

Gramsci broadens the dimension of his sociolinguistic approach applied to the study of the linguistic policies pursued by the dominant classes. In other words, this approach also includes the problematic related to semiological writing systems analyzed as facts emerging from determined types of organization and the diffusion of culture. The same *function* that was performed in medieval Europe by a linguistic system was in China performed by the system of writing. In other words, this function consisted in transmitting the culture of a certain dominant class not rooted in the popular and national cultural and linguistic reality. Starting from the polemics against Esperanto in 1918 and going on with the reflections on the linguistic history of Italian culture and the notes on Chinese culture, Gramsci's thought developed until informally elaborating a methodological scheme of sociolinguistic research. This scheme, based on the analysis of the relationships between communication (oral and written) and cultural organizational modalities, engages a wide-ranging thematic related both to the description of present conditions and to historical precedents.

Now, (chronologically) the last topic I have to deal with is the *Notes* devoted to "grammar" in the last notebook—namely, the twenty-ninth. These notes, as I said, should have constituted the ground for a wider and more organic examination. The point of departure (and the objective) of these notes is still the polemic against Croce and idealism, that is, the analysis of Croce's essay "This Roundtable Is Square," where Croce wanted to demonstrate the theoretical groundlessness of grammar. But what is not "grammatically exact" can be justified "as an element of a vaster and inclusive representation." As a matter of fact, "the proposition [this roundtable is square] can be non-logical, contradictory, in itself, but at the same time, 'coherent' in a vaster picture" (i.e., that in which, as we would say today, are included other significant elements, like contexts, situations and the pragmatic scopes of communication). Since idealistic philosophy does not acknowledge grammar as having scientific status, because it does not allow it in the sphere of spiritual cognitive activities, it is not able to adequately answer the question: "What is grammar?" Gramsci provisionally answers that "grammar is 'history' or 'historical document:' it is the 'picture' of a determined phase of a certain national (collective) language [*linguaggio*] [historically formed and continuously developing itself] or the basic traits in a picture." This is the way Gramsci defines the kind of synchronic-descriptive grammar that documents a determined historical phase of a certain language [*lingua*] (it must be noticed that, according to Gerratana's critical edition of the *Prison*

Notebooks, Gramsci himself adds the reference to diachronic historicity in the quotation above only later on). This way of defining grammar does not exhaust all of its modalities. Gramsci as a sociologist of language [*linguaggio*] feels the need to reformulate the question in more adequate terms: "How many forms of grammar can exist?" First of all, there exists an "immanent" grammar, that is, those rules almost unconsciously practiced by the speakers. Moreover, "one can say that each of us has his/her own grammar." Furthermore, as a matter of fact, there exists a nonwritten normative grammar constituted by all those interventions and judgments ("by reciprocal monitoring, teaching and censorship that surfaces in questions like: 'What did you mean or want to say?' 'What do you mean?' 'Make yourself clearer' etc., through caricature, mockery, etc.") enacted by the speakers, who, going through a series of actions and reactions, tend to create a certain "grammatical conformism" reproducing a linguistic norm of prestige ("subaltern classes try to speak as the dominant ones and the intellectuals"). If, on the one hand, normative nonwritten grammar bears the characteristic of being spontaneous, on the other hand, written normative grammar represents a planned intervention over an entire national territory and over all the "linguistic volume in order to create a national unified linguistic conformism." Written normative grammar, however, cannot do without historical grammar or without the history of language, of which it is intended to propose an "exemplary phase" as the only one worthy of representing the common language of a certain nation.

Normative grammar equals historical grammar the same as politics equals history in a relationship of complementary necessity. The "exemplary phase" of normative grammar is indeed determined by a series of historical, and hence not only linguistic, factors. This phase is chosen on the basis of a politico-cultural will: "Normative written grammar is therefore always a 'choice,' a cultural direction.' In other words, normative written grammar is always an act of cultural-national politics" that, even though, on the one hand, tends to organize and centralize spontaneous and inorganically diffused tendencies in society, on the other, should not reasonably find cultural and political forces opposed to it on principle. Put in another way, if the intervention meant to unify the dominant class is based on real processes of popular participation that tend to overcome particularism and tend to cultural and linguistic unification, an opposition on principle to such an intervention must be considered anachronistic and reactionary. It is necessary, however, to be aware of the factors that act both in the direction of the irradiation of linguistic innovations and in that of the creation of the "national linguistic conformism in the large national masses." Gramsci lists these factors in detail; they are: (1) schools; (2) newspapers; (3) artistic and popular writers; (4) theater and sonorous cinema; (5) radio; (6) any kind of public reunion, included the religious ones;

(7) the "conversational" relationships between the various more or less learned strata of the population; and (8) local dialects and regional speeches. All these factors—both the ones that innovate and the ones that only diffuse linguistic innovations—are effectively implied in the real process of formation and diffusion of a certain Italian linguistic type effectively spoken in a period when the formation and the enlargement of the ruling class have determined, as Gramsci says, "the necessity of establishing deeper and well-built relationships between ruling groups and the popular-national masses, that is, of reorganizing the cultural hegemony."[52] But, as Gramsci concludes (reformulating his discourse in Ascoli's terms), the complexity of the historical process of formation and diffusion of a unified linguistic type is such that an organized intervention can be considered "decisive" in order to surely reach "a *determined* unified language: a unified language will be obtained if this language is a necessity. An organized intervention will speed up the time of the already existing process." In other words, an organized intervention must consensually respond to the real conditions and cultural and linguistic needs of the entire mass of the speakers.

One of the ways to realize an organized intervention is the accomplishment of the "political act" consisting in the school system's adoption of a written normative grammar. Croce's and Gentile's idealism tended to exclude such types of intervention, so devaluating the role of grammatical teaching in schools:

> In reality, the national-popular mass is excluded from learning the educated language, since the highest level of the ruling stratum, which traditionally speaks the [national] "language," passes it form generation to generation, through a slow process that begins with the first stutterings of the child under the guidance of its parents, and continues through conversation (with its "this is how one says it," "it must be said like this," etc.) for the rest of one's life: in reality, one "always" studies grammar, etc. (through imitating admired models, etc.) In Gentile's position there is much more politics than one could believe and a lot of unconscious reactionary thought . . . there is all the reactionism of the old liberal conception.[53]

Gramsci places the concepts of grammar defined above in the social reality of the scholastic situation and, beyond the polemic contingency, he focuses on one of the central knots of every program of linguistic education. "Immanent" grammar exists in "real life" and is what in a more modern way we would now call speaker competency. This kind of grammar acts in a much less conscious way when the speakers belong to the lower classes, whereas at the level of the upper classes it is more conscious for the speakers in terms of cultural selection. Excluding "normative" written grammar (we would say: grammatical theory) from scholastic teaching, means the subtraction of a rational instrument from the mass of the speakers. Yet this is an instrument needed to develop one's own linguistic competencies and to elevate oneself to a higher level of consciousness. Those who belong to the high classes, and who have the adequate cultural instruments at their disposal to develop their own rational competencies, can, instead, reach this level of competence even independently of teaching. Yet Gramsci asks, "Even if one admits that traditional normative grammar were not sufficient, is this a good reason not to teach any 'grammar,' that is, not to engage oneself with the speeding up of learning how to speak in a certain linguistic realm in any way, yet letting 'one learn the language [*lingua*] within the living language [*linguaggio*]' (or whatever other similar expression by Gentile or the Gentilians one would like to use)?"[54] In fact, whereas, on the one hand, Croce, for whom grammar is excluded from the theoretical activities of the spirit, justifies it on the level of practical activities, on the other, Gentile excludes grammar even from the practice of educative intervention. Gramsci's polemic against Gentile is, at the same time, political and theoretical: his is a sociological position that goes against an essentially naturalistic conception of language [*lingua*] that, by arguing in favor of linguistic spontaneity, subtracts an instrument central to the formation of their hegemony—the linguistic one—from the popular masses. The contents of this notebook (Lo Piparo is right)[55] cannot be read without taking into account the other prison notebooks, where Gramsci develops his political thought about the modalities in which organized workers can gain power in civil society and the modalities of exercising their ruling role before their complete conquest of state power.

NOTES

1. Franco Lo Piparo, *Lingua intellettuali in Gramsci* (Bari: Laterza, 1979).
2. Lo Piparo, 15.
3. Luigi Ambrosoli, "Nuovi contributi agli 'Scritti giovanili' di Gramsci," *Rivista Storica del Socialismo* 3 (1960): 545–50 [referenced in English translation in Antonio Gramsci, *Selections from Cultural Writings*, ed. David Forgacs and Geoffrey Nowell-Smith, trans. William Boelhower (London: Lawrence & Wishart, 1985), 26n.4, hereafter SCW. For a list of abbreviations, see pages ix–x]. On November 17, 1930, Gramsci writes to his sister-in-law Tatiana: "Ten years ago I wrote an essay on the language question according to Manzoni, and that required a certain research into the organization of Italian culture, from the time when the written language (the so-called medieval Latin, that is, Latin written from 400 AD until 1300) became completely detached from the language spoken by the people, which Roman centralization having come to an end, was fragmented into numberless dialects." Antonio Gramsci, *Letters from Prison*, vol. 1, ed. Frank Rosengarten, trans. Raymond Rosenthal (New York: Columbia University Press, 1994), 360, hereafter LP1. It is hard to believe that Gramsci would find time to write such an essay in 1920, the

year in which the factories of Turin were occupied. It has perhaps to be dated back to the year 1918; Leonardo Paggi, *Antonio Gramsci e il moderno principe* (Rome: Editori Riuniti, 1970), 76. Maybe the elaboration of the thesis for Gramsci's university diploma constituted the nucleus of this "essay." Alternatively, and more probably, as Lo Piparo (8) hypothesizes, this essay would be the introduction to the volume *Scritti sulla lingua italiana* [Writings on the Italian Language] by Manzoni that Gramsci should have had published in the *Collezione dei classici italiani* [Collection of Italian Classics] edited by G. Balsamo-Crivelli for the Press UTET, as indicated by a 1918 booklet by the same press (and as noted by Giancarlo Bergami, "Gustavo Balsamo-Crivelli," *Belfagor* 30 [1975]: 537–38). Gramsci's essay is, unfortunately, considered lost.

4. Renzo De Felice, "Un corso di glottologia di Matteo Bartoli negli appunti di Antonio Gramsci," *Rivista Storica del Socialismo* 7 (1964): 169–79.

5. Matteo Baroli, "Un po' di sardo," *Archeografo Triestino* 29 (1903): 129–55.

6. Guido Melis, ed., *Antonio Gramsci e la questione sarda* (Cagliari: Della Torre, 1975), 45–46.

7. See Melis, 44, 47. Almost all the words that Gramsci lists are from the geographical area where the "Logudorese" dialect is spoken; Max L. Wagner, *Dizionario etimologico sardo* (Heidelberg: Winter, 1960–1964).

8. Giulio Bertoni and Matteo Bartoli, *Breviario di neolinguistica* (Modena: Società Tipografica Modenese, 1925), 70.

9. LP1, 89.

10. LP1, 84. For a different translation, see Antonio Gramsci, *Letters from Prison*, trans. Lynne Lawner (New York: Harper and Row, 1973), 79.

11. Lo Piparo, 57.

12. In Ambrosoli, 548–50.

13. Antonio Gramsci, *Selections from Cultural Writings*, ed. David Forgacs and Geoffrey Nowell-Smith, trans. William Boelhower (Cambridge, Mass.: Harvard University Press, 1985), 27, hereafter SCW. [These articles and the debate of which they were interventions are available at www.andreamontagner.it/?p=43.]

14. SCW, 27.

15. SCW, 27.

16. SCW, 27, translation altered slightly.

17. "It had transpired that a scholar of the history of the language, Graziadio Isaia Ascoli, had set some thirty pages against the hundreds of pages by Manzoni in order to demonstrate: that not even a national language can be created artificially, by order of the state; that the Italian language was being formed by itself and would be formed only in so far as the shared life of the nation gave rise to numerous and stable contacts between the various parts of the nation; that the spread of a particular language is due to the productive activity of the writings, trade and commerce of the people who speak that particular language." SCW, 28. See Lo Piparo about the influence of Ascoli on the formation and thought of Gramsci.

18. Cited in Ambrosoli, 548.

19. Frederick Engels, "Note: The Franconian Dialect," in *Karl Marx and Frederick Engels: Collected Works*, vol. 26 (London: Lawrence & Wishart, 1990), 81–107.

20. Antonio Gramsci, *Quaderni del Carcere*, four volumes, ed. Valentino Gerratana (Turin: Einaudi, 1975), 5, hereafter QC. Q1§0. [To facilitate locating passages

in various translations and anthologies, we use the standard method of providing the Notebook (*Quaderno*) number, in this case 1, followed by the section number, §. See the introduction, page 12, for discussion. We will indicate the English translation, if used.]

21. Q29§9, QC, 2351.

22. See Giuseppe Carbone, "I libri del carcere di Antonio Gramsci," *Movimento Operaio* 4 (1952): 640–89, here 653.

23. LP1, 160.

24. Lo Piparo, 49ff.

25. As the Soviet scholar E. Ja. Egerman ("Voprosy lingvistiky v teooreti eskix trudax Antonio Gramsci," *VJa* 4, no. 5 [1954]: 114–15) says: "He [Gramsci] understood how harmful the neo-linguists, who transform positivism into the new form of neo-idealism, are to Italian linguistics. Therefore, reelaborating the methodological questions of linguistics, Gramsci does not criticize the theories of the neo-grammarians as much as the reactionary conception of the so-called idealist neo-linguists." As a matter of fact, in the prison notes, the polemic against linguistic positivism seems quite vague and essentially reduced to a repetition of stereotyped formulas (linguistics "narrowly conceived as a natural science," "the vocal apparatus physiologically conceived," etc.). In reality, the picture Gramsci had of the neo-grammatical method derived, above all, from the terms of the polemic set up by Bartoli. Gramsci was not exactly aware of the fact that there was not as great a distance between the neo-linguistic and neo-grammatical method as appeared on the level of militant polemic. In fact, both methods use the same logical paradigm to explain linguistic change and innovation—a paradigm that, in turn, uses inductive and statistical laws. Thus, I would not insist on the real anti-positivism of Gramsci's linguistic thought nor would I accept Lo Piparo's (80) epistemological continuity between the theories of the neo-grammarians and the positivist Marxism of the Second International. On the contrary, what must be noticed is Gramsci's interest in a typical product of German anthropo-linguistic positivism, namely, in the book by F. N. Finck, *Die Sprachstämme des Erdkreises*, third ed. (Leipzig: B. G. Teubner, 1923), which, in the years 1929–1931, he translated completely in the translation *Notebooks B* and *C*. Valentino Gerratana provides an articulated philological description of them (QC, 2437–38) and I hope I will soon be able to fulfill my commitment to publish this translation.

26. Q3§74; Antonio Gramsci, *Prison Notebooks*, vol. 2, trans. Joseph Buttigieg (New York: Columbia University Press, 1996), 70, hereafter PN2.

27. Q3§74, PN2, 71.

28. In a famous article, Croce engaged in a battle to demolish Bertoni's conception highlighting its contradictory inconsistency from Croce's philosophical point of view. Benedetto Croce, "La filosofia del linguaggio e le sue condizioni presenti in Italia," *La Critica* 39 (1941): 169–79.

29. Q3§74, PN2, 71. For a different translation, see SCW, 174.

30. Hermann Paul, *Principien der Sprachgeschichte*, fifth ed. (Halle: Niemeyer, 1920). Translation based on Hermann Paul, *Principles of the History of Language*, second ed., trans. H. A. Strong (London: wan Sonnenschein, Lowrey, 1888).

31. Q6§71, Antonio Gramsci, *Prison Notebooks*, vol. 3, trans. Joseph Buttigieg (New York: Columbia University Press, 2007), 52, hereafter PN3.

32. Lo Piparo, 101–2.

33. Q6§71, PN3, 52.

34. Lo Piparo, 104.

35. Q11§24, Antonio Gramsci, *Selections from Prison Notebooks*, ed. and trans. Quintin Hoare and Geoffrey Nowell Smith (New York: International Publishers, 1971), 451, hereafter SPN.

36. Lo Piparo, 103–51.

37. Bertoni and Bartoli, 94.

38. Perry Anderson, "The Antinomies of Gramsci," *New Left Review* 100 (1976/1977): 18; Christine Buci-Glucksmann, *Gramsci and the State*, trans. David Fernbach (London: Lawrence & Wishart, 1980), 174–85; Luciano Gruppi, *Il Concetto di Egemonia in Gramsci* (Rome: Editori Riuniti, 1972), and Q7§33.

39. Q10II§12, SPN, 365.

40. Q6§71, SCW, 177.

41. Q10§44, SPN, 349, translation altered, see QC, 1330.

42. Q6§62; for a slightly different translation, see PN3, 45.

43. See Albero Cirese, *Intellettuali, Folklore, Istinto di Classe* (Turin: Einaudi, 1976), 65–105.

44. Q11§12, SPN, 325.

45. See Antonio Carrannante, "Antonio Gramsci e i Problemi della Lingua Italiana," *Belfagor* 28 (1973): 551–52.

46. Renée Balibar and Dominique Laporte, *Le Français National* (Paris: Hachette, 1974).

47. PN2, 72–76.

48. Q3§76, PN2, 73–74.

49. Q3§76, PN2, 73–74.

50. Q29§7, SCW, 187–88.

51. Q5§23, PN2, 286.

52. This sociolinguistic thematic is broadly explored by De Mauro; however, Gramsci is only used marginally and only quoted twice. Tullio De Mauro, *Storia Linguistica dell'Italia Unita* (Bari: Laterza, 1970).

53. Q29§6, SCW, 187, translation altered.

54. Q29§6, SCW, 187.

55. Lo Piparo, 256.

3

Language from Nature to History: More on Gramsci the Linguist

*Tullio De Mauro**

<table>
<tr><td>

Spesso a cuori e a picche
ansiose bocche
chiedono la verità.
Principi e plebe
vengono qua:
Madame de Tebe
le carte fa.

</td><td>

From hearts and spades
anxious mouths
often ask for truth
Princes and commoners come
Madame of Tebe
reads the cards

</td></tr>
</table>

M. Lombardo, *Madame de Tebe*[1]

1

Today, we can understand that the relevance of the amount of space Antonio Gramsci devoted to language [*linguaggio*] in his historical and theoretical reflections is not only biographical or quantitative. Sozzi, Rosiello and Carannante's pioneering studies are well behind us.[2] A linguist would be surprised when confronted with such an articulate and original view of Italian linguistics and, especially, of language [*linguaggio*] and of written national languages [*lingue*] (as evident in the way I presented Gramsci's contribution in one of my earlier works, *Storia Linguistica dell'Italia Unità* [Linguistic History of United Italy]).[3] By the early 1970s, this had already given way (not only in my experience) to more systematic attention to the strength of some of the points in Gramsci's linguistic thought—namely,

* Translated from "Il Linguaggio dalla Natura alla Storia: Ancora su Gramsci linguista," in *Gramsci da un Secolo all'Altro*, ed. Giorgio Baratta and Guido Liguori (Rome: Editori Riuniti, 1999), 68–79. Translated by Rocco Lacorte with assistance by Peter Ives.

that human language [*linguaggio*] is constantly innovative and metaphorical, which means one should regard language from a semantic point of view in both ordinary and scientific languages. Gerratana's edition of Gramsci's *Prison Notebooks*[4] was decisive in that it enabled the reconnecting of fragments, like Lo Piparo's study at the end of the 1970s.[5] The amazement or silence about Gramsci's interest in linguistics that has long predominated Gramsci studies since Gobetti's times has now given way to a diffused consciousness about Gramsci's interest in linguistics. There is a renewed need to understand the role and the limits of this specific linguistic interest with respect to his thought taken as a whole and to understand its vitality within the scholarship.

This interest is not exclusively Italian anymore. It is shared by linguistics internationally. If, at the end of the 1980s, Niels Helsloot's work was a thankful, but still an isolated appearance, Gramsci's name now appears—finally—in the very technical *International Encyclopedia of Linguistics* (1993) and a large lexical entry in the *Lexicon Grammaticorum: Who's Who in the History of the World Linguistics* is devoted to him.[6] Moreover, British, North American and French scholars who study the theme of "language and power" and that current, which proudly titles itself "critical linguistics,"[7] explicitly tie themselves to Gramsci. We can now approach this side of Gramsci's heritage with a less troubled and stirred mind.[8]

2

It is important to remember and stress that Gramsci came to language [*linguaggio*]—namely, to linguistic critical reflection—through many paths and was stimulated by heterogeneous experiences. It is not possible to substitute a Gramsci seen as entirely devoted to books of linguistics for the Gramsci seen as a mere Marxist ideologue that dominated the old vernacular gramsciology, or for the Gramsci seen as a pure politician that one can find in recent works. Gramsci's world was rather much wider and various, and his way of approaching linguistic facts was a vital one, as I tried to show in my preface to Lo Piparo's book twenty years ago (to tell the truth, without much of an impact). Here, I will enumerate some of Gramsci's crucial experiences, namely, the real linguistic experimentation that he was very conscious of:

1) First of all, his personal experience as a youth, where his dense Sardinian dialects met, or rather clashed with, Turin's linguistic reality. Turin was still in fact divided by a dense set of dialects, although they were very different from those of Sardinia, and an imminent use of regional Italian (a dialect mechanically Italianized, Gramsci would say

later, echoing a bias diffused in De Amicis and Terracini's Turin) and of learned spoken Italian, the first signs of which were manifested in Turin and Naples in the 1910s (whereas in Rome, it had been spoken for centuries).

2) Gramsci's long and intense experience as a theatre critic, his reflections on dialects and language and on verbalism, mask and gesture, as well as on cinema.

3) Gramsci's experience writing for newspapers seeking to fuse more learned local and national and, later, international political groups, with the urban proletariat. Gramsci was conscious of this experience and he reflected on it, as evident in his notes on journalism. This was an intense and original experience, as attested to by Paolo Spriano.[9]

4) Gramsci's glottological studies at the school of Matteo Bartoli, who was an original figure within early twentieth-century linguistics. Bartoli made Gramsci study the processes of innovation and consolidation of linguistic innovations, the linguistic repercussions of innovative centers' socioeconomic, cultural and political prestige, and traditional German, French and, in Italy, Ascoli's historical linguistics.

5) Gramsci's relationship to Turin's logicians and pragmatists, who were the first to discuss semantics in Italy and to pay crucial attention to the relationships between the semantics of ordinary, daily languages and the construction of the symbolic and scientific ones. It is thanks to the latter, more than to his teacher Bartoli, that Gramsci comes to know the *Essai de Semantique* [Essay on Semantics] by Michel Bréal.

If we look at all these experiences together, and, furthermore, if we think of Gramsci in Vienna or in Moscow, we can see that they are all experiences of "translation": translation from dialect into a multilingual urban world and—especially—vice versa; translation from the language [*linguaggio*] of politicians and ideological intellectuals into clear journalistic writing; translation of learned experiences and exigencies of workers (who were comrades) into general political guidelines; and later, translation of intellectual Italian culture—from Machiavelli to Ascoli to Croce—into the European language of the philosophy of praxis and retranslation of the latter into terms that are Italian not only phono-morphologically but also culturally and semantically; translation of Gramsci himself from the world of humanistic, idealistically orientated culture fraught with spiritualism and anti-scientism into the world of (even idealistic international) culture, of techniques, of natural sciences—a world that he understood and that, again, he retranslated, freeing it from any scientistic residue, from any Lorian idolatry of technical instruments. Before acting as a theoretician, "Antonio the Hunchback"[10] himself lived through these linguistic conflicts and the experience of overcoming them. In this respect, his was really and

literally the non-erudite philosophy of a varied and direct praxis. His readings of linguistics—Ascoli, Bréal, Bartoli and, do not forget, Croce—cata-
lyzed this non-erudite philosophy, but his raw materials were constituted
by his life and his activities as an intellectual.

                                    3

The first coalescence of those experiences took place during the final years
of World War I, while Gramsci was about to write his graduation thesis with
Bartoli on Ascoli, Manzoni and the linguistic situation of a recently united
Italy. In the meantime, he was combining an aspect of his commitment
to socialist and workers' organizations and his approach to the great texts
of classical German philosophy and of Marx. When in 1920 the publisher
UTET entrusted him with an edition of Manzoni's linguistic writings, he
had not abandoned his thesis proposal yet.

It is in those years that one of Gramsci's articles appeared in a politically
activist newspaper. Gramsci writes:

> Manzoni asked himself: now that Italy is formed, how can the Italian language
> be created? He answered: all Italians will have to speak Tuscan and the Italian
> state will have to recruit its elementary teachers in Tuscany. Tuscan will be
> substituted for the numerous dialects spoken in the various regions and, with
> Italy formed, the Italian language will be formed too. Manzoni managed to
> find government support and start the publication of a *Novo dizionario* which
> was supposed to contain the true Italian language. But the *Novo dizionario* re-
> mained half-finished and teachers were recruited among educated people in all
> regions of Italy. It had transpired that a scholar of the history of the language,
> Graziadio Isaia Ascoli, had set some thirty pages against the hundreds of pages
> by Manzoni in order to demonstrate: that not even a national language can
> be created artificially, by order of the state; that the Italian language was being
> formed by itself and would be formed only in so far as the shared life of the
> nation gave rise to numerous and stable contacts between the various parts of
> the nation; that the spread of a particular language is due to the productive
> activity of the writings, trade and commerce of the people who speak that
> particular language.[11]

As one can see, Gramsci still regarded Italian linguistic history in historical,
"idiographic" and particular terms—that is, apparently according to Ascoli's
perspective.

With regard to this latter remark, however, it is necessary to make a
twofold consideration. At this stage of his experience, Gramsci has already established, in an historical way, the terms of a certain dialectic
between society and language to which he will later return. Moreover,

besides Gramsci's evident retrieval of Ascoli's positions, it would seem undeniable that, at this stage, he also recognized the way in which Ascoli's positions are becoming his own and are being represented by Croce.

In 1900, Croce had already written the following in his *Tesi fondamentali di un'estetica come scienza dell'espressione e linguistica generale* [Fundamental Theses of Aesthetics as Science of Expression and General Linguistics]:

> Language is perpetual creation; what is expressed at one time in words is not repeated save in the reproduction of what has already been produced; ever new impressions give rise to a continually changing set of sounds and meanings, that is, to ever new expressions. To search for a model language is, then, to look for a *motionless motion*. . . . It is not only without good reason that the most ardent supporter of this or that solution to the problem of the *unity of the language [lingua]* (be it the adoption of a Latinate, fourteenth-century, or Florentine language, or whatever else) when he comes to speak, in order to communicate his views and to make them understood, feels reluctant to apply his *theories*; since he senses that to substitute the Latin, fourteenth-century, or Florentine words for those of a different origin which correspond to his natural impressions, would be to falsify the genuine form of the truth; so that from being a *speaker*, he would become a *conceited listener to himself*, from a *serious* man, a *pedant*; from a *sincere* person, a *histrionic* one.

The question of the *unity of language* continually crops up because, as it is posed, it is *insoluble*, being founded on a false conception of what language is. It is not an arsenal of beautiful finished weapons, and it is not a *vocabulary*, which is a collection of abstractions, that is to say, a cemetery of corpses more or less progressively updated.

We would not want, by this somewhat brusque way of cutting short the question of a *model language*, or of the *unity of the language*, to appear less than respectful to the great throng of writers, who have for centuries discussed it in Italy.[12]

Croce, the young scholar, uses these paragraphs almost verbatim with only a few typographical corrections, in a volume entitled *Estetica come scienza dell'espressione e linguistica generale* [The Aesthetic as the Science of Expression and of the Linguistic in General] published by Sandron in Palermo. This volume, as is known, shocked Bartoli because it came close to plagiarizing him; he even recommended it to his students. This version of the text was not changed in the subsequent editions published by Laterza. But in the first version (1900), this passage is followed by one (quoted below) where Croce posited the premises for an historical rethinking of what the question of language had been. In this earlier version, he writes with more vivacity and uses concrete and openly politico-social references, reminiscent of Pontano.[13] The subsequent versions of the *Estetica* are more sober and he attenuates the politico-social references. Here is the continuation of the passage quoted above from the 1900 version:

> [We would not want to appear less than respectful . . .] especially to the last great promoter of it [the *unity of the language*], Alessandro Manzoni. I will add that, in my opinion, the true problem troubling Manzoni was *aesthetic* and was not a problem of *aesthetic science*, of *literature* or of the *theory of literature*, of *effective speaking* and *writing* and not of *linguistic science*. Manzoni's theory was rigorous, logical and quite sophisticated, but it was wrong because its practical solution looked like a scientific thesis, which it could not by definition be. Rejecting this thesis does not mean affirming that Manzoni and his followers were working on an empty terrain. Under Manzoni's banner, the spiritual needs of Italy in the new era, the needs of unity and democracy, the reaction against the pompous formalism of old Italy, and so on and so forth, emerged on the battle field. What was at stake were *new impressions* demanding new expressions. This situation was serious, although Manzoni's scientific thesis, which was put forward in order to justify these new needs, was inadmissible. Moreover, the question [of the unity of the language] that had been solved practically, remained theoretically unresolved or was badly resolved by means of the false conception that Florentine authors were the repository of the only real Italian linguistic tradition. Anyone who speaks or writes in Italy nowadays has felt the effectiveness of the movement promoted by Manzoni; even his adversaries felt it. As is the case . . . not infrequent in history: beneficial movements are made by means of erroneous theories.[14]

The interpretation Croce draws out from Manzoni's position is close to the reading provided by Graziadio Isaia Ascoli (whom Croce knew and even appreciated as a prose writer) in the *Proemio* [Preface] that he used to begin the publication of the journal *Archivio Glottologico Italiano* [Italian Glottological Archive]. In the less precise editing of the *Estetica*, the distance between Ascoli and Croce's interpretations of Manzoni's position seems to increase. Yet Croce's conclusive words added in the *Estetica* to the passage mentioned above (from his previous *Tesi*) definitely sound like Ascoli's: "The social need for an easier understanding can only be satisfied by the diffusion of culture and by the growth of communication and of intellectual exchanges between people."[15] Gramsci certainly already knew about these passages because of their clarity, grounding, source and location; he keeps them in his mind through his last notebook.

Three decades later, the linguist Alfredo Schiaffini and Antonio Gramsci find themselves far enough from those texts to consider the question of language with the detachment of the historian, in the former case in a specialized journal, *Italia Dialettale* [Italian Dialect], and the latter, notes written in prison.

The intention of historicizing the old question of language is present in both Gramsci and Schiaffini. They both highlight the objective components of the discussions among the intelligentsia. Schiaffini unfolds his analysis paying attention to objective linguistic conditions (the secular persistence of dialectal heterogeneity, Tuscany's lack of hegemonic capability after the sixteenth century, lack of spoken Italian outside Tuscany) and to the inevitable questions regarding stylistic choices imposed by those conditions on Italian writers, including Manzoni (who was also conscious of these questions). Moreover, as is known, the subsequent historical studies have deepened, specified, and confirmed the interpretive lines Schiaffini had enunciated.

4

In the *Notebooks*, Gramsci's emphases are partly different. In the prison notes, the question of language in Italy is a central knot of the "nexus of questions" that the historian of Italian reality can provide to those reflecting on the interplay of forces regulating life in society, not so much *en historien* but rather *en philosophe*—even though as a philosopher of "praxis." The shift of Gramsci's focus from history and the history of Italian linguistics to general theory, from idiographic to nomographic, appears evident above all in Notebook 29, Gramsci's last one, written in 1935 and entitled "Notes for an Introduction to the Study of Grammar."

As I recalled elsewhere, Giuseppe Giarrizzo has formulated a suggestive interpretive hypothesis regarding this matter. What Gramsci attempted to elaborate in his mind during the period of his stay in Vienna and in Moscow, and during the rise of the PCI [the Italian Communist Party] was a general national Italian response to the dramatic demands of the international communist movement and of the forthcoming fascisms.

This general hypothesis can be integrated with other considerations that are more specifically connected to the questions regarding the relationships between language, nationality and classes, which have been recently and rightly pointed out by Giancarlo Schirru, a young scholar from Rome. These questions are alive in international socialism in early 1920s. Lenin's article *Sulla Cooperazione* [On Cooperation] was published in 1923, in which he supports the necessity of developing alphabetization and culture as necessary complements of socialist politics. Lenin's *Die Nationalitätenfrage und die Sozialdemokratie* [The National Problem and Social Democracy] came out in 1924 and was bitterly discussed by Kautsky and later by Stalin. These vital questions arise while the two great multilingual Austro-Hungarian and Ottoman empires are collapsing and new nationalities and languages are acquiring relevance, and while the Soviet Union starts a great alphabetization process of its population targeting the most disparate languages spoken in the country. All these

languages are transformed from being almost exclusively oral to also being written languages. The alphabetization process occurs starting from the
written languages and only later from the teaching of the Russian language.
It must be noted that William McKey and Miguel Siguan, two of the major
scholars of the processes of alphabetization in bilingual areas, have recently
stressed, in *Bilinguisme et Education* [Bilingualism and Education], what I
have always held: the great experience of the Soviet linguistico-scholastic
politics is an exemplary one.

What fascism tried to kill—and effectively contributed to keeping
smothered for a long time by imprisoning Gramsci—was the proliferation
of a whole philosophical and anthropological theoretical view of social
and cultural life and of the forms through which human beings forge
techniques (yet, in Gramsci as well as in [Antonino] Pagliaro's eyes, language is precisely the following: a technique of expressing and elaborating
symbols). Thanks to these techniques history is constructed on the basis
of nature. This view, if I am not wrong, is perfectly attuned with those Lev
Vigotskij [Vigotsky] and Jean Piaget. Karl Bühler and the Prague Structuralists, the psychologists of *Gestalt* and cognition and Ludwig Wittgenstein
were pursuing (or pursued) it in different environments. As with Hegel
(who is quoted far more than Engels in the *Prison Notebooks*—as Kant is
quoted more than Trotsky, Gentile more than Lenin, Croce more than
Marx—yet this is not because Gramsci had to be careful as a prisoner),
for Gramsci, "hand and word" sustain, materialize and project the human
capacity of intervening in the order of nature, turning it to human needs as
much as possible and transforming, in some way, its value. Starting from
the vital natural base, human beings become historical subjects thanks to
these techniques.

A "fundamental point," for Gramsci, is to understand "how historical
movement arises on the ground of the structure."[16] It is not so much the
objectivity of the real that is central for him, as he writes:

> but humanity forging its methods of research, continually correcting those
> of its material instruments which reinforce sensory organs and logical instru-
> ments of discrimination and ascertainment (which include mathematics): in
> other words culture, the conception of the world, the relationship between
> humanity and reality as mediated by technology. . . . Without humanity's
> activity, which creates all, even scientific, values, what would "objectivity" be?
> A chaos, i.e., nothing, a void, if one can indeed say that, because in reality, if
> one imagines that humanity does not exist, one cannot imagine language and
> thought.[17]

During the historical evolution of the human species, these techniques
become economic-productive activity, cultural heritage, language and political dimension.[18]

There is no pan-lingualism in Gramsci, as there is no economism. What Gramsci wants to investigate passionately and enlighten us by teaching is the nexus and the circularity of these elements: that is, the capability of transforming raw materials into new products. This means that, for Gramsci, the economic-productive element is interwoven with the element of invention and cultural elaboration, and both cannot subsist without being woven into the capability of linguistic elaboration and communication and with the construction of life in common in both the ethnic and national dimensions of life.

Within this circle, which is vital for individuals and society, language and linguistic conformism constitute only one link; although the circle is broken without it. It can be hypothesized that Gramsci's readings of Bréal and of the semantics of the Turin pragmatists and his reflections on the direct experiences of communication were valuable in enabling him to better understand Hegel, and thus, that the role of language cannot be eliminated from constituting, articulating and organizing the historical life of societies. This allows us to understand the value of the subject of linguists' analytical, historical and descriptive inquiries. Croce, pushed by dramatic theoretically external factors of the fight against the obtuse savagery of fascism and Nazism, will follow Gramsci along this path, even though much later. In a new light, he valorizes institutions and "abstractions," the pursuit of life's activities, of literature and its civil ethos, and, finally, of the place of the "language of linguists" in the life of society.

5

Thus, for Gramsci, the events in Italy become a case study for the laboratory of his prison notes. Gramsci shifts from idiographic and particular to the general and "nomographic." In the last *Notebook*, Gramsci develops a social and political theory of grammar, which is meant to be a model (as Lo Piparo thought) or a complement (as it seems to me more correct to interpret) of a theory of society, culture and politics. In this notebook, Italy appears a little larger than the "terrestrial flower bed" Dante sees from paradise, because "the linguistic fact, like any other historical fact, cannot have strictly defined national boundaries, but . . . history is always 'world history' and . . . particular histories live only within the framework of world history."[19]

In a specific and successful way, "the archangel sent to destroy the neo-grammarians" delineates the relationships between: (1) immanent grammaticality (always present when people talk and want to understand); (2) "implicit" (as we say) or "lived" (as Lombardo Radice said) immanent and normative grammar, which is created in a group within and for mutual understanding; and (3) "written" (as Gramsci says), "explicit" (as we say today) or "reflected" grammar (as Lombardo Radice said). The latter is always a political act and, if adequate, leads to the constitution of more or less temporary written national languages.[20] In some sense, one can find in this grammatical view of Gramsci's the same picture drawn by Saussure in his third *Course* (an obvious comparison since both Gramsci and Saussure stem from Bréal), but viewed from the opposite perspective. Whereas one can observe a neverending mobility of immanent grammars in Saussure, even though concealed by the apparent inertness of written languages with respect to the vital and primary self-making and -unmaking of spoken *langue;* one can observe a neverending mobility of political situations and of the political effects springing out of the constitution of relatively inert written languages, which emerge by historic-political necessity from the mobile dynamics related to the permanent innovativeness of speaking. Saussure's third *Course* [in *General Linguistics*] seems to tell us, "Be aware of the always fluid spoken and not only written language!" while Gramsci seems to tell us, "Be aware of the modalities through which written languages constitute themselves, namely, as great political events!" As in an ideal school in Athens, the two directions diverge, even though both equally and clearly delineate the same objective picture of the linguistic universe.

Gramsci adds, always generalizing and probably criticizing the progressive affirmation of those bureaucratic aspects emerging within cultural and linguistic policies of Stalin's age:

> Since the process of formation, spread and development of a unified national language occurs through a whole complex of molecular processes, it helps to be aware of the entire process as a whole in order to be able to intervene actively in it with the best possible results. One need not consider this intervention as "decisive" and imagine that the ends proposed will be reached in detail, i.e., that one will obtain a *specific* unified language. One will obtain a *unified language,* if it is a necessity, and the organized intervention will speed up the already existing process: in any case, if the intervention is "rational," it will be organically tied to tradition, and this is of no small importance in the economy of culture.[21]

For Gramsci, the historical recuperation of the Italian language question stems from this general vision. This issue becomes an example, a valuable, personally experienced, first-hand example, though not more than an example:

> Manzonians and "classicists." They had a type of language which they wanted to make prevail. It is not correct to say that these discussions were useless and have not left traces in modern culture, even if the traces are modest. Over the

last century a unified culture has in fact been extended, and therefore also a common unified language. But the entire historical formation of the Italian nation moved at too slow a pace.[22]

And again Gramsci returns to a conclusion of a more general character. Locked in prison, Gramsci does not look only at his own country, but rather at the more vast world of humans: "Every time that the question of language surfaces, in one way or another, it means that a series of problems are coming to the fore: the formation and enlargement of the governing class, the need to establish more intimate and secure relationships between the governing groups and the national-popular mass, in other words to reorganize the cultural hegemony."[23]

These memorable words became known in 1950, through the publication of these pages in *Letteratura e Vita Nazionale* [Literature and National Life]. In Italy, they meant the achievement of a high goal and a demanding cultural and intellectual yardstick for the best minds to confront—writers like [Italo] Calvino, [Carlo Emilio] Gadda or [Pier Paolo] Pasolini, some scholars of linguistics, educators like Don Lorenzo Milani, who in the second half of the century addressed the questions of the linguistic organization of Italian society or more general reflections on the role language plays in history and human life.

Today, as I was recalling at the beginning of this piece, these questions are being translated into other languages and appear to have a broader attraction for those who work in the educative dimension or attend to theoretical studies on language and culture: like the tongue in cheek refrain, which Gramsci loved, *Princes and people come: Madame of Tebe reads the cards.*

NOTES

1. Quoted in M. L. Straiero, *Un Ritornello Amato da Gramsci,* in *Osteria* (Milan: Dischi del sole, 1969).

2. Bartolo Tommasso Sozzi, *Aspetti e Momenti della Questione Linguistica* (Padova: Liviana, 1955). See Rosiello, this volume, chapter 2, and Antonio Carannante, "Antonio Gramsci e i problemi della lingua italiana," *Belfagor* 28 (1973): 544–56.

3. Tullio De Mauro, *Storia Linguistica dell'Italia Unita* (Bari: Laterza, 1963).

4. Antonio Gramsci, *Quaderni del Carcere,* four volumes, ed. Valentino Gerratana (Turin: Einaudi, 1975), hereafter QC.

5. Franco Lo Piparo, *Lingua, Intellettuali, Egemonia in Gramsci* (Bari: Laterza, 1979).

6. Harro Stammerjohann, ed., *Lexicon Grammaticorum: Who's Who in the History of the World Linguistics* (Tübingen: Max Niemeyer Verlag, 1996).

7. [Both expressions in quotation marks appear in English in the Italian text.]

8. [The latter expression comes from Giambattista Vico, *La Scienza Nuova* [The New Science].]

9. Paolo Spriano, *Antonio Gramsci and the Party: The Prison Years*, trans. John Fraser (London: Lawrence & Wishart, 1979).

10. [De Mauro is using Gramsci's nickname to recall the hardships and health problems of Gramsci's childhood leading to his hunch condition.]

11. Antonio Gramsci, "A Single Language and Esperanto," in *Selections from Cultural Writings*, ed. D. Forgacs and G. Nowell-Smith, trans. W. Boelhower (Cambridge, Mass.: Harvard University Press, 1985), 28, hereafter SCW. There is a list of abbreviations on pages ix–x.

12. Benedetto Croce, *Tesi fondamentali di un'estetica come scienza dell'espressione e linguistica generali*, Memoria letta all'Accademia Pontaniana, Naples, Stabilimento tipografico dell'Università, 1900 (but actually published in 1901!), 80–81. [This translation is based on Benedetto Croce, *The Aesthetic as the Science of Expression and of the Linguistic in General*, trans. Colin Lyas (Cambridge: Cambridge University Press, 1992), 163–84, translation altered slightly.]

13. [Giovanni Pontano, 1426–1503, poet and writer known for his supple, pragmatic style.]

14. Croce, *Tesi Fondamentali*, 81.

15. See Croce, *The Aesthetic*, 164. Translation altered.

16. Q11§22, Antonio Gramsci, *Selections from Prison Notebooks*, ed. and trans. Quintin Hoare and Geoffrey Nowell Smith (New York: International Publishers, 1971), 431, hereafter cited as SPN. [To facilitate locating passages in various translations and anthologies, we use the standard method of providing the notebook (*Quaderno*) number—in this case 11—followed by the section number, §. See the introduction, page 12, for discussion. We will indicate the English translation, if used.]

17. Q11§37, Antonio Gramsci, *Further Selections from the Prison Notebooks*, ed. and trans. Derek Boothman (Minneapolis: University of Minnesota Press, 1995), 292.

18. On Croce, see Q10§54II, SPN, 351–54.

19. Q29§2, SCW, 181.

20. Q29§2, SCW, 181–82.

21. Q29§3, SCW, 183.

22. Q29§3, SCW, 183.

23. Q29§3, SCW, 183.

4

Linguistics and the Political Question of Language

*Stefano Gensini**

In the *Introduction to the Second Course of General Linguistics* (1908–1909), one can find Saussure's metaphor of language as a "vessel not in dry-dock but on the sea." This metaphor contains much more than a generic instance of sociohistorical contextualization of linguistic facts. There is a radical rupture with the tradition of positivist and neo-grammatical tradition in this metaphor, in a historical moment of both very dense theoretical and meta-theoretical reflection, where linguistics starts to constitute itself as science, while including itself in the class of the semiological disciplines. For the neo-grammarians, in fact, the society-language pair, though ever reaffirmed, did not go beyond the borders of a conventional and, therefore, a substantially static relationship. In this relationship, languages, as given entities, are placed alongside human communities, which nominally and mechanically signify them. On the contrary, for Saussure, "'This social nature' [of signs] is one of its internal, not one of its external, elements"[1]: The *collectivity of speakers* is defined as a constitutive principle of the functioning of language, in a historical time and space. This collectivity is the real historical agent that continuously establishes, disaggregates and reaggregates, the functional relationship of value within the linguistic system through social practices, in which the infinite individual linguistic acts (paroles) intertwine.

It can even seem odd rereading certain pages of the *Course* that, to some materialistically oriented authoritative scholars, the lesson of the master from Geneva may have appeared tarnished by idealistic abstractness. In

* Translation of "Linguistica e Questione Politica della Lingua," *Critica Marxista* 1 (1980): 151–65. Translated by Rocco Lacorte with assistance by Peter Ives.

reality, *against* the founder of scientific linguistics [Saussure] and, *notwith-standing* his programmatic indications, the great part of twentieth-century reflection in the field of linguistic sciences consisted of the effort of exclud-ing from theory the bothersome presence of the "speaker" (or, better, of the speakers)—who, for Saussure, were the "prime principle" of his scientific construction—namely, the notion of arbitrariness, that is, of the radical impact of history and society on linguistic facts, as clearly distinct from the notion of conventionality.[2] After all, this is what Noam Chomsky's great journey consisted of: the elaboration of an idea of language as an (innate) self-regulating syntactic mechanism, which is, by definition detached from semantic implications and programmatically referred to "an ideal speaker-listener, in a completely homogenous speech-community, who knows its language perfectly."[3] Chomsky consistently eliminates all the "grammati-cally irrelevant conditions" (among which he mentions mistakes, distrac-tions, changes of interest or of attention) that belong to mere individual *performances* and that do not effect the generative schematics of *competence* that are not pertinent from a theoretical point of view. Therefore, Chomsky sees language as a kind of mathematics: it doesn't matter *who* or why, or for what goal, the linguistic operation is performed. The living world of historico-natural languages fades into a neutral balance of calculations. The dialectical nature of the relationship individuals-society (*parole*-language[*lingua*]), which Saussure viewed as an always opened weaving between regularities and infractions and of innovation and conformism,[4] is destroyed and flattened on the level of abstract *competence*, which must be presupposed as innate in the biological sense, in order to assure com-munication. In this way, however, both Noam Chomsky and his followers went back to that kind of despised *empiricism* which some had wanted to free linguistic science from forever.[5]

Certainly, we can see all of this today. Thanks to the joint efforts of those who continue Saussure's teaching—open to the sharpest logico-epis-temological tradition of European thought—it was possible to elaborate the tools which do not throw out the social dimension of linguistic facts and to limit the intrusions of the culture of Chomskianism, revealing its internal incongruence. It seems to me, however, that one can find a rather interesting politico-cultural problem in the backdrop of these theoretical phenomena.

I am alluding to the fact that Chomsky's theoretical construction corre-sponded to, and somewhat formalized, a certain condition typical of intel-lectuals in the United States of America, notwithstanding their pacifism and progressive nature. A propos one can consider the open scission Chomsky makes between the theoretical work of the linguist and the "analysis of the social and political questions" in the notorious *Intervista su Linguaggio e Ideologia*.[6] Chomsky's declared intention is to take the mystifying presence of the technicians away from the realm of politics and to demonstrate the concrete public dimension that does not need specialization, but rather "only some Cartesian good sense." This is certainly one way to react against the condition of politics conceived as mere technique and manipulation of power which is typical of the American world. Yet one can well suspect that Chomsky remains fully within the ideological schemes of the traditional separation of the intellectual from society, despite the merits he acquired through his generous democratic and anti-imperialist struggle. In fact, it seems that for him, on the one hand, politics, which is the arena of empirical things, only needs to be illuminated by Enlightenment's *raison* (that *works by itself*, rather aristocratically outside of any political perspective which is or could be organized). On the other hand, the academic profession of a linguist is removed from social tensions in principle. Anyone who studies the marginal languages of New York's ghettoes and the relationships between linguistic analysis, social situation of the speakers and scholastic condition does "a nice thing," which is yet "evident and banal" on the theoretical level.[7] William Labov's sociolinguistics (which we will return to later) has a practical interest "on the level of education." But, for Chomsky, it does not enter the conceptual realm: "It remains something obscure, at this level," because, from the beginning, he negated the linguistic pertinence of the social element, that is, concerning who speaks and why one speaks. For Chomsky, the formal aspect of theory and the isolated condition of the American intellectual truly seem to come together and designate in their own way, a less than brief epoch of the culture of linguistics in these years.

The Chomskian *revolution* consisted in what has been said above, socially and theoretically. If these considerations make sense, this revolution seems to have been a sort of "preventive counterrevolution" in the field of linguistic sciences (to paradoxically continue the metaphor). This is not the place to recall the intoxication of scientism and formalism that this revolution has brought not only to the United States, but also to some European universities, including Italian ones. Moreover, many European universities and some of the Italian ones that were intoxicated by this linguistic formalism and by scientism, while looking for mediations with other cultural currents, have not succeeded in overcoming the perfect (and yet unacceptable) rigor of the American master. Yet the situation is clearly changing today. After years of adjustments and theoretical compromises, of progressive modification to the *standard* Chomskian model, and of the breaks within Chomsky's school, there is a profound tendency to recover the analytic direction inspired by historical and empirical experience that we will discuss below. After sixty years, the vitality of Saussure's teaching, and, even beyond Saussure, of the relevance of the sociohistorical component seems to be reemerging.

In this picture, of particular interest is the direction provided by Bruce Derwing in his *Transformational Grammar as a Theory of Language Acquisition* (1973).[8] He is a scholar who went through the entire Chomskian experience and who got to the point of radically refuting it. Derwing severely criticizes the TGG[9] both on the technical and on the epistemological level, destroying one by one all the bricks of Chomsky's theoretical construction: innatism and linguistic universals, the concept of *rule*, the notions of competence and execution and the structure of his theory itself.

It is vital that we focus on two of these points. First of all, the discovery that Chomsky's construction is not verifiable (which is something that has particular importance since Chomsky's theory affirmed the introduction into linguistics of the unverified linguistic procedure of scientific rigor *through* the extreme complexity of its mathematical apparatus). Facing an established epistemological tradition that, from Popper to Bachelard, views the nature of scientific discourses as being disposed to *falsification* in an explicit and methodical way—insofar as their possibility of becoming social and their possible "cumulative" character would consist of being disposed to falsification. "Chomsky's philosophy of linguistics is imbued with the idea that theories are tested by inquiring whether the data at hand are or are not *compatible* with a transformational-generative description; rarely does one find a transformationist exposing the basic tenets of TGG to falsification 'in every possible way,' or exposing them to 'the fiercest struggle for survival' against equally well-conceived and well-developed alternative accounts."[10]

The second point concerns, instead, Derwing's positive proposal "toward a redefinition of linguistic research." Reexamining the classical modeling of linguistic processes introduced by communications' engineering,[11] Derwing becomes aware that the moment of "codification" and of "decoding"—namely, the initial and final moments (i.e., those of the sender and of the recipient) of the linguistic process are its decisive moments, despite the fact that the attention of the linguists falls on what is usually observable: the message as objective.

This point is decisive because the entire well-known theory of the "functions" of language (from Bühler to Jakobson and Halliday) is based on the theoretical equivocation that language *per se* possesses some opportunities which can be enumerated and described in a closed set, however large. The various imprints of objectivism and organicism characterize not only linguistic structuralism, but, among other things, many of its transpositions in the arena of literary criticism derived from this theoretical equivocation. Derwing's conclusion is therefore of the highest interest, to the extent that it recognizes the source of linguistic unities—"at whatever 'level'" they would be recognized—in the consideration and in the unifying activity of the speaking subjects: in other words, of the "language user." Moreover, as he continues, in a more explicit way: "The explanation of the form of utterances is not to be found in the utterances themselves (though these provide helpful clues), but within the language user. . . . It is impossible to determine what the structure of a language is without broaching the question how that structure functions, since language has no structure independent of the process."[12] In our view, this is a way to go back to Saussure's awareness, which was our starting point: namely, language viewed as a vessel which is no longer in the dry-dock, but in the midst of the sea, where the shape of the hull no longer counts, and whose course cannot be foreseen; language made for the reality of usage, ploughed by many and unforeseeable currents, and tied to the specificity of the situations and of the concrete speakers.

Derwing here finds himself—whether conscious or not—in agreement with the theoretical break performed by Wittgenstein in his *Philosophical Investigations*. In this work, Wittgenstein substitutes the notion of meaning elaborated by Frege and traditional logic (and, as he says, even by the author of the *Tractatus Logico-Philosophicus*—i.e., Wittgenstein!) with an idea of the processes of *signifying*,[13] in which words are brought back to their daily usage (so allowing philosophy "to rest") and to the possibility of being practiced by the users, which does not tolerate being confined to a restricted number of "language games."[14] In this manner, Derwing lays the foundation that allows an escape from the conception of linguistic facts that we called organicistic—this is what John Lyons does not succeed in doing with his vigorous manual of *Semantics I-II*, where the recovery of the philosophy of ordinary language and of Wittgenstein's operationalism, on the one hand, and of Austin's and Searle's operationalism, on the other, only serves the goal of attributing one *variable* (the social one) among others to language and not of theoretically reconsidering its intrinsically sociohistorical nature, insofar as it is a semiologic system.

I am glad that such a conclusion comes from North America because it returns to the core of the problem—better than Chomsky or the post-Chomskians—namely, to reframe linguistics on the renewed grounds of social and historical theory in an experimental dimension, proceeding through hypotheses and exact verifications. Yet it is here that Derwing's program shows its limits or its inevitable historical twists. I am alluding to his proposal of substantially reformulating linguistics as a branch of psychology. It no longer seems, however, that Chomsky (who, in the last years, has been the main supporter of the psychological nature of language) is behind Derwing's theoretical proposal. Rather, it seems that Derwing's is a non-Chomskian and experimental interest in "the problems concerning linguistic behaviors and processes."[15] It is, however, noteworthy that Derwing's return to *the speaker* does not make him aware of the data (which for Chomsky were already "irrelevant") that today seems to stimulate more robust sectors of the research on language (as we will soon show): namely, that regarding the social influence of linguistic facts, the sociocultural stratifications of the environment, and the weave of idiomatic and dialectal varieties in the competence of single individuals and of the communities. Derwing's choice therefore shifts to the psychological ground, which, certainly, has a fundamental importance.[16] However, in a more articulated theoretical framework, experiences and empirical works which are the patrimony of the last decades would find opportune development.

The volume *Per Saussure contro Saussure*[17] [For Saussure against Saussure], by Annibale Elia, can be useful to broaden the horizon and clarify the contorted cultural itinerary of the linguistic sciences in this century. Well aware of the epistemic and methodological importance of the social notion of language elaborated by Saussure, Elia documents very precisely the motifs concerning the progressive eclipse of the "social" in post-Saussurian philosophy of language. The inauthentic, rigid, dehistoricized Saussure, emerging from his pupils' deficient reconstruction of the *Cours de Linguistique Generale*, has helped, as Elia explains, the simultaneous divorce between linguistic theory and social theory, which has been performed—even though under different, but deep down similar, perspectives—by European and American structuralism. In the famous [Prague School's] "Theses of 1929," one could see the beginning of a dangerous and philosophically compromising teleological trend of interpreting the Saussurean conception of linguistic change. There was also a misunderstanding of the methodological and non-organic character of the synchrony/diachrony dichotomy which departed from Saussure's already fully developed awareness of the intrinsically *historical* character of every moment of the life of a *langue*.[18] On both sides of the Atlantic Ocean, the nonsocial and nonsemantic nature of research perspectives correspond to each other: while Trubetzkoy bracketed *meaning*, in order to get at an advanced analysis of the *signifier* of the linguistic sign and laying an initial rigorous theorization of the concept of distinctive oppositions as found in his *Principles* [*Grundzüge*],[19] Bloomfield and his followers reject meaning as inaccessible to objective analysis, which, under the behaviorist point of view, could be explained only on the ground of observable data. The theoretical value of these two instances is certainly very different, but the results that each of them achieves are not dissimilar. It can now be well understood (as Elia shows convincingly) how Chomsky's theoretical effort rises from such bases. After all, the project of the GGT brings to its extreme consequences the goal that characterized various sectors of language research, not solely the American. The aim of achieving a "Parmenidean" model of language, namely, a closed system which can refer back to a fixed number of operations is the kind of *objet*[20] that calms the linguist down. This is the case at both the theoretical level (where formal work on objects of study which are informal by nature is terribly complicated), and on the professional level taken in a broader sense (where it is not necessary to look outside the laboratory and to consider the "accidental" and not entirely foreseeable moment of linguistic usage).

In different spheres, linguistic theories have run across the uncomfortable world of social phenomena. This is the case in Sapir, Malinowski and Firth's anthropology; in Weinreich's dialectology, which is devoted to the complex moment of the "contact" between languages; and of William Labov's sociolinguistics. In this fashion, as Elia writes, "In the 1960's, a revaluation of sociality—conceived above all as variation—in the linguistic theories and methodologies was achieved."[21] The most authentic interpretation of Saussure's conception of language—in opposition to the one often proclaimed—was therefore rediscovered on the ground: it is this interpretation that, between 1957 (the year in which the *Sources Manuscripts* of the *Course on General Linguistics* [*Cours de Linguistique Generale*] came to light) and today, scholars such as Godel, De Mauro, Engler and Prieto have brought to the fore, making, as we said above, the concept of arbitrariness its pivot.

The case of Labov—an author that, in my view, needs further valorization—is quite singular. In the essays recently gathered for the Italian public (*Il Continuo e il Discreto nel Linguaggio*[22] [The Continuous and The Discrete in Language]), Labov strongly criticizes rigidly categorical conceptions of language, for which the linguistic structure would be "an ensemble of discrete categories, which are invariant and qualitatively defined."[23] He traces this conception back to a continuous line of thought that goes from Saussure to Chomsky. Differently from many "classic" structuralists working on *language in use*,[24] Labov is aware that those who view linguistic phenomena through such categories neither succeed in explaining nor want to explain the infinite *variants* and *particularities* of the concrete linguistic practice in "marginal" social situations, which are very far from the ideal speakers as portrayed in the tradition of the generative linguists. It is clear that Labov's attack addresses more the vulgarizations of Saussure (which were already mediated by Chomskism) than Saussure himself. But this is not the point. What counts is Labov's claim, which is already theoretical despite Chomsky's dismissal; a claim concerning the "continuous" nature of the object, language. In other words, the nature of language is intrinsically informal, specifically, social and manipulative. Moreover, the problem Labov posits—to construct a "theory of the limits" capable of understanding "how discrete categories can be imposed on the continuous substance of the world"[25]—seems to me analogous to the one briefly mentioned above, concerning how to provide rigorously a theory with the means by which a not entirely calculable object, such as a natural language, can be described.

I believe that it is not by accident that Labov's experience has been welcomed in Italy (also because of what his professional profile as a linguist presupposes; it seems to me that he constitutes a novelty in the recent cultural tradition in the United States).[26] The possibilities for linguists pursuing "ideal" models of communicative competencies are reduced in America, by the politico-cultural emergence of the linguistic questions rooted in the varied inheritance of dialects and idioms of minorities, and in Italy, the dramatic sociocultural fractures that exist. No wonder that Italian scholars turned their interest to Labov's research and, vice versa, since their interest coincided with the substantial nonpenetration of the most famous hypotheses by Bernstein, regarding the "compensation" of the so-called linguistic deficit in Italy. Whereas Labov's model is programmatically "open" and politically unequivocal, Bernstein has in mind a concept of language that is closed and mechanically connected to social class conditions. The tight homology Bernstein establishes between "low" classes and "restricted code," on the one hand, and, on the other hand, between middle classes and "elaborated code," excluding a reciprocal permeability between these two levels, has rightly appeared fallacious on the theoretical level, falsified on the historical level (it is enough to think of the sociolinguistic dynamics in Italy in this century), and politically functional for a conservative view of society. For a full critique of Bernsteinism, one can refer to the *Manuale di Sociolinguistica* [Manual of Sociolinguistics] by Norbert Dittmar[27] that is constructed on the grounds of an interesting perspective of "ideology critique"—which is not common among linguists—and that seems deficient only in the sense that it is affected by a certain schematism in the assessment of Labov's experience.

To tighten the various separate and wandering threads of this discussion, we will use the assistance of the important work, *Lingua, Intellettuali, Egemonia in Gramsci*[28] [Language, Intellectuals, Hegemony in Gramsci] by Franco Lo Piparo, with an engaging preface by Tullio De Mauro. In this essay the object of analysis is pushed back or rather qualitatively modified. The object does not concern university professors, but a politician and great intellectual [Antonio Gramsci]: a theoretician and strategist of the proletarian revolution in the West. What is the meaning, or meanings, of this type of change of analysis?

The answer (I am trying to summarize and interpret Lo Piparo's perspective) can perhaps be the following: with Gramsci, linguistic questions are definitively taken out of the realm of any kind of specialist, and are inserted deeply in the analysis of how society functions. Language appears as the real terrain where civil and political society intersect, as the site of socialization or separation of experiences, knowledge and needs. Likewise, language appears as the decisive dimension of politico-cultural stratification of the class system that crosses and defines the ways of thinking and feeling of entire populations from common sense to scientific theories of reality. Finally, language appears as the concrete space for every possible hegemony—namely, the site and condition of the "intellectual and moral reformation of the masses" of which the socialist revolution in Italy must consist.

In this way, Lo Piparo both connects the case of Gramsci in the contemporary theoretical dispute, which is internal to linguistic sciences, and launches it again into the more complex historico-political debate, which, for several years, has characterized the reflections of Marxists in and outside of Italy.

Lo Piparo's starting point is seriously and solidly philological. He presents the information he finds in Gramsci's biography concerning his formation as a linguist, which, except for a few sporadic and partial exceptions,[29] was never fully developed. Gramsci, before becoming a political leader, develops in Bartoli's school of "neo-linguistics." He studied theory and the history of language in a moment in which there is a struggle between the neo-grammarian and historicist tendencies and he became excited about the polemic between Manzoni and Ascoli, adhering to the latter's historiographic perspective. Lo Piparo reconstructs with great care the materials that Gramsci certainly read and those that he probably read. Lo Piparo provides an abundant quantity of bibliographical references, with respect both to the Italian linguistic tradition and to the French sociology of Meillet and Gilliéron. Moreover, he comes to formulate the hypothesis that this liberal-linguistic formation does not fade in the mature Gramsci—the Marxist and the secretary of the PCI—but rather constitutes and characterizes some of the central categories of the *Notebooks*: namely, the theory concerning intellectuals and, through it, the notion of *hegemony*, which seems to have a substantial antecedent in the linguistic notion of *prestige*. In this fashion, Lo Piparo recuperates, for the rich legacy of Gramscian studies, one of the original points of the work-plan announced by Gramsci in the letter to Tania of March 19, 1927 (where second, after "a study of Italian intellectuals, and their origins etc.," Gramsci mentions "a study of comparative linguistics! Nothing less"),[30] and Gramsci's conceptual connection between the unpopularity of Italian literature, the question of a national language, the need for an intellectual reformation of the masses, the unpopularity of the Risorgimento and so on as he announces it in the famous "nexus of problems."[31] The linguistic moment (that Gramsci elegantly introduces through the mischievous label of something *für ewig*) is therefore seen as one of the nodal passages of Gramsci's thought and of his complex prison inquiry of an historical and political nature. This is how Lo Piparo puts the synthesis:

> A solid theoretical chain in which every link that is necessary is formed by the theoretical and methodological study of comparative linguistics (i.e. cultural prestige as a cause of language change and diffusion), the theory and history of the intellectuals (i.e. intellectuals as producers and bearers

of prestige-hegemony), the definition of the concept of the State (i.e. the force of cohesion and the national popularity of the State as the effects of its intellectuals' capability of prestige-hegemony and of the social groups that represent it), and the question of language [*lingua*] (i.e. the means by which the cultural and linguistic history of Italy is proven and exemplified). The same problem is at stake in all four topics: how a nation-people-state is formed and organized and what invisible threads give rise to and unite it. Language and the reflection on language have an essential—decisive—place in this problem, which Gramsci did not disregard, nor can we.[32]

With this formulation, and above all with the many detailed analyses he carries out in his essay, Lo Piparo introduces a perspective in the study of Gramsci which is new in many respects. Anyone who is familiar with the state of research on Gramsci today—after the volumes by Paggi, Badaloni, Buci-Glucksmann and after the Conference in Florence in 1977—sees the grand "fusion of the sources" Gramsci performs in the mature phase of his theoretical reflection which becomes deeper and is enriched in Lo Piparo's study.

Yet maybe Lo Piparo did not develop some possibilities that his analysis opened. This is partly due to the specific delimitation of his project.[33] The first step, of course, was to fully highlight the consistency of the linguistic dimension in Gramsci (in this respect, Lo Piparo's essay really represents a point of no return). Yet I have the impression that his discovery of what we have called above the liberal-linguistic component of Gramsci's formation sometimes leads Lo Piparo to "flatten" Gramsci into his earlier cultural experiences. For instance, if it is true that Ascoli, against Manzoni's linguistic centralism from above, claims the rights and "economic-cultural" spaces of civil society, it would still be risky to conclude that Gramsci's concept of hegemony can only be applied to civil society itself. Gramsci's enlargement of the concept of state, which he performs in relation to the turning point represented by world capitalism, shifts the hegemonic struggle onto more complex levels. The forms and contents of this struggle—as Buci-Glucksmann and Gerratana have shown well—are certainly not indifferent to the historical and political subjects that fight it. On the one hand, I understand Lo Piparo's preoccupation with not reducing the notion of hegemony to a passive Soviet derivation and to give value to all the historical and cultural *Italian* components that constitute it. Yet, on the other hand, there are analogous risks in pushing back the date of the genesis of Gramsci's notion of hegemony. The notion of hegemony must always be considered in relation to the background only of what, according to me, is decisive for a man like Gramsci, namely, that he is first of all a political leader. A propos, what must be taken into account is the concrete historical situation Gramsci faced, the immense structural and institutional transformations of the 1920s and 1930s together with the rise of state capitalism, the new articulations coming to light within the range of the intellectual functions, and the necessity to elevate at these levels the struggle of the communists. The notion of hegemony progressively acquires more and more definition within this situation, namely, in a very complex weave of historical analysis, theoretical reflection, and revolutionary planning. Regarding the relationship between Gramsci and Lenin, it seems to me that recent studies have validated Togliatti's suggestion of 1957. He argued that Leninism taught the leader of the Italian working class the full primacy of politics, which was a decisive theoretico-practical direction for the Italian working class that had been closed in the *impasse* occurring between Reformism and Maximalism.[34]

In a word, once Lo Piparo's knowledgeable contribution is positively absorbed, I think that his position must be broadened through consideration of how Gramsci's role as a politician had, in turn, an effect on his formation as a linguist.[35] Far from impoverishing the dimension of language, this exalts and strengthens it, adding components that could not be present in the theoretical nucleus elaborated by Ascoli and Bartoli. And vice versa, it allows the articulation of the political perspective on levels of analysis and of intervention not thought of until Gramsci—and unfortunately also not after him.

Thus, the problems related to the question of hegemony, in the time when the State was expanding, unfold through language [*linguaggio*] (taking this word in the strong sense that it has for Gramsci: namely, culture, form of civilization, popularity, "microcosm and metaphor" of the social, as Lo Piparo[36] writes) in a closer connection between civil society and politics. It is along the lines of linguistic-cultural relationships which the following struggle is fought: that the proposition that the way out of the historical crisis is in terms of a passive revolution (which would be constructed starting from the factories through the Taylor-Fordist reorganization of the modes of production) and the proposition of a transition to socialism viewed as an "anti-passive revolution."[37] The leading democratic role of the producers shifts from the workplace to the ethico-political dimension, and includes all the cells of the social organism: but the conquest of a spontaneous linguistic "conformism"—namely, of a common and diffused *critical* consciousness of the masses—is the intermediate connection of this shift.

What has been learned *after* Gramsci on some points should also be stressed. Think of his attitude toward dialects: even though Gramsci fully understood their anthropological and sociohistorical value, he seemed to view them only as heritage from the past—namely, like the consequence of the lack of hegemony of the city over the country, as Lo Piparo has noted. Therefore, Gramsci sees the dialects as destined to be overcome by the national language during its expansive stage that will occur within an overall politico-cultural rise of the working classes. In this case, differently from Ascoli and from De Sanctis himself, Gramsci does not seem interested in a pedagogical and political perspective which takes into account *bilingualism* (his famous letter to Teresina, in fact, must not be interpreted as an indication of scholastic policy, but rather as a position of real oscillation of Gramsci's thought). Is this situation equivalent to the one described in Gramsci's pages on the relationship between master and pupil, characterized[38] by an essential distrust of the "reciprocity" of teaching and by an element of *dirigisme*?

Today, after the experiences of this century, we regard the question of dialects in a different fashion, both at the politico-institutional and at the scholastic level. There is a growing possibility of the consolidation of the dialects and of cultural expansion that would be part of a conquest of the major means of communication and of culture, and therefore, above all, of a national language (even today only 25 percent of the Italians claim to always use the Italian language in and outside their homes). This is what the many didactic and theoretical experiences of linguistic democratic education are teaching us (I am thinking of the long and hard work by the MCE [Movimento di Cooperazione Educativa—The Movement of Educative Cooperation] and by the CIDI [Centro Iniziativa Democratica Insegnanti—Center for Teachers' Democratic Initiative], and of the indications provided by the "10 theses for democratic linguistic education," which moreover acknowledge Gramsci's linguistic conception as one of their more significant components).[39]

In any case, Lo Piparo does well in stressing that the pages devoted by Gramsci to dialect and folklore are the most radical denial of what has been pretentiously referred to as Gramsci's "populism." Yet it seems to me that in the past years this particular thesis of Lo Piparo's has not been very welcome.

Returning to more general considerations, I believe that it should be now clear that Gramsci's reflections on language must be interpreted according to a twofold fashion. Regarding the contemporary problems of linguistic sciences, Gramsci's suggestions about language have at least two important implications. The first concerns the level of historiography: Gramsci draws a dense and precise interpretive outline of the linguistic events in Italy, developing Ascoli's conception. The perspectives that Gramsci opens have been substantially verified by the most recent studies, recovering the depth of Gramsci's analysis. They are linked to the following topics: the substance of the dialects and how they are rooted in local cultures; dialects being tied to a worldview and to a way of participating in "parochial" social life (this implies, in turn, a consequent linguistic-cultural polycentrism in Italy); the fact that the Italian language is extraneous to the great masses, which is an aspect of the nonpopular character of the state and of the Italian nation; the role of the press, of religious, political mass organizations and of the trade unions in diffusing the national language, and the analysis of the means by which "linguistic conformism" of a given population can be established;

and the observations on the "Italianizing jargon" coming to light in the popular classes. The second implication concerns a more theoretical level. Here, it seems to me, the picture Gramsci draws of the language/society relationship contributes to important progress in our knowledge about this. Gramsci's positions agree with the major accomplishments of the linguistic sciences of the twentieth century specifically; his diagnoses of "external linguistics" (to use Saussure's term); his notion of "immanent grammar" as distinguished from normative grammar and perception of the political meaning of the latter; his discovery of the permanently *metaphorical*—semantically open—nature of language and the socially manipulable character of historico-natural languages; and more generally his incredibly acute examination of the relationships between language and worldview, and language and the way thought is organized. Classic names can be listed again like Saussure; the great Soviet psychologist, Lev S. Vigotskij; the Wittgenstein of the *Philosophical Investigations* and scholars like De Mauro, Prieto and Godel. They provide the trajectory of work in which Gramsci has the place of a master who tends to place the reflection on language in the perspective of an intrinsically critical and sociohistorical science.

Gramsci's contribution to linguistic questions must, however, be assessed on a more overall political level. In other words, Gramsci is always, first of all, a revolutionary thinker and an organizer of real forces—that is, a political militant who grew through class and party experience, gathering all the components of his formation and culture under the great question arising in the 1930s: how to talk about the revolution in the West in the stage of the world crisis of the revolutionary process and during the complex restructuring of capitalistic power, both on the economico-social level and of the state in and outside Italy.

The linguistic dimension—like all the other social and cultural points Gramsci is interested in, past and present, and that he analyzes (from the intellectuals to Fordism, from literature to the Risorgimento and the southern question)—permeates the *Notebooks* as a *political* question, namely, as one of the levels on which the possibility of transforming Italy into a socialist country is at stake.[40] Thus, this problem rebounds to the present, where, in times of very deep sociocultural mutations, of radical modifications in the civil and cultural structure and in the tendencies and experiences of great masses of humans, the *question of language* [*lingua*] has already exploded on the national level. This question is intermingled with the political struggle and the social life of Italy on an infinite number of levels: in the schools, where from the nineteenth century on, because of ministry programs and the repressive attitude of the teachers, the reigning phobia of dialects is one of the main reasons for the exclusion of the popular masses from the right to education and from the real possibility of knowing and controlling society; in local life, in the cities in the towns in the neighborhoods—where the often-dramatic weave between the heritage of dialects and the national language must be summed up with the presence of three million citizens speaking a language other than Italian (not only the speakers of Greek, German and French, but also some half a million workers from the Third World with their cultures and idioms); in the factories and in the big cities of the north-central part of Italy—where the great internal immigration of the masses coming from the south has opened the immediate battle front concerning understanding and being understood and the struggle for language; in the Italian civil reality taken as a whole—characterized by a terrifying level of instruction (76.6 percent of Italians did not have more than an elementary school diploma and 32.4 percent of them had not finished any level of education), by a massive regression to semi-illiterate condition of previously literate subjects and by a simply deficient diffusion of literature and press (Italy is the worst in Europe, even lower than Spain)[41]; inside the trade unions and the political parties— where every day a linguistic problem shows up as a need to *understand* and to break the fracture between the learned and the masses.

With respect to these facts, I think that Gramsci's teaching is first of all valuable as an indication of how to grasp the nonextrinsic—but rather hegemonic and political—sense of the linguistic questions however they manifest themselves. It is also valuable to the extent that it presents an object of political analysis and an objective to work on. Insisting on these aspects may perhaps seem superfluous or tautological, but I have the sense that—even among us—an essentially rhetorical (and therefore easier) way of assessing the linguistic facts is still in fashion.

I believe that this leads to a stagnation of our capabilities to relate to reality and therefore to transform it. Thus, what Gramsci writes in a crucial moment of his reflection in prison should be reread. He questions himself about the relationship between common sense and philosophy, concerning the struggle for hegemony leading to "collectively attaining a single cultural 'climate'":

> Once philosophy is conceived as a conception of the world and philosophical activity is not to be conceived [solely] as the "individual" elaboration of systematically coherent concepts, but also and above all as a cultural battle to transform the popular "mentality" and to diffuse the philosophical innovations which will demonstrate themselves to be "historically true" to the extent that they become concretely—i.e., historically and socially—universal—then the question of language [*linguaggio*] and languages [*lingue*] must be "technically" put at the forefront of our enquiry.[42]

NOTES

1. Ferdinand de Saussure, *Saussure's Second Course of Lectures on General Linguistics (1908–1909)*, ed. and trans. Eisuke Komatsu and George Wolf (Oxford: Pergamon, 1997), 14a.

2. See note 65 by Tullio De Mauro in the Italian edition of Ferdinand de Saussure, *Corso di linguistica generale*, ed. and trans. Tullio De Mauro (Bari: Laterza, 1967).

3. Noam Chomsky, *Aspects of the Theory of Syntax* (Cambridge, Mass.: MIT Press, 1965), 3.

4. Ferdinand de Saussure, *Course in General Linguistics*, ed. Charles Bally and Albert Sechehaye, trans. Wade Baskin (New York: McGraw-Hill, 1966), 13–17. This is discussed and developed in the essay by Daniele Gambarara, "Il circuito della *parole* e il modo di riproduzione delle lingue" [The Circuit of *Parole* and the Way of Reproducing Languages], in *Studi Saussuriani* [Studies on Saussure], ed. R. Amacker, Tullio De Mauro and Luis J. Prieto (Bologna: Il Mulino, 1974), 133–64.

5. See the valid arguments of Piero Caracciolo, "Teorie linguistiche ed epistemologia marxista" [Linguistic Theories and Marxist Epistemology], and Franco Lo Piparo, "Teoria linguistica e oggetto linguistico" [Linguistic Theory and Linguistic Object], in *Linguistica Semiologia Epistemologia* [Linguistics, Semiology, Epistemology] (Rome: Bulzoni, 1972), 81–91 and 93–99.

6. Noam Chomsky, *Intervista su Linguaggio e ideologia* [Interview on Language and Ideology] (Bari: Laterza, 1977), 8–10.

7. Chomsky, *Intervista*, 55.

8. Bruce L. Derwing, *Transformational Grammar as a Theory of Language Acquisition* (Cambridge: Cambridge University Press, 1973).

9. [TGG refers to "transformational-generative grammar," which is the grammar of a natural language as deduced following Noam Chomsky's linguistics.]

10. Derwing, 236–37. The citations are from K. R. Popper, *Logica della Scoperta Scientifica* [The Logic of Scientific Discovery] (Turin: Einaudi, 1970), 24. Derwing could have also quoted the very different attitude one can find in Hjelmslev's *Prolegomena*, where the principle of "adequateness" of theory opportunely sides—as a factor "having an equivalent importance" to—the one of the "arbitrariness" of theory, [translated into Italian as] *I Fondamenti della Teoria del Linguaggio* (Turin: Einaudi, 1968), 17.

11. See the classical work by C. E. Shannon and W. Weaver, *The Mathematical Theory of Communication* (Urbana: University of Illinois Press, 1949), which is recalled by the psychologist G. A. Miller, *Language and Communication* (New York: McGraw-Hill, 1951), which is at the base of the famous scheme by Jakobson.

12. Derwing, 306.

13. [In the paragraph above, Gensini plays with the meaning of the Italian words *significato* (signified, meaning) and *significare* (signifying, to signify), where respectively the former conveys a static meaning and the latter a dynamic one, thus associating the first word to the traditional way of conceiving meaning.]

14. See the beautiful paragraph 23 in the *Philosophical Investigations* and, on the entire matter, Tullio De Mauro, *Introduzione alla Semantica* [Introduction to Semantics] (Bari: Laterza, 1971), 189ff.; C. H. Brown, *Linguistica Wittgensteiniana* [Wittgenstein's Linguistics] (Rome: Armando, 1978).

15. Derwing, 353. Regarding the psychological nature of language, one should see Chomsky's review of B. F. Skinner, *Verbal Behavior*, now included in the reading of F. Antinucci and C. Castelfranchi, *Psicolinguistica: Percezione, Memoria e Apprendimento del Linguaggio* [Psycholinguistics: Language Perception, Memory and Learning] (Bologna: Il Mulino, 1976), 21–65.

16. An instance of the importance of the psychological ground for linguistic facts should be noted in the work of a great student of Vygotskij, A. R. Luria, which synthesized the studies of the very active psycholinguistic Soviet school: *Problemi Fondamentali di Neurolinguistica* [Fundamental Problems of Neurolinguistics] (Rome: Armando, 1978), and *Corso di Psicologia Generale* [Course of General Psychology] (Rome: Editori Riuniti, 1979), especially 296–365. On the historical role and the achievements of Vygotskij's school, see L. Mecacci, *Cervello e Storia* [Brain and History] (Rome: Editori Riuniti, 1977).

17. Annibale Elia, *Per Saussure contro Saussure* (Bologna: Il Mulino, 1978).

18. [*Langue* is Saussure's notion of language as a system, as opposed to *parole*, which is language in use.]

19. N. S. Trubetzkoy, *Principles of Phonology*, trans. Christiane Baltaxe (Berkeley: University of California Press, 1969). [Gensini uses *tratto pertinente*, which Baltaxe translates as "distinctive oppositions" to distinguish it from Trubetzkoy's colleague and friend Roman Jakobson's use of "distinctive features," which, although parallel, should be distinguishable.]

20. [Gensini uses the French *objet*, meaning both "object" and "aspiration" or "aim."]

21. Elia, 103.

22. William Labov, *Il Continuo e il Discreto nel Linguaggio* (Bologna: Il Mulino, 1977).

23. Labov, 33.

24. Labov, 190.

25. Labov, 23.

26. See his contribution to an important conference of the SLI in 1974 in *Aspetti Sociolinguistici dell'Italia contemporanea*, ed. Simone and G. Ruggiero (Rome: Bulzoni, 1977).

27. Norbert Dittmar, *Manuale di Sociolinguistica* (Bari: Laterza, 1979) (German original edition: Frankfurt, 1973).

28. Franco Lo Piparo, *Lingua, Intellettuali, Egemonia in Gramsci* (Bari: Laterza, 1979).

29. The contributions by Luigi Rosiello are, among these exceptions, of particular relevance. His first one was delivered at the Conference on Gramsci in 1958.

30. Antonio Gramsci, *Letters from Prison*, vol. 1, ed. Frank Rosengarten, trans. Raymond Rosenthal (New York: Columbia University Press, 1994), 83.

31. Antonio Gramsci, *Quaderni del Carcere*, four volumes, ed. Valentino Gerratana (Turin: Einaudi, 1975), 2107ff., hereafter QC. A list of abbreviations is on pages ix–x. Q21§1 [To facilitate locating passages in various translations and anthologies, we use the standard method of providing the notebook (*Quaderno*) number—in this case 21—followed by the section number, §. See the introduction, page 12, for discussion. We will indicate the English translation, if used.]

32. Lo Piparo, 155.

33. Lo Piparo, 11.

34. See, for example, R. De Felice, *Serrati, Bordiga, Gramsci* (Bari: De Donato, 1971), or the contributions to *Lavoro Critico* [Critical Activity], no. 9 (1977). The centrality of *political praxis* is referred back to the problematization of the theoretical instances of Marxism in the fundamental work by Leonardo Paggi, "La teoria

generale del marxismo in Gramsci" [The General Theory of Marxism in Gramsci], in the *Annali Feltrinelli*, 1973, in particular 130ff.

35. An analogous suggestion is given by Tullio De Mauro in his "Preface" to Lo Piparo's book, who insists on the effects Gramsci's political, cultural, and human experience—which he had as a journalist, a militant and leader of the PCI, and a knower of the Italian sociocultural reality—should have had on his "theoretical linguistics."

36. Lo Piparo, 246.

37. See Buci-Glucksmann's paper, at the Conference in Florence, "Sui problemi politici della transizione: Classe operaia e rivoluzione passiva" [On the Political Problems of the Transition: Working Class and Passive Revolution], in *Politica e Storia* I (Rome: Editori Riuniti, 1977), 120ff.

38. Q10II§44; SPN 350.

39. [The MCE is an association linked to the Federation internationale de l'Ecole Moderne established in Italy in 1951 (influenced by the ideas of Célestin and Elise Freinet) working toward a pedagogy for the people. Its goal is to create class environments where reciprocal listening and authentic communication between children and teachers can occur, in order to promote global development. Among the founders and members of the MCE were teachers and educators like: G. Tamagnini, A. Fantini, A. Pettini, E. Codignola and later B. Ciari, M. Lodi and many others (see www.mce-fimem.it/index1.htm, accessed on June 26, 2007). The CIDI is an association of teachers from all kinds and levels of schools and disciplines that works to reform the education system. Its objective is to realize a democratic school attentive to the cultural needs of the students (see www.cidi.it/index.php, accessed on June 26, 2007).]

40. On this issue, see De Mauro—for whom Gramsci's is "a *political* theory of language, a theory of language as an always mobile and fluid result or of the currents of consensus that plough and keep the body of a given society united in its parts and to the tradition" ("Preface" to Lo Piparo, xv–xvi)—and Emilia Passaponti in the essay that introduces her anthology of Gramsci's writings on language to be published by Prismi, in Catania, and entitled *Gramsci and Language*. See also E. Passaponti, "Gramsci e le questioni linguistiche," in *Lingua, Linguaggi e Società*, ed. Stefano Gensini and M. Vedovelli (Florence: Manzuoli, 1978), 106–15.

41. See the rich documentation De Mauro gathered in his *Storia Linguistica dell'Italia Unita* [Linguistic History of United Italy], vol. 1–2 (Bari: Laterza, 1976), and in the essay "La cultura" [Culture], in *Come Siamo, come Eravamo 1968–1978* [How We Are, How We Were 1968–1978] (Bari: Laterza, 1979). The data on literacy that I cited (i.e., the last available: 1971) come from the ISTAT source; see them discussed in detail under the political and scholastic viewpoint in the volume by the same author: *Scuola e Linguaggio* [School and Language] (Rome: Editori Riuniti, 1977), 114ff.

42. Q10§44, QC, 1330–31. Antonio Gramsci, *Selections from Prison Notebooks*, ed. and trans. Quintin Hoare and Geoffrey Nowell Smith (New York: International Publishers, 1971), 348–49.

5

Gramsci the Linguist

Utz Maas *

In the widespread interest in Gramsci, the linguistic element still plays, at least outside of Italy, a subordinate role—even though Gramsci was a trained linguist (and thus, an exception in the workers' movement) and pursued his linguistic project until the end of his life. Gramsci's linguistic-theoretical considerations can offer a point of departure for recommencing the discussion about a materialist theory of language that seems to have been exhausted in recent years. I want to stimulate such a reception of Gramsci's thought with this contribution, on the one hand, by reconstructing his argumentation in its historical context (and thus opposing the tendency of playing with decontextualized citations from the available selected editions, which is unfortunately still difficult to avoid in the German-speaking world), and, on the other hand, by developing further the implications of Gramsci's thoughts.[1]

THE DIFFICULTIES OF THINKING ABOUT LANGUAGE IN THE TRADITION OF THE WORKERS' MOVEMENT

Linguistic questions are traditionally marginal in left-wing discussions, if not even suspect. Like all cultural approaches, they meet the suspicion of displacing the primacy of the social question. This is even more the case for

---

* Translation of "Der Sprachwissenschaftler Gramsci," which originally appeared in *Das Argument*, Heft 167 (1988): 49–64, and republished in Utz Maas, *Sprachpolitick und Politische Sprachwissenschaft* (Frankfurt: Suhrkamp, 1989), 165–89. Reprinted with the kind permission of the publishing house. Translated by Peter Thomas.

questions of language: left-wing discussions are loaded with deep-seated reservations with respect to linguistics, which must surely be rooted in traumatic school experiences with grammar lessons. This discursive constellation can be traced back to the First International: political reflection or the attempt to elaborate its scientific-analytical foundation was at that time determined by the reaction to romantic-lyrical nationalism, above all in student circles, which sought a point of departure for a new political organization in linguistic criteria. The new national states were supposed to follow the postulate of "one language—one nation."[2]

Marxist analysis, on the other hand, aimed at the *real*, the social, the relationships that were merely covered over by "superficial" linguistic-cultural differences ("the workers have no country"). Thus we can explain the cheeky—to put it mildly—remarks about the Romantic movement in, for example, the *Rheinische Zeitung*. However, with the organization of the workers' movement and as the more *political* questions were discussed, the clearer it became to Marx that a simple reduction of linguistic problems was not possible. The reason for a more thoroughgoing concern with this question was the analysis of the liberation movements that mobilized the early workers' movement: the Polish and then the Irish. Here, Marx recognized a relative dead weight of cultural organizational forms. In the case of the Irish question, this even provoked him to an outburst of free trade dogma. At the same time, analysis of the real difficulties of political-revolutionary undertakings (above all, consideration of the Paris Commune) led him to pose concrete political organization as an important question. Similarly, the social integration of the existing trade union organizations (above all, the English) compared to the "revolutionary elan" of the marginal movements became a problem for him.

This led to a displacement that can be observed in Marx's and Engels's political writings in their numerous daily political contributions during their last years, and particularly in their letters. In the Second International, questions of culture moved into the foreground. However, they were always posed with a view to the world revolution: in the meantime, mobilizing as well as hindering cultural factors, including linguistic differences, were to be accommodated. This constellation then necessarily became worse under the conditions of "socialism in one country," leading to the dogmatically imposed doctrinal versions of the Third International. Lenin had certainly seen the "residue" of the linguistic problem that was suppressed by this accentuation, but in his writings he limited himself to scheduling a systematic position of argumentation for this reflection.[3]

This absence continues to take its revenge today: the repressed complex of a political analysis of linguistic questions can be seen in the theoretical scandal of the absence of an analytically clear position vis-à-vis the advent of regionalist movements (with the symptoms of the "dialect wave" here in

Germany) or, even more dramatically, the emergence of "tribalist" tendencies in the revolutionary movements of the Third World. What one finds here are rather helpless recourses to citations from the classics with more or less moral-opportunistic concessions on the organizational-strategic level. In this perspective, we can see a particularly interesting aspect of Gramsci's thought. Unlike these movements, he didn't force his thinking into these templates and didn't treat language problems abstractly "from above," from the perspective of the existing or even of a future state, but from the perspective of social reproduction.

Gramsci brought particular presuppositions to this undertaking. Oriented toward Lenin's thought and practice, he took up the tradition of the Marxist workers' movement. However, as a trained linguist, he had, like almost no other in the workers' movement before or after him, the conceptual instruments for analyzing questions of language systematically.[4]

But for Gramsci, there was another decisive feature: as a Sardinian, he was immediately forced to deal with the contradictions of the Italian social modernization process. He could thus treat his analytical undertaking as a working out of his own subjective contradictions.[5]

Gramsci left behind no closed theoretical work regarding linguistic questions, as he left little regarding other problems. His remarks must therefore be read in their particular context and should not be used as familiar quotations. This is the case with his early journalistic articles, written in the spirit of the organization of a revolutionary movement, just as for the later *Prison Notebooks* in which he reflected on the political defeat of the workers' movement—and at the same time, according to a remark in a letter, sought to put his considerations into a form *für ewig.*[6] The problem of language is continually found in a prominent position throughout his whole work. Until the very end, he had a plan for a historical-linguistic sociological presentation of Sardinian. For Gramsci, this undertaking was an indispensable part of his overall revolutionary project of the liberation of thought in the universal (critical) clarification of everything that is sedimented in an unclear form in "common sense" [*Alltagsdenken*],[7] because otherwise it would always break out into action again as irrationality. To this extent, it required a systematic treatment from the "professional revolutionary" (which was how he conceived of himself), even more so, however, because for him such a critical liberation of thought was a revolutionary act.

THE LINGUISTIC-POLITICAL POINT OF DEPARTURE: "POPULAR LANGUAGE"

The linguistic and thus educational relations in Italy led Gramsci to analyze a problem of cultural reproduction that appeared to have already been overcome in other bourgeois societies: the establishment of a national language and its anchoring in the popular education system. The debates of the Second International stood under the augury "knowledge is power" and thus the appropriation of the *cultural legacy* that was monopolized in the state apparatuses of education; popular literacy appeared to have been accomplished right up to the "margins" of society with the establishment of compulsory education. The pedagogical discussion of the late nineteenth century, however, knew better: even if it usually did not put in question the high or literary languages (high German, high French, etc.), it nevertheless clearly saw how illusionary an imposed official language [*Oktroi*] was that didn't use the resources of the learner. In Germany, all throughout the nineteenth century there was the debate about language instruction that "picked up" the students' spontaneously developed linguistic abilities (thus, as a rule, their dialect) and led them to a controlled appropriation of the literary language by means of reflection on the contrast between dialect and high language. In the last quarter of the nineteenth century, these methodological considerations were extended with the methodology of comparative linguistics and in particular their application to linguistic geography.[8] In Italy, these debates were virulent after unification in 1861. On the side of the linguists, Graziadio Isaia Ascoli took up a position that brought to bear for Italy what were then the leading developments of German linguistics (neo-grammarians). He turned decisively against the then-propagated "Jacobinism" that comprehended the Risorgimento as an historical zero point and demanded the imposition of an artificial literary language, which was claimed to be predetermined due to the literary prestige of Tuscan (Alessandro Manzoni). In opposition, Ascoli provided a consistent linguistic-sociological argumentation. He showed that behind and within the question of the choice of the linguistic form there was the social problem of the socialization of education, in the foreground of which was the literacy of the great popular masses. Looking to historical development in Germany, Ascoli propagated literacy on the basis of the spontaneous language of the learner. He began from the supposition that becoming literate (for example, in a dialect) could be carried over to another language (the national language) unproblematically, because he saw in general the elaboration of a normative literary language as the endpoint of such a development.[9]

The Italian situation was and is still in certain respects more complex than the German one. Linguistic relations in Italy are distinguished by the extreme dialectal oppositions between north and south. There wasn't a national cultural movement comparable to that which has taken place in Germany since the seventeenth century. In Germany, this movement, as a development of cultural decentralization, has devalued *all* regional forms in comparison to the literary language of "high German." In Italy, language forms exist that are indeed closely related to Italian, but which are not to be assigned to it (Sardinian and Ladin), as well as the non-Romantic minorities of Albanian and Greek. Finally, the prestige-charged Tuscan literary dialect, in the wake of Dante and completely detached from the development of linguistic relations, functions as an additional factor hindering a national development, because reference to it explicitly excluded the real social centers of Rome and the north Italian industrial zones from the high cultural horizon. This confused cultural situation correlated with one of the highest rates of illiteracy in Europe.[10]

This exerted an enormous pressure on Italian cultural politics. In the 1920s, language pedagogy finally officially changed to the use of the dialectal resources of the students. The methodological postulate "from dialect to language" became official school policy (formulated by Guiseppe Lombardo Radice). It was also retained as a constitutive component part of the forced modernization policy of fascism under Gentile's ministry until 1931.[11]

As a linguist, Gramsci was familiar with these debates: in his early remarks on it, he explicitly named Ascoli as an authority. In an essay of 1918, he virtually paraphrased Ascoli's argumentation.[12] He developed, in a Crocean mode, the argument already presented by Ascoli, beginning from the "living" language (*lingua vita*) and counterposing "organic development" against the aloof "cosmopolitan" intellectuals. The linguistic form is precisely not arbitrarily available for linguistic political measures; it is not transparent for the therein "transported" content; rather, it is a determinate articulation of the relevant praxis which is itself an historical product. Linguistic form must be created after and then further developed in a creative process.[13] How closely Gramsci was oriented to Croce in his earlier writing is demonstrated by repeated comments that the particular language form under consideration can only be judged according to the standard of the historically possible optimal embodiment in aesthetic literature.[14]

However, it was not a purely theoretical debate for Gramsci. He knew these problems as lived problems; this disrupts the extent of his Croceanism from the beginning. As a Sardinian who had to make his career in Italy at the expense of his own language, he had to live out these tensions himself. Stimulated by his teacher, Bartoli, he made it the object of his early scientific work (his early letters home to his family in Sardinia contain detailed questions regarding his home dialect).[15] The later letters show that the theme remained a "living" one for him. Time and again he interspersed Sardinian expressions in these letters: whether in an excurse about dialect names for lizards in a letter to Tatiana (June 2, 1930); as intimate greetings to his son, Giuliano; but above all in the letters to his mother or those that are related to his mother, particularly her culinary specialties.[16]

We can see how much the problem struck him above all in his pedagogical recommendations to his relatives. These letters, which were after all written as texts *for readers*, have in this regard perhaps a heavier weight than the notes in the *Prison Notebooks*. He prided himself on having rehearsed Sardinian songs with his son, Delio. In the same letter to Teresina of March 26, 1927, he disapproved of his niece, Edmea, for not being able to speak Sardinian (unlike his nephews).[17] Almost as example of his agreement with the position taken up by the contemporary reform pedagogy on language development, he demanded that this should be played out spontaneously in the natural environment in which children are born. Edmea's development confirmed that *ex negativo*: she clearly had difficulties with orthography.[18]

Language is the expression of *lived experiences* (*esperienze vissute*),[19] it is connected with them, and thus is not to be leapfrogged in development—otherwise, there will be hybrid results, a linguistic mishmash.[20] However, Gramsci was a long way from any romanticism of rural living and nostalgia for dialects. The dialect was for him a more intimate linguistic terrain, which stood at the beginning of development—but which as a life-form that reversed the signs of development necessarily became a fetter. The life-form that is written into the dialect "ties life to the church, to the family," as he wrote drastically in an essay of 1917[21]—conversation in dialect was sufficient for this life-form, but not however for its transformation.[22]

THE LINGUISTIC-POLITICAL MIRAGE: UNIVERSAL LANGUAGE

Gramsci was thus not unfamiliar with the themes of the Jacobin discourse or the devaluation of dialects as antiquated. They were also dominant in the linguistic discourse of the workers' movement in the tradition of the French revolution. Since the First International they were not only a theoretical theme, but also present in a practical form: the "ancestors" had to struggle permanently with practical language questions, at international conferences as well as in contact with different sections, but also inside these, where regional teams continually naturally formed that practiced policies of linguistic exclusion (particularly against migrant workers). In certain aspects, these practical problems of the International were reflected in the abstract way in which linguistic questions were articulated in programmatic expressions. At the congresses of the First International the liberation of humanity by stages already in the present was demanded—for example, by means of the practice of an international language. These projects were nurtured by a multiplicity of projects for an international language, among which Esperanto was only one. The demand for a universal language that corresponds to human linguistic nature (often in connection with the radical orthography reform emphasized as "natural" or a demand for "phonography") was propagated as a struggle against the *unnatural* limitation of human nature by the bourgeois states and their educational apparatuses. In the Roman federations such efforts had a certain significance; Gramsci also had to deal with them in his Turin section.[23]

His clearest early expressions on the linguistic problematic occur in this context. In a polemical article of 1918 against the Esperanto movement, he explicitly makes recourse to the authority of linguistics.[24] He argues fundamentally against any way of approaching questions of language "from above," both in terms of Esperanto in the international context and in terms of the imposition [*Oktroi*] of an artificial national language in the national context. This can only be a formal state instrument of oppression (Gramsci takes aim here explicitly at purist attempts to exclude the variety of dialects). Here there is also the notion of language as expression of *lived experiences*, already noted above. Instead of making the linguistic form an ostensible problem, it must be a case of building up a new culture that entails a correspondingly new language. He denounced the opposed efforts as "cosmopolitanism." The realization of the project of an international language is thus for Gramsci fundamentally linked to the realization of socialism.[25]

Already a year before, in another article in the context of his militant engagement in the Turin workers' movement, Gramsci clarified where he thought political linguistic reflection had to set to work: in the overcoming of the cultural barriers against social participation, in the struggle against illiteracy.[26] Pointedly, he asserted that when the limitation of the local horizon is written into the dialectal language and life-form, obligatory school requirements can't achieve anything either: they can certainly force school attendance, but not the transformation of a way of life in which *writing* is necessary and has meaning, that is, the urban life-form (of the city dwellers). Only from the perspective of this way of life does the development of language have its place; only here does there emerge "the necessity of writing and language" (both of which here characteristically stand against the dialect).

However, Gramsci displaces the problem not simply from the ostensible formal debate to the *underlying* social question. Rather, he is interested in the cultural determinations lying *in* the linguistic form. He continued this interest also in prison. The continuity of his thoughts, but also the clarity he gained, is demonstrated when, for example, he writes in Notebook 11:

> Someone who only speaks dialect, or understands the standard language incompletely, necessarily has an intuition of the world which is more or less limited and provincial, which is fossilised and anachronistic in relation to the major currents of thought which dominate world history. His interests will be limited, more or less corporate or economistic, not universal.[27]

A language-form expresses the experiences of a community. It cements the categories of experience in which the members of a community recognize each other and which make possible for them the unproblematic coordination of activity and agreement among each other—at the price of the reproduction of these structures. In this sense, Gramsci always says that language belongs together with the life-form *organically*, that every language [*linguaggio*] "contains the elements of a conception of the world and a culture." With that, however, language represents at the same time a *limitation* of praxis, which is to be overcome through educational work in the perspective of its universalization. Universal in this sense, however, does not mean *formally* the same for all. The development of a national language is the development and sublation of particularism even if in national form: this remains related to the family of dialects that "dwell" under its roof; the local limitations will be overcome, without however losing the ground of the lived experiences. Culture is for Gramsci in this sense linked to linguistic translatability, which for him, to a certain extent, by definition only occurs between national languages, related to the universal contents that are articulated in culturally specific forms. For the dialects, as symbolic expression of particular cultural praxes, that is excluded.[28]

LIBERATION OF LABOR, LIBERATED LANGUAGE

Gramsci overcomes the aporia of the language debate of his times (which remains operative to a certain extent even today) by mediating "dialectically," on the one hand, the Romantic emphasis that stressed the spontaneity of the natural tongue (the dialect) with, on the other hand, the Enlightenment-Jacobin pathos of progressiveness of the universal language. In order to do this he uses the vitalizing terms of *lived* praxis: the *life* of language and *organic* cohesion. The linguistic-political question was presented to him not as a decision between competing linguistic forms or varieties, but rather as *work* on the language, as working out of the potential of spontaneous linguistic forms and thus at the same time as their valorization. The dialect is not to be repressed, but also not to be jumped over. Rather, it is to be *elaborated* into a universal language that is not a completely other language, or a fixed form as such (thus Gramsci's polemic against any form of purism!), but a flexible instrument in the life-forms in transformation. The elaboration of language is therefore for him necessarily linked to the socialist social project.[29]

Here we find the same emphatic mode of argumentation that we also encounter in Marx's writings, which sometimes makes it difficult to separate analytical from empirical statements. Education doesn't mean the appropriation of something completely other, but rather the development of the potential that the learners bring along with them. Thus the *Prison Notebooks* are pervaded by formulations such as "all men are intellectuals," which function as pointed comments of the scandal that characterizes an organization of society in which this fundamental human determination is not valid and operative. They are thought as contra-determinations for the analysis of the existing (and insofar, precisely those that have to be transformed) relations: "Not all men have the function of intellectuals in the society."[30] But intellectual potential is also manifested in the praxis that is not correspondingly valorized: namely, in common sense [*Alltagsdenken*], with its contradictions. Lived experience is the necessary point of departure for any educational work and thus also for any linguistic work. Rendering coherent spontaneous philosophy, the philosophy of the nonphilosophers, can only succeed through objectivization in language [*linguaggio*]. This is the reason for the close linkage of *language* and *writing*, in opposition to dialects: the communal praxis of oral *conversation* is embedded in the flux of the immediate happening, of the interactive constellation. Only through the objectivization of language in writing do the heterogeneous moments become comprehensible and linguistic critique becomes accessible.[31]

Language is not a fixed formally definable system, but rather, liberated praxis. Gramsci's remarks about working on language must be read together with his extensive comments on the liberation of labor (cf. above all the articles from the time of the Turin factory councils). Praxis necessarily contains moments that exceed its (externally determined) organization in the reproduction process; liberated praxis develops these surplus moments.[32] With the development of the capitalist production process (which for the young Gramsci is still an inevitable law), workers increasingly appropriate the intelligence entrapped in the means of production. They are thus pressured into forms of self-organization (thus also to a transformation of the language praxis on the job), which tendentiously increases their access to moments of the social organization of labor. They become intellectuals, who shape the forms of labor organization in employment itself: liberation of labor, valorization of labor as intellectual and liberation of language constitute a situation whose realization is only possible in communism.[33]

LINGUISTIC-THEORETICAL GENERALIZATIONS

Gramsci had thus found a theoretical starting point that enabled him to overcome prevalent short-circuited reductions of linguistics. Nevertheless, we still should not expect to find a closed theoretical system. We should not only attend to the "passages" in which the word *language* itself appears, for it is precisely in these that Gramsci is caught up in the vitalistic forms of expression of the early twentieth century. One must work out his linguistic theory to a certain extent against the written word.[34]

Gramsci's argumentation is based on a radical historicization of the concept of praxis, which he comprehended on the basis of the current material conditions of reproduction. In this context, language praxis (spoken language) becomes comprehensible as an exceptional moment.[35]

The point of departure is perhaps most evident in the early writings on the factory councils. Labor is determined by, respectively, the relations of production and the *culture* linked with them. In a very optimistic argument that sounds like something from the *Proletkult*, Gramsci comprehends the development of capitalism as an increasing displacement of organizing activities into production itself. The decisions are then no longer made outside, but by the producers themselves, the qualified factory workers and the "technical intelligence."

Here is the criterion for an analytical concept of *intelligence*: organizing intervention in production. Capitalist property and domination relations, however, in the end prevent the realization of the free disposal of intelligence in the production process, because the state power apparatus secures external determination in production; the final liberation of labor is therefore only possible as a form of liberated living together (he speaks expressly of *convivenza umana*)[36] in communist society. Intelligence stands here against the purely instrumental dimensions of the labor process (*operare tecnicamente, industrialmente*), for the moment of autonomy.

In the later works, Gramsci then grasped the analysis of the industrial labor process more realistically and defined the analytic concept of intelligence more exactly. In a radicalization of these considerations, he subsumed the activities of the "Taylorized intelligence" to be addressed "intellectually" as totally externally determined activity under *operare tecnicamente*; in this sense he speaks of the school as an intellectual Taylorization, which precisely does not develop the above-addressed intellectual-linguistic potential of the students.[37]

For Gramsci language is to be analyzed against the background of self/ external determination. Where this is externally determined, the potential of the language is reduced to the more or less ritualized reproduction of forms of intercourse. Linguistically, it can be largely substituted by nonverbal gestures, as in communicatively trusted interactions; here we encounter Gramsci's dictum of the narrowmindedness of local forms of speech. It is otherwise if the relations are not reproduced behind the backs of the subjects, but are instead controlled by them. A *symbolic* control is then particularly necessary, if, as in more developed social forms with a developed social division of labor, the relations are not immediately manageable, but only become accessible through a symbolic synthesis.

That is valid for the self-ascertainment of the conditions of action no less than for the assurance of social consensus, insofar as it is not only a case of conformity, which is possible pre-linguistically or at the "zero point" of language to a certain extent in relations of external determination, but is a case of organized efforts for the transformation of relations.[38]

A further consideration here can highlight the short-circuit of the linguistic-theoretical functionalisms, often also presented as "materialist": genetically, languages can be developed out of the conditions of the coordination of action (that is also to be tracked ontogenetically, where social praxis is antecedent for the child who orients himself on the praxis of the parents). But *when* the categories of language praxis are developed, they exhibit a symbolic *excess* over the functional finalizations, which *can* be used for the making sense and ascertainment of the goals of action. This process is repeated in a more potent form with writing, which is similarly learned in communicative relationships (and thus is perhaps also socially developed), which, however, has potentials for the development of processes of meaning that are free, released from the communicative stress of interaction. Admittedly, the realization of potentials does not follow inevitably from being practiced, as demonstrated by everyday ("phatic") speaking as well as utility-writing (communicative marks as substitute for oral communication). Not by chance, Gramsci linked discussion of the developed language to writing in the binomian formula *alphabet* and *language* [*linguaggio*].

The linguistic-theoretical approaches of Gramsci are thus to be taken up culturally and analytically: as dynamic analysis from the perspective of the liberation of praxis but also from the perspective of the limitations that are immanent to the historical language forms and relations (thus Gramsci's determined opposition to 'all projects that codify language forms normatively).

LANGUAGE AND INTELLIGENCE:
TRADITIONAL AND ORGANIC INTELLECTUALS

The following comments are related to Gramsci's own formulations quite loosely. They are only to be taken in regard to his analysis of the intellectuals in which he clarifies in particular the relation of analytical and empirical concepts. Similar to Marx (one thinks of the opalescent category of the "total worker"), Gramsci has great difficulties in making a division of the two categories; in his early writings, this is not even present.[39]

Gramsci's essay on "The Southern Question" of 1926 plays a key role for the development of his thought in this regard (incidentally, it was the last work that he prepared for publication, first published in Paris in 1930).[40] Conceptual clarification occurs here, which is then later strengthened in the *Prison Notebooks*, under the pressure of the changed political problem: how was it possible that fascism could take power? (Here, differently from in the *Prison Notebooks*, Gramsci does not yet assume a fundamental defeat of the workers' movement, but a "transitional period.") Intelligence plays a key role in this context, both as a socially comprehensible group (*gruppo or strato sociale*), which he can identify as people (here he plays ironically with the suffixes—*iotti, iali* and so on, which is hard to approximate in German [or English]), as well as in an analytical sense, as the question regarding the articulation of social consciousness. He thus turns, more or less explicitly, against any type of economistic reduction of consciousness and emphasizes the relative autonomy of the linguistic problematic.[41] Articulation can integrate praxis in social reproduction; however, it can also destabilize it and "disarticulate" the "ruling bloc" (that is the role of the left intellectuals); finally, it can also articulate a revolutionary praxis (that is the role of intellectuals in the communist parties). He defines here the social function of intellectuals as social cement [*soziales Bindemittel*] (*collegamento organico*).

As a social group, the intellectuals are related to their social environment, embedded in the noncontemporaneous development of society. The "traditional intellectuals" (for Gramsci, the "great intellectual," Croce is a prime representative) work in the sense of social reproduction as it still determines relations in the south. They thus stabilize in the first instance the dominant relations of the great landowners. The left intellectuals in the (large) cities of the industrialized north, on the other hand, are organically linked to the emancipatory struggles of the working class.

The social function of intellectuals thus results from how they act upon social oppositions of interests. Here the empirical concept overlaps with the analytical one. "Organic intellectuals" are—in an analytical sense—the intellectuals involved in social reproduction (indispensable for it). The task of left intelligence is to disarticulate the ruling discursive structures that guarantee the reproduction of relations, that is, to undertake an educational work that rearticulates these discursive structures in the perspective of social transformation.[42]

To a certain extent, the empirical composition of intellectuals forms the material basis for their social role, as Gramsci shows particularly clearly for the formal-universal European orientation of the "intellectuals of the south." These intellectuals jump over the necessary critical development of common sense [*Alltagsdenken*] and channel its revolutionary potential into the reproduction of existing relations. In the same context Gramsci makes very clear how the heterogeneity of commonsense functions—for example, when he shows the collusion of the traditional peasant anticlericalism with actual control by the Catholic hierarchy.[43]

These contradictions are amalgamated diffusely in concrete praxis, not least insignificantly precisely in a discursive praxis that occurs on the basis of the local forms of communication. The "shadows of the church" inscribed into the dialect then fulfill their regulative function of sieving experience.

"Traditional intellectuals" like Croce therefore function as organic intellectuals, despite the fact that their role had been superannuated by the capitalist development of Italy, because they contribute to the reproduction of the bourgeois state in the sense of the noncontemporaneity of development in a "modern" way: the rebellious moments of the peasant "popular culture" is disarticulated by the organic intellectuals of the great landowners; a progressive politics requires their rearticulation, which applies "nationally" to the commonalities of the north Italian proletariat and the south Italian small farmers and workers (the islands, in particular Sardinia, belong in the way of thinking of the south). The role of intellectuals in an analytical sense is thus determined by their key function in the development of linguistic potential.

By monopolizing descriptive language relations as articulated praxis, the traditional intellectual functions for the benefit of the reproduction of capitalist relations in the cultural apparatuses (Gramsci speaks in this context sarcastically of intellectuals as the "commissars" of the system). Such an intellectual helps a language representation to achieve social validity, based upon aesthetic virtuosity in dealing with the complex norms of the school language. For the majority of the population, however, these are founded in the obligatory school confrontation with the inferiority problems that were traumatic for them, and are the basis for the meritocratic consensus of social reproduction.[44]

An historical linguistic analysis that begins from Gramsci's premises will therefore treat language not on the basis of its aesthetic appearance. It is aimed against the existence of a particular layer of professional purveyors of sense. Its goal is the reappropriation of intellectuals and thus also language by the producers themselves.[45]

LINGUISTIC REFLECTION AND POLITICAL INTERVENTION

Gramsci was no pure theorist; he wrote as a politician, as a "professional revolutionary," as he described himself on numerous occasions. This consideration of intellectuals and language also responds to a practical-political problem: in the early writings, the problem of the organization of workers' struggles on the left wing of the party; in prison, the problem of the analysis of the defeat of the workers' movement by fascism and the mechanisms of social reproduction that fascism stabilized.

However, it was precisely fascism—or rather collusion with fascist power on a mass basis—that demanded a clarification of the connection of language and intellectuals: the corporative mechanisms of the fascist system built upon the limitation of social critique that were inscribed in the local language forms.[46]

Gramsci's perspective is not that of antimodernist resentment, of anti-statal revolts (which is nevertheless still noticeable in the young Gramsci). That makes him extraordinarily contemporary, not only due to the already-initially noted continuity of objective problems. In a confused discussion, however, Gramsci is now being reclaimed precisely by those who refer to positions "on the basis of the stomach." This is precisely what Pasolini (whose *Scritti Corsari* has enjoyed such success in Germany) does, for example, in a fascinating way (in Germany, at any rate). Pasolini articulates the revolts against the "americanization" of life, which he explicitly refers to as "fascism." As impressive as is his analysis of the expropriation of popular culture, for which he also reclaims explicitly Gramscian premises,[47] so little is his gesture of revolt in the sense of Gramsci's analytical project. What is ambivalently present in Gramsci's early writings is unequivocal in Pasolini: the rebellious gesture stands against the externally determined homogenization of everyday language (noticeably, Croce's opposition of the dominance of communicative and expressive language is present in Pasolini).[48] In the position of retreat is the oral, as a natural state to a certain extent, as a barrier against writing, which for him necessarily refers to statal control. What is lost in this emotionally charged opposition is that which Gramsci had worked out in his continual confrontation with the contradictions of his own early position: that linguistic reflection should be related to the potentials of humans, to the possibilities of an educational work that leads to the liberation of labor and thus to the liberation of language.[49] On the way to this, there is still much analytical work that needs to be done.

NOTES

1. On the contemporary relevance of Gramsci, see Giorgio Baratta, "Gramsci befrien," *Das Argument*, Heft 162 (1987): 236–49. In Italy, Gramsci has since become one of the standard references in linguistic-sociological discussion: cf. Tullio De Mauro, *Storia Linguistica dell'Italia Unita*, two vols. (Bari: Laterza, 1963; second edition 1976), and *Lingua e Dialetti nella Cultura Italiana da Dante a Gramsci* (Florence: Casa editrice G. D'Anna, 1980), or the extensive anthology of Maurizio Vitale, *La Questione della Lingua* (Palermo: Palumbo, 1978). In the German Democratic Republic [East Germany], Klaus Bochmann has now created the preconditions for linguistic work on Gramsci: on the one hand, with his selected volume 1984; on the other hand, with the organization of a conference on Gramsci in Leipzig in 1986 (see my conference report in *Das Argument*, Heft 164 (1987): 564). I am indebted to the contributions to this conference, particularly those of Jürgen Erfurt and Michael Grabek, for important stimuli for the following essay. I am also grateful to Michale Bommes for critical remarks on a first version of the manuscript.

2. This is not the place to trace the history of political reflections on language, which is still to be written. In agreement regarding the structure of this argument are such opposed movements as, in Germany, the nationalism of "Turnvater" Jahn and the *Burschenschaften*; in Italy, Mazzini; in the Slavic world, Bakunin and others. Some references to the Marxist wing's confrontation with these positions until the end of the Second International can be found in Utz Maas, *Sprachpolitk und Politische Sprachwissenschaft* (Frankfurt: Suhrkamp, 1979), 66–112.

3. In the question of the self-determination of nations, central for political organization (above all in confrontation with the Jewish "Bund"), Lenin differentiated between the national (to a certain extent congruent with the state) form of political organization of a party and the content of its politics, of the "international culture" (see Vladimir I. Lenin, "Critical Remarks on the National Question," in *Lenin Collected Works*, vol. 20 (Moscow: Progress Publishers, various years), 33–51. Subsequently, this was turned into a dogma to a certain extent, which Stalin repeatedly developed: "national in form, but socialist (international) in content"—developed extensively, for example, in Joseph Stalin, "Political Report of the Central Committee to the Sixteenth Congress of the C.P.S.U. (B.), June 27, 1930," in *Works*, vol. 12 (Moscow: Progress Publishers, 1949), 242–365.

4. Franco Lo Piparo, *Lingua, Intellettuali, Egemonia in Gramsci* (Bari: Laterza, 1979), has reconstructed in detail Gramsci's development as a linguist and the traces of his linguistic formation in later work. Extensive references here are therefore unnecessary. In the labor movement the obvious parallel is Engels, who, as an autodidact, reaped the harvest of the philology of his day in an extraordinarily capable manner: he applied his knowledge not only to the *Plattdeutsch* relations he knew (where his original linguistic-sociological considerations today are being rediscovered), but also in relation to the Irish, in order to undertake foundational studies for daily political interventions. The parallel of Engels and Gramsci would be an attractive object of investigation.

5. For a linguistic-sociological overview of the development of linguistic relations in Sardinia, see Eduardo Blasco Ferrer, *Storia Linguistica della Sardegna* (Tübingen: Niemeyer, 1984). In the workers' movement, there is in this respect an informative parallel to Gramsci: Rosa Luxemburg, whose sensibility for linguistic-political problems is undoubtedly linked to her marginality as Pole in the political constellation of the time (see Maas, *Sprachpolitik*, 66–112).

6. Antonio Gramsci, *Letters from Prison*, vol. 1, ed. Frank Rosengarten, trans. Raymond Rosenthal (New York: Columbia University Press, 1994), 83, hereafter LP1, and vol. 2, hereafter LP2. A list of abbreviations is on pages ix–x.

7. [Maas uses *Alltagsdenken*, literally meaning "everyday thinking," as the German translation of Gramsci's *senso comune*.]

8. See Heinrich Menges, "Mundart in der Volksschule" in *Encyklopädisches Handbuch der Pädagogik*, vol. 5, second edition, ed. W. Rein (Langensalza: H. Beyer, 1906), 941–82; Rudolf Hildebrand, *Vom deutschen Sprachunterricht in der Schule und von Deutscher Erziehung und Bildung Überhaupt* (Berlin: Klinkhardt Verlag, 1867 [1947]); and Rudolf von Raumer, "Der Unterricht im Deutschen," in *Geschichte der Pädagogik*, vol. 3/2, ed. Karl von Raumer (Stuttgart: Walter de Gruyter, 1852), 17–151.

9. See Graziado Isaia Ascoli, *Scritti sulla Questione della Lingua*, ed. C. Grassi (Turin: Einaudi 1975).

10. De Mauro, *Storia Linguistica*.

11. On this late development, particularly in fascism and the volte-face of fascist language politics, see Gabriella Klein, *La Politica Linguistica del Fascismo* (Bologna: Il Mulino, 1986). In general, the pedagogical concept of Lombardo Radice was expressly oriented to Croce, who was also a central reference for Gramsci. The parallels between the linguistic politics of Italian and German fascism would be worth its own investigation, since the analogies highlighted by Klein need to be differentiated. In at least the first phase of stabilization of its domination, German fascism integrated at least the functionaries of the corresponding organizations successfully with policies that allowed the autochthonous language forms to be used.

12. Antonio Gramsci, "A Single Language and Esperanto," in *Selections from Cultural Writings*, ed. D. Forgacs and G. Nowell-Smith, trans. W. Boelhower (Cambridge, Mass.: Harvard University Press, 1985), 26–31, here 28–29, hereafter SCW.

13. See Benedetto Croce, *The Aesthetic as the Science of Expression and of the Linguistic in General*, trans. Colin Lyas (Cambridge: Cambridge University Press, 1992 [1902]).

14. SCW, 27.

15. See Giansiro Ferrata and Nicolo Gallo, eds., *2000 Pagine di Gramsci*, vol. 2 (Milan: Il Saggiatore, 1964), 161.

16. LP1, 372–74, and LP2, 19–21. See also the undated letter Ferrata and Gallo, 435.

17. LP1, 88–91.

18. See the letter to Carlo, December 31, 1928, LP 1, 329–30.

19. SCW, 29.

20. LP, 89.

21. Antonio Gramsci, *Scritti Giovanili, 1914–1918* (Turin: Einaudi, 1958), 81ff.

22. It is notable that at the same time Ferdinand de Saussure characterized the contradictory dynamic of linguistic development with the same term: the tension between "the spirit of the church" (*esprit du clocher*), marked by the dialectal border, and the power of social intercourse tending toward the universalization of the form of intercourse. See Ferdinand De Saussure, *Course in General Linguistics*, trans. Wade Baskin (Glasgow: Collins, 1974), 205.

23. On this discussion of phonography, Utz Mass, "Die Schrift ist ein Zeichen für das, was in dem Gesprochenen ist: Zur Frühgeschichte der sprachwissenschaftlichen Schriftauffassung," in *Kodikas/Code* 9 (1986): 247–92, 281–83.

24. SCW, 27–31.

25. In his argumentation Gramsci notably agrees with contemporaneous discussion in Soviet linguistics that was similarly confronted by the problem of mass literacy and the unification of a national language. There is, however, no evidence that he had knowledge of the works of Voloshinov, Polivanov and others.

26. Gramsci, *Scritti Giovanili*, 81ff.

27. Antonio Gramsci, *Quaderni del Carcere*, four volumes, ed. Valentino Gerratana (Turin: Einaudi, 1975), 1377, hereafter QC. Q11§12. [To facilitate locating passages in various translations and anthologies, we use the standard method of providing the notebook (*Quaderno*) number—in this case 11—followed by the section number, §. See the introduction, page 12, for discussion. We will indicate

the English translation, if used; in this case, Antonio Gramsci, *Selections from Prison Notebooks*, ed. and trans. Quintin Hoare and Geoffrey Nowell Smith (New York: International Publishers, 1971), 325, hereafter SPN.]

28. Gramsci continues in the indicated passage: "While it is not always possible to learn a number of foreign languages in order to put oneself in contact with other cultural lives, it is at least necessary to learn the national language properly. A great culture can be translated into the language of another great culture, that is to say a great national language with historic richness and complexity, and it can translate any other great culture and can be a worldwide means of expression. But a dialect cannot do this." The accent lies here on the *great*—that is, universal culture—not on formal translatability, which naturally also exists between dialects, as is made clear by the usual multilingualism of peasant communities in multiethnic regions (here translatability consists to a certain extent in relation to the divided particularity of the way of life).

29. In this sense Gramsci is also consistent in practical questions of agitation: against any form of populism, he insists that agitation in fact must be uncompromising (and consequently also difficult). Related to the language of the workers, the argumentation must always be in advance of where they are in their thought or language; see "Culture and Class Struggle," in SCW, 31–34; on the idea that linguistic work is educational work, see "The Problem of the School," in SCW, 39–41.

30. Q12§1, SPN, 9.

31. Q11§12, SPN, 323–25.

32. Q8§204, QC, 1063.

33. See the articles "The Instruments of Labor" and "The Factory Council," in Antonio Gramsci, *Selections from Political Writings 1910–1920*, trans. John Matthews (Minneapolis: University of Minnesota Press, 1990), 162–66 and 260–64, hereafter SPW1. See also "L'opera di fabbrica," in Antonio Gramsci, *L'Ordine Nuovo 1919–1920* (Turin: Einaudi, 1954), 80–84. Gramsci sketches out here a "culture analysis" of labor, which implies a linguistic analysis—and which consequentially thus establishes educational work as a necessary component part of everyday revolutionary work.

34. Gramsci would certainly have approved of such an enterprise. As the often-ironic, self-satirizing formulations show, his plan *für ewig* was distant from any fixing of a canonical text; see also his introductory note to Notebook 11, where he states that his notes were written with a running pen and would probably be radically changed upon further examination (QC, 1365), which surely regards not only citations from other sources. Above all, however, it corresponds to the methodical core established by Gramsci himself, *to live* Marxist thought, just as he established as exemplary for Lenin and the Bolsheviks who had made the October revolution against Marx's *Capital*, as he provocatively wrote in 1918 (in "The Revolution against *Capital*," in SPW1, 34–37).

35. Here and on the following points see Utz Maas, "Als der Gesit der Gemeinschaft eine Sprache fand," *Opladen* (1984): 195–201.

36. SPW1, 263.

37. Q4§49, PN2, 210. With the keyword "Taylorism" (in certain respects synonymous with Fordism and Americanism), Gramsci analyzed later capitalist development (in opposition to his early expression close to *Proletkult*) as an ever-increasing

appropriation of the organizing moments of labor by capital (cf. Notebook 22). It is at any rate notable that the same emphatic formulations about intellectuals occur in completely different contexts (and certainly without knowledge of Gramsci), namely in Victor Klemperer. He turned against the "nazistic" dumbing down of the intellect and reclaimed it for social rebuilding; in this he distinguished the analytically valued concept of intellectuals from the ascription of social status: "One can be a stone tapper and nevertheless at the same time an intellectual . . . much more common with us is the other limit case, that one is by profession the most learned intellectual worker, and nevertheless only a stone tapper and no intellectual" (Victor Klemperer, "Die Rolle der Intellektuellen in der Gesellschaft," in *Aufbau 2* (1946): 682–86, here 685).

38. That is the vanishing point of the control of linguistic relations, but not however that of pregiven indoctrination, the manipulation by the establishment of ideas in people's heads. See Maas, "Als der Gesit."

39. Such a distinction is already present in Gramsci's most important point of reference, Ascoli, who does not regard single groups of people as the correlate for the social development of linguistic relations, but who speaks explicitly of the intellectual apparatus of society: "apparato intellettuale della nazione" (Ascoli, *Scritti*, 22).

40. SWP2, 441–62.

41. SWP2, 458ff.

42. Also here, Gramsci operates explicitly as a linguist. He enjoys transferring naïve "popular etymologies" to intellectual opponents, for example, when they anxiously make a pub sign of the Albanians (*skipetari*) into a gathering place of "strikers" [*scoperanti*] (SPW2, 458). Above all, he makes clear here that the reference for language analysis lies in the articulated experiences, not in the linguistic form: thus he refers to the fact that the same song that Sardinian soldiers had sung before and after their deployment against striking Turin workers was charged with entirely different meanings due to their experiences in the confrontation (SPW2, 447ff).

43. Antonio Gramsci, *La Costituzione del Partito Comunista 1923–1926* (Turin: Einaudi, 1971), 152–56.

44. That is the core of Gramsci's analysis of linguistic purism and its role in the obligatory popular school. The theme has been developed in Richard Sennett and Jonathan Cobb, *The Hidden Injuries of Class* (Cambridge: Cambridge University Press, 1972).

45. Maurice Godelier, *The Mental and the Material* (London: Verso, 1996), undertakes the systematic attempt to comprehend organic intellectuals as a productive factor in social (re-)production—against the schematic differentiation in the dualisms of base/superstructure or praxis/ideology. The constitutive function of intellectuals is to be differentiated from its specific comprehensibility in the historical social forms of organization, particularly if this organizing knowledge/ability is monopolized by determinate social layers (thus, by intellectuals in the sense of a social stratification—for example, castes of priests). Godelier puts the accent on the real use-value of the thus monopolized intelligence for the masses, whose life-level is immediately linked to this organizing achievement. This use-value is the basis of legitimation for the privileged way of life of the (traditional) intellectuals—bought by the expropriation of the knowledge of the producers.

46. Italian fascism carried on the pro-dialect pedagogy until 1931. As mentioned, German fascism also understood itself as nurturing the "autochthonous" culture. In Germany, the change in cultural politics came about due to the pragmatic necessities of the strengthened centralism of the war economy. This is arguably similar to Italy, where the synchronization with the increase of German influence is surely not accidental. Gramsci's analysis of the social function of rural intellectuals can be carried further. In Germany, it is striking that the functionaries who sought to nurture the dialects saw their field of efficacy, if it was related to the schools at all, in the high schools [*Gymnasien*]—not, however, in that place where working on and valorizing linguistic potentials articulated in dialect could actually count—that is, in the primary schools.

47. As he says, in a Gramscian sense [*senso gramsciano*], Pier Paolo Pasolini, *Freibeuterschriften*, trans. Thomas Eisenhardt (Berlin: Wagenbach, 1978), 227.

48. Pier Paolo Pasolini, *Ketzererfahrungen*, trans. Reimar Klein (Munich: Hanser, 1979), 21.

49. That doesn't speak against Pasolini's attempt to valorize dialects socially, as he undertook with his own poetry in dialect (for example, the cycle *Nuova gioventù* of 1975). It does however go against the romanticization of the dialect, which *in itself*—that is, not as intellectual raw material of educational work—but with all that which is articulated in dialect is taken up positively (for example, the direct equation of dialect—life—revolution: see Pasolini *Freibeutschriften*, 229). Incidentally, Pasolini himself made clear his one-sidedness in comparison to Gramsci; in his cycle "Gramsci's Ashes," he says: "The scandal of contradicting myself, to be with you [Gramsci] and against you, with you in my heart, in light, against you in the darkness of the guts." Additionally, Pasolini also gave an extraordinarily sensitive interpretation of Gramsci's early works on linguistic questions, cf. his attempt at a "Marxist linguistics" (Pier Paolo Pasolini, *Gramscis Asche* [Munich: Piper, 1984], 51–77.

6

Gramsci from One Century to Another

Interview with Edoardo Sanguineti by Giorgio Baratta *

This interview took place just prior to the International Gramsci Society conference in Naples in October 1997, "Gramsci from One Century to Another." Edoardo Sanguineti[1] notes that the current political and cultural situation demands positing again the question of "national-popular" but now within the overall tendency that, following Etienne Balibar, we may call "postnational." The claim for the "national-popular" in our postnational situation is not a contradiction: it is rather a sign of the very delicate condition informing the tension, already very strong in Gramsci, between "particular histories," the "southern question" and the "universal" dimension of human society.

DEAR SANGUINETI, WHAT IS THE RELEVANCE OF THE MARXIAN HERI-
TAGE AND OF COMMUNISM IN YOUR INQUIRY ON THE QUESTION
OF GRAMSCI'S LANGUAGE AND THE ROLE OF LANGUAGE IN HIS
WRITINGS?

Gramsci repeatedly posits the question of languages and asks himself if reaching a universal language is possible. Two things seem very clear to me. For Gramsci, the fundamental content of the philosophy of praxis and of historical materialism certainly means the end of, and the overcoming of, class struggles, and the advent of communism. This is not something we believe today, but Gramsci believed it. For him, according to this perspective, the very fundamental and essential point was,

---

* Translated by Rocco Lacorte with assistance by Peter Ives.

however, the unity of humankind. Gramsci meant it to be a cultural unity, in the sense that the day in which class perspective will come to an end, there will not be conflicting cultural multiplicities anymore. Human beings will collaborate within a unified framework and within what Marx used to talk about but cautiously without saying anything substantial—something that is an object of a dream. He knew what it was not, although he was cautious enough not to pretend to know what it was to be. Even Gramsci very cautiously and "in some way" tries to indicate "that thing" as unification and eventually—"in some way"—as the homologation of humankind. Gramsci observes that there exists a case of universal artificial language, namely, mathematics. Sciences have the advantage of prefiguring in some way the future linguistic unification of humankind. In mathematics all humans communicate: it is the only universal language. Moreover, taking as a starting point the primacy of humans' unification as a real task, I think Gramsci would have answered the question "For what purpose do we do a revolution?" with "In order to universalize the human genre."

WAS NOT GRAMSCI USING LANGUAGE IN A VERY PARTICULAR AND PRAGMATIC—IN SOME SENSE SOCRATIC—WAY?

Language is an instrument for interexchange, communication and, at the same time, for creating identities. Therefore, language has, on the one hand, an internal and cohesive function, and on the other, a communicative and very open use. If I were asked whether he assesses these two aspects of language as equivalent or if he has a different take on their roles, without a doubt, I would answer that Gramsci proposes an unbalanced view, sharply in favor of the communicative one. A parallel or cautious analogy could be drawn between how Giacomo Leopardi writes the entire *Zibaldone* and Gramsci writes the *Notebooks*.[2] There is almost catastrophic evidence of a sort of tic or monomania. What is, in fact, reiterated the most in Gramsci's *Notebooks*? I don't mean what concepts or ideas are reiterated, but what linguistic modality appears most frequently? The question must be answered saying that Gramsci reiterates expressions like "so to say," "in some sense," "in a certain respect," "if so we would like to say" and "for some aspect," as a tic or almost as a *lapsus*. In other words, Gramsci never rests, never says "That's it."

Never.

He had a truly obsessive idea about any fetishism or ideology conceived as false consciousness of words. Indeed, language is really always in danger of being overturned into false consciousness, because what is often lacking is precisely Gramsci's obsessive caution, expressed through the various "in some sense," "it may be said so." To make words rigid, to take them as things is a major cause for troubles. Words are not things. They go through a perpetual transformation in which communication is always, in some way, precarious, namely exposed to misunderstanding, and full of consequences because to say is truly to do.

WHAT IS THE ROLE OF THE QUESTION OF LANGUAGE IN GRAMSCI'S THOUGHT?

After Lo Piparo's book, the origin of the word "hegemony" became not the specific subject, but the emblem and symbol of Gramsci's question on language. Where does the word "hegemony" come from? From Lenin or from Ascoli? This question became a standard debate. This is not to say that Lo Piparo is wrong if it is demonstrated that hegemony comes from Lenin and that Leninists are right. On this matter I should intervene almost for family reasons. I am the father of Federico [Sanguineti], who wrote and published a university thesis—*Gramsci and Machiavelli*—part of which was devoted to demonstrating, without arguing against Lo Piparo, that the concept of hegemony comes from Lenin, specifically documenting this through articles by Lenin that Gramsci published in *L'Ordine Nuovo*. Yet, at some point, if we connect this question to Gramsci's idea of "translating," we may ask ourselves if it is superfluous to question whether hegemony comes from Lenin or from Ascoli, although it has some relevance in terms of philology and documentation. On the contrary, we must stress how concepts coming from different worlds and from heterogeneous mental systems, "in some sense," come to coincide, because Gramsci does not have any superstitions about words: the reason for this is in that—as it is the case of an honest linguist of our century—he purifies words from any magic or enchanting residue. A verbal coincidence must not immediately cause us to draw associations of the analogical kind, but can suggest—as [Lucien] Goldmann would have said—principles of homology, which mean something else: namely, something other than imaginative and suggestive similarities—that is, symmetries which are "in some way" structural. A given symmetry exists and can be fertile for further developments, but it does not allow just making two things overlap onto each other. In this case, we are dealing with elements that reinforce each other.

Gramsci is a linguist, yes, but a linguist who is very conscious of what the question of language means; as one of his famous propositions says, language is immediately connected to other questions. Which ones? Gramsci himself does partly provide some of them, but, perhaps, it could be said that the question of language is somewhat connected to all other questions.

If so, the question of language is *the one* issue connected to all the other ones, this means that it is right to start from it.

AND WHERE DO WE GET WITH THIS?

We get to one of the principal theories of *culture*, in a strong sense of this word, conceived as a global attempt to grasp the concrete historical-social existence of humans as it appears in light of historical materialism. What Gramsci is interested in is intellectual and moral reform. This cultural re-form means reform of the concrete way humans exist. This is what Gramsci aims to achieve when he claims that every language question is connected, *internally*, not externally, to other questions.

This claim coincides therefore with the shift to Gramsci's idea of a nexus of problems. This is at the base of the apparently unstructured structure of the *Notebooks* when they are compared to certain ideals of how a work should be constructed. He stresses immediately that it is not possible to shift continuously from one thing to another. The day in which we succeed in truly reconstructing the drafts of the *Notebooks*—including all of Grams-ci's annotations, the exchanges back and forth between notebooks, the circularities, the stratifications (precisely the same way people have begun to approach Leopardi's *Zibaldone*)—and seeing how they are sedimented, we will also have a philological confirmation of Gramsci's method (in the narrowest and most rigorous sense of the term: philological).

NOTES

1. Edoardo Sanguineti is a poet, writer, scholar and translator, one of the major intellectuals in Italy today. He was born in Genova, on December 9, 1930. His uncle, the musician and musicologist Luigi Cocchi, met Gobetti and Gramsci, and collaborated with the magazine *L'Ordine Nuovo.* Sanguineti was a member of the neo-vanguard group "Gruppo 63," whose intellectuals were inspired by Marxism and structuralism and meant to experiment with new forms of expression breaking the traditional literary and rhetorical schemes.

2. [Giacomo Leopardi (Recanati 1798–Naples 1837) was one of the most im-portant poets, writers and philosophers in Italy. *The Zibaldone* is a massive 4,526 pages, written between 1817 and 1832, in which Leopardi would write notes, observations, thoughts amd memories, mainly concerning philosophical, literary, linguistic and political topics. *The Zibaldone* as well as the *Prison Notebooks* were not conceived as books. Sanguineti notes that there can be established an analogy both and in the way Leopardi's *Zibaldone* and Gramsci's *Prison Notebooks* were written and in the cautious attitude the two authors show in dealing with the several matters they think and write about.]

II

LANGUAGE, TRANSLATION, POLITICS AND CULTURE

7

Translation and Translatability: Renewal of the Marxist Paradigm

Derek Boothman *

> See *Marx's analysis in the Holy Family* where it turns out that *Jacobin phraseology corresponded perfectly to* the formulas of *classical German philosophy.*
>
> Antonio Gramsci[1]

> *If Herr Edgar compares French equality with German "self consciousness,"* for an instant he will see that *the latter principle expresses in German,* i.e. in abstract thought, *what the former says in French,* that is, in the in the language of politics, and of thoughtful self-observation.
>
> Karl Marx and Friedrich Engels[2]

To claim that the question of translatability and translation are an important part of Gramsci's prison reflections may seem at first sight strange and even exaggerated. Wolf Haug, editor and chief translator of the German edition of Gramsci's *Prison Notebooks*, has, however, very shrewdly observed that "Gramsci's concept of 'translation' and 'translatability' leads into the

* This chapter is a modified version of the second chapter of *Traducibilità e Processi Traduttivi. Un caso: A. Gramsci linguista* (Perugia: Guerra edizioni, 2004), and of the last chapter "Traduzione e Traducibilità" of the collectively authored volume *Le Parole di Gramsci* (Rome: Carocci, 2004), of the regular "Seminario Gramsciano" of the Italian Section of the International Gramsci Society, with additional comments included from papers read at the XII Congress of the Italian Society for the Philosophy of Language ("Tradurre e Comprendere: Pluralità di Lingue e di Culture," Piano di Sorrento, September 2005) and at the 120th Congress of the Modern Language Association (Philadelphia 2004), the full text of which is to be published in the review *Italian Culture.* Work from the end of 2004 has been supported by a research grant dealing with "translation as the locus of encounter and of conflict," awarded jointly by the University of Bologna and the University's Department of Interdisciplinary Studies on Translation, Languages and Culture (SITLeC).

very center of his conceptual network."[3] This chapter will be devoted to analyzing the development of the concept in the *Notebooks* and indicate why the subject is a key one for Gramsci and for the renewal of Marxism and progressive thought in general.

The relatively few pages of the prison writings in the *Notebooks* that Gramsci dedicates explicitly to translatability are, paradoxically, among those that have given most problems to the translator. The present writer is not alone among translators of Gramsci in having experienced these difficulties. The very first translator of a selection of the *Notebooks*, Carl Marzani, went so far as to deny that Gramsci's use of the term "translate" had a great deal to do with what translators do in practice. For Marzani, Gramsci's concept of "translate" is near to that of "to transpose, to find correspondence or differentiations among the 'idioms' of various countries," where for Marzani "idioms" are "the cultural ensemble, the ways of thinking and acting in a country at a given time."[4] All this is true, but what Gramsci meant by translatability and translation goes further and deeper than this and it is that "something extra" which is important for understanding why translatability is a key concept. We shall examine here why there have been difficulties in understanding what Gramsci was getting at in his notes on the "translatability of scientific and philosophical languages," as he says, or to put it in other words, the theoretical possibility and the practice of translating not only between different natural languages but also between different paradigms, or discourses, to use a term that has become fashionable, and therefore be able to update the Marxist paradigm itself.

THE FIRST THREE PARAGRAPHS
OF NOTEBOOK 11, SECTION V

Gramsci devotes the fifth section of Notebook 11, a notebook on philosophical problems and one of the crucial "monographic" notebooks, to giving final and definitive form, insofar as things could be definitive for him, to the notes on translatability. In this context it should be noted, of course, that "scientific" is not to be taken in the very narrow sense of the so-called exact sciences, as is often the case in the English language, but in the broader sense that includes the social and "human" sciences.

There is an explicit comment in Notebook 10 on the close connection between his concept of translatability, explained in Notebook 11, and the writings contained in Notebook 10, almost exclusively devoted to the philosophy of Benedetto Croce, the dominant figure in Italian idealist philosophy in the first half of the twentieth century. Very near the beginning of the second part of Notebook 10 under the heading "The Translatability of Scientific and Philosophical Languages," Gramsci states that "the notes written under this heading are in fact to be brought together in the general section on the relationship between speculative philosophies and the philosophy of praxis."[5] He thus makes it very clear indeed that he sees the possibility of translating the one into the terms of the other, and an important part of the polemic with Croce is in fact Gramsci's critique and then *translation* of Crocean concepts, purged of their idealist content, into his own philosophically realist and materialist paradigm. It is important to know how Gramsci reached this position, and we shall here attempt a reconstruction of the background to this operation, with passing mention of important similar approaches developed since Gramsci's time and, at the end and for the sake of illustrative comparison, a couple of examples from non-Gramscian sources of translation between paradigms in the social sciences.

By way of "preface" to the three key paragraphs on translatability, Gramsci cites as his starting point Lenin's observation at the Fourth Congress of the Comintern in 1922 (referring back to resolutions approved at the previous year's Third Congress: "Vilich [Lenin], in dealing with organizational questions, wrote and said (more or less) this: we have not been able to 'translate' our language into those of Europe."[6] Lenin went on to say, in a comment not recalled by Gramsci, "We have not learnt how to present our Russian experience to foreigners."[7] In Gramsci's note on Lenin, we see the nature of the objections raised by Marzani— namely, that "translate" seems used in a broad and metaphorical sense as compared with the act of re-expressing concepts in another natural language, and the word "language" itself is used to indicate the culture of a given country. It is, however, to be noted that for Gramsci language and culture are always very closely intertwined, a national language being the expression of a national culture, and for him the two become near-synonyms.

After the prefatory comment on Lenin in Q11§46, the argument contained in Q11§48 is substantially recast as compared with the first draft (Q4§42, October 1930), which is probably the reason why Gramsci introduces an intervening text (Q11§47) by way of defining his aims.[8] Gramsci asks in Q11§47 whether "the mutual translatability of the various philosophical and scientific languages is a 'critical' element that belongs to every conception of the world, or whether it belongs (in an organic way) only to the philosophy of praxis, being appropriable only in part by other philosophies." This then acts as a prelude to the conclusion reached in Q11§49, with the intervening long paragraph Q11§48 carrying the main thrust of the argument.[9] We shall now try to reconstruct the background to these paragraphs on translatability before going back to illustrate Gramsci's solution to the problem he poses.

TRANSLATABILITY OF PHRASEOLOGY OR OF LANGUAGES?

Gramsci first mentions translation between paradigms in the very first note-book: in Q1§44 we read, in regard to Giuseppe Ferrari, one of the main, but, as Gramsci observes, "ignored" agrarian experts of the Action Party in nineteenth-century Italy, that he "was not able to translate 'French' into 'Italian,'" not of course as national languages but as national realities, as different ideological discourses.[10] Then in the same paragraph, Q1§44, but several pages further on, Gramsci for the first time cites Marx in the context of what he goes on to develop as his concept of translatability, noting that, for Marx, "Jacobin phraseology" corresponded to the formulas of classical German philosophy (February 1930). In the rewritten version of 1934, in Notebook 19, he speaks this time of Marx's analysis of "Jacobin language" and "Hegel's admission, when he places as parallel and reciprocally trans-latable the juridico-political *language* of the Jacobins and the concepts of classical German philosophy."[11] The salient points to note are that the earlier phraseology becomes, four years later, Jacobin language (*linguaggio*) and that while, in the first draft, their phraseology "*corresponded* perfectly" to the formulas of classical German philosophy, in the C-text says explicitly that they are "parallel and reciprocally *translatable*." In these examples and in others discussed here Gramsci uses the word "language" (*linguaggio*, the Italian term for a natural language being, instead of *lingua*) in the sense of what, after Thomas Kuhn, one of the most authoritative late twentieth-century historians and philosophers of science and someone to whom we shall return later on, may be defined as a paradigmatic discourse or, simply, a paradigm.

In the other pair of texts which have already been mentioned, the C-text Q11§48 and its corresponding A-text, Q4§42, the chronologically earlier one begins somewhat peremptorily with the assertion that Marx *shows* or *demonstrates* that "the French political language used by Proudhon cor-responds to and can be translated into the language of classical German philosophy."[12] Somewhat similarly in Q3§48 (June–July 1930), Gramsci observes that for Marx "the political formulas of the French Revolution are reducible to the principles of classical German philosophy."[13] In the later C-text version of Q11§48, instead of the "show" or "demonstrate" of Q4§42, Gramsci uses the verb *afferma* (to "claim" or "assert"), while the rest remains essentially unaltered.[14] It thus appears that what was accepted in the first draft as a demonstration comes over in the later, more authorita-tive, C- text of Notebook 11 more as a thesis on translatability that has to be proved. Probably in one way the substance does not change much but, when he comes to group together the various C-texts on translatability, he seems to be wanting to give greater rigor to his argument, proceeding logi-cally one step after the other rather than with simple affirmations. In this particular case, as compared with its A-text, Q11§48 shows greater care and is more refined linguistically, and at the same time the claims are more cautious and more dubitative in nature. In the A-text, for example, the statement about the correspondence of the Jacobins and classical German philosophy "seemed" to Gramsci "very important for understanding the innermost value of historical materialism," while in the C-text, "very important" remains to describe the correspondence and translation which existed between the two national paradigmatic discourses and which served, more simply as compared with the A-text, "for understanding certain aspects of the philosophy of praxis."[15] The first version is polemical above all with Croceanism, while the second one contains a criticism of "mechanistic abstractions," presumably having in mind the Bukharin's Marxism, the target of Gramsci's critique in an earlier part of the same Notebook 11. Gramsci then adds a reflection regarding the possibility that this "critical principle" of translatability can be juxtaposed with "analogous statements"—in other words, whether it could be generalized further.

At this point, he seems to distinguish between *two forms of translatability*, a first and more restricted type which, however, still connects up with the same set or series as the examples discussed by Marx, which represent the second, more general, form of translatability. The first type, "very limited" in its scope, refers to the "particular languages of different scientific personalities"; although "language" (once again *linguaggio*) is a term used in the first draft, this particular comment is present only in the second draft and is perhaps indicative of a greater attention and recognition in the later draft to the implications of technical languages as such. In the more cautious wording of the C-text, Gramsci asks himself if a translation of technical languages is not a step toward "the vaster and deeper problem implicit in the assertion contained in the *Holy Family*" of Marx. (There is a much more peremptory affirmation in the first draft that the more limited type of translation "belongs" to the same set as Marx's more general propositions.)

The differences between Gramsci's A- and C-texts are often subtle, and sometimes subject to reconsideration, and not always linear in development and unambiguous. One factor that seems to have influenced Gramsci between the earlier and later versions of this is his reasoning on the language of Machiavelli, someone for whose intellect and paradigmatic discourse he had the highest respect and took very seriously. This comes over in a number of places, perhaps first of all in Q5§127, a B-text not copied and revised elsewhere, and written only a matter of weeks after Q4§42. In this paragraph of Notebook 5, Gramsci observes that "if one had to translate the notion 'Prince' as it is used in Machiavelli's book into modern political language," a series of distinctions would have to be made, among whose possibilities "'Prince' could be translated in modern terms as 'political party'" if one were dealing with the establishment of a new type of state.[16] The notion of translation appears here as that of a single term and not yet as a fully fledged question of the language of discourse.

Jumping forward to what seems to be the next occasion that Gramsci returns to this subject of Machiavelli and translation, we see that, in a letter to his sister-in-law, Tania, of March 14, 1932, and therefore apparently about six months before Q11§48, he asks whether Machiavelli had not

> expressed in political language what the mercantilists said in terms of economic policy. Or could one even go as far as to maintain that in Machiavelli's political language . . . there appears the first germ of a physiocratic conception of the State and that therefore . . . he might be considered a precursor of the Jacobins?[17]

Only just a few weeks after this letter to Tania, again relying on Francioni's dating of the various parts of the *Notebooks*, Gramsci wrote another paragraph on Machiavelli (Q8§162, April 1932), in which he claims that if one demonstrates that Machiavelli "aimed at creating links between city and countryside," such as to

> incorporate the rural classes into the State, one will also have shown that, implicitly, Machiavelli had in theory overcome the mercantilist stage and already had some traits of a "physiocratic" nature—that he was thinking, in other words, of a politico-social environment which is the same as that presupposed by classical economy.[18]

This time the question is no longer just a terminological one, but involves an entire theoretical discourse that Gramsci seems to become fully aware of only in the spring of 1932. Indeed, only a few months earlier, at the end of 1931, he discussed in Q8§78 the economic implications of the political theories of Machiavelli without considering the concept of translatability, while in the C-text version (Q13§13, probably the earlier part of the period mid-1932 to 1934) he asks himself whether "Machiavelli's essentially political language can be translated into economic terms, and to which economic system it could be reduced."[19]

Be this as it may, it is in the passages quoted from the letter to Tania and from the paragraph Q8§162 on Machiavelli as an economist that one sees Gramsci beginning to ask himself what really lies behind the concept of the translatability of languages—that is, of paradigmatic discourses. It is not a question of merely translating terms and concepts belonging to the same subject matter, but first of all recognizing that two different subjects, political theory and economics, can have fundamentally equivalent postulates, can be mutually comparable and in consequence can be reciprocally translatable, due consideration being given to the different eras and events of the countries considered. We are here, it appears, at a halfway house, between a narrower view of translation and the more general one.

The comments cited here on the economic implications of Machiavelli's political language were written in a two-year period from autumn 1930 through mid-1932. These paragraphs, which also contain comments on the views of the liberal economist, Luigi Einaudi, on translation problems of the paradigms of experts working in the same field, offer a key to a clearer understanding of the reasons that induced Gramsci to introduce into his C-text, Q11§48, modifications as compared with the earlier A-text, Q4§42. In the later version Gramsci seems to attach more weight and credence to Einaudi's words, cited in both these paragraphs, on the ability of the pragmatist philosopher and mathematician, Giovanni Vailati, to

> translate any theory whatsoever from the language of geometry to that of algebra, from the language of hedonism to that of Kantian ethics, from the pure normative terminology of economics into the applied perceptive one.[20]

In the first version Gramsci limits himself to the comment that "two individuals produced by the same basic culture believe that their opinions differ simply because they use *different terminologies*"; the second text reads "two 'scientists' who owe their cultural formation to the same background think they are upholding different 'truths' just because they employ a different *scientific language*."[21] The emphasis is added here in the two quotes to bring home the difference: the earlier "terminology" becomes a full-blown "language" in the later draft. It is indeed true that these languages may be limited, as Gramsci says, to different "scientific personalities" and questions of personal or group "jargon" may be involved but, as he goes on to say immediately afterward, between two scientists who use different languages, "we do not say that there is not a difference between them nor that this difference is not without significance," an acknowledgement that is not to be found in the A-text. And, for further confirmation of this change in perspective, one may recall the similar difference between the A-text (Q1§44, dating February–March 1930) and its corresponding C-text (Q19§24, dating from 1934) where "Jacobin phraseology" becomes the "juridico-political language of the Jacobins."[22]

This recognition of the real difference between discourses passes through the type of reasoning that we have seen in the extracts from the paragraphs on Machiavelli at the same time as taking account of the seriousness of a scholar such as Vailati, treated in the *Notebooks* with far greater respect than other Italian pragmatists.

Yet further evidence of a change in perspective comes from another difference in the wording used. Again comparing paragraphs 4§42 and 11§48, the earlier draft reads that, for the historian, two national cultures

> are interchangeable: each one is reducible to the other; they are mutually translatable. This "translatability" is not perfect in all details (including important ones); but "deep down" it is.[23]

While in the more authoritative second draft, it is the word "perfect" that is put in inverted commas by Gramsci while those around the word "translatable" disappear. As a hypothesis, it seems in the 1930 A-text that Gramsci judges the translatability of two cultures as metaphorical, when compared with the similar operation between two natural languages, whereas in the C-text, there is full recognition of the reciprocal translatability between civilizations, of their reducibility of one to the other. It has to be emphasized however that this is a hypothesis and other paragraphs may suggest otherwise, as in Q1§44 and its rewritten version found in Q19§24, where the term "translating" is in inverted commas in the later draft but not the earlier one, which instead have the names "French" and "Italian" in inverted commas while "translate" is without them.[24] One has here to take account of the fact that "French" and "Italian" are used in both these extracts not as the names of natural languages but of national realities and experiences. In the later C-text version, the verb "translate," written between inverted commas, seems to indicate a double process: the culture of one nation is expressed in the national language which, in its turn, is the object of translation into another language, the material mode which expresses the culture of the second nation.

TRANSLATABILITY IN A GENERAL
SENSE AND IN A LIMITED SENSE

Translatability in a general sense, as observed above, corresponds to the possibility suggested by Marx of translating between two national cultures—that is, the ways, at first sight apparently disparate and unconnected, in which national cultures may express fundamentally the same concepts. To the two national cultures, French and German mentioned up to now, in Q10II§9 Gramsci, following Lenin's *Three Sources and Component Parts of Marxism*, adds the third one of English political economy:

> one of the most interesting and fecund subjects for research yet to be carried out concerns the relationship between German philosophy, French politics and English classical economy. One could say in a sense that the philosophy of praxis equals Hegel plus David Ricardo.[25]

A similar position to this one that brings English classical economy onto the scene is expressed in the letter to Tania of May 30, 1932, in which Gramsci asks a question not really to her but for her to pass on to the great economist who was his main intellectual and financial supporter in the prison years, Piero Sraffa, in Cambridge: did Ricardo have, Gramsci wonders, an importance for the history of philosophy, contributing to directing Marx and Engels "towards surmounting Hegelian philosophy and to the construction of their new historicism, purged of all traces of speculative logic"?[26] Among the problems to be studied, Gramsci then goes on to list in the paragraph here cited from the *Notebooks* those of establishing "the connection of Ricardo with Hegel and Robespierre" and "how the philosophy of praxis has arrived, from the synthesis of the three living currents to the new conception of immanence." He makes a generalization of the same theme in Q11§65, where he states that the three activities of philosophy, politics and economics are "the necessary constituent elements of the same conception of the world" and there must therefore be a "convertibility from one to the others and a reciprocal translation into the specific language proper to each constituent element."[27]

The more "limited" form of translatability, moreover, consists in translating within one discipline the *language* used by one theorist into that of another, where once again it must be recalled that "language" (*linguaggio*— i.e., a technical discourse) in contexts of this kind may be substituted by "paradigm." These are examples of the translatability Gramsci has in mind when he gives Q11§48 the heading *Giovanni Vailati and the Translatability of Scientific Languages*. During the 1920s, there is a striking example probably not known to Gramsci. Quantum mechanics, then a newborn branch of physics, gave rise to the two different formulations, wave mechanics and matrix mechanics, which both described, in different formal mathematical languages, the same reality. After some controversy and acrimony over physical and also fundamentally aesthetic questions, in 1926 Erwin Schrödinger, the physicist after whom the wave equation is named, proved them to be alternative forms of the same theory.

Returning to the examples that Gramsci takes from Luigi Einaudi's discussion of Vailati, in a B-text (Q10II§20, June 1932) devoted to economic questions rather than translatability, Gramsci observes that these examples are very similar to one discussed by Engels in his preface to the third volume of Marx's *Capital*. The "vulgar economist" Wilhelm Lexis arrives in Engels's view at an explanation of the profits of capital that "amounts in practice to the same thing as the Marxian theory of surplus value . . . this theory is merely a paraphrase (*Umschreibung*) of the Marxian."[28] The paraphrase (or transcription) adds weight to what Gramsci maintains regarding translation between technical discourses or languages: both "orthodox economics" and "critical economy" (as Gramsci calls Marxist economics here) deal with the same problems, and one has to demonstrate that "the critical solution is the superior one." In this paragraph, too, Vailati's work is referred to when Gramsci comments that, in recognizing the validity of Vailati's work, Einaudi "implicitly admits the mutual translatability of these languages," a reciprocity that, however, does not mean that two languages are symmetrical and may be used indifferently.[29]

The concept of asymmetry is assumed as an axiom by Gramsci when, in the above-mentioned paragraph Q10II6iv of May 1932, he claims that speculative philosophies are reducible to the philosophy of praxis as a political moment which the latter "explains 'politically,'"[30] the element of asymmetry clearly giving precedence to the philosophy of praxis as compared with other rival philosophical approaches. This comes out strongly in the main group of paragraphs on the subject of translatability. The paragraphs pose the question of "whether the mutual translatability of the various philosophical and scientific languages is a 'critical' element that belongs to every concept of the world or whether it belongs (in an organic way) only to the philosophy of praxis." The conclusion is expressed in different words from those of Q10II§6iv, just a few months previously, but the substance seems the same. As Gramsci states in 11§47, "It seems that one may in fact say that only in the philosophy of praxis is the 'translation' organic and thoroughgoing."[31] However, this time, before arriving at his conclusion Gramsci offers an explanation: in order for there to be translatability between two civilizations, a given expression must correspond to an earlier stage of the civilization that translates it; alternatively, the two civilizations must be at a more or less similar level of development and in this case the languages, while different, such as classical economy, philosophy and politics, must reflect the same basic processes that characterize their respective national societies. In the argument contained in this particular paragraph, translation from a less to a more advanced society is excluded. The reason for this is fairly obvious: the concepts used in, say, a neolithic society can be understood, even though with great difficulty, by a more "advanced" society, but it would undoubtedly be far more difficult, for example, to explain to a neolithic hunter the nature of quantum mechanics.

A less extreme example which may be read in the context of translatability is contained in a note Q9§52 (June 1932) which has been almost entirely ignored. After an explanatory introduction Gramsci observes that

> two men whose thought is fundamentally identical, but who have lived separate from each other and in very different conditions, end up by having great difficulty in understanding each other, thus creating the need for a period of work in common that is necessary for retuning themselves to the same note. If this necessity is not understand one runs the banal risk of indulging in useless polemics, on merely "verbal" questions when much more important issues are at stake.

As observed in the introduction to Gramsci's paragraph, when two or more people do not understand each other, it is not (only) the lexis that divides them but rather their different experience, or form of life, to use a Wittgensteinian term.

On this subject of translation between radically different communities an article by two British researchers, Len Doyal and Roger Harris, is of interest. In his *Word and Object*, W. V. O. Quine posed the question of how two people belonging to radically different societies could fully understand each other. The solution offered by Doyle and Harris is that language acquires its purchase on reality through its involvement and its intimate link with practical activities, and that the most important of these activities (i.e., those which involve the production and reproduction of life) by their very nature "possess a measure of intelligibility in and of themselves," which is equivalent to saying that understanding takes place through human praxis, through labor in common.[32] Certain idealist philosophers arrive at a similar conclusion, as for example Ernst Cassirer, who agrees with Humboldt's position that the reason that people understand one another is to be sought in the fact that

> by touching the same link in each other's sense perception and concepts, by striking the same key in each other's spiritual instrument. . . . When . . . the link in the chain, the key of the instrument is touched in this way, the whole organism vibrates and the concept that springs from the soul stands in harmony with everything surrounding the individual link, even at a great distance from it.[33]

It is clear that Gramsci reaches similar conclusions to those of Doyle and Harris in Q11§49, where, among other things, he states that "two fundamentally similar structures have 'equivalent' superstructures and are mutually translatable whatever their particular national language."[34]

It should however be noted that this quotation contains differences as compared with its A-text, Q8§208 (February–March 1932), which turn out to be substantial toward the end of the C-text, where Gramsci attaches the "tranquil theory" of Kant to the moderates of the Risorgimento. In an "orthodox" vision of translation, the reference to the Risorgimento might be considered a side issue, but here it is not. For Gramsci, this stems directly from his concept of translatability and is an example of it. As he writes in this paragraph, the influence of classical German philosophy made itself felt in Italy through the Moderates but, as he specifies elsewhere, it was not just the Moderates who attempted to give a national interpretation of the movements in France and Germany. There is a certain ambiguity and lack of clarity in his comment in Q10II§41x (late summer–autumn 1932) to the effect that between Croce-Gentile and Hegel a linking tradition Vico-Spaventa-(Gioberti) was formed, in other words the translation of Hegel was made to pass through these thinkers. It is not clear why here Gramsci puts Gioberti's name in brackets. It would seem that Gramsci had some doubts about him, which are also indicated by the fact that there is no mention of him in the first draft (Q4§56, November 1930) of this note and, a few pages after the C-text (Q10II§41xiv), he is still considered as fundamentally a Moderate who tempered conservatism and innovation. On the other hand, Gramsci clearly acknowledges Gioberti's post-1848

Jacobinism and in fact says so explicitly in the conclusion to Q17§9 (August–September 1933) where, in commenting on Gioberti's volume *Rinnovamento* (*Renewal*), Gramsci recognizes that Gioberti "shows himself to be genuine Jacobin, at least in theory."[35] Gramsci notes that Gioberti himself was fully aware that in both France and Germany the same result had been reached by different means (Q17§18iii, September 1933) and, to quote his words on this: "Gioberti's note is of interest where he says that classical German philosophy and French materialism are the same thing in *a different language*."[36] Expressing this in other words, Gioberti was aware of the translatability of German and French philosophical languages and himself managed to effect a translation into Italian through what Gramsci calls an "extract from the history of philosophy," a part of the legacy of Hegel and of the progressive current in France.

"TRANSLATING" AND "TRANSLATABILITY"

At this point, it is of use to look at the way in which the words "translate" and "translatability" are used in other paragraphs of Gramsci's notebooks, so as then to be able to sketch out a model of his notion of translatability. We shall refer most of all to Notebook 10 and its corresponding A-texts, following in general the chronological order of the C-texts, with other notes being cited afterward.

Croce and Religion (Q10I§5, May–June 1932)

At the start of this paragraph Gramsci defines Croce's conception of religion and "faith":

> For Croce . . . every philosophy, that is to say every conception of the world, in so far as it has become a "faith," i.e., is considered not as a theoretical activity (the creation of new thought) but as a spur to action (concrete ethico-political action, the creation of new history), is therefore a religion.[37]

Before going on to indicate how this might be *translated*, "one cannot but emphasize that a faith that cannot be translated into 'popular' terms shows for this very reason that it is characteristic of a given social group."[38]

Here the act of translation is from the specialized discourse of a restricted group or class to a more general one comprehensible to the people as a whole. This is a type of translation for which elsewhere he praises the activity of Martin Luther in popularizing the teachings of the Christian Bible. In Luther's case, this involved as an essential step the translation of sacred texts from natural languages in which they were passed down (Hebrew, Greek and Latin) to the one actually spoken by the common people in sixteenth-century Germany. In this paragraph of Gramsci's, the action is not the operation carried out between natural languages, but the aspect of making a culture widely accessible. As he wrote in a letter to Tania of December 1, 1930, for the great popular masses the religious Reformation at first assumed "coarse and even superstitious forms," but at the same time its aspect of moral and intellectual renewal represented "the beginning of all modern philosophy and civilization"[39] and the philosophy of praxis for him had the equivalent task in modern times.

Definition of the Concept of Ethico-political History (Q10I§7, May–June 1932)

Again in a C-text where there is no equivalent to these words in a previous draft, Gramsci observes that a question to resolve is that

of translating speculative language into historicist language, i.e. of seeing whether this speculative language has a concrete instrumental value, superior to previous instrumental values.[40]

This represents one very clear indication of what he intended by what we have termed "interparadigmatic translation." There are terms which with very little or with no modification may be used in different paradigms because they correspond to reality as the human species understands it, irrespective of class, gender and so forth. This is what Gramsci means by an "instrumental value," corresponding to a "bare objective notion" around which there is however always some "system of hypotheses which go beyond the mere objective fact" (Q11§38),[41] but where this is judged to be a minimum in the case of "instrumental values" (more common in the exact than in the human sciences, of course). What makes the translatability of a philosophical paradigm more arduous lies in its more marked ideological content.

Croce and the Philosophy of Praxis (Q10I§11, May–June 1932)

In this B-text, we have the demonstration that Gramsci thought translatability was possible in both directions between rival paradigms:

Just as the philosophy of praxis was the translation of Hegelianism into historicist language, so Croce's philosophy is to a quite notable extent the retranslation into speculative language of the realist historicism of the philosophy of praxis.[42]

At this stage, only weeks before he gave final form to his notes on translatability, there is no explicit comment about any asymmetry involved in translating between one type of paradigm and another. But he perhaps gives a foretaste of this when he writes, with reference to whether Crocean philosophy in Italy could "offer the premise for a renewal of the philosophy of praxis in our times," that it is "worthwhile looking afresh at the position and putting it forward in a critically more developed form." In other words he considers that a "revised" and updated translation of Croce into the philosophy of praxis is necessary, adapting Crocean philosophy like Hegel's was by "the first theorists of the philosophy of praxis"—that is, Marx and Engels.

The Nexus between Philosophy, Religion, Ideology (Q10II§31i, June– August 1932)

Certain subjects alluded to in Q10I§11 are now taken up again, such as what it means to be the "heirs of classical German philosophy":

> From speculative philosophy a "concrete and historical" philosophy, the philosophy of praxis, had been arrived at, whereas Croce has translated the progressive acquisitions of the philosophy of praxis back into speculative language, and in this retranslation lies the best of his thought.[43]

If the heirs of the tradition of classical German philosophy are the modern workers' movement, this for Croce meant the negation of philosophy, while for Gramsci the "heir continues the work of the predecessor, but does so in practice, deducing an active will that attempts to transform the world." For Engels, Gramsci says, "History is practice (experiment, industry); for Croce history is still a speculative concept."[44] The identity of history and philosophy in Croce is his way of presenting the problem posed in the *Theses on Feuerbach*; in other words, Croce has here interpreted in a different way and retranslated the *Theses on Feuerbach* into his own speculative language.

Religion, Philosophy, Politics (Q10II§41i, August 1932)

Again here we have an example of translation within the same paradigmatic discourse (a "limited" rather than more general form of translatability), once again dealing with the forms that the philosophy of praxis has to assume in order to be assimilated by a mass public.

> Just as popular catholicism can be translated into the terms of paganism, or religions that, because of the superstitions and witchcraft by which they are or were dominated, are inferior to catholicism, so this inferior quality philosophy of praxis can be translated into "theological" or transcendental terms, i.e., those of pre-Kantian and pre-Cartesian terms.[45]

The last words are a reference to the criticism made of historical materialism by Croce at the Oxford Philosophy Congress of 1930, in polemic with the Soviet delegate and People's Commissar Anatoly Lunacharsky. While Gramsci wrote in the letter, already cited above, to Tania of December 1, 1930, that Croce was of the opinion that the whole of "historical materialism marks a return to the old . . . medieval theologism, to pre-Kantian and pre-Cartesian philosophy,"[46] in the paragraph of the Notebooks discussed here, his response to Croce is that this so-called return was not historical materialism itself but an "inferior quality" though historically necessary translation of it carried out in order to spread its doctrines.

Gramsci makes use of a similar argument regarding the popularization of historical materialism, in Q8§226, repeated and slightly amplified in Q10I§13, note 3, where he quotes the words of the medieval humanist Alberti in his observation:

> Speculative history and the need to use less sophisticated instruments. Leon Battista Alberti wrote of the mathematicians: "They measure the shapes and forms of things in the mind alone and divorced entirely from matter. We, on the other hand, who wish to talk of things that are visible, will express ourselves in cruder terms."[47]

It is necessary to express oneself in very precise and refined terms, but it is also necessary to use another type of language in order to explain what one means to an audience that has to struggle to master certain types of discourse. It is perhaps not out of place to quote the words of Wittgenstein in a similar context dealing not with popularization but with the nature of language itself:

> The more narrowly we examine actual language, the sharper becomes the conflict between it and our requirements. . . . The conflict becomes intolerable, the requirement is now in danger of becoming empty. We have got onto slippery ice where there is no friction and so in a certain sense the conditions are ideal, but also, because of that we are unable to walk. We want to walk, so we need *friction*. Back to the rough ground.[48]

For Wittgenstein, language itself is imprecise, so the problems of popularization are also inherent in any type of language, which seems to reduce the problem of translation from high to popular culture to one merely of a degree of difference between them rather than a qualitative, insuperable gulf.

Croce's Speech at the Oxford Philosophical Congress (Q7§1, November 1930)

Gramsci deals up the question of Croce's speech at Oxford not just in Notebook 10 but also in the earlier Notebook 7, whose very first paragraph takes up the question of translatability.

The translation of the terms of one philosophical into the terms of another philosophical system, just like the translation of the language of one economist into the language of another economist, has limits, and these limits are determined by the fundamental nature of philosophical systems or of economic systems. In other words, such translation is possible within traditional philosophy, whereas it is not possible to translate traditional philosophy into terms of historical materialism or vice versa.[49]

Here Gramsci is very close to saying that some of the limits on translatability stem from the nature of language [*lingua*, or *langue* for Sassure] itself, and are certainly due to the nature of the various systems that are expressed in a given language [*linguaggio*, which in Gramsci is not used in really the same sense as Saussure's *langage*].

He then goes on to say that

the principle of mutual translatability is an inherent "critical" element of historical materialism, inasmuch as it presupposes or postulates that a given stage of civilization has a "basically identical" cultural and philosophical expression, even though the language [*linguaggio*] of the expression varies depending on the particular tradition of each "nation" or each philosophical system.[50]

This formulation is then repeated in Q11§47, for which Q7§1 serves as an A-text, just as it is also the A-text of Q10II§41i, discussed in the immediately preceding section to this one.[51] More or less at this point, the texts of Q7§1 and Q11§47 begin to diverge, and it is solely in the later text that we read:

It is to be seen whether translatability is possible between expressions of different stages of civilization, in so far as each of these stages is a moment of the development of another, one thus mutually integrating the other, or whether a given expression may be translated using the terms of a previous stage of the same civilization, a previous stage which however is more comprehensible than the given language, etc.[52]

THE GRAMSCIAN MODEL OF TRANSLATABILITY

Gramsci's concept of translatability has as one of its origins the ideas that started to circulate in the 1790s, and were then taken up by Marx, about the equivalence of what, on the surface, seemed to be two separate national discourses in France and Germany. But the equation formulated by Gramsci is more articulated than the simple equivalence between two languages or national cultural discourses. His model involves the intervention of another factor that he maintains is essential for making one national culture translatable in the terms of another—namely, the similarity between the structures themselves ("structures" or "bases" in the Marxist sense) of two or more societies dealt with, either a current similarity or a similarity between the present stage of development of one society and a past one of another one. The interposition of the structural aspect of a society mediates, and maybe complicates, the task of translation between two or more societies. As he notes in Q11§48, "Translatability is not 'perfect' in every respect, even in important ones (but what language is exactly translatable into another? what single word is exactly translatable into another language?) but it is so in its 'basic' essentials."[53] Bearing this in mind, and taking account of the "vertical nature" of Marx's structure-superstructure metaphor, a simple model of how Gramsci envisages the process of translation may be illustrated by figure 7.1, below

In this model, translation between two natural languages is not a direct process carried out by going "horizontally" from natural language 1 to natural language 2, by trans*fer*ring words from one to the other, as may be inferred etymologically from the Latin verb whose "literal" meaning for us is "to carry across" (trans-*late* or trans-*fer*, from the irregular verb "to carry" whose parts are: *fero, ferre, tuli, latum*). A model was current in the 1970s in which Eugene A. Nida and C. R. Taber, biblical scholars and authors of an authoritative early modern study of translation theory and practice, suggested figure 7.2.[54]

To their great credit, Nida and Taber recognize that the "transfer" process between the intermediate stages X and Y involves not merely linguistic but the all-important question of cultural reinterpretation. One of their striking examples of this is how to translate the expression "lamb of God" into a culture like that of the Inuit of the Arctic and semi-Arctic regions, where a lamb is a rare and exotic and, perhaps until recently, an unknown animal. The "seal of God," having some of the same ritualistic overtones, is their ingenious translation equivalent.

In his Marxist approach Gramsci regards translation as an act in which, from the propositions expressed in natural language 1, one descends through the appropriate levels of the superstructure to the "base" or "structure" of a society that has or has in the past had a "fundamentally similar" structure,

Natural Language 1		Natural Language 2
⇕		⇕
inserted into the context of a paradigm or national cultural discourse (e.g. French politics)		inserted into the context of cultural discourse (e.g. German philosophy or English classical economy)
⇕		⇕
Given stage of socio-economic development	⇔	Equivalent stage of socio-economic development

Figure 7.1. A Simplified Model of the Translation Steps between Two Natural Languages

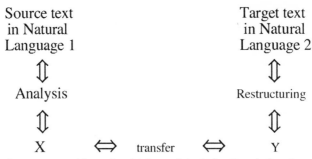

Figure 7.2. Nida and Taber's Model of the Translation Process

in order then to carry out the reverse, ascending, procedure to arrive at the "surface" constituted by natural language 2. It is when one gives due consideration to this question, an approach that is consistent with Nida and Taber's, that one explains the process in material, and, indeed, materialist, terms.

In the normal sense of the term "translation," a process that illustrates quite neatly our model derived from Gramsci is provided by the classical analysis of the Melanesian language and customs of the Trobriand Islands (N.E. New Guinea) carried out in the 1920s by the linguist-anthropologist Bronisław Malinowski. In a conversation of a friendly nature (interpersonal, or "phatic," to use the technical term introduced by Malinowski) words serve among the islanders to reinforce the links necessary for ensuring successful fishing and thus to ensure the production of the material conditions for life: language as used here is a "mode of action" to quote Malinowski.[55] The "surface" linguistic level is intimately linked with the "structural" level of their society, that is, with the social relations of production. If we can say that there is complete interpersonal understanding among the islanders, or among members of another community, one cannot (always or perhaps even often) say the same about the community and an outsider. There exist problems in translating into another language the phatic conversation of the islanders. A "horizontal" passage from Melanesian to, say, English is clearly inadequate and in order to be more real (even if not "perfect," to use Gramsci's description) the translation and understanding must pass through the intermediate stages of a model such as that proposed on the basis of Gramsci's translatability notes.

The model suggested here as a first summary interpretation of Gramsci's position involves different national cultures but does not fully take into account any mutual relationship and influence of one on another. Some time after the set of notes in paragraphs 46–49 of Notebook 11, he returns to the subject in Q11§65 (written between the end of 1932 and the beginning of 1933), a paragraph headed "Philosophy-politics-economics," and having few significant modifications as compared with its A-text (Q4§46, October–November 1930). Both these paragraphs refer explicitly to what is contained in other ones on translatability (Q4§42 and the later paragraph to the series Q11, paragraphs 46–49). In the later, more developed, note of Q11§65, Gramsci observes that if the three activities of the heading are

> the necessary constituent elements of the same conception of the world, there must necessarily be, in their theoretical principles, a convertibility from one to the others and a reciprocal translation into the specific language proper to each constituent element. Any one is implicit in the others, and the three together form a homogeneous circle.[56]

A further comment may be added to this observation, found in Q10II§9. In this paragraph of Q10, in order to explain precisely how the three "movements" or "moments" lie at the origin of the philosophy of praxis, Gramsci asks whether "each of these three movements has contributed respectively to the elaboration of the philosophy, the economics and the politics of the philosophy of praxis" or whether, instead it is the case

> that the philosophy of praxis has synthesized the three movements, that is, the entire culture of the age, and that in the new synthesis, whichever moment one is examining, the theoretical, the economic, or the political, one will find each of the three movements present as a preparatory "moment"? This is what seems to me to be the case. And it seems to me that the unitary moment of synthesis is to be identified in the new concept of immanence.[57]

Q10II§9 continues by noting that it is the discovery by Ricardo of the "formal logical principle of the 'law of tendency'" that implies a new conception of necessity and of freedom. It is then the philosophy of praxis, in carrying out a translation has also "universalized Ricardo's discoveries . . . drawing from them, in an original form, a new conception of the world."[58] This, in Gramsci's view, guarantees Ricardo a position in the history of philosophy, a position that, without this explanatory background, left Sraffa less than convinced.

The reconstruction and explanation offered here lies, in my view, at the basis of the "homogeneous circle" that, applied to translatability, gives rise to a more complex model than that illustrated in figure 7.1 and is here illustrated diagrammatically in figure 7.3, where, purely for reasons of simplicity, the arcs of circles have been substituted by the straight lines of the triangles.

A scheme such as that of figure 7.3 allows the passage from the structure, using Marx's metaphor, to the language (*linguaggio*, paradigmatic discourse) characteristic of a given national culture (German classical philosophy, French politics, English classical economy) and then to the corresponding natural language (*lingua*), here German, French and English. The possible paths of

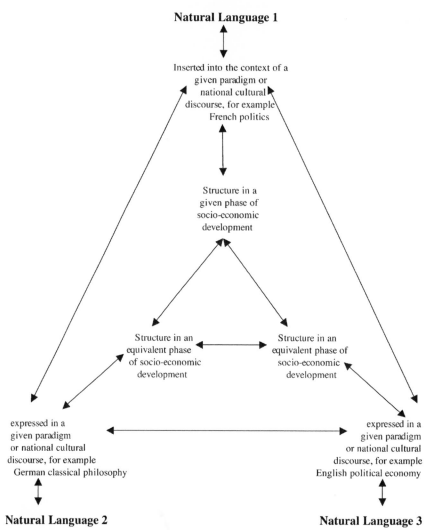

Figure 7.3. The Gramscian Model of Translation between Paradigms and Cultural Discourses

reciprocal interactions are shown by two-way arrows, in other words between discourses [*linguaggi*] either between the respective structures for two or more nations, or between the structure and respective discourses that "depend" on or "belong" to each particular structure. Furthermore, a philosophy like the philosophy of praxis has links, which it explicitly recognizes, both with the different structures and with what in the diagram is called the "paradigm or national cultural discourse" and, in theory, is able to explain them and incorporate them into its discourse—that is, translate them (Q10II§9).[59]

The type of model outlined here on the basis of Gramsci's writings in the *Notebooks* on translatability helps explain at a theoretical level why, between two or more natural languages, or in the development in time of just one language,

> in translations . . . there is never identity between the terms of the languages being compared, or at least that what identity there seems to be at the beginning of the exercise (Italian "rosa" = Latin "rosa") becomes increasingly more complicated as the "apprenticeship" progresses, moves increasingly away from the mathematical scheme and arrives at a historical judgement or a judgement of taste.[60]

The first draft has almost identical wording except for the ending, where it reads "it reaches the historical or psychological level in which nuances, 'unique and individual' expressiveness prevail" (Q1§153, May 1930).[61]

It should come as no surprise that, in a volume that Gramsci had in prison, *Science at the Cross Roads,*[62] with its celebrated—or perhaps notorious—essay "Theory and Practice from the Standpoint of Historical Materialism," attacked by Gramsci in Notebook 11, part II, the Soviet delegates to the London congress on the history of science and technology developed their analysis of the social roots of science, thereby providing a link between the structure of a society and the scientific theories and, going up in the scale of abstraction, the discourses-languages on whose terrain they are born. In the example of the more limited type of translation, that between scientific languages, Gramsci suggests that the translation that the philosophy of praxis makes when it translates other philosophies into its own terms is more thoroughgoing and complete ("organic"), while in the opposite direction the translation is defective and incomplete.

For languages in the sense of paradigmatic discourses that are contemporaneous with each other, there can exist what the philosopher of language Ferruccio Rossi-Landi calls a "homology" (i.e., not simply a similarity but a correspondence between two manifestations that springs from the fact that they have their roots in an essence common to both of them).[63] One may think here of recent examples such as the various guises adopted by modernism, postmodernism and minimalism in the various countries where they have held sway. Gramsci uses to affect the near-identical argument that structures of society at similar stages of development give rise to different "manifestations," in his case cultural discourses that are characteristic, each of its own national society. For two or more such paradigms, which may exist in different eras or in the same one, and which attempt to explain the same phenomena, in Gramsci's view, the often radical reinterpretation of concepts, conducting them to the same "essence" (to use Rossi-Landi's metaphor) or "base/structure" (to use Marx's) makes these paradigms in the human and social sciences translatable.

This stance, it ought to be noted, is different from the early work of Thomas Kuhn, when, in putting the emphasis on the incommensurability of paradigms in the physical and exact sciences, he almost always denied that translatability was possible in these fields.[64] From the mid-1970s onward, however, Kuhn modified this initial position, in part by reconsidering his initially stark and almost absolutistic concept of paradigm. In an essay of 1974, "Second Thoughts on Paradigms," he recognizes that competing schools, typical of the social sciences, all possess paradigms and that their work is not, as he thought in his seminal 1962 *Structure of Scientific Revolutions*, merely a sign of a pre-paradigmatic phase.[65] From there it is but a short step to recognize that translatability is possible between such paradigms and a couple of years later, in his 1976 essay, "Theory Change as Structure Change," we find him saying that "comparing theories becomes in part a problem of translation." In such activity "translation always and necessarily involves imperfection and compromise" and that the translator has to "repeatedly shift the choice of word and phrase" to capture the aspect of the original that s/he has to preserve at a given moment. Kuhn continues, in almost Gramscian language, by saying that it is upon compromises of this sort that "the translation of one theory into the language of another depends,"[66] thereby explicitly recognizing the existence of translatability between theories. Thus, although he did not know of Gramsci, or at least of this aspect of Gramsci's work, these two major figures in part converged in their lines of analysis and their judgments on translatability. Tullio De Mauro, one of Italy's most distinguished linguists, takes the argument one stage further by noting that the greater the degree of internal reducibility (to axioms, etc.) of a science (i.e., the nearer we get to the "hard" sciences), "the more difficult it is to render its phrases in a less reducible field of knowledge." He then goes on to state explicitly that the cultural and political science fields, that is, the ones that most involved Gramsci's reflections, are sciences at the opposite end of the spectrum to the "hard" sciences.[67] In consequence, not only their phrases but also their technical terms are more easily translatable from the scientific language of one school into that of another.

SOME IMPLICATIONS OF GRAMSCI ON TRANSLATABILITY: CONCLUDING REMARKS

The British linguist Raymond Firth commented that "wherever and whenever we enter into the speech of someone else, or of our own past, we are really translating."[68] In terms argued in more detail by Emilio Betti the discourse of other people is "accepted as an exhortation," to use one's own world knowledge to "retranslate and re-express" with one's own "mental categories the idea [the discourse] gives rise to"—in other words, when one listens to the words of another person, one is in actual fact translating into the schemes of one's own world the concepts that belong to the schema of the other person.[69] In this sense we are carrying out that type of fundamental translation which may be called zero-level or zero-degree, which Gramsci follows up with what he defines as a "first degree" of translatability, which is not between natural languages as such but between, at first, what he considers as merely different terminologies (Q4§42), then, after reasoning on both Machiavelli (see Q8§162 in particular, and also the letter to Tania of December 1, 1932) and the Italian pragmatist Giovanni Vailati, realizes is actually between scientific languages or discourses. The various schools of thought attempt to describe the same reality not only through different *terminologies* but different scientific *languages*, as he notes in the definitive C-text, Q11§48.

There is a high degree of abstraction in Gramsci's translatability notes but, at the same time, he also "descends" to the practical level, as one sees from the comments above taken from Q1§153 and Q16§21. Figure 7.1 is an attempt to show that the passage from one language to another, here in the sense of natural languages, cannot be a direct passage from one to the other but is instead mediated, to a greater or lesser extent as the case may be, by the nature of the societies, both in their structures and in the superstructures arising on them in the various societies and which characterize the discourses of each of these societies. This seems to represent the next level up for Gramsci in the degree of complexity of translatability.

But then, in the eleventh notebook in particular, he takes a big step forward. He realizes the full potential of what Marx had said in the *Holy Family* about classical German philosophy and French political practice expressing fundamentally the same processes, and to these discourses he adds from Lenin the third element, that of English classical economy in the figure of Ricardo. Starting from Marx's metaphor of structure (base) and superstructure, he realizes that these three discourses reflect in some way deeper-lying processes at work within their respective societies and that, given that the societies are basically the same stage of economic and social development (i.e., they have "fundamentally similar structures"), their superstructures are "equivalent," and thus these superstructures, including most of all here the discourses that characterize them, "are mutually translatable whatever their particular national language" (Q11§49). Hence we arrive at the most abstract degree or level of translatability, which figure 7.3 attempts to summarize diagrammatically.

In Notebook 11 Gramsci clarifies and makes explicit his concepts of translatability between different technical languages (*linguaggi*) or paradigms, but then he applies this method of his in practice elsewhere in the *Notebooks*. Nowhere is this more apparent than in the "twin" notebook to

Q11—namely, Q10—on the philosophy of Benedetto Croce, in regard to various aspects of Croce's philosophical and historical paradigms (the term *paradigma* is used explicitly by Gramsci in this respect). But it is not just an exercise carried out with Croce's discourse. It is also the technique Gramsci applies for the examination, critique and incorporation—in other words, the *translation*—of important concepts from the discourses of thinkers such as Piero Gobetti, the Turinese left liberal who was editor of *La Rivoluzione Liberale* and a collaborator on Gramsci's review, *L'Ordine Nuovo*, Edgar Quinet, historian of the French Revolution, Vincenzo Cuoco, Neapolitan patriot and others.

Lest it be thought that this process is limited to Gramsci, and thus as sort of "quirk," it may be pointed out that similar processes were being carried out in the intellectual ferment of the same years. Heidegger's reworking in *Being and Time* of key concepts of Lukács's *History and Class Consciousness* was analyzed explicitly in the 1960s as a problem of translation from one paradigm to another by Lucien Goldmann.[70] More recently, Richard Wolin has written in similar terms of this same relationship. The young Marcuse who, it may be remembered, was a pupil of Heidegger, carried out a similar operation by reinterpreting certain concepts of the latter's discourse and in effect translating the reinterpreted forms into his Marxist discourse, in order to arrive, according to Wolin, at what some would call a "Heideggerian Marxist" position.[71]

In Q7§33 Gramsci observes that "at the advent of a regulated society," when "political society" with its aspect of dominance is superseded, Marx's conception of the world will also be superseded. In other words, this means that some future philosophies will be able to "translate" not only other philosophies of the past but also the current-day philosophy of praxis in order to incorporate them into a higher synthesis. Both the incorporation of concepts from outside Marxism and this prediction of the supersession of Marx's conception of the world are examples of what Carl Marzani rightly said was "The Open Marxism of Antonio Gramsci," the title of his selection from the *Notebooks*. And it should also be stated explicitly that this open aspect makes Gramsci's Marxism qualitatively different from any conception of Marxism as a closed system, and specifically much of the system that in the Soviet Union and elsewhere in the countries of "real" or "actually existing" socialism went under the name of Marxism-Leninism.

Summing up in a sentence a wider significance of Gramsci's work on translatability, it may be seen that in his overall approach, he was far in advance of his times and heralded the ideas sketched out by a philosopher of science of the stature of Thomas Kuhn, at the same time that he was also a forerunner, without the experts in the field being aware of it, of the important so-called cultural turn in translation studies that took place internationally in the 1980s.

NOTES

1. Antonio Gramsci, *Prison Notebooks*, vol. 1, trans. and ed. Joseph Buttigieg (New York: Columbia University Press), 147, hereafter PN1. [There is a list of abbreviations on pages ix–x. To facilitate locating passages in various translations and anthologies, we use the standard method of providing the notebook (*Quaderno*) number—in this case 1—followed by the section number, §. See the introduction, page 12, for discussion. We will indicate the English translation, if used.]

2. Karl Marx and Friedrich Engels, *The Holy Family*, in *Collected Works*, vol. IV, trans. Richard Dixon and Clemens Dutt (London: Lawrence & Wishart, 1975), 5–211, here 39.

3. Wolfgang Fritz Haug, personal communication, March 22, 2006.

4. Carl Marzani, "Preface" to Antonio Gramsci, *The Open Marxism of Antonio Gramsci*, ed. and trans. Carl Marzani (New York: Cameron Associates, 1957), 59.

5. Q10II§6iv, Antonio Gramsci, *Further Selections from the Prison Notebooks*, ed. and trans. Derek Boothman (Minneapolis: University of Minnesota Press, 1995), 306, hereafter cited as FSPN.

6. Q11§46, FSPN, 306. The words of this definitive C-text, written like the other paragraphs on translatability of section V of Notebook 11 in the late summer or autumn 1932, are to all intents and purposes the same as those of the first draft A-text, Q7§2, dating to November 1930; all dates quoted here that regard the *Notebooks* are taken from the chronological analysis, Gianni Francioni, *L'officina gramsciana* (Naples: Bibliopolis, 1984), 140–46.

7. Vladimir Lenin, *Collected Works*, vol. XXXIII (London: Lawrence and Wishart, 1966), 430–31.

8. Q11§47 is listed as a B-text (i.e., one for which there is no previous first draft), but it is actually a C-text, for which see below, QC, 1468.

9. FSPN, 306–13.

10. PN1, 140.

11. Q19§24, SPN, 78.

12. Antonio Gramsci, *Prison Notebooks*, vol. 2, ed. and trans. Joseph Buttigieg (New York: Columbia University Press, 1996), 191, hereafter cited as PN2.

13. PN2, 51.

14. FSPN, 307.

15. In the absence of a verb in the C-text, the expression "seemed to me" of the A-text is replaced editorially in the critical edition of the *Notebooks*, QC, simply by "is," an interpolation repeated in the translation by the current writer, who at the time was not aware of these subtleties. FSPN, 307.

16. PN2, 382.

17. Antonio Gramsci, *Letters from Prison*, two volumes, ed. Frank Rosengarten, trans. Raymond Rosenthal (New York: Columbia University Press), 150–51, hereafter cited as LP2 for volume 2, and LP1 for volume 1. Here the translation is amended to substitute "economic policy" [*politica economica*] for the mistaken "political economy."

18. FSPN, 164.

19. Antonio Gramsci, *Selections from the Prison Notebooks*, ed. and trans. Quintin Hoare and Geoffrey Nowell Smith (New York: International Publishers, 1971), 143, hereafter cited as SPN.

20. See FSPN, 306, and PN2, 191.

21. FSPN, 308, by "scientists" [*scienzati*], Gramsci means two scholars in general.

22. PN1, 147, and SPN, 78.

23. PN2, 192.

24. PN1, 140, and SPN, 65.

25. SPN, 400.

26. LP2, 178.

27. SPN, 403, autumn 1932 or very beginning of 1933.

28. Friedrich Engels, "Preface" to Karl Marx, *Capital, Vol. III* (London: Lawrence & Wishart, 1967), 10.

29. FSPN, 184.

30. FSPN, 306.

31. FSPN, 307.

32. Len Doyal and Roger Harris, "The Practical Foundations of Human Understanding," *New Left Review* I, 139 (1983): 59–78, here 78.

33. As quoted from Humboldt in Ernst Cassirer, *The Philosophy of Symbolic Forms, Volume 1: Language*, trans. Ralph Manheim (New Haven, Conn.: Yale University Press, 1953), 160.

34. FSPN, 312.

35. Antonio Gramsci, *Selections from Cultural Writings*, ed. David Forgacs, trans. William Boelhower (Cambridge, Mass.: Harvard University Press, 1985), 248, hereafter cited as SCW.

36. FSPN, 313, emphasis added.

37. FSPN, 338.

38. FSPN, 339.

39. LP1, 365.

40. FSPN, 344.

41. FSPN, 293.

42. FSPN, 355.

43. FSPN, 385.

44. FSPN, 385.

45. FSPN, 403.

46. LP1, 364.

47. FSPN, 358.

48. Ludwig Wittgenstein, *Philosophical Investigations*, trans. G. E. M. Anscombe, ed. G. E. M. Anscombe and Rhush Rees (Oxford: Blackwell, 1953), §107.

49. Antonio Gramsci, *Prison Notebooks*, vol. 3, ed. and trans. Joseph Buttigieg (New York: Columbia University Press, 2007), 153, hereafter cited as PN3.

50. PN3, 153.

51. This correspondence is not stated in the critical edition of the Notebooks, but was accepted by its editor, Valentino Gerratana, in conversation with the Gramscian scholar Fabio Frosini; oral confirmation of this came during a session of the Seminario Gramsciano of the IGS Italia when the subject matter of this chapter was first presented in February 2003.

52. FSPN, 307, translation altered to give the more precise term "translatability" instead of "one can translate."

53. FSPN, 309.

54. Eugene Nida and C. R. Taber, *The Theory and Practice of Translation* (Leiden: Brill, 1974), 33.

55. C. K. Ogden and I. A. Richards, *The Meaning of Meaning* (London: Kegan Paul, Trench, Trubner, 1946), 315.

56. SPN, 403.

57. SPN, 399–400.

58. SPN, 401.

59. SPN, 399–400.

60. Q16§21, after February 1934; SCW, 384–85, translation altered.

61. PN1, 233.

62. Nikolai Bukharin, *Science at the Cross Roads: Papers Presented to the International Congress of the History of Science and Technology by the Delegates of the U.S.S.R.* (London: Kniga, 1931).

63. Ferruccio Rossi-Landi, *Semiotica ed Ideologia*, second edition (Milan: Bompiani, 1994), 249–51.

64. Thomas Kuhn, *The Structure of Scientific Revolutions* (Chicago: University of Chicago Press, 1962), 129–30.

65. Thomas Kuhn, *The Essential Tension. Selected Studies in Scientific Tradition and Change* (Chicago: University of Chicago Press, 1977), 295n.4.

66. Thomas Kuhn, *The Road since Structure: Philosophical Essays 1970–1993*, ed. James Conant and John Haugeland (Chicago: University of Chicago Press, 2000), 189–90.

67. Tullio De Mauro, "Linguaggi scientifici," in *Studi sul Trattamento Linguistico dell'Informazione Scientifico*, ed. Tullio De Mauro (Rome: Bulzoni, 1994), 309–25, here 317.

68. Raymond Firth, "Linguistic Analysis and Translation," in *Selected Papers of J. R. Firth 1952–59*, ed. F. R. Palmer (London: Longman, 1968), 77.

69. Emilio Betti, "Di una teoria generale dell'interpretazione," in *Diritto e Potere—Il problema dell'interpretazione e dell'applicazione del diritto*, vol. I, ed. R. Orecchia (Milan: Giuffrè, 1966), 53–54.

70. Lucien Goldmann, *Lukács and Heidegger*, trans. William Q. Boelhower (London: Routledge and Kegan Paul, 1977), 10–13 and 27.

71. Richard Wolin, *Heidegger's Children* (Princeton, N.J.: Princeton University Press, 2003), 135.

8

Aunt Alene on Her Bicycle: Antonio Gramsci as Translator from German and as Translation Theorist

Lucia Borghese *

> A skilled translator should be able not only to translate literally but also to translate the conceptual terms of a national culture into the terms of another national culture, that is, such a translator should have a critical knowledge of two civilizations and be able to acquaint one with the other by using the historically determined language of the civilization to which he supplies the informative material.
>
> Antonio Gramsci[1]

Antonio Gramsci wrote this letter to his wife Julca in September 1932 to encourage her to work in the field of translation, an activity which Gramsci himself had pursued for three years while jailed in Turi, believing—in his own words—that we should commit "all our forces" to translation. Gramsci's experience as a translator lasted from 1929 to the early part of 1932. Subsequently, in his letter to Julca, he formulated his idea of translation as deeply rooted in his overall political and philosophical theory, most maturely expressed in the *Prison Notebooks*. As we shall see, this proposition was sometimes applied by Gramsci himself, and it is a corollary to the fundamental and universal proposition that he had deduced from the Marxian theory: in fact, Gramsci considered Marx's theory to be indispensable to the historiographical methodology of historical materialism, according to which "two fundamentally similar structures have 'equivalent' superstructures, whatever the particular national language."[2]

---

* Translated from Lucia Borghese, "Tia Alene in Bicicletta: Gramsci Traduttore dal Tedesco e Teorico della Traduzione," *Belfagor* 36, no. 6 (November 1981): 635–65. Translated by Sabrina Fusari with some assistance from Derek Boothman.

In other words, Gramsci relied on Marx's by-now classical "distillation of the French political terms . . . into the language of German philosophy,"[3] in arguing that in the international sphere:

> two national cultures, the expressions of two fundamentally similar civiliza-
> tions . . . for the historian . . . can be mutually translatable, the one reducible
> to the other. Certainly, this translatability is not "perfect" in every respect, even
> in important ones (but what language is perfectly translatable into another
> language? what single word is exactly translatable into another language?) but
> it is so in its "basic" essentials.[4]

The principle that the superstructures, or cultures, are mutually translatable implies a judgment of historical value: according to Gramsci, this is a critical element of the philosophy of praxis—it is, in fact, a primary assumption that Gramsci claims for the philosophy of praxis, and is confirmation of its anti-dogmatic nature. Testimony to this is Gramsci's purpose, as stated even as far back as the *Ordine nuovo* period—namely, to "translate into Italian historical language" the postulates of international communism.[5] This approach reflects Gramsci's refusal of a "mathematical" scheme—in the sense of a rigid and abstract one—in his political theses and actions and, consequently, his need to find a "historical and psychological" schema to express them in a concrete and flexible way. Translation thus becomes a necessary criterion of mediation between two cultures, or conceptions of the world, which can critically mediate between the multiple and ever-changing faces of reality, and protect against all kinds of "metaphysical" rigid thinking: translation allows us to prevent contingent truths from being considered absolute and becoming fossilized as ideologies. In a certain sense, then, the concept of translation gives us a measure of Gramsci's "absolute historicism."

The methodology used by Gramsci to translate Lenin's political works by adapting them to the specific situation of Italy was also applied, with pedagogical intent, to literature. Implicitly Gramsci recognizes that language—as a social microcosm—is the vehicle of a conception of the world entrusted to the word as metaphor in a perennial, almost Heraclitean, state of becoming.

Gramsci first and foremost wanted to be a translator: with his theoretical and practical work, he laid the foundations for an idea of communism not as an imported product different in form from the political and social reality that it aimed to modify, but having the same form, and being viable due to its being an original "translation." Furthermore, although translation seems so different from the subjects that he tackled in his most mature work, Gramsci proved to be a translator in the real sense of the term. Besides translating a number of narrative texts from the Russian, Gramsci also translated several philological and literary texts from German: a compendium of linguistics by Franz Nikolaus Finck, part of a collection of Goethe's poems and prose writings, the first year of the conversations between Goethe and Eckermann, a series of articles on American and French literature, an anthology of writings by Marx and nearly a couple of dozen of the Brothers Grimm's fairy tales.

These translations are still unpublished[6] for no justified reason: an exception is an anthology of Gramsci's writings entitled *Favole di libertà* [Tales of Freedom],[7] which includes what is claimed to be Gramsci's translation of some of the Grimms' fairy tales. However, this version is the result of a blatant manipulation of Gramsci's manuscripts, which in our opinion one cannot yet consider to be published. An analysis of these neglected manuscripts with the aim of clarifying their subjects, putting them in chronological order, understanding their purpose and defining their inherent characteristics, will demonstrate that this alleged "minor work" is actually rich in meaning and goes beyond mere erudite curiosity.

THE ISSUE OF GRAMSCI'S MANUSCRIPTS

The exclusion of Gramsci's translation notebooks (A, B, C, D and part of Notebooks 7 and 9) from the various editions of his work may be indirectly traced back not only to the unsystematic way in which they were published, but also to editorial policies which, in reflecting the various phases of the political and cultural landscape of the Italian left, influenced distribution of the work in the postwar era. After the initial publication, with somewhat dubious selection criteria, of both the early and the mature writings, subsequent additions[8] became necessary when from time to time there appeared in newspapers or reviews unpublished works, whose attribution to Gramsci was sometimes doubtful or controversial. The selection was wide-ranging, but fragmentary and incomplete: not only did this lead some commentators to hazardous conclusions and instrumental distortions of Gramsci, but it also rekindled and legitimated the old debate about the fragmentariness of Gramsci's prison writings, first raised by Benedetto Croce when he observed that the *Notebooks* did not contain "that kind of synthesis whereby thought separates, combines and integrates in a coherent whole."[9]

Only very recently has a systematic reorganization of Gramsci's work begun, and materials have been integrated, put in chronological order and provided with the necessary critical commentary. Before that, Gramsci's works were seen as lacking a systematic "mechanical exteriority," although they did have their own "inner coherence."[10] This work was started by Giulio Einaudi in 1975 with the critical edition of the *Prison Notebooks* edited by Valentino Gerratana, and is still continuing today with the unabridged publication of Gramsci's early writings.[11]

Yet the critical edition of the *Notebooks* is also incomplete, as it includes only twenty-nine notebooks (two of which are abridged) out of thirty-three that were written by Gramsci. The missing parts include Gramsci's "translation exercises," which according to the editor were supposed to have a predominantly "therapeutic" function, while the author reflected on and organized the ideas that he would then go on to develop. It is therefore clear that the issue of how to organize Gramsci's writings was tackled from the very beginning, but was put aside due to a misplaced functionalist attitude (the introduction reads "they would make an already hefty edition unnecessarily heavier") when it was decided that the excluded writings were "clearly beyond the work plan that Gramsci set himself."[12] However, a simple comparison between Gramsci's translations and the originals—an entirely respectable endeavor for a critical edition—would have revealed the contrary. Even the critical edition only offered, with some inaccuracies, a description of the excluded parts, but did include several examples taken from Marx's writings that were judged to be "more directly connected with the issues dealt with in the *Notebooks*." The exclusion was explained—perhaps too casually—by remarking that those sections of the *Notebooks* did not "go beyond the immediate purpose that they were intended to serve."[13]

Venturing into unexplored territory is always a daunting and difficult challenge, especially if the final decision is to eliminate some parts of a work and leave the remaining ones to express an organic thought. In this case the risk was that of undermining the very premises on which a critical edition is based by sanctioning—unintentionally, of course—the fragmentary character of the *Notebooks* rather than transcending it. It is indeed our belief that only by publishing the work in its entirety can its inner coherence be guaranteed, thereby allowing readers to explore the genesis and original articulation of Gramsci's thought.

It is reasonable to contend that Gramsci's translations are not exempt from errors and inaccuracies, and that, due to their being work in progress (all texts are first drafts, often not reread),[14] they are far below the *optimum* required for publication. However, an essential hallmark of Gramsci's entire prison writings is their provisional and incomplete nature, since they represent an unsystematic collection not originally thought of for publication, at least not in the form in which we know them (Gramsci himself once observed that posthumous editions of unpublished works require considerable care). And, indeed, for a correct interpretation of the *Notebooks*, one cannot avoid reconstructing their chronology, and even less, their structure in its entirety.

Nevertheless, it would be senseless to argue that these heterogeneous versions have an independent value and an intrinsically organic character. This would be like considering a cut-off limb as independent of the body that it belongs to, asking it to do things that only the whole can do. Gramsci's translations are documentary evidence of the methodical study of languages that had begun in his youth, an interest that he had cultivated at university when he attended Arturo Farinelli's lectures on German classical and Romantic literature,[15] and Matteo Bartoli's linguistics course.[16] As such, Gramsci's translations are directly connected with the themes dealt with in the *Notebooks*, and in many ways they bridge the gap between past and present, between Gramsci, culture-hungry at the beginning of his journalistic career in Turin, and Gramsci as a Marxist theoretician of "disinterested" reflection.

In 1932, now an expert due to his prison segregation, Gramsci wrote a letter to his wife—who had remained "on the margins of life's flow" for several years—to encourage her to resume the study of music, a fundamental part of her education. This would allow her to relive her past with greater critical consciousness, since "it often happens that when returning to our past experiences, with all the wealth of hindsight, we do make important discoveries."[17] Might it be that Gramsci—as an erstwhile student of linguistics—followed a similar path with his translations?

These translations of his cast a bridge between his university apprenticeship and pre-Marxist period, but also anticipate issues and concepts that were developed at a later date. It is therefore necessary to take the translations into account when we analyze Gramsci's writings in an overall perspective, as recommended by Gerratana when he wrote that "[e]verything that made Gramsci the man that he was, from the ways in which he was moulded and his development, relives in the *Notebooks*, and it is in this reliving that it can be judged, examined in detail and developed."[18]

If we follow this course, it soon becomes clear that the excluded texts do contribute to an enrichment of Gramsci as a thinker and as a man, revealing indeed entirely new facets of his thought. Not only do they clarify his preferences and interests, but they also complement his linguistic theory and pedagogical concepts. His translations should therefore be considered to be in an "organic" relationship with the rest of the *Notebooks*, since they fall within the realm of his overall social theory, especially where the translation of the Grimms' tales is concerned. The chronology allows us to view Gramsci's translations as following a path from the simple to the complex, from mere "exercise" to a conscious design, and from philology to political pedagogy.

THE CHRONOLOGY OF GRAMSCI'S TRANSLATIONS

Gramsci's translations are generally assigned to the 1929–1931 period and can be dated and ordered chronologically approximately, despite the objective difficulty that all have found in dating the prison writings, due to his having worked simultaneously on different notebooks, and completed them at different stages. However, an understanding of the order in which different sections were written—based on an orthographic analysis, a comparison with the *Letters*, and an analysis of grammar and style—may provide further insight into the chronology of other entries in the *Notebooks*, the dates of which are still uncertain.[19]

Notebook A contains the translation of a special issue of *Literarische Welt* (October 14, 1927) on American literature, and several articles on Zola which had appeared in the same weekly journal on September 30, 1927[20]; following on with no interruption in the writing, the subsequent parts of this notebook contain fifteen tales of the Brothers Grimm,[21] numbered progressively by Gramsci himself, thus seeming to confirm the hypothesis that the order of presentation of these writings reflect their chronology.

Notebook B contains, in order, the next tales of the Grimms (eight complete and one unfinished), the rough copy of a letter to Julca—which can be dated between November 14 and 23, 1931[22]—and the first part of a short volume on linguistics by F. N. Finck, *Die Sprachstämme des Erdkreises* [The Linguistic Families of the World] (Teubner: Leipzig-Berlin, 1923). In fact, only part of Notebook B (as concerns the remaining tales, which are numbered consecutively) was written after Notebook A, as appears from the translation of Finck's essay, which adopts a particular stylistic trait typical of Gramsci's pre-prison writings, as reported by Gerratana (letter "t" being written with a long oblique stroke across it)[23]; therefore, this translation should not be accepted to be only antecedent to the preceding tales in Notebook B, but also earlier than the entire Notebook A, where this stylistic trait is not used. What certainly comes after the tales is the letter to Julca, which begins on the sixth (!) line of the reverse side of sheet 23, after an interrupted letter, from which it is separated with a line drawn in pen.[24]

Notebook C begins with a series of English exercises,[25] and the rest of Finck's text, which is translated in its entirety with the same stylistic traits described above. Subsequently, the even pages contain a series of poems by Goethe[26]: based on the frequency of the letter "t" written with a stroke across, these translations may be contemporary with the first part of the translation of Finck. On the odd pages, instead, the poems alternate with the first year of *Gespräche mit Eckermann* [Conversations with Eckermann], where his previously used spelling conventions, with double consonants, appear only occasionally.[27] The two groups of writings, on and by Goethe, were produced at different times, as appears not only from the form of the letter "t" and from the more recent spelling conventions in the *Gespräche*, but also from the order of presentation of the texts in the *Notebooks*: although the translations of Goethe's poems alternate with the writings on Goethe, the former are obviously earlier. It should also be noted that the second part of Finck's translation, which follows on the first part contained in Notebook B, was written before the translation of the *Gespräche*. In fact, Notebook C, distinguished by the more or less marked presence of the characteristic form of the letter "t," must predate Notebook A, where the old style has disappeared completely; however, Notebook C is more recent than the first part of Finck's translation, and comes after the continuation of the Grimms' tales contained in Notebook B.

Notebook 7 contains an almost-complete translation of an anthology of Marx's writings, *Lohnarbeit und Kapital*,[28] although the passages appear in a different order from the original: the increased rarity of stroked "t"s (which now appear only occasionally when the consonant is doubled) suggests that this notebook should be more recent than the translations of Finck and those of Goethe's poetry, and almost certainly more recent than the *Gespräche*, but it should predate Notebook A, where there are no characteristically stroked "t"s, and also predate the parts of Notebook B which represent a continuation of Notebook A (the tales and the rough copy).

Gramsci's translations from German[29] may therefore be ordered as follows:

1. Notebook B: Finck, first part (sheets 23^r–100^v).[30]
2. Notebook C: Goethe's poems (page 99 and sheets 100–176, only on the even pages) may be at least partly contemporary with the Finck translation.
3. Notebook C: Finck, second part (sheets 7–48).
4. Notebook C: *Conversations with Eckermann* (sheets 49–98, 101–75, only on the odd pages, and 177–94).
5. Notebook 7: the translations of Marx (sheets 2^r–34^r) may be partly contemporary with the *Conversations*.
6. Notebook A: "Die literarische Welt" (sheets 1^r–50^v).
7. Notebook A: Grimm, fifteen tales (sheets 51^r–99^r).
8. Notebook B: Grimm, eight complete and one incomplete tale, continuation (sheets 1^r–23^r).
9. Rough copy of letter to Julca, written between November 14 and 23, 1931 (sheet 23^{rv}).

Although there are very few references to this order of contents in the *Letters from Prison*, they still seem to confirm its correctness, sometimes with quite precise chronological details. The earliest possible date for the beginning of the translations is indicated in the letter to Tania of February 9, 1929. In this letter Gramsci informed his sister-in-law that he had obtained permission to write in his cell, and that he had started the translation work that he had envisioned for a long time. On November 18, he wrote her: "At present, I'm translating only from German, because I don't want to overtax my memory and disperse my attention, but next year, when I'll have completed the German program I have set for myself, I'll take up Russian again in depth."[31] However, Gramsci's "German program" kept him busy until after the end of 1931.

At that time, as the letter to Tania of December 16, 1929, clearly demonstrates, Gramsci was working on Finck's text, and he was translating the chapter entitled *La Lingua dei Negri Africani* [The Language of the Black Africans] (Notebook C). Finally, Gramsci's request for *Lohnarbeit und Kapital* was recorded on March 24, 1930, and he quoted a passage from this work in a letter to his brother Carlo on August 25.[32] The translations from this collection are therefore likely to have been written between the summer and autumn of 1930. Gramsci still had before him the numerous articles from the *Literarische Welt*, so his translation of the tales could hardly have started before 1931. Although the exact date of its beginning remains unknown, the translation of the tales was certainly interrupted between November 14 and 23, when Gramsci wrote to Julca instead of finishing the translation of the last tale that he had begun. The rough copy of this letter represents, therefore, the earliest possible date for the Grimm texts and for all of Gramsci's translations from German.

This chronology is further supported by evidence of Gramsci's increased linguistic skills as his translation work progressed: his fluency in German had improved (as shown by his gradually improving understanding of verbal forms and idiomatic phrases that were previously mistranslated), and he had developed a smoother style of writing. In fact, after a series of technically pedestrian translations, Gramsci attempted an unexpectedly original adaptation of the tales (*Märchen*) for their intended readership.

Notebook D contains only the beginning of the second draft of the tales: the second draft was supposed to consist of a transcription and stylistic revision addressed to the children of his sister Teresina, as results from the letter that he wrote to her on January 18, 1932. However, fate decided otherwise: the draft was interrupted after two pages for no apparent reason, and was never resumed. The prison authorities may have forbidden Gramsci to send the manuscript to his sister. This suggestion, first made by Gerratana, seems to be confirmed by Gramsci's use of "if" when he promised the tales to Teresina: "I'll . . . send them to you, if I get permission."[33]

For obvious reasons of space, our analysis is limited to the implications of Gramsci's "translation exercises" for some of the main topics of the *Notebooks*; in particular, we concentrate on the translation of the Grimms' *Märchen*, which marks the conclusion of Gramsci's translation project, both chronologically and conceptually. With his adaptation of the Grimms' fairy tales or popular tales for children,[34] Gramsci wanted to give his personal *"contribution to the imagination of the little ones,"*[35] and although the second draft was never completed, his contribution does stand as a concrete educational proposal, as well as an example of the "translatability of philosophical and scientific languages" that he dealt with in the *Notebooks* during the same period.[36]

FROM "MIMESIS" TO INTERPRETATION

Only recently has recognition been granted to the importance of Gramsci's linguistic interests, formerly often a source of embarrassment for those who felt somehow obliged to justify its presence throughout his early and his mature writings. Here most of the credit goes to Franco Lo Piparo, whose enlightening book traces the fundamental import of linguistics "in the formation of all the main Gramscian concepts: that of the national-popular, the intellectuals, folklore, hegemony, political society, civil society, consent."[37] For Gramsci, linguistics was "not simply a *Nebenfach*" ("subsidiary subject") as Tullio De Mauro observes in his introduction to Lo Piparo's work, "but a pivotal point, a fundamental element of all his theoretical reflection."[38] And his study of foreign languages and their literature, resumed in jail and culminating in his translations from the culturally most significant languages, should also therefore be considered as a way "to put oneself in contact with other cultural lives."[39] His aim was clearly to acquire the necessary concrete analytical elements, and the wide array of instruments necessary for historical inquiry, in order to analyze the complex interaction between the history of a language, cultural apparatuses and society. According to Gramsci, "linguists are essentially *historians* . . . they study languages precisely in so far as they are not art, but the 'material' of art, a social product, and the cultural expression of a given people."[40]

Gramsci recognized that his knowledge of foreign languages, albeit sufficient to "speak and especially to read,"[41] was limited: this is why he resolved to pursue a "systematic" study not only of German and Russian, but also of English, Spanish, Portuguese and Rumanian. He was not allowed to write or make any notes in the early stages of his imprisonment and so, at the beginning of his work (among the four "homogeneous" subject matters that he intended to give a treatment of *für ewig*, in the manner of Goethe, was "a study of comparative linguistics"[42]), it seems logical that he tried to make the most of his time and energies in conducting a preparatory study that could be of use for his project without necessitating any written notes.

It is neither by chance nor out of unreasonable punctiliousness that, on October 3, 1927, Gramsci reiterated his request for Finck's book (the first that he had set out to translate). He did not want to content himself with the other book by the same author (*Die Haupttypen des Sprachbaus* [The Main Types of Language Structure], Leipzig 1909) that the bookseller had wrongly sent to him. Nor is it a mere coincidence that in the same letter Gramsci asked not only for *Die Sprachstämme des Erdkreises*, the most complete classification of languages that was available at the time, but also for Giulio Bertoni and Matteo Giulio Bartoli's *Manualetto di Linguistica* (in actual fact *Breviario* rather than *Manualetto*), the programmatic manifesto of the new approach to linguistics founded by his former professor Bartoli.

Bartoli's *Breviario* provided Gramsci with a methodology: in fact, "Bartoli's innovation lies precisely in this: that he has transformed linguistics, conceived narrowly as a natural science, into an *historical science*, the roots of which must be sought 'in space and time' and not in the vocal apparatus in the physiological sense."[43] Finck's learned work effectively complemented Bartoli's insofar as his classification, far from being mechanical and arbitrary, was based on ethnic and geographical distribution of linguistic phenomena, thus making it possible to devise an implicit and tentative historical profile of these phenomena. The complementary nature of the two works, both of them anti-positivistic and anti-evolutionist, is further confirmed if we consider that, in Gramsci's own words, Bartoli's work "paved a new way in the idealistic sense,"[44] whereas Finck's took in hand and developed *Romantik* philosophical intuitions by declaring that there was a direct relationship between language and culture, thought and language. (Fink had in fact been a follower of [Wilhelm von] Humboldt, and was also strongly indebted to Steinthal.[45])

In criticizing naturalistic scientism, Finck opposed (much as Gramsci did in his early and mature writings) the neo-grammatical stance that language processes can be explained through predictable intrinsic laws. Instead, Finck saw language as the expression of worldviews and cultures, inseparable from human activities, as shown in the introduction to *Die Sprachstämme des Erdkreises*:

> Since language as an entity is not independent of human beings, it cannot exist, develop and disappear without the aid of human beings. In fact, any given language (such as German) is nothing but a sum of activities which appear more or less similar and homogeneous: not even a single one of them can result [derive][46] from another, but all should be attributed to the human beings who perform these activities (Notebook B, sheet 29[rv]).

This is a passage from Gramsci's translation of Finck[47]: the exaggeratedly painstaking effort he put into translating the whole work can only be explained by a deep interest in this matter, which is further confirmed by his use of Finck's work for various *noterelle di cultura* ("brief notes on culture"). According to Gramsci, culture is always connected with language and writing; Finck's acute observations on popular and elite varieties, dialect fragmentation or homogeneity of the languages he examined must have proved valuable in ascertaining the existence, or absence, of a national culture in different countries, and in understanding how a national culture could be attained. Thus, the "Esperantistic" value that Gramsci attributes to Chinese ideograms, insofar as they "have no organic connection with any particular language," suggests a series of considerations about "the so-called universal conventional languages in so far as they are not the historical expression of any particular, necessary conditions, become an element of social stratification, and of the fossilization of certain strata": the conclusion is that China cannot have a "widespread popular culture."[48]

The translation notebooks include about fifty poems from Goethe's biographical anthology entitled *Über allen Gipfeln* (about twenty of these translations were revised and corrected by Gramsci on the basis of a previous translation of Benedetto Croce's),[49] as well as a section of the *Conversations with Eckermann*. These translations complement Gramsci's notes on Goethe, while demonstrating his renewed interest in him, which had been stimulated by Farinelli and, later on, by Croce. Indeed, as early as 1917–1918, Croce had induced Gramsci to popularize Goethe's humanistic message in the organs of cultural renewal that he had given rise to.[50] At the time, Gramsci was the young editor of *Il Grido del Popolo* and had just begun his activity as a leader of the Turin working class, but his "elective affinity" with Goethe continued for the next twenty years and was further developed in the *Notebooks*.

Against this backdrop, the translations of "Goethe as creator" and "Goethe as artist" (Notebook C, 49) confirm that Gramsci's "aesthetic admiration"[51] for Goethe was fed by his unlimited intellectual curiosity about the poet's "exceptional character." Indeed, for Gramsci, Goethe was a modern poet insofar as he managed to express "in serene and classical form . . . his confidence in man's creative activity, in nature seen not as an enemy or as an antagonist, but as a force to be understood and dominated, relinquishing without regret our faith in those 'ancient fables' in which the still-present perfume of poetry renders them even deader as beliefs and faiths."[52]

The active role of human beings in history and, consequently, the refusal of any kind of spontaneous teleology, providentialism or "superstition" are, according to Gramsci, the salient and intertwined features of Goethe's humanism.[53] These features, first identified in Gramsci's journalistic work, were subsequently the object of his reflection in the *Letters* and in the *Notebooks* (and not by chance is Goethe often quoted in the section entitled "History and Anti-history"), and were also compared symbolically with the myth of Prometheus, as it appears from the modern version of the myth, that Goethe reproposed in his hymn, the subject of one of Gramsci's prison translations. The lines "Qui siedo, e formo gli uomini a mia immagine, una schiatta che mi somigli nel soffrire, nel piangere, nel godere e nel gioire, e nel non curarsi di te, al par mio!" / "Here I will sit, forming men after my own image, a race that resembles me in suffering, weeping, enjoying and rejoicing, in paying no attention to you, just as I do!" (Notebook C, 148 and 150, interlinear variant) concludes the Titan-demiurge, a rebel against God, sealing his own fate with a totally human self-affirmation.

In Gramsci's view, the victory of the Russian revolution established the role of people as becoming "at last . . . the makers of their own destiny" and it is possible to see the figure of Prometheus behind the obscure "watchmaker of the revolutions," the bringer of fire who was summoned to ensure that the mainspring of change be "not a mechanical fact like unease, but . . . the audacity of thought which creates increasingly higher and more luminous social myths."[54] In an article against the harsh tax increases brought in by the Italian government, Gramsci had described Prometheus as a "liberator" and a "revolutionary": "Prometheus is the unknown inventor of the match. Prometheus is the symbol of the human spirit, never content with what has been already obtained, but constantly striving to improve and replace the good with the better, and even the better with the best . . . so that an ever-increasing number of human beings should enjoy well-being, be freer from the chains of natural laws."[55]

As a symbol of the human spirit, the myth of Prometheus stands as a metaphor for history when Gramsci makes use of it in his critique of the positivist version of Marxism that emerges from Bukharin's *Popular Manual*,[56] which Gramsci considered a narrowminded "metaphysics of matter" that had lost contact with thought. Gramsci's long digression about the myth of Prometheus aims at challenging Bukharin's trivialization of bourgeois culture, and is fully consistent with his intention to advance a philosophical refoundation of Marxism.[57] In comparing Goethe's hymn dedicated to Prometheus with the incomplete drama, Gramsci accepts Leonello Vincenti's chronology, according to which the drama was written after the hymn.[58] However, unlike Vincenti (a Germanist who links the titanism of Prometheus to Goethe's religious crisis), Gramsci tries to explain it with Goethe's need to expand to work as an artist, work that for the poet coincides with action. From this perspective, the later nature of the drama is then demonstrated by its greater complexity, by the greater, more constructive awareness that fuels Prometheus's rebellion: in the drama, the protagonist is seen "not merely as a rebel titan, but rather as a 'homo faber,' conscious of himself and of the meaning of his own actions."[59]

Prometheus thus becomes a moral and social myth. An awareness of humanity's historic task is the only antidote against all forms of teleology. This belief, prefigured in the coupling "history and anti-history" (the core subject of Gramsci's philosophical writings and the red thread that runs through the *Notebooks*), is also at the basis of Gramsci's original "adaptation to the present" of the Grimms' tales.

As far as Marx's texts are concerned, rather than making generic remarks regarding their connection with the subjects dealt with in the *Prison Notebooks*, it is thought preferable to concentrate on a number of differences between the original and the translation which, however small, should not be considered unimportant. The first difference can be found in the title of a chapter of *Manifest der Kommunistischen Partei, Bourgeois und Proletarier*, that, significantly, Gramsci translates as *Teoria della Storia* [Theory of History] (Q7, sheet 4). This variation seems programmatic in nature if it is related to Gramsci's project to "rehabilitate" Marx by freeing him from the vulgarizing schemes imposed on him by both revisionist and orthodox Marxists, who had confined Marxist thought to the narrow constrictions of historical reconstruction: Gramsci's intention was rather to restore the philosophical value of historical materialism as an instrument for analyzing political processes as they actually unfold. According to Leonardo Paggi, Gramsci achieves this aim by "re-establishing the concept of the antagonistic social relations of production occurring when one social class replaces another in the direction of society [*Bourgeois und Proletarier*], and by attributing philosophical value to this concept as capable of laying the foundations for a *general theory of history*."[60]

Gramsci subsequently specified that the multiplicity and specificity of historical reality does not affect the legitimacy of this theorization, because "the philosophy of praxis is realized through the concrete study of past history and through present activity to construct new history": however, "*a theory of history and politics can be made,* for even if the facts are always unique and changeable in the flux of movement of history, the concepts can still be theorized."[61] The new title that Gramsci chose for Marx's chapter in 1930 therefore represents a nonnegligible point of reference within the chronology and development of his thought.

The second difference can be found in the following chapter, whose title *Forderungen der Kommunistischen Partei in Deutschland* was translated—and put in historical perspective—by Gramsci as *Esigenze della Politica Tedesca Prima del 1848* [Needs of German Politics before 1848] (Q7, sheet 10^v).[62] These changes announce Gramsci's evolution from apprenticeship to mastery as translator: what was initially an "exercise" became a pedagogical project based on a precise method reflecting Gramsci's political view of translation: Gramsci had actually put his views on translation into practice since 1925 as secretary of the PCI, when he had started developing his programmatic approach to translation.

At that time, in his Italian translation of Bukharin's introduction and first chapter of *Popular Manual* (published in German in 1922) for a school of the Communist Party, Gramsci had modified a passage in which historical materialism was defined—in accordance with the positivistic approach of the book—as the "general doctrine of society and the laws of its development, that is sociology"[63]: Gramsci replaced this definition with a new one underlining the philosophical value of historical materialism as *theory of history*, thus anticipating, in many ways, his own considerations in the *Notebooks*.

GRAMSCI AND THE "KINDER- UND HAUSMÄRCHEN"

In 1927, in a letter to Tania, Gramsci wrote: "I am now reading the fairy tales of the brothers Grimm, which are very elementary,"[64] referring to Reclam's small book entitled *Fünfzig Kinder- und Hausmärchen*, an abridged edition of the Grimms' much larger collection. Gramsci had known of the Grimms' tales for at least ten years, having read the unabridged edition in Italian. Although there is no explicit reference to this, his knowledge of the tales is documented by two articles written in 1917, where Gramsci summarizes "the tale of that boy who went off around the world to learn the exact meaning of the banal expression to 'have goose flesh'" and gives a partial summary of *Clever Hans* (*Der Gescheite Hans*).[65] This tale is not included in the Italian abridged editions that were on sale at the time and that Gramsci might have known; the probable source, instead, is Salani's unabridged 1908 collection.[66]

In two polemical articles (the first one was against Teofilo Rossi, the mayor of Turin; the second one argued against the theatre of horror, the "Italian Guignol," that was headed for a quick demise, according to Gramsci), the tales of the Brothers Grimm are used as an ethical gauge against which reality can be assessed, a demonstration of Gramsci's pedagogical intent as inseparable from his political commitment, as would be shown in paradigmatic form in his translations in 1931.

This side of his work, carried out even unbeknownst to his family, comes out only in a letter to his sister: "I have translated from German, as an exercise, a series of popular tales, exactly like the ones we liked so much when we were children," he wrote to Teresina on January 18, 1932, "and that actually resemble them to some extent, because their origin is the same. . . . I'll make sure to copy them in a notebook and send them to you as soon as I get permission, as *my contribution to developing the imagination of the little ones.*"[67] Since he never transcribed the tales, this project was long believed—different from what Gramsci himself states in the letter—to have remained in the realm of good intentions. However, we now know that the project had already been set down in its essential lines, and required only some stylistic revision.

Gramsci's caution led him to write this letter in a vaguely allusive tone: optimistic self-censorship led him to sacrifice any details or clarifications regarding his ambitious and enigmatic promise of a personal "contribution to developing the imagination of the little ones." If this cryptic prison message of his was not enough for overcoming the censors' mistrust, and if he never managed to send his family the fairy tales that he had promised, nevertheless, when these folktales are carefully analyzed and given their legitimate place in the context of the whole of Gramsci's work, these neglected *Notebooks* will stand as his unalienable and highly eloquent contribution and, to the maligned translator, author's rights will finally be accorded. Since the purpose of Gramsci's translation of the tales emerges clearly from the manuscripts, the above is implicit in the almost imperceptible, yet significant, departures from the original texts, clearly destined to change the nature of his translation "exercises" into a concrete pedagogical proposal.

The reasons for choosing some tales rather than others, and changing their original order, still remain in the realm of hypothesis. It is impossible to ascertain to what extent Gramsci had chosen to concentrate on well-known characters (the first part contains in the main the best-known tales), to follow his own personal taste (stories of talking animals and metamorphoses are frequent in the second part) or to what extent his choice was determined by unconscious processes or simply by linguistic elements (some of the tales he did not include were in dialect, and it cannot be excluded that the ones selected were those that Gramsci remembered best in Italian).[68] It is certainly remarkable that his collection starts with the story of that young but anonymous personage who travels the world to learn about fear—the same story that had attracted his attention in 1917 when he wrote the polemic article mentioned above. This tale is paradigmatic of the individual's self-formation and of how a person grows up by overcoming fear, but the symbolic meaning possibly escaped Gramsci (much as it did even Bettelheim), and he decided to give a name to the protagonist: what the Brothers Grimm call *Märchen von Einem, der Auszog, das Fürchten zu Lernen* [The Story of the Youth Who Went Forth to Learn What Fear Was], becomes *Storia di Uno, Giovannin Senzapaura, Che Partì di Casa per Imparare Cos'è la Pelle D'Oca* [The Story of a Youth, Johnny Lackfear, Who Set Off from Home to Learn the Meaning of Goose Flesh], based on the title of an Italian folktale.

The choice of this and other titles reveals Gramsci's attitude as a writer of children's fiction, as demonstrated by the *Story of the Hedgehogs* that he wrote later on for his sons Delio and Giuliano, together with other short stories and animal and rural fables that are characterized by an almost classical sober style.[69] Consciously ignoring the popularized Italian version of Snow White (*Sneewittchen*, currently translated as *Biancaneve*), Gramsci entitled this tale *Nevina* [The Little Snow Girl] and made Tom Thumb (*Daumesdick* or *Daumerling*: the two names reflect the older tale by Perrault) even smaller, by changing the popular Italian title *Pollicino* [Little Thumb] into *Mignolino* (or its variant *Mignoletto* [Thumbling]), a more comic, almost caricatural name. If these can well be considered to be the kind of small poetic license that most translators sometimes indulge in, the manuscripts actually contain a series of microscopic "betrayals," interpolations and molecular substitutions, the changes remaining, however, functional to the public for whom the translations were destined, and their philological arbitrariness is outweighed by their cultural importance.

In the fifteenth tale translated, *Die Zwölf Brüder* [The Twelve Brothers], the birth of a sister and the intention of the father to kill the twelve brothers is heralded by a *red* flag, a typical signal of danger and death. In his translation, however, Gramsci consistently changes the red color into *black*, the choice being so systematic it cannot be considered an oversight. Writing for his sister's children, Gramsci must have decided to transform the symbol of death in the original tale by making it understandable in his contemporary context: in other words, Gramsci translated this symbol into the "Italian historical language," with a transparent allusion to current political events.

The twentieth tale that appears in first draft is *Rumpelstilzchen* (Rumpelstiltskin), which Gramsci had significantly chosen to open the collection that he had promised to his sister. The text undergoes two major changes, converging to give it a local flavor, so that almost by accident, as it were, the Germanic world of the *Märchen* becomes more familiar to their young Sardinian readers. We here give the original, followed by Gramsci's version:

"Heisst du vielleicht *Rippenbiest* oder *Hammelswade* oder *Schnürbein?*" Aber es antwortete immer: "So heiss ich nicht." Den dritten Tag kam der Bote wieder zurück und erzählte: "Neue Namen hab ich keinen einzigen finden können; aber wie ich an einen hohen Berg *um die Waldecke kam*, wo Fuchs und Has' sich gute Nacht sagen."[70] ["Perhaps your name is Shortribs, or Sheepshanks, or Laceleg," but he always answered, "That is not my name." On the third day the messenger came back again, and said, "I have not been able to find a single new name, but as I came to a high mountain at the end of the forest, where the fox and the hare bid each other good night"].[71]

Ti chiami forse *Catarrino, Saltamontone, Trombatore* ma egli rispondeva sempre: "Non mi chiamo così." Il terzo giorno ritornò il messaggero che raccontò: "Non ho potuto trovare neanche un nome nuovo, ma mentre attraversavo un'alta montagna *nel paese di Pastinarca*, dove la volpe augura la buona notte *alle galline*" (Notebook B, sheet 14ʳ).

The unusual names suggested by the messenger (*Catarrino, Saltamontone* and *Trombatore* [Little Monkey, Ram's Leap, Trumpeter]) are reminiscent of the Sardinian language, and this is even more true of *paese di Pastinarca*, an archaic name for an imaginary rural community, probably derived from the fusion of the noun *arca* (ark) and the verb *pastinare*[72]: Gramsci thus changes the setting of the tale by replacing the foggy atmosphere of Northern forests with a more familiar imagery of the Sardinian countryside, like his native Ghilarza, culminating in the substitution of a wild hare with more homely animals such as hens. The association between a fox (*volpe*) and a brood of hens is of course more natural in popular Mediterranean imagery, and well attested in the popular literature of the nineteenth century.

Gramsci thus aims at transforming the *Märchen* into "popular folktales" by adopting the "historically determined language of the civilization to which he [the translator] supplies the informative material": however, he went beyond his original intention of adapting the tales to a Sardinian environment, easily recognizable from the very first story translated. It was only somewhat later on, when he was well into the translation work, that he developed and executed a more ambitious plan: the translation of common sense, imbued with fatalism and "superstition," into a secular and nonreligious, *rational* common sense.

In fact, his more ostensibly obvious, radical intervention on the original text of the *Märchen* concentrates precisely on their religious element, which is increasingly secularized by Gramsci, first one would say in an experimental way but then, starting from the fifteenth tale onward, in a scrupulously systematic way. All the spiritual elements—not only explicit references to God, but all direct or indirect references to the idea of transcendency, any residue whatsoever of divine providence—are expunged from the tales or replaced with references to nature, all explicable in terms of rationality.

As early as the sixth tale, the God of the Christians is replaced with a mythological figure: the cry *Ach Gott!*[73] becomes *Per bacco* [By Jove], without any metaphysical references (Notebook A, sheet 69ᵛ); elsewhere, the reference to an unfathomable providence (*befahl sich Gott* ["said a prayer"],[74] is simply omitted (sheet 77ʳ), whereas another *Ach Gott* is rendered with an almost blasphemous *Per dio* [My God!] (sheet 86ʳ). However, in the first tales this attempt at secularization seems to be just an experiment, since most religious expressions actually remain unchanged.

Starting from *Little Brother and Little Sister*, the fifteenth tale in Gramsci's manuscript, all metaphysical references disappear and allusions to the idea of providence are deliberately expunged from the text regardless of their being actual references to religion or stereotypical set phrases which have entered into use to indicate fear, happiness or surprise, but which, although they have lost their old meaning, still retain an echo of their original religious sense. Below is a list of the religious expressions that appear in the *Märchen* with the secularized variants introduced by Gramsci (table 8.1).[75]

Nothing seems to escape the translator's attention in this secularizing process, not even the most "innocent" line, in *Hänsel und Gretel*, where Gramsci deliberately ignores the supernatural connotation of the word *himmlisch* [heavenly], and translates it as a perfectly rational and realistic weather word: *Der Wind, der Wind, das himmlische Kind* ["The wind, the wind, the heaven-born wind"][76] often translated by professional [Italian] translators with phrases that render—or even reinforce—its religious meaning (so that the wind is variously defined as "il celeste bambino"/ "the heavenly child," "il divino bambino"/ "the divine child," or even "il bambino mandato da Dio"/ "the God-sent child" or "il bambinello Gesù"/ "Baby Jesus"),[77] is simply

Table 8.1.

German Reclam Edition	Gramsci: Notebook A
"Dass Gott erbarm, wenn das unsere Mutter wüsste! Komm, wir wollen miteinander in die weite Welt gehen" (*Brüderchen und Schwesterchen*, page 28).	"Se nostra madre lo sapesse! Vieni, andremo insieme per il vasto mondo," *Fratellino e Sorellina*, sheet 95ᵛ ("If our mother only knew. Come, we will go forth together into the wide world." *Brother and Sister*. Gramsci omits the initial "God pity us").
Abends, wenn Schwesterchen müde war *und sein Gebet gesagt hatte*, legte es seinen Kopf auf den Rücken des Rehkälbchens (page 60).	Alla sera, quando sorellina era stanca (*omission*), metteva la sua testina sulla spalla del capriolino, sheet 96ᵛ ("In the evening, when the sister was tired, she laid her head upon the roe's back": Gramsci omits "and had said her prayers").
Sprach der König: "Ach *Gott*, was ist das?" (page 65).	Disse il re: "*Ahimè*, cosa capita?," sheet 98ᵛ (The king said: "Alas, what is happening?": Gramsci substitutes for "Ah God, [Good heaven] what is this?").
und hatte in dem Augenblick *durch Gottes Gnade* das Leben wiedererhalten.	e in quell momento riacquistò la vita ("and at the same moment she received life again": Gramsci omits "and by God's grace").

Notebook B

German Reclam Edition	Gramsci: Notebook B
"*Du lieber Gott*," sagte das Mädchen, "im Winter wachsen ja keine Erdbeeren" (*Die drei Männlein im Walde*, page 67).	"*Per carità*—rispose la fanciulla—le fragole non ci sono d'inverno," *I Tre Omini della Foresta*, sheet 1ᵛ ("*Oh dear*," said the girl, "there are no strawberries to be found in winter." *The Three Little Men in the Wood*: Gramsci changes the words "Dear God").
"Sei getrost, liebes Schwesterchen, und schlaf nur ruhig ein, *Gott wird uns nicht verlassen*" (*Hänsel und Gretel*, page 78).	"Cara sorellina, consolati e dormi tranquilla: tutto andrà bene per noi," *Giannino e Ghitina*, sheet 6ᵛ ("Be easy, dear little sister, and go to sleep quietly; everything will be fine for us." *Hansel and Gretel*: Gramsci substitutes for "God will not forsake us").

"Weine nicht, Gretel, und schlaf nur ruhig, *der liebe Gott wird uns schon helfen*" (page 83).

"*Lieber Gott*, hilf uns doch," rief sie aus, "hätten uns nur die wilden Tiere im Wald gefressen" (page 87).

"*Gott hat verboten*, dass der Vater seine Tochter heirate, *aus der Sünde* kann nichts Gutes entspringen, und das Reich wird mit ins Verderben gezogen" (*Allerleirauh*, page 201).

zog den Mantel von allerlei Rauchwerk an und machte sich Gesicht und Hände mit Russ schwarz. *Dann befahl sie sich Gott* und ging fort und ging die ganze Nacht.

"Non piangere Ghitina, e dormi tranquilla; *ce la caveremo anche questa volta.*" sheet 7v ("Don't cry, Gretel, and go to sleep quietly; *we will make it* this time too." Ibid.: Gramsci substitutes for "the good God will help us").

"*Ahimè*, chi ci aiuterà?" esclamava—"almeno le fiere ci avessero divorati nella foresta," sheet 9r ("*Alas*, who will help us now?" cried she; "if only we had been devoured by wild beasts in the wood": Gramsci substitutes for "dear God, do help us").

"*La natura non permette*, che il padre sposi sua figlia; *da un tale abominio* non potrebbe risultare nessun bene, e tutto il reame ne sarebbe portato alla rovina," *Millepelli*, sheet 16v ("Nature has forbidden a father to marry his daughter, no good can come from such a crime, and the kingdom will be involved in the ruin." *Allerleirauh/All-kinds-of-fur*, or *Catskin*: Gramsci substitutes the alternative "nature" for "God" and "abomination" for "sin" ["Sünde"]).

"indossò il mantello fatto di tanti pezzettini di pelle vellosa, e si tinse di nero la faccia e le mani con la fuliggine. Uscì di casa in tale truccatura [così truccata] (*omissione*) e camminò tutta la notte," sheet 17r ("She put on her mantle of all kinds of fur, and blackened her face and hands with soot. In that disguise [disguised in that way] . . . she set forth and walked the whole night': Gramsci omits "she commended herself to God").

and effectively translated by Gramsci as *il vento, il vento, figlio dell'aria* ["the wind, the wind, child of the air"] (Notebook B, sheet 8ʳ).

Gramsci even eliminates those passages in which the author's comments on the characters and plot seem to endorse a fatalistic attitude, implicitly leading the reader to conclude that human fate is not determined by human actions, but by some metahistorical force (blind or providential) abstracted from any rational determination. This seems the only possible explanation for the remarkable absence, in Gramsci's manuscripts, of the following expressions: "Ja, es gibt viel Trübsal und Not auf der Welt!" ["Truly, there is much worry and affliction in this world"],[78] "In den alten Zeiten, wo das Wünschen noch geholfen hat" ["In olden times when wishing still helped one"],[79] "Ach, du schöne Königstochter, wie soll's mit dir noch werden!" ["Alas, fair princess, what is to become of thee now!"].[80]

There is just one expression that escaped Gramsci's attention: the phrase "Geh nur in Gottes Namen" ["For Heaven's sake, just go in peace"],[81] in the last unfinished tale, is not eliminated but translated literally as "Va pure in nome di dio" / "go now, in God's name" (Notebook B, *Gente Furba* [Wise Folks], sheet 21ᵛ). This may have been just an oversight, but we believe that there is a complex link between the missing secularization process, the sudden interruption of Gramsci's translation work, and the rough of copy of his letter to Julca (which has been considered as the earliest possible date, the *terminus ante quem*, for Gramsci's translations). Since the tale's date was inferred from the draft of the letter (between November 14 and 23, 1931, as we have seen), the cause of its interruption cannot be a ban imposed by the prison authorities subsequent to January 1932. The translation of *Gente Furba* was still under way when Gramsci started writing this letter to Julca. In fact, the two texts come one after the other almost without interruption, except for a sketchy, almost accidental line drawn in pen; furthermore, the tale and the letter are remarkably similar in subject matter, and this may suggest that Gramsci was so upset as a result of the tormented connection he had made between the subject of the story and Julca that he was distracted from the secularization work he had begun and decided to put it off indefinitely.

The tale is the story of two women: one is so foolish that she causes her husband's ruin, whereas the other is a widow who lets herself be convinced that she can be of use to her husband by sending clothes and money to him "in Heaven." The absurdity of this situation is based both on the contrast between the pious illusion of the widow and the inevitability of death, and on the preposterous candor with which she goes to every effort to keep up a relationship that exists solely in her own mind: Gramsci's translation does not however reflect the author's sardonic irony. Just before there was about to enter the scene the third fool in the tale (a man who thinks he can build a bridge to a dimension with no return),[82] Gramsci jotted down the draft of his letter (the first and only rough copy written in prison). Upset by Julca's persistent silence and by their mutual misunderstandings (Julca's last letter, as Gramsci remarks at the start, dated back to "over three months ago"), he pours out all his uncontrollable anguish at the lack of communication with his wife, and complains about the absurdity of "a relationship between phantoms":

> It seems to me that we have increasingly become phantoms for each other, unreal beings, outside time and space, like conventional and faint (crystallized) memories of a short period of time spent together; we no longer understand our mutual needs, we do not even know how to keep up a flow of common feelings between us any longer, we are not a source of strength for each other (Notebook B, sheet 23^{rv}).

This is arguably the most genuine of Gramsci's letters to Julca; unlike the other letters, it was not written on the day and at the time prescribed by the prison's rules, but on the spur of emotion—an unprecedented case—directly in the translation notebook. We may even note that the shift from fiction to reality is not marked by changes in handwriting or style, and in addressing himself to his wife, Gramsci continues the imaginative language of the tale. Evidence of this comes from comparing the draft quoted above with the letter to Julca of November 30, 1931, which uses in part the rough copy. The reason underlying the absurd relationship has clearly been rationalized (in the meantime Gramsci had learned that a letter from Julca had arrived), and is this time dealt with in the more detached language of someone who has regained control of his emotions. The spontaneous outpouring of emotions now turns to an explicit reproach: "I believed that a certain communality in our lives would still be possible, that you would help me not to lose contact completely with the life of the world; at least with your life and that of the children. Yet it seems to me, and I say this even though I must cause you much pain, that you have helped to intensify my isolation, making me feel it more bitterly."[83]

The rough copy might even be seen as an unexpected, paradoxical twist in the conclusion of the Grimms' tale. Gramsci's abandonment of his translation work, and perhaps even the secularization that was missing from *Gente Furba*, would thus seem to connect back with reality breaking into the dimension of fable.

EUTHANASIA OF A TRANSLATOR

At this point we must necessarily illustrate briefly the inexplicable—or perhaps only too explicable—treatment reserved to these translations. Only the data that emerge from the analysis of the texts, from a scrupulous juxtaposition of the manuscripts with the German edition that Gramsci had with him in jail, matched against his letter to Teresina, and then taking into consideration all the other secondary comparisons, justify an interest in its own right in Gramsci's translation of the *Märchen*. However, these data were blatantly overlooked by the editors of the Vallecchi anthology, Elsa Fubini and Mimma Paulesu, referred to above.[84] As Carlo Muscetta declares in his introduction to that anthology, no "linguistic study of Gramsci's results as a novice translator" was performed (it should be noted that Gerratana's dating of these manuscripts generically to 1929 led the editors to believe that the tales had been translated then). For this unconvincing anthology, Gramsci's manuscripts were not compared with the German original but with Clara Bovero's Italian version, and "corrected" on the basis of this latter. The editors, after defining their principles ("since these are however translations, we made changes when we thought it wise for the sake of textual clarity and legibility"[85]), made between twenty and forty "interventions" on each page of the volume. What emerges is a castrated version of Gramsci, who, clearly subject to the inexorable knife of the cosmetic surgeon aimed at eliminating unevenness and at masking flaws, has been rendered all but unrecognizable, albeit not unworthy for the "common reader."

Based on these premises, Muscetta believed that the "common reader" would consider Gramsci's translations to be "far from unworthy," and is repeatedly at pains to point this out to any possible "experts" or "specialists," certain that they would "regret" the fact that the translator had not continued his stylistic revision (that of Notebook D), a revision pursued with militant zeal by the editors who deemed themselves worthy of taking Gramsci's place.

It is therefore unsurprising that Muscetta, who was unaware of the changes that Gramsci had made to the Grimms' tales (the only objective data that cannot be ignored on pain of failure of any initiative whatsoever), tried to look for psychoanalytic explanations. In order "to evaluate the reasons for his [Gramsci's] choices," Muscetta turned his analysis to the "subjective condition" of the translator, trying all means to unravel the subconscious reasons for his choice of certain tales rather than others, based on their hidden symbolic meaning.

The result is a psycho-critical interpretation, as hurried as it is implausible, explicitly influenced by Bettelheim (a fashionable author, and an obligatory point of reference for the study of folktales), where the subjects of the traditional *Märchen* are related to the concerns, both documented and undocumented, of Gramsci as a man and as a prisoner. This operation is not devoid of those hagiographic overtones that still persist and which, despite all the criticism that they have received, are still in general currency. As already emphasized, this is a foolproof method to decree the death of an author.

It is really not necessary to resort to Gramsci, for the "-nth" patched-up version of the *Märchen*, a work that has already been subjected to countless attempts at popularization for the delight of children or for the edification of the "common reader." The result is an abominable hybrid which makes it impossible to appreciate Gramsci's intentions even from the formal point of view—an element which seems to rank very high in the editors' priorities. Instead, this would actually represent the most negligible aspect of Gramsci's translation whose importance, as we have seen, lies elsewhere. And the questions that they raise are totally different.

AN ALTERNATIVE PROJECT

Why did Gramsci decide to secularize the Grimms' tales? What was the purpose of this "betrayal"? Seemingly his intention was that of not, through the agency of the tales, instilling an ideologizing element into his nephews, an operation which is particularly effective in early childhood, as he had already realized at the time of his journalistic activity. However, the question poses itself of how such a simplistic and apparently ingenuous removal of the "obstacle" on the part of the mature Gramsci can be reconciled with his belief—expressed often in his writings—that ideology transmitted by religion should be demystified not by ignoring it, but by historicizing it.

Gramsci had already tackled this subject in the articles of his early period. In 1916 he had written that "metaphysical needs produced by tradition, the instinctive legacy of thousands of years of terror and ignorance of the reality surrounding one" can only be overcome by explaining them and only by understanding them as an "object of history" can one recognize their "vacuity."[86] This concept resurfaces in 1933, in a discussion with Julca concerning the education of their elder son, especially in reference to his reading matter. After asking his wife "why Delio got the idea" of reading Harriet Beecher Stowe's novel *Uncle Tom's Cabin*, Gramsci was concerned to know whether someone would be able "to *historicize* it for him, by setting the religiosity and emotions with which this book is permeated in their proper space and time," in the knowledge that this is a "very difficult task to do for a boy (to do seriously, of course, and not with the usual generalizations and commonplaces)."[87]

However, in 1933 Delio was already nine years old, whereas the intended readers of the tales that Gramsci had translated in 1931–1932 (the eldest being about seven) were still at the stage where children "besides images and representations they begin to form logical connections."[88] His nephews' young age may have led Gramsci to prefer a process of secularization to a rational explanation, which must of its nature require the use of previously acquired historical categories. Furthermore, according to Gramsci, "fables and tales such as those of the Grimm brothers" fall within the vast and stratified domain of folklore.[89] Therefore, the religiosity of these texts, here understood as that "disaggregated common sense" which is always the product of a series of inorganic historical sedimentations, did not seem to him inseparable, as in Beecher Stowe's novel, and thus immovable from the context of folktales, without detriment to the "popular" content that he deemed to be particularly appropriate for the emotions and mentality of children.

Given the age of his nephews, the secularization of the tales was not only "consistent with the aim," but also perfectly coherent with Gramsci's pedagogy, if one takes account of his dislike of educational orientations that lead children to "fantasize about pseudoscientific hypotheses," and his firm belief that students should be "led back onto a path that permits the development of a solid and realistic culture, purified of all traces of rancid and stupid ideologies."[90] When writing to his family, Gramsci never got tired of quoting Engels's idea that "man is entirely an historical formation, obtained by coercion,"[91] and declared—implicitly and explicitly—that human nature does not exist as an abstract and immutable entity, and even intellectual tools are not innate, but acquired historically: therefore, it is necessary to counter environmental influences with an educational program that reconciles "spontaneity" with "discipline." Gramsci believed that children, especially in infancy and elementary education levels, should be taught "dogmatically (relatively speaking, of course) the basic elements of the new conception of the world, in opposition to the conception of the world conveyed by the traditional environment (folklore in its full scope)."[92]

The declared need to cultivate a certain "dogmatism" in the early stages of education without stifling the child's "spontaneity" is coherent with Gramsci's polemic against idealism: his criticism was particularly addressed at the abstract libertarianism of Gentile, who assigned the formation of individuals to an "natural" unraveling of innate inclinations, but in fact finished up by subjecting them to an environmental determination that was more dogmatic and authoritarian than any "conscious leadership." Gramsci wrote about Gentile's theory of education:

> The new pedagogy has concentrated its fire on "dogmatism" in the field of instruction and the learning of concrete facts—i.e., precisely in the field in which a certain dogmatism is practically indispensable and can be reabsorbed and dissolved only in the whole cycle of the educational process. . . . On the other hand it has been forced to accept the introduction of dogmatism *par excellence* in the field of religious thought, with the result that the whole history of philosophy is now implicitly seen as succession of ravings and delusions.[93]

In other words, Gramsci criticized the fundamental mystification approved by Gentile, who, from a nonreligious perspective, considered religion to

correspond with the Hegelian spiritual infancy of mankind, and had introduced it as a compulsory subject in elementary schools in 1923, extending
this correspondence to any nonmetaphorical infancy. Gramsci believed
that this attitude meant abandoning the notion of educating. The weakness
of idealism was thus reconfirmed in the "school question," in which no
attempt was made "to construct a conception which could take *the place of
religion* in the education of children."[94]

For the tales to represent a real "contribution to developing the imagination of the little ones," thus constituting an alternative pedagogical program, it was not, therefore, enough to eliminate religion, the providential
vision of life: it was also necessary to *replace* it with the first elements of the
new conception of the world in order to promote logical abilities and at
the same time lay the foundations for a future historicization of religion. In
this case, Gramsci played the role of *excubitor*, of supervisor, through a third
party: he was forced to express his thought ambiguously, the only way open
to him, and managed to perfect his contribution with happy intuition, by
relying on Teresina's comprehension.

If one reads the rest of his letter to Julca concerning their son's readings,
one realizes that Gramsci is criticizing his wife's pedagogic shortcomings as
too close to the Geneva school. In contrast with this, he describes the figure
of the exemplary teacher, the mystagogue or initiator—as exemplified in
the past in figures like De Sanctis, Renato Serra and Arturo Farinelli—not
into esoteric mysteries, but an initiator who furnishes the instruments for
exorcizing them.[95] According to Gramsci, Julca's inability to "successfully
historicize" the novel for Delio came from her emotional, noncritical attitude, which relegated her to a "subaltern rather than a leading position.
That is, you assume the position of someone incapable of historically criticizing ideologies by dominating them, explaining and justifying them as a
historical necessity of the past; of someone who, brought into contact with
a specific world of emotions, feels attracted or repulsed by it, remaining
always within the sphere of emotion and immediate passion."[96]

These explicit pedagogical guidelines also cast light on Gramsci's "coded"
instructions transmitted by letter to his sister (January 18, 1932), which
are often quoted but remain incomprehensible outside the context of his
translations. A more in-depth reading reveals new aspects that would be
impossible to grasp on a superficial reading:

*Perhaps the person who reads them will have to add a pinch of irony and indulgence
in presenting them to the listeners, as a concession to modernity.* But how does this
modernity present itself? The hair will be bobbed, I imagine, and the songs
will be about "Valencia" and the mantillas of the women of Madrid, but I am
sure there will survive old-fashioned types like Aunt Alene and Corroncu and
my little tales will still find a suitable environment. Anyhow I don't know if you
remember: I always used to say, when I was a child, that I would have liked to

see *Aunt Alene on a bicycle*, which proves that *we had fun comparing the troglodytes with the relative modernity of that time; even though it was beyond our immediate environment, this never ceased appealing to us and arousing pleasant sensations in us.*[97]

Through the use of irony, Gramsci introduces a significant new element into the traditional relationship between narrator and public: on the one hand, he reaffirms a constant element of popular short stories—that is, their being transmitted orally—while on the other hand he almost anticipates Brecht's *V-Effekte* [*Verfremdung-Effekte*]—the estrangement, or alienation, effects introduced by Brecht in epic theater—by using irony to break the illusion and act as an antidote to empathy. With an ironic attitude, attraction or repulsion no longer remain within "the sphere of emotions and immediate passion" and the public is therefore prevented from developing an unconditional attachment to the character's story, and this distancing "spirit of cleavage" is seen as a necessary condition for a critical, potentially revolutionary, conscience to develop.

The narrator's "estrangement" approach enables Gramsci to free the text from the fixity stemming from magic and timelessness, and at the same time frees the public from an attitude of uncritical, passive reception, typically facilitated by the magical atmosphere of fairy tales with their intention of orienting readers by disorienting them. The originality of Gramsci's intuition consists of relying not so much on the content of the tales to perform an educational task (and it is well known that Gramsci distrusted openly educational literature), but on a formal element which gives them a particularly open character. This becomes particularly evident if we consider that Gramsci's estranging procedure is conceived of as the basis for "an historical, dialectical conception of the world, which understands movement and change . . . and which conceives the contemporary world as a synthesis of the past, of all past generations, which projects itself into the future."[98] Due to its intrinsically anti-teleological nature, irony is the magical key to the doors of history.

The screen provided by irony allows the establishment of a double perspective that, enlarging the structure of the work, also widens its legibility by appealing to the listeners to participate actively: this perspective entails, on the one hand, the dimension of univocality of the work and of its characters, and on the other hand, the dynamic polyvocality of the relationship between the work and current reality. By juxtaposing literature and reality, past and present, by comparing two worlds that are similar and different at the same time—the archaic and immobile world of the tales (the "troglodytes") and the dynamic, complex and inevitably contradictory reality of the province of Sardinia (a mixture of "troglodytes" and "modernity" or, to maintain Gramsci's metaphor, "Aunt Alene on her bicycle")—his nephews would be able to acquire, together with the first logical instruments of thought, an embryonic historicist approach.

Gramsci's pedagogical advice to his sister can actually be interpreted as an attempt to use the tales to reproduce on a different level—in an elementary way—the conditions and modes of learning the historical method that he had acquired through the study of dead languages. Indeed, for Gramsci, Greek and Latin were, paradoxically, appropriate instruments for developing a historical consciousness precisely by virtue of their double, ambiguous nature as "the dead who are still alive,"[99] representing at the same time "a fossil museum" and an organism that continually comes to life again: it is this characteristic that allows Latin and Greek to promote "a historicizing understanding of the world and of life, which becomes a second—nearly spontaneous—nature, since it is not inculcated pedantically with an openly educational 'intention,'"[100] without leading to simplifications and generalizations.

The Grimms' tales could be read from an "estranging" perspective by using the historical method, no longer the exclusive prerogative of the study of Latin, which is but one of its many possible fields of application. Indeed, Gramsci envisaged that the historical method could be used for "the study of any science, since it enlarges the mind and shapes concrete mentalities."[101] An "estranging" reading of the tales makes it possible to transfer the historical method from the micro-social to the macro-social dimension, and from the linguistic field to that of the study of folk traditions: in 1932, when Gramsci wrote that "it will be necessary to replace Latin and Greek as the fulcrum of the formative school,"[102] he was probably also referring to his own pedagogical project, where he had already tested this process of substitution.

At the time he was editor of the *Grido del Popolo*, Gramsci had used the principle of *panta rhei* ["everything is in flux"] to argue against the Esperantists, asserting the living flow of language, and it was this fundamental teaching he intended to transmit to his nephews. The Heraclitean principle—the key to understanding Gramsci's pedagogical conception and his entire thought—can also be found elsewhere in the *Notebooks*, where he focuses on the double nature of language (both a "living thing" and "a museum of fossils of life and civilization")[103] whose ambivalence is expressed and guaranteed by this perennially metaphorical weave. It is almost as if, as a linguist, Gramsci had decided to translate the relation, implicit in the metaphor, and indicative of historical and social change, but at the same time of continuity between past and present, through a literary screen that reflected its expandable and multifaceted nature, allusive as it is to historical development.

Irony lends further meaning to the mechanical process of secularization of the tales, integrating it, insofar as it overturns their original providentialism, and introduces once again a historicizing perspective which seemed to have been lost in the elimination of the religious element. Gramsci thus replaces "metaphysical needs" with the "absolute secularization and earthliness of thought," as postulated by the philosophy of praxis, laying the basis for the formation of a historical consciousness able to "trace the thread

of the new conception of the world."[104] To ancestral confessional religion
he opposes the only "faith" he had believed in since his youth which, in
Crocean terms, he defined as a "secular religion"—namely, history.

Used as a didactic instrument (partly Socratic and partly Brechtian *avant
la lettre* but, as we have seen, most of all Gramscian) irony thus becomes a
dialectical element of knowledge and liberation, thus "developing the imagination of the little ones" that, for Gramsci, represented a point of arrival,
since it coincided with a "spontaneous" creativity that was the paradoxical
result of the use of a rigorous "discipline" intended as a "conscious direction" in education.

It should be noted that, despite their familiar and occasional character,
Gramsci's translations are consistent with the theoretical framework found
in the *Notebooks*, thus confirming the substantial overall coherence and
unity of inspiration of Gramsci's entire prison writings.[105] In these translations there converge, translated into practice in an almost paradigmatic
way, the various remarks and reflections on linguistics, on folk traditions,
on pedagogy and on political culture that Gramsci was engaged in making
during those years and on which he was subsequently to go into greater
depth, all directed toward his inquiry into the political value of culture, the
function of schools, and the role of the intellectuals in society.

Gramsci's pedagogical project itself is an attempt to accomplish the
two-fold task that is implicit in Marx's proposal—taken from the theses
on Feuerbach that Gramsci had translated in prison and that he so often
quoted in his letters to his family—on the need to "educate the educator." Gramsci, as an advocate of active pedagogy, believed that the task of
education cannot be separated from the historically determined environment which it addresses, and to which it must conform (hence the need
to translate the *Märchen* as folktales—that is, to adapt them to the cultural
tradition and mentality of their public, by rewriting them in Italian "historical language"). In fact, the main aim of education must tend toward
transforming, molecularly but progressively, the environment and the
dominant conception of the world (hence the substitution of a providen-
tialist vision of the world with historicism, and of common sense, imbued
with "superstition," with the philosophy of praxis). Yet again, in Gramsci,
pedagogy and politics coincide: his alternative project, too, enters into a
wider political design.

NOTES

1. Antonio Gramsci, *Letters from Prison*, two volumes, ed. Frank Rosengarten,
trans. Raymond Rosenthal (New York: Columbia University Press, 1994), vol. 2, 207,
hereafter cited as LP1 and LP2. There is a list of abbreviations on pages ix–x.

2. Antonio Gramsci, *Quaderni del Carcere*, four volumes, ed. Valentino Gerratana (Turin: Einaudi, 1975), 1473, hereafter QC. Q11§49. [To facilitate locating passages in various translations and anthologies, we use the standard method of providing the notebook (*Quaderno*) number—in this case 11—followed by the section number, §. See the introduction, page 12, for discussion. We will indicate the English translation, if used.] Antonio Gramsci, *Further Selections from the Prison Notebooks*, ed. and trans. Derek Boothman (Minneapolis: University of Minnesota Press, 1995), 312, hereafter cited as FSPN. The critical edition of the *Prison Notebooks* does not include a complete index of Gramsci's own notes, which can be found in "Quaderni dell'Istituto Gramsci/Sezione Toscana," no. 1, Bibliographical exhibition, Biblioteca Nazionale Centrale (December 8, 1977–January 28, 1978).

3. Q4§3, Antonio Gramsci, *Prison Notebooks*, vol. 2, ed. and trans. Joseph Buttigieg (New York: Columbia University Press, 1996), 142, hereafter cited as PN2.

4. 11§48, FSPN, 309; the same concept is in Q4§42.

5. *Duemila pagine di Gramsci*, ed. G. Ferrata and N. Gallo, two volumes (Milan: Il Saggiatore, 1964), vol. I, 720. The first acknowledgment of the importance of translation in Gramsci's work is Leonardo Paggi, *Gramsci e il Moderno Principe* (Roma: Editori Riuniti, 1970).

6. [They are now included as the first volume of the *National Edition* of Gramsci's Collected Works, presented publicly on April 30, 2007, by the Italian president, Giorgio Napolitano.]

7. Antonio Gramsci, *Favole di Libertà*, ed. Elsa Fubini and Mimma Paulesu (Florence: Vallecchi, 1980).

8. For Gramsci's early writings, see Antonio Gramsci, *Scritti 1915–1921*, ed. Sergio Caprioglio (Milan: Il Corpo, 1968), and *Per la Verità*, ed. R. Martinelli (Rome: Editori Riuniti, 1974).

9. Benedetto Croce, *Quaderni della Critica* 10 (1948), 78–79.

10. See also Eugenio Garin, *Gramsci nella Cultura Contemporanea*, in *Studi Gramsciani*, second edition (Rome: Editori Riuniti, 1969), 400.

11. The first volume, entitled *Cronache Torinesi 1913–1916*, edited by Sergio Caprioglio, appeared in 1980. [This work was then carried to completion, and careful philological work is now being done, at the time of publication of this translation, to establish definitive texts for the National Edition of Gramsci's writings.]

12. Valentino Gerratana, "Introduction" to QC, xxxvii.

13. Gerratana, xxxviii.

14. This is evident from several inaccuracies (for example, repetitions of the same word) that Gramsci could have corrected if he had reread the text.

15. In 1912–1913, Gramsci had attended the lectures of Farinelli, for whom the first chair in German literature had been created in 1907. In some of his earliest articles, Gramsci had praised Farinelli as "a true master of life and of humanism" (*Scipio Slataper*, in *Avanti!* XX, 101 (April 10, 1916), now in *Cronache torinesi*, op. cit., 251): following Hegel, Farinelli conceived history as history of the spirit, and was among the first in Italy to understand the importance of thought in early German Romanticism. While in prison, however, Gramsci's praise turned to blame when he discovered that his professor had gone over to fascism.

16. Bartoli and Gramsci developed a close cooperation: in the young Gramsci, a brilliant student of linguistics who carried out research for Bartoli on Sardinian

terms, and had decided to write his final dissertation on comparative linguistics, Bartoli saw his successor. One of Gramsci's regrets was that of having interrupted his linguistic studies.

17. LP2, 244–45.

18. Gerratana, xxxvi.

19. [This type of analysis was in fact carried out in Gianni Francioni, *L'Officina Gramsciana* (Naples: Bibliopolis, 1984). It is an essential reference work for all serious Gramsci scholars, with the proviso that some members of the collective that worked under Gerratana think that it added only rather marginally to what they had deduced (translator's note based on information from Gerratana's collaborators).]

20. Gerratana's contention that all the articles belong to the same issue of the journal (that of October 14) is therefore inaccurate, QC, 2430.

21. The tales are translated from the Brothers Grimm, *Fünfzig Kinder- und Hausmärchen* (Leipzig: Verlag von Ph. Reclam Jun., n.d.) (the authors are Jacob and Wilhelm Grimm, not Karl and Jacob, as inaccurately reported in Q, 2431, by Gerratana, who unwittingly perpetuated a mistake that is frequent in Gramscian literature. This confusion was initiated by a careless commentator who, not knowing the first names of the authors of the *Tales*, reported them incorrectly. The Reclam volume reproduces the 1912 fiftieth edition of the Kleine Ausgabe first published in 1825 as an abridged edition of the Grimms' much larger 1812–1815 collection, last revised by Wilhelm Grimm in 1858 (tenth edition). Gramsci probably owned this book before being arrested in 1926, because, unlike other texts, there is no trace of his asking either Tania or his brother Carlo to send it to him. It is impossible to ascertain whether Gramsci had received the book from Sperling & Kupfer, the Milan bookshop where Gramsci's friend Piero Sraffa had opened an account for him, since, unfortunately, the bookshop and all its documents were destroyed during the war.

22. In the rough copy, which was partly used for his letter of November 30, 1931, Gramsci writes that his last communication with Julca had taken place "on August, 13, over three months ago." However, as his letter to Tania of November 23, 1931, clearly demonstrates, Gramsci knew that a letter from his wife had arrived at the prison of Turi in the intervening time, although it had not been forwarded to him yet. The rough copy cannot therefore have been written after November 23.

23. In our opinion, this is a leftover (persistent, though in any case to disappear) from an entire series of consonants with strokes through (p, r, q, etc.), especially when written as capitals or used at the beginning of sentences.

24. If Gramsci had written the rough copy of this letter before the translation of the tales—or in any case before its sudden interruption—there would be no point in leaving five blank lines. Furthermore, the handwriting and several elements within the text, and in Gramsci's family life, suggest that the letter was written after the tales, as we shall see.

25. A few pages with a list of words and the beginning of a translation of Milton.

26. From an anthology of Goethe's writings: *Über allen Gipfeln: Goethes Gedichte im Rahmen seines Lebens*, ed. E. Hartung (Munich: Wilhelm Langewiesche-Brandt, 1922).

27. J. P. Eckermann, *Goethes Gespräche mit Eckermann*, ed. F. Deibel (Leipzig: Insel-Verlag, 1921).

28. Karl Marx, *Lohnarbeit und Kapital: Zur Judenfrage und andere Schriften aus der Frühzeit*, second edition (Leipzig: Verlag von Ph. Reclam Jun, n.d). In this collection, the passage entitled *Über Goethe* was said to be Marx's, but it was in fact written by Engels.

29. We are not considering Gramsci's translations from Russian, based on Rachele Gutman-Polledro and Alfredo Polledro's *Antologia Russa* (QC, 2397-99), which are in Notebook 9, due to our limited knowledge of this domain. As concerns their chronology, the letter to Julca of October 1, 1933, seems to suggest that Gramsci had completed these translations by 1930: "For various reasons it's been almost three years since I've read a line in Russian, and I have forgotten much of what I used to know (which in fact was not much)." LP2, 320.

30. The pages are numbered only on the recto side, as in Notebooks A and 7: therefore, for the sake of clarity, we specify whether each sheet should be intended as recto (r) or verso (v), an indication which was also used, albeit inaccurately, by Gerratana (see QC, 2389, 2430, 2435, 2439, 2442).

31. LP1, 292-93. [The word "only," necessary for the sense, and included in the Italian original, has here been added to the translation published in *Letters from Prison*.]

32. The passage of *Über Feuerbach* (*Theses on Feuerbach*) on the need to "educate the educator" is quoted again by Gramsci on May 14, 1931, in a letter to his sister Teresina, LP2, 364.

33. LP2, 130. [Rosenthal's *Letters from Prison* translation errs here in reading "*as soon as* I get permission," which does not correspond to the Italian of the letter as reported here: "*if* I get permission."]

34. LP1, 112, and LP2, 129.

35. LP2, 130, emphasis added.

36. [That is, the first drafts of these notes, whose final version (FSPN, 307-12) dates to summer 1932.]

37. Franco Lo Piparo, *Lingua, Intellettuali e Egemonia in Gramsci* (Bari: Laterza, 1979), 11.

38. Tullio De Mauro, "Preface," in Lo Piparo, ix.

39. Q11§12, Antonio Gramsci, *Selections from the Prison Notebooks*, ed. and trans. Quintin Hoare and Geoffrey Nowell Smith (New York: International Publishers, 1971), 325, hereafter cited as SPN.

40. Q6§71, Antonio Gramsci, *Selections from Cultural Writings*, ed. David Forgacs, trans. William Boelhower (Cambridge, Mass.: Harvard University Press, 1985), 177, hereafter cited as SCW. Emphasis added.

41. LP1, 112.

42. LP1, 83.

43. Q3§74, SCW, 174, emphasis added.

44. Q3§74, SCW, 174.

45. Steinthal, a Hegelian and Humboldtian, also contributed to Labriola's background in theoretical linguistics.

46. Henceforth the interlinear variants in the quotations from Gramsci's manuscripts will be indicated within square brackets.

47. [Here, of course, retranslated into English.]

48. Q5§23, PN2, 285. In discussing the problem of Chinese morphology, Gramsci writes that "it is necessary to check Finck's booklet on the major types of languages" (Q5§23, PN2, 288). However, this was not the book that Gramsci himself translated in prison, as Gerratana specifies (see QC, 2672), but *Die Haupttypen des Sprachbaus*, which he had probably sent back to his wife after receiving it by mistake (see LP1, 145-46).

49. In prison, Gramsci had a copy of Benedetto Croce, *Goethe*, second edition (Bari: Laterza, 1921), but he never quoted this book as a source for his own translations; however, a number of interlinear corrections reveal that he did refer to this work, sometimes by rewriting his entire translations based on Croce's. Gramsci often described Croce as a master of style, and this holds true for his translations too.

50. Gramsci intended to lay the foundations for an ideological renewal within the Socialist Party by putting to good use "the progressive legacy of the Western bourgeois civilization," in other words by "appreciating the efforts made by humanity to free itself from idolatries and ancestral or mythological taboos" (Giancarlo Bergami, *Il Giovane Gramsci e il Marxismo 1911-1918* [The Young Gramsci and Marxism 1911-1918] [Milan: Feltrinelli, 1977], 55). In this period of intense educational initiative, Goethe was a continual point of reference for Gramsci: his works were read and discussed at the "Club di vita morale" ("Club of Moral Life," the discussion circle that Gramsci had founded in Turin at the end of 1917 with Andrea Viglongo, Carlo Boccardo and Attilio Carena) as the club's library demonstrates, but they were also dealt with in *Il Grido del Popolo* (*The Cry of the People*, a small provincial newspaper that Gramsci transformed into a cultural and philosophical weekly journal). In his articles for *Il Grido del Popolo*, Gramsci mainly concentrated on Goethe's most "modern" aspects, which he analyzed in more depth in the *Notebooks*.

51. LP2, 38.

52. Q9§121.

53. There springs spontaneously to mind the reference to Lukács's thought and the importance for him of Goethe, considered as the greatest representative of those humanistic ideals born of the struggle for the development of personality through social action.

54. "L'orologiaio," *Il Grido del Popolo* (August 18, 1917), xxii, n.682, now in *Scritti Giovanili 1914-1918* (Turin: Einaudi 1958), 126.

55. "Prometeo monopolizzato," *Avanti!* XXI no. 19 (January 19, 1917), now in *Cronache Torinesi*, 711-12. Emphasis added.

56. [Gerratana (QC, 2539) states that in all probability the edition that Gramsci was able to receive in prison was the 1927 French translation *La Théorie du Matérialisme Historique* of the 1921 Russian original. Gramsci had to refer to it for censorship reasons with a gloss, translated in *Selections from the Prison Notebooks* as the "Popular Manual"; in English the book is *The Theory of Historical Materialism* (Ann Arbor: University of Michigan Press, 1969).]

57. In the sense intended by Leonardo Paggi, *La Teoria Generale del Marxismo in Gramsci*, in *Storia del Marxismo Contemporaneo*, ed. Aldo Zanardo (Milan: Feltrinelli, 1973).

58. Vincenti relied on an essay written by Julius Richter. More recent studies suggest that the hymn is in fact a shorter version written after the drama.

59. Q8§214, for a partial translation, see SPN, 471–72.

60. Paggi, *La Teoria Generale*, 1332. Emphasis added.

61. Q12§26, SPN, 427. Emphasis added. See also Q4§13, PN2, 155.

62. Amongst the data that arise from careful textual analysis, one element should be pointed out that goes beyond philology, one whose significance may be assessed adequately only in the light of the question raised in 1967 at the Congress of Gramscian Studies in Cagliari. In reply to a question by Norberto Bobbio, Gerratana highlighted the difference between Marx's and Gramsci's concepts of "civil society": according to Gerratana, Bobbio's contention that Gramsci had derived his own concept of "civil society" directly from Marx is not in contradiction with the fact that, in the *Notebooks*, Gramsci had translated "a series of extracts from *On the Jewish Question* . . . one of the main essays in which Marx marked the distinction between 'civil society' and the 'political state.'" Gerratana supported this statement by adding that "the German phrase *bürgerliche Gesellschaft* is translated by Gramsci as 'società borghese,' or 'bourgeois society,' rather than 'civil society'" (*Gramsci e la Cultura Contemporanea*, ed. P. Rossi [Rome: Editori Riuniti, 1969], 170). Although this is true in general (the same rendition can also be found in Gramsci's other translations from Marx's anthology), in the second translated text entitled *Il materialismo storico*—and only in this text—twice consecutively Gramsci corrected this phrase: this may have happened in the rereading process, possibly after a comparison with the French translation that Gramsci had quoted elsewhere (Q7, sheet 28ʳ). Contrary to his habit of keeping the first solution and adding an interlinear variation, in this case Gramsci crossed out the phrase "bourgeois society" and replaced it with "civil society": his change of mind still remains a mystery.

63. Quoted in Paggi, *La Teoria Generale*, 1335.

64. LP1, 112.

65. I wish to thank Sergio Caprioglio for pointing out the two articles. The first one, *Il Tramonto di Guignol* [The Twilight of Guignol], *L'Avanti* (March 13, 1917), is now in Antonio Gramsci, *Letteratura e Vita Nazionale* (Turin: Einaudi, 1950), 276–78, and the second one, *Le Tessere e la Favola del Furbo*, *Avanti!* XXI, 59 (February 28, 1917), only recently attributed to Gramsci, is in the volume Antonio Gramsci, *La Città Futura (1917–1918)*, ed. Sergio Caprioglio (Turin: Einaudi, 1982).

66. Gramsci was almost certainly aware of the centenary of the Grimms' tales (*Märchen*), which was celebrated the same year that he attended Farinelli's lectures on German classics and Romantics and to which space was given over in the Italian press. See also my article, *Antonio Gramsci und die Brüder Grimm*, in the collectively authored volume *Brüder Grimm Gedenken* III (Marburg: Elwert, 1981).

67. LP2, 129–30. Emphasis added.

68. We give a list of the translated tales and, in brackets, their original titles preceded by the numbers with which they appear in Reclam's edition of the *Märchen*. Notebook A—1. *Storia di Uno, Giovannin Senzapaura, Che Partì di Casa per Imparare Cos'è la Pelle D'Oca/ The Story of the Youth Who Went Forth to Learn What Fear Was* (3. *Märchen von Einem, der Auszog, das Fürchten zu Lernen*); 2. *Il Lupo e i Sette Caprettini/ The Wolf and the Seven Little Kids* (4. *Der Wolf und die Sieben Geisslein*); 3. *Cenerentola/ Cinderella* (14. *Aschenputtel*); 4. *Cappuccetto Rosso/ Little Red Riding Hood* (17. *Rotkäppchen*); 5. *I Quattro Musicanti di Brema/ The Bremen Town Musicians* (18. *Die Bremer Stadtmusikanten*); 6. *Mignolino/ Tom Thumb* (20. *Daumesdick*); 7. *Il Pellegrinaggio di Mignoletto/ Thumbling's*

Travels (21. *Daumerlings Wanderschaft*); 8. *Elsa la Furba/ Clever Elsie* (19. *Die Kluge Else*); 9. *Nevina/ Snow White* (27. *Sneewittchen*); 10. *Gianni e la Felicità [Fortuna]/ Hans in Luck* (33. *Hans im Glück*); 11. *La Contadinella Furba/ The Peasant's Clever Daughter* (33. *Die Kluge Bauerntochter*); 12. *La Figlia di Maria/ Our Lady's Child* (2. *Marienkind*); 13. *Il Re dei Ranocchi/ The Frog King* (1. *Der Froschkönig, Oder der Eiserne Heinrich*); 14. *I Dodici Fratelli/ The Twelve Brothers* (7. *Die Zwölf Brüder*); 15. *Fratellino e Sorellina/ Little Brother and Little Sister* (9. *Brüderchen und Schwesterchen*). Notebook B—16. *I Tre Omini della Foresta/ The Three Little Men in the Forest* (10. *Die Drei Männlein im Walde*); 17. *Le Tre Filatrici/ The Three Spinners* (12. *Die Drei Spinnerinnen*); 18. *Giannino e Margheritina [Ghitina]/ Hansel and Gretel* (11. *Hänsel und Gretel*); 19. *Rosina [Rosaspina], Ossia la Bella Addormentata nel Bosco/ Sleeping Beauty [Little Briar-Rose]* (24. *Dornröschen*); 20. *Rumpelstilzchen/ Rumpelstiltskin* (28. *Rumpelstilzchen*); 21. *Il Cane e il Passero/ The Dog and the Sparrow* (29. *Der Hund und der Sperling*); 22. *Millepelli/ All-Kinds-Of-Fur* (31. *Allerleirauh*); 23. *Il Forasiepe [Re di Macchia] e L'Orso/ The Willow-wren and the Bear* (38. *Der Zaunkönig und der Bär*); 24. *Gente Furba/ Wise Folks* (39. *Die Klugen Leute*).

69. Originally in *Lettere dal Carcere*, Gramsci's tales for children were published in a separate collection, Antonio Gramsci, *L'Albero e il Riccio*, ed. G. Ravegnani (Rome: Editori Riuniti, 1966).

70. Brothers Grimm, 188.

71. [We have taken the English quotations from widely available sources; obviously other translations exist and those used may not always correspond to the ones known by readers, for example, the guesses at Rumpelstiltskin's [Rumpelstilts-kin's] name are sometimes rendered "Bandy-legs, Hunchback, Crook-shanks" (Harmondsworth: Penguin, 1996), 143.]

72. Carlo Battisti and Giovanni Alessio's *Dizionario Etimologico Italiano* reads, "pastinare = rivoltare, divellere la terra, v. dotta (lat. pastinare), con continuatori popolari nei nostri dialetti meridionali compreso il sardo" ("pastinare = to dig and plough the earth, formal lexis [from Latin, pastinare], finding a continuation in Southern dialects, including Sardinian").

73. Brothers Grimm, 134.

74. Brothers Grimm, 173.

75. [In this table, translator's notes are added to explain the words substituted or changed by Gramsci.]

76. Brothers Grimm, 85.

77. These quotations are taken respectively from: Jakob Grimm, *Cinquanta Novelle per i Bambini e Per le Famiglie*, trans. Fanny Vanzi Mussini (Milan: Hoepli, 1897); *Le Novella per Tutti* (Florence: Salani, 1908); Jakob Grimm, *Fiabe*, trans. Dino Provenzal (Milan: Istituto Editoriale Italiano, 1914); Jakob Grimm, *Biancaneve e Altre Novelle*, trans. A. Mazzoni (Florence: Bemporad, 1922).

78. Brothers Grimm, 133; see Notebook A, *Mignolino*, sheet 69^v).

79. Brothers Grimm, 7; see Notebook A, *Il Re dei Ranocchi [The Frog King]*, sheet 89v.

80. Brothers Grimm, 203; see Notebook B, *Millepelli*, sheet 17^v. The same holds true for untranslated expressions such as "dem alles glückte, was es anfing" ["for everything it did turned out well"] (Brothers Grimm, 130; see Notebook A, *Mignolino*, sheet 67^v) and "begegnete ihm ja eine Verdriesslichkeit, so würde sie doch gleich wieder gutgemacht" ["if he did meet with any vexation it was immediately

set right"] (Brothers Grimm, 214, see Notebook A, *Gianni e la Fortuna*, sheet 82ʳ).
The remaining—very few—omissions in Gramsci's translation of the Grimms' tales
are probably oversights.

81. Brothers Grimm, 241.

82. At this point in the Grimms' original fable the word used is "Himmel" /
"Heaven."

83. LP2, 106.

84. Gramsci, *Favole di Libertà*.

85. Carlo Muscetta, "Introduction" to Gramsci, *Favole di Libertà*, xxxiii.

86. Antonio Gramsci, "La storia," *Avanti!* XX (August 29, 1916), 240, now in
Cronache Torinesi, 513–14.

87. LP2, 318, emphasis added [and translation modified].

88. LP1, 301.

89. Q8§135, PN3, 314.

90. LP2, 370 [altering the translation by using the more exact "culture" instead
of "education"].

91. LP1, 302.

92. Q4§50, PN2, 211.

93. Q12§2, SPN, 41.

94. Q11§12, SPN, 329, emphasis added.

95. Antonio Gramsci, "La luce che si è spenta" [The Light That Has Been Ex-
tinguished], in *Il Grido del Popolo*, no. 591 (November 20, 1915), now in *Cronache
torinesi*, 23–26.

96. LP2, 318 [translation modified replacing "dominant" with "leading"].

97. LP2, 130. Emphasis added.

98. Q12§2, SPN, 35.

99. Antonio Gramsci, "La difesa dello Schultz," *Avanti!* XXI, no. 328 (November
27, 1917), now in *Scritti giovanili*, 134.

100. Q12§2, SPN, 39.

101. Gramsci, "La difesa dello Schultz," 135.

102. Q12§2, SPN, 39.

103. Q11§28, SPN, 450.

104. Q11§27, SPN, 465.

105. In this respect, it would be extremely important to collect the entire corpus
of Gramsci's translations in a single volume. This would provide a useful integration
and a long overdue complement to the critical edition of the *Notebooks*.

9

On "Translatability" in Gramsci's *Prison Notebooks*

*Fabio Frosini**

The theme of translatability of languages [*linguaggi*] is evidence of a strong link to the philosophical status of Marxism. The radical form of translation, that is, the one that makes possible all other translations, is the translation of philosophy into politics. Translation, if regarded from the correct point of view (that of Marx), is a "reduction"; if regarded from the mistaken point of view (that of idealism), it is an "overturning [*capovolgimento*]."

As it is known, Gramsci devoted the fifth section of Notebook 11 to the "Translatability of Scientific and Philosophical Languages." This section does not have a title, even though Gramsci refers to it in Notebook 10 as "the notebook concerning the 'Introduction to the Study of Philosophy.'"[1] Moreover, "Notes for an Introduction and a Beginning to the Study of Philosophy and the History of Culture" is written as a title on the top of the *recto* side of page 11, which could be understood to refer to the entire section. In other words, the theme concerning the translatability of languages constitutes an integral part of Gramsci's project of rethinking philosophy. Or better, to use Gramsci's explanation, the philosophy-culture couplet, in the precise sense that he used it, should be understood in the light of the "equality of, or the equation between, 'philosophy and politics,' thought and action," that is, a philosophy of praxis for which "everything is political, even philosophy or philosophies . . . and the only 'philosophy' is history in action, life itself."[2] The presence of the couplet, philosophy-culture, in the notebook devoted to the "introduction to philosophy" is not extrinsic, but rather coincides with the philosophical nucleus of Marxism, insofar as only

* Translated from "Sulla 'Traducibilità' nei Quaderni di Gramsci," *Critica Marxista* 6 (2003): 1–10. Translated by Rocco Lacorte with assistance by Peter Ives.

thinking of philosophy as joined with the "culture" in which it is immerged and against which it reacts, reforming and transforming that "culture," will it be possible to fully grasp philosophy's specific *reality*. This specific reality of philosophy consists in an unending work of the transformation of "common sense," which is where philosophy gains relief, as happens with a picture of a landscape.

As can be seen with little more than a superficial glance, the theme of the translatability of languages brings forth a strong connection with the *philosophical status of Marxism*. Gramsci fully explicates this connection in a passage from Notebook 10, wherein he refers to the title of the fifth section of Notebook 11. This passage is in Notebook 10II§6iv entitled "Translatability of Scientific and Philosophical Languages":

> The notes written under this heading are in fact to be brought together in the general section on the relationships between speculative philosophies and the philosophy of praxis and their reduction to this latter as a political moment that the philosophy of praxis explains "politically." Reduction of all speculative philosophies to "politics," to a moment of the historico-political life; the philosophy of praxis conceives the reality of human relationships of knowledge as an element of political "hegemony."[3]

The note containing this passage of Gramsci's, which is divided in four parts, is extraordinarily important from a theoretical point of view. This entire note is entitled "Introduction to the Study of Philosophy." In his first point, entitled "The Term 'Catharsis,'" Gramsci draws an initial account of his reflection on this Aristotelian concept, which he takes from Croce's aesthetics. He affirms that the term "catharsis" can be appropriated by the philosophy of praxis to point out "the passage from the purely economic (or egoistic-impassionate) to the ethico-political moment"—that is, the *hegemonic*—even stating that "to establish the 'cathartic' moment becomes therefore . . . the starting-point for all the philosophy of praxis."[4] In this way, according to Gramsci, "The cathartic process coincides with the chain of syntheses which have resulted from the evolution of the dialectic,"[5] that is, of the dialectical unfolding that Marx defined through the extreme terms of its ideal oscillations—by the two criteria he enunciated in the Preface of 1859 to the *Critique of Political Economy*. Gramsci summarizes these two criteria in the following way:

> One must keep in mind the two points between which this process oscillates: that no society poses for itself problems the necessary and sufficient conditions for whose solution do not already exist or are coming into being; and that no society comes to an end before it has expressed all its potential content.[6]

The space of catharsis—that is, of hegemony or of historical initiative—is delimited by two slopes: the *new* that comes to light and the *old* that perishes—by conditions that are only *negative*. In other words, for Gramsci, historical materialism establishes the conditions in which something either will *not* be able to come to light at all or will *not* be able to perish; it does not extend to the affirmative level of *prediction*. Thus the centrality of "catharsis" in the philosophy of praxis consists indeed of it being an *integral part of historical materialism*. Catharsis is the specific form human freedom assumes within historical materialism. Consequently the only possible predictive statements will be the ones formulated in terms of catharsis— namely, not in predictive terms, but rather in terms of open and alternative possibilities. In this way, both fatalism and determinism are banished in any of their possible forms.[7]

The same reference to the two criteria of the Preface of 1859 was already present in a previous note, Q7§20, which Gramsci transcribed together with others in Q11§22. In this note, Gramsci pointed out that in the *Popular Manual*, the theory of historical materialism of Bukharin "does not deal with a fundamental point: how does the historical movement come to light from the structures? This is indeed the crucial point of historical materialism."[8] He continues recalling the two fundamental criteria of Marx's Preface mentioned above to conclude:

> Only on these grounds can all mechanistic views and every trace of superstitious belief in "miracles" be eliminated. On these grounds also one must pose the problem of the formation of social groups and of political parties and, in the final analysis, of the function of great personalities in history.[9]

"This ground" is therefore what in Q10II§6 (but also in other texts contained in Q10I) Gramsci calls "catharsis" and what allows one to *think politics*, and within politics the role "of the great historical personalities," who always belonged to the *idealistic* philosophy of history (remember Napoleon, "spirit of the world on horse back").[10]

It is in the context of this reflection that one must read the subsequent part of Q10II§6: "II. The Subjective Conception of Reality and the Philosophy of Praxis" that has as a corollary "III. Reality of the External World." In fact, Gramsci presents the philosophy of praxis as capable of "translating" idealistic philosophy into realistic terms thanks to the concept of catharsis, namely, of highlighting and giving value to what is *historicity* (i.e., *politics*) in idealism, even though in the form of a "philosophical romance."[11]

The "translation" Gramsci speaks about in "IV. The Translatability of Scientific Languages" is therefore closely tied, on the one hand, to the problem of *praxis* or politics—that is, to the problem of the enigma represented by "historical movement" on the basis of the structure—and, on the other, to the theme concerning the comparison between the philosophy of praxis and idealism. Gramsci's two-fold articulation of his discourse on translation is analogous to Marx's theoretical reasoning in his *Theses on Feuerbach*. In *Thesis 1* he says, "Hence, in contradistinction to materialism, the *active* side was developed abstractly by material-ism—which, of course, does not know real, sensuous activity as such."[12] When, in fact, Gramsci writes that "the philosophy of praxis conceives the reality of human relationships of knowledge as an element of politi-cal 'hegemony,'"[13] he does nothing but call attention to the specific value that must be assigned to the "active side" Marx speaks about in *Thesis 1*. Yet Gramsci's specific claim demands that this active side is "translated" into a *worldly* language—that is, it is grasped according to its specific *real-ity* (i.e., as the *production of hegemony*).

Exactly as Marx could not have appropriately grasped the "active side" represented by the concept of *Thätigkeit* [activity] had he not already possessed the idea of *sensuous* activity (which is irreducible to idealism), the philosophy of praxis could not have grasped the concept of *cathar-sis* without already possessing the idea of the *unity of theory and practice*, which indeed negates what is *idealistic* in the concept of catharsis. In fact, as Marx's concept of "sensuous activity" contains his detachment from idealism thanks to the notion of the "real basis," which he elaborated in *The German Ideology*, in the same manner, Gramsci's idea of "'equality' of, or the equation between, 'philosophy and politics,' thought and action,"[14] which he elaborated in the *Prison Notebooks*, radically puts into question the abstract unity of the principle, which is at the basis of Croce and Gentile's idealism. For them—and they are in complete agreement on this specific point—unity is the principle (i.e., the *form*), and only as such can it also be the result—namely, history or matter. For Gramsci it is the reverse: unity can only be a result, and therefore only a material unity, that is, transitory and contingent. As seen above, Gramsci does not negate the role of form. Rather, he rethinks it as a function of the potentiality or of the realization (which nothing can guarantee, to the extent that it belongs to the sphere of "catharsis") of the potentials which are present in matter (i.e., in social relationships).

TRANSLATION OF POLITICS AND POLITICS OF TRANSLATION

According to Gramsci, the concept of the *unity of theory and practice* would be reduced to a procedure of mechanical transposition or to a "simple game of 'generic schematisms,'"[15] if *translatability* did not coincide with it. In this statement, Gramsci refers to the way the Pragmatists deal with the problem of language as a cause of errors and with the translatability of scientific languages. Beyond this superficial or "weak" (as it has also been called recently)[16] level of translatability, there is a deeper and more important one that is necessary to understand in order to grasp the entire meaning of translatability. Gramsci formulates this deeper level in the *Notebooks*, wherein he conceives it as a relationship between national cultures:

> Translatability [of philosophical and scientific languages [*linguaggi*]] presupposes that a given stage of civilization has a "basically" identical cultural expression, even if its language is historically different, being determined by the particular tradition of each national culture and each philosophical system, by the prevalence of an intellectual or practical activity, etc.[17]

Taking into account this hierarchical articulation of the theory of translatability, it can be said therefore that the "fundamental" equivalence between the languages [*linguaggi*] of different sciences and philosophies is nothing but the particular case of a wider fact. Namely, of the fact that since each culture—on the level of national cultures—is always complete as such and does not have expressive deficiencies, the different national traditions will have to be decoded as different forms of response to historical problems, which are fundamentally identical—provided that they are regarded as related to forms of civilization that are comparable and *insofar as* they are comparable. What follows from this is the relativization of diverse languages [*linguaggi*] and (given the unity of theory and practice) a clarification of their *uniquely* political character.

The radical form of translation, the one that makes all others possible, is the *translation of philosophy into politics*—namely, the peculiar understanding of the "reality" of "human relationships of knowledge" according to their specific unfolding *in their various national contexts*, that is, the *way* philosophers—and in general intellectuals—realize the unity of philosophy and common sense in light of their respective national traditions and languages [*linguaggi*].

This should not lead to the conclusion, however, that Gramsci thinks of the "reduction" of philosophy (and of culture in general) into politics as an operation of *ideological unveiling*. For Gramsci, the critique of ideologies is something that is far more complex and cannot be reduced to this moment, that is to say, only to its simple and elementary presupposition. Once this translation of philosophy into politics is done, what must be highlighted is the *specific* function of the couplet, philosophy-culture, which is indeed the level grasped in the space of *catharsis*.

I will come back to this point later when I try to show that there is a very strong anti-reductionism present in the concept of translatability. This helps Gramsci free himself from any temptation to think of the realm of theory in terms of detachment from the radical nature of political praxis—a temptation which is evident here and there in the first year in which Gramsci worked on his *Notebooks*. Before showing this anti-reductionism, I would like to discuss another passage in which Gramsci articulates the nexus

between translatability and praxis on the level of hermeneutical criteria that
are indispensable to realize correct translations:

> *Philosophy—politics—economics.* If these are constitutive elements of a single
> conception of the world, there must necessarily be, in the theoretical prin-
> ciples, convertibility from one to the others, a reciprocal translation into the
> specific language of each constitutive part: each element is implicit in the oth-
> ers and all of them together form a homogeneous circle (cf. the earlier note on
> "Giovanni Vailati and scientific language").[18]

Some criteria for inquiry and critique follow from this statement, which are
useful to the historian of culture and ideas:

> A great personality may happen to express his most creative thought not in
> what would seem to be, from an external classificatory point of view, the most
> "logical" context but in another place where it would appear to be extraneous
> (Croce, I believe, has made this critical observation quite often in different
> places). A politician writes about philosophy; it could be that one should look
> for his "true" philosophy in his political writings instead. In every personality
> there is one dominant and predominant activity; it is in this activity that one
> must look for his thought, which, in most cases, is *implicit* and sometimes in
> contradiction with what is stated *ex professo*. To be sure, this criterion of histori-
> cal judgment entails many pitfalls of dilettantism, and it must be applied with
> great caution, but that does not negate the fact that the criterion is pregnant
> with truth.[19]

The criterion of translatability is capable of highlighting real connections
that are independent of, and in disagreement with, those apparent from
formalistic consideration. Regarding formalistic approaches, Gramsci refers
back to Croce's conception of historiographic categorization and its aver-
sion to genre. But the presupposition, from which Gramsci's anti-formalism
springs, is anti-Crocean. Gramsci does not argue in favor of the unity of the
spirit, but rather for the unity of theory and practice and therefore the idea
that true philosophy can be found in the realm Croce defined as economic.
In other words, the "homogeneous circle" Gramsci is speaking about is not
the expressive circle of [Croce's] distincts, since its unity does not reside in
the *form*, but—as shown above—in the *matter* and hence is always a possible
unity (i.e., a unity to be realized). This is what Gramsci writes in a passage
from Q7§35, which I already quoted above regarding the "equality or equation between 'philosophy and politics,' thought and action":

> Nor have the "faculty of reason" or the "mind" created unity, and they cannot
> be regarded as a unitary fact since they are a formal, categorical concept. It is
> not "thought" but what people really think that unites humans and makes
> them different.[20]

Given all this, there is no criteria, fixed or unfixed, from which to locate the centrality of one "element" or ordering principle to compare the other "elements." Rather, such a principle has to be found and explained continuously, continually motivated, and thus, will be *particular* and indeed profoundly *historical* (precisely in the sense that history = matter). That is, it must be deeply tied to the *biography* of individuals as well as, on a national scale, the *unrepeatable* way the relationship between culture and society is realized in given contexts. As one can see, Gramsci's discourse on national cultures—that is, on the *culture-activity or the form of civilization that predominates* in each culture cannot be separated from the problem represented by the necessity "for the historian of culture and ideas," to develop some "criteria for inquiry and critique" capable of preventing the "dangers of dilettantism" represented by the tendency to forge keys capable of opening all doors or to reduce history to some formulas which Gramsci stigmatizes (in agreement with [Antonio] Labriola and the "revisionist" Croce) since his time in Turin.[21]

What are these *canons of inquiry and critique?* An answer can be found in Q7§81:

> *Types of periodicals. Foreign contributors.* One cannot do without foreign contributors, but foreign collaboration should also be organic and not anthological, sporadic, or casual. In order for this kind of collaboration to be organic, the foreign contributor must not only be knowledgeable about the cultural currents in their country; they also have to be able to "compare" them with the cultural currents in the country where the periodical is published, that is, they need to know that country's cultural currents and understand its national "discourse" [*linguaggio*]. The periodical (or, rather, the editor-in-chief of the periodical), then, must also mold the foreign contributors so that this organic integration can be achieved. . . . The type of [foreign] contributor being discussed here does not exist "spontaneously" but must be formed and cultivated. Opposed to this rational way of thinking about collaboration is the superstition of having among one's foreign contributors leading figures, the great theoreticians, etc. One cannot deny the usefulness (especially commercial usefulness) of having marquee names. But form a practical point of view, the advancement of culture is much better served by the type of contributor who is totally in tune with the periodical and who knows how to translate a cultural world into the discourse [*linguaggio*] of another cultural world; someone who can discover similarities even where none are apparent and can find differences even where everything appears to be similar, etc.[22]

Gramsci had already expressed this concept clearly in Q1§43:

> *Types of periodicals.* . . . Patient and systematic "repetition" is the fundamental methodological principle. But not a mechanical, material repetition: the adaptation of each of basic concept to diverse peculiarities, presenting and

re-presenting it in all its positive aspects and in its traditional negations, always ordering each partial aspect in the totality. Finding the real identity underneath the apparent differentiation and contradiction and finding the substantial diversity underneath the apparent identity is the most essential quality of the critic of ideas and of the historian of social development.[23]

It must be noted that *both* passages are devoted to "Types of Periodicals." In fact, for Gramsci, the periodicals are at the same time centers for the irradiation of a unitary "language" [*lingua*] and of "translation," both to the extent that they "translate" national cultures (think of the political, but also of the poetic foreign texts published in *L'Ordine Nuovo*) and to the extent that they "translate" certain themes into the language of a specific *public*, which they not only intend to reach and educate, but also *help come to light*.

The relationship between scientific and philosophical languages [*linguaggi*], which the Pragmatist recognized, is nothing but a particular manifestation of the problem of a national linguistic unity. This problem can be dealt with correctly only if actively formulated in terms of linguistic "unification." Yet, given the equivalence of language [*lingua*] and ideology, this relationship is correctly posited only if it is thought of as an active process of *ideological* unification (recall the passage cited above: "It is not 'thought' but what people really think that unites humans and makes them different.") Even in the notes written in the early prison years one can see that the generating center of Gramsci's thoughts was the unity of theory and practice conceived as an historical self-creation. In fact, if we examine Q4§33 ("The Passage from Knowing to Understanding to Feeling and Vice Versa") we have Gramsci's formulation of the problem concerning the unification of the intellectuals and the people, that is, as a unification of "knowing" and "feeling" (i.e., of "reason" and "sentiment"). He returns to this theme many times in the *Notebooks*, wherein he discusses the relationship between the "solid" convictions needed for action and the theoretical "understanding" of the problems tied to action itself.[24]

FROM REDUCTION TO TRANSLATION

We can now return to the theme concerning the relationship between philosophy and politics in the light of the translatability of national cultures. To pursue this goal, it will be useful to start from Q3§48, in which the relationship between "spontaneity" and "conscious direction" is paralleled with that between "philosophy" and "common sense":

> In this regard, a fundamental theoretical question arises: can modern theory be in opposition to the "spontaneous" sentiments of the masses? ("Spontaneous" in the sense that they are not due to the systematic educational activity of an al-

ready conscious leadership but have been formed through everyday experience in the light of "common sense," that is, the traditional popular conception of the world: what is very tritely called "instinct," which is itself a rudimentary and basic historical acquisition). It cannot be in opposition: there is, between the two, a "quantitative" difference—of degree not quality; it should be possible to have a reciprocal "reduction," so to speak, a passage from one to the other and vice versa. (Remember that I. Kant considered it important to his philosophical theories to be in agreement with common sense; the same is true of Croce. Remember Marx's assertion in *The Holy Family* that the political formulas of the French Revolution are reducible to the principles of classical German philosophy.)[25]

Gramsci's reference to the equation, which was formulated in Marx's *The Holy Family*, between German speculative philosophy and French political intuitive thought ("If Herr Edgar [i.e., Bruno Bauer] compares French *equality* with German 'self-consciousness' for an instant, he will see that the latter principle expresses *in German*, i.e., in abstract thought, what the former says *in French*, that is, in the language [*lingua*] of politics and of thoughtful observation.")[26] This reference recurs many times in the *Notebooks* and is one of his favorite references when he deals with the theme of translatability. It condenses the entire complex problematic in which Gramsci frames this problem, even though it does so with an evocative formula. The comparison between French culture and German culture is, in fact, in a certain way, paradigmatic because of their respective relationship to philosophy and to politics, to theory and to practice. There was already a lively comparison between the French and the Germans before Marx and Engels (and later Gramsci will take note of it on the grounds of Croce's essay "La Preistoria di un Paragone" [The Prehistory of a Comparison], which he summarized in Q8§208).[27] Both in the *Lectures on the History of Philosophy* and on the *Lectures on the Philosophy of History*, Hegel affirmed that insofar as the German people and the French people are *opposed*, they are the ones that fully express the present form of the spirit of the world each according to its own peculiar way. On the one hand, the Germans express the present form of the spirit of the world in a philosophy that "contains the revolution in the form of thought"; on the other, the French expressed it by conducting the revolution in political practice and translating the "concept" into "effectual reality."[28]

Evidently, Marx and Hegel are not saying the same thing. An enormous problem is raised by the differences between Marx and Hegel's position (i.e., that concerning the relationship between the philosophy of praxis and speculative philosophy). This problem is already formulated in some way in Q3§48, where Gramsci recalls Kant and Croce's aspiration to reach an agreement between their own philosophies and common sense, adding the passage from *The Holy Family* mentioned above. Both the case of Kant and Croce and the case of Marx concern the unity between philosophy and common sense, but they formulate this unity in opposite ways. By comparing France and Germany, Marx stresses the primacy of political praxis over self-consciousness, whereas for Kant, Croce and Hegel the comparison between France and Germany or between common intellect and philosophy[29] explicates the fact that a unity between these two moments *is always already there*, because it corresponds to a *principle*—namely, to the form of human reason and spirit.

The reference to the comparison between the French and the Germans is therefore ambivalent because it refers to the idea of *speculation*, insofar as this comparison can mean both a reduction of speculation to abstraction (primacy of politics) and, on the opposite hand, the discovery within abstraction of a form (or supreme form) of *praxis* (the primacy of philosophy conceived as *Thätigkeit*—i.e., as creativity). While Gramsci never takes the second path, his route often crosses the first one, even though he detaches himself from it thanks to his balanced position contained in the notion of translatability, in which (if this notion is *thought* profoundly) neither of the two moments can prevail over the other or can be assumed to be the original one.

The heaviest traces of Gramsci's tendency toward "politicization" can be found in Notebook 1, which is not by accident, at the same time, the laboratory in which the concept of translatability comes to light.[30] It is enough to refer to Q1§44 (transcribed in Q19§24), in which for the first time the reference to French politics and German classical philosophy appears. Yet the group of texts, Q1§150 and 151 (transcribed together in the same note, Q10II§61, but in reverse order) and Q1§152 (transcribed in Q10II§60), is even more interesting. These texts must be read together with the subsequent one, Q1§153 (transcribed in Q16§21), entitled "Conversation and Culture." In this note Gramsci returns to the theme concerning the diffusion of a homogeneous way of thinking, articulating it from the viewpoint of the "research of a pedagogical principle." He concludes this note with some considerations on translation from Latin and Greek into Italian conceived as an exercise which is mechanical only at the beginning, but that soon becomes a "comparison" and a "translation" of one culture into another (this confirms the connection between the theme I am dealing with now and that concerning the "diffusion" of culture).[31]

Let's now go back to Q1§150–152. In these notes what occurs is a sort of backwards movement. Gramsci starts by considering, on the one hand, the relationship between the bourgeoisie and proletariat and, on the other, the intellectuals, strongly devaluating the latter. The intellectuals "create" the concept of a modern state conceived as an "absolute" since in this way they make their own historical position absolute and at the same time they react against the French Revolution ("reaction national-transcendence," etc.). In this way, Gramsci explains philosophical idealism as a theoretical absorption of revolutionary innovations and as the thought that fertilizes post-Napoleonic Europe. Thus the currents "that seem most autochthonous, in that they appear to develop a traditional Italian current"[32] are indeed the ones that are "Jacobin" in the worst sense in Italy of the Risorgimento. The national tradition they develop is made by nothing other than "culture" (that of the Italian intellectuals' cosmopolitism) which is not able to truly unite the people-nation.

Note the conceptual couple formed both by the intellectuals making their position absolute and by the reaction to the revolution. The first element in this couple is the hegemonic one. The second has almost no autonomy. That is why Gramsci's conclusion is harsh, even though formulated in the form of a doubt:

> The question is very complicated and full of contradictions; therefore, it is necessary to study it more thoroughly on a historical basis. In any case, Southern intellectuals during the Risorgimento appear clearly as the scholars of the "pure" state, of the state in itself. And whenever intellectuals seem to "lead," the concept of the state in itself reappears with all the "reactionary" retinue that usually accompanies it.[33]

In the next note, Q1§151, mentioned above, Gramsci deepens the theme concerning the relationship between France and the other countries of Europe.

> Another important question . . . is that of the function that intellectuals believed they had in this smoldering political ferment of the Restoration. Classical German philosophy is philosophy of this period and it enlivens the national liberal movements from 1848 to 1870. Consider, in this respect, how Marx reduces the French maxim "liberté, fraternité, égalité" to German philosophical concepts (*The Holy Family*). This reduction, it seems to me, is extremely important theoretically; it should be placed next to what I have written on the *Conception of the state from the point of view of the productivity (function) of the social classes.*[34] What is "politics" for the productive class becomes "rationality" for the intellectual class. What is strange is that some Marxists believe "rationality" to be superior to "politics," ideological abstraction superior to economic concreteness. Modern philosophical idealism should be explained on the basis of these historical relations.[35]

The entire last paragraph is omitted when Gramsci writes the C-text (yet the variants of these texts are generally of fundamental importance). The reason for this omission is that, in this way, Gramsci eliminates the ambivalence present in this passage and in the previous one mentioned above by affirming only one of the two components: the political one. In this way, Gramsci allows a reading of the equation of *The Holy Family* in terms of a "reduction" of the abstraction to politics conceived as the unveiling of ideology, so that philosophical idealism as a whole is deprived of any *reality*; politically, philosophical idealism becomes synonymous with *reaction* and, theoretically, it becomes nothing other than politics deprived of substance.

In Q1§152, Gramsci explicates this last aspect by providing Marx's (actually Engels's) image about Hegel as the one who "has men walking on their heads."[36] Hence, Gramsci is concerned with the idea that if translation is regarded from the correct point of view (that of Marx), it is a *reduction*, whereas, if it is regarded from the mistaken point of view (that of idealism), it is an *overturning* [*capovolgimento*—literally a head-turn]. That is, the relationship between philosophy and politics is analogous to the one between ephemeral illusion and solid reality. Yet this way of positing the problem is at odds with Gramsci's fundamental theoretical intention at the base of his *Notebooks*—namely, that of fighting against theoretical and political economism and sectarianism. In fact, in the second draft of these sections, Gramsci radically downsizes his previous statements, rereading them in the light of the concept of translatability.

Yet it is impossible not to see that the idea of translatability—that is, the problem regarding the unity between theory and practice—is already present in the notes mentioned above, which Gramsci writes in his earlier prison years, thanks to the structural ambiguity contained in the way he thinks of translation. That is, sometimes he thinks of translation as the correspondence between theories and sometimes as their overthrowing [*capovolgimento*]. In other words: the affirmation that the relationship between France and Germany is a relationship between politics and rationality corresponds to a negative statement about "rationality" only if the fact that rationality is an overturning [*capovolgimento*] of politics is equivalent to assigning to this overturning [*capovolgimento*] a merely *privative* reality (as nonconcreteness, nonhistoricity, etc.). And vice versa, the affirmation that the relationship between France and Germany is a relationship between politics and rationality turns into a very different statement when the overturning [*capovolgimento*] is seen as a form of translation, that is, as a way to realize that the *same* politics that was being carried out in Germany and in France (in different ways and with specifically different ends, especially from the perspective of their *class* differences). To put it in Gramsci's own terms, this form of translation can then be seen as a form of "hegemony," even though its sign [as in the mathematical plus and minus signs] is inverted [*rovesciato*], the same as the Jacobins' "permanent revolution" is inverted into the "passive revolution" of the Moderates.

Gramsci's concept of "passive revolution" (which he announces, not by mere coincidence, in Q1§150 and 151 by referring to the "formation of modern states in Europe as 'reaction—national transcendence' of the French Revolution and Bonapartism [passive revolution],"[37] points out the start of his reevaluation of the overturning [*capovolgimento*] in terms of *translation* (i.e., his own understanding of the positive and not privative political nature of abstraction). Once this new viewpoint is achieved, the concepts Gramsci already elaborated in Notebook 1 can be reread (i.e., explicated or "translated") in a different way. Thus, in Q8§208, which is entitled "[Reciprocal] Translatability of National Cultures," Gramsci will even be able to trace Marx's version of the comparison between French politics and German classical philosophy back to Hegel's and to find the "source" of the fundamental philosophical idea of Marx's *Theses on Feuerbach* in Hegel's comparison, namely, the unity of theory and practice:

> This passage from Hegel is, I believe, the same one that Marx specifically refers to in the *Holy Family* when he cites Proudhon against Bauer. But the passage from Hegel, it seems to me, is much more important as the "source" of the view, expressed in the *Theses on Feuerbach*, that the philosophers have explained the world and the point now is to change it; in other words, that philosophy must become "politics" or "practice" in order for it to continue to be philosophy. The "source," then, of the theory of the unity of theory and practice.[38]

Gramsci obviously puts the term "source" in quotation marks. This makes it far more significant that he used the term. He doesn't intend to claim that Hegel enunciated the theory of the unity of theory and practice, but rather that *indeed* his answer—the overcoming of the French Revolution—is contained in the comparison French-Germany, namely, that by placing himself on the terrain of "passive revolution," he produced some *knowledge effects* critically appropriable by historical materialism. "The reality of human relationships of knowledge" consists of the double productivity (both theoretical and practical) of philosophy, which is synthesized by the notion of *hegemony*.[39]

NOTES

1. Antonio Gramsci, *Further Selections from the Prison Notebooks*, ed. and trans. Derek Boothman (London: Lawrence & Wishart, 1995), 318–19, hereafter cited as FSPN. Q10II§60. [There is a list of abbreviations on page ix–x. To facilitate locating passages in various translations and anthologies, we use the standard method of providing the notebook (*Quaderno*) number—in this case 10, part II—followed by the section number, §. See the introduction, page 12, for discussion. We will indicate the English translation, when used.]

2. Q7§35, Antonio Gramsci, *Prison Notebooks*, vol. 3, ed. and trans. Joseph Buttigieg (New York: Columbia University Press, 2007), 187, hereafter cited as PN3. Not long ago, Domenico Jervolino talked about "a very strong link between praxis and translation" in Gramsci [see introduction, page 9]. On this subject see,

however, above all, the essay by Maurizio Lichtner, "Traduzioni e metafore in Gramsci" [see chapter 10, this volume]. Moreover, the relationship between hegemony and translatability is stressed by André Tosel, *Filosofia Marxista e Traducibilità dei Linguaggi e delle Pratiche* [Marxist Philosophy and the Translatability of Languages and Practices], in *Filosofia e Politica: Scritti dedicati a Cesare Luporini* (Florence: La Nuova Italia, 1981), 235–45 [see also chapter 16].

   3. Q10II§6iv, FSPN, 306.

   4. Q10II§6i, Antonio Gramsci, *Selections from the Prison Notebooks*, ed. and trans. Quintin Hoare and Geoffrey Nowell Smith (New York: International Publishers, 1971), 366–67, hereafter cited as SPN. Translation altered slightly, see QC, 1244. Emphasis added.

   5. Q10II§6i, SPN, 367.

   6. Q10II§6i, SPN, 367. Translation altered slightly, QC, 1244.

   7. I would speak about catharsis as "prediction" in the critical sense, which is specifically Gramsci's, that Nicola Badaloni assigned to this term (in his *Antonio Gramsci: La filosofia della prassi come previsione* [Antonio Gramsci: The Philosophy of Praxis as Prediction], in *Storia del marxismo*, ed. E. Hobsbawm, vol. III, 2 [Turin: Einaudi, 1981]) rather than of catharsis as "mediation" as André Tosel did (in A. Tosel, *Philosophie de la praxis et dialectique* [Philosophy of Praxis and Dialectic], in *La pensée*, no. 237 (1984): 105). For the same reason, I believe that Tosel's critique of the notion of catharsis cannot be accepted (see Tosel, 1981, 242ff). Moreover, Tosel himself implicitly revised his critique in *Marx en Italiques* (Mauvezin: Trans Europe Repress, 1991), 147–49.

   8. Q7§20, PN3, 171.

   9. Q7§20, PN3, 171.

   10. See Leonardo Paggi, "Da Lenin a Marx" [From Lenin to Marx], in *Le Strategie del Potere in Gramsci. Tra fascismo e socialismo in un solo paese 1923–1926* [The Strategies of Power between Fascism and Socialism in Only One Country 1923–1929] (Rome: Editori Riuniti, 1984), 461–66, on the relationship between historical materialism and political science in the *Prison Notebooks*. It should be recalled that in the well-known letter to W. Borgius of January 25, 1894, Engels mentioned the problem of the appearance of the "so called great men" in history, in order to deprive the causality/necessity nexus of its significance and to reduce the former to an appearance of the latter (*Karl Marx and Frederick Engels: Collected Works*, vol. 50 [London: Lawrence & Wishart, 2004], 264–67), and hence in a direction which is different from Gramsci's. Gramsci recalls the letter to Borgius in Q4§38, (QC, 462; PN2, 184) a propos of the notion of "ultimate analysis" and therefore in an anti-economistic sense.

   11. Q8§217, 1079.

   12. [Frosini takes his quotation from Gramsci's translation of *Thesis 1* (see QC, 2355). See Karl Marx and Frederick Engels, *The German Ideology*, ed. C. J. Arthur (New York: International Publishers, 1970), 121.]

   13. Q10II§6, FSPN, 306.

   14. Q7§35, PN3, 187.

   15. Q11§47, FSPN, 307.

   16. Derek Boothman, *Traducibilità* [Translatability]. Paper delivered at the seminar on the lexicon of the *Prison Notebooks* of the IGS [International Gramsci Society]

Italia, Rome, February 23, 2003, in www.gramscitalia/html/seminario.htm. [See also chapter 7 in this volume and Derek Boothman, *Traducibilità e Processi Traduttivi* (Perugia: Guerra Edizioni, 2004), 61–65.]

17. Q11§47, FSPN, 307. [Frosini added "of philosophical and scientific languages."]

18. Q4§46, PN2, 196. He dealt with Vailati in Q4§42.

19. Q4§46, PN2, 196.

20. Q7§35, PN3, 186.

21. See Q4§38, 463, on Engels's critiques to economism within historical materialism. For these aspects in the young Gramsci, see Leonardo Paggi, *Antonio Gramsci e il Moderno Principe* [Antonio Gramsci and the Modern Prince]; *I. Nella crisi del Socialismo Italiano* [I. In the Crisis of Italian Socialism] (Rome: Editori Riuniti, 1970), chapter 1.

22. Q7§35, PN3, 211–12.

23. Q1§43, PN1, 128–29.

24. See Q1§29, QC, 23ff., "Sarcasm as an Expression of Transition among Historicsts"; Q4§40, QC, 465, "Philosophy and Ideology"; Q4§45, QC, 471ff., "Structure and Superstructure"; Q4§61, QC, 507, "Philosophy-ideology, Science-doctrine" (the last paragraph of this note is very important); Q7§37, QC, 887, "Goethe"; Q8§175, QC, 1047, "Gentile"; Q11§62, QC, 1488ff., "The Historicity of the Philosophy of Praxis."

25. Q3§48, 330–31, PN2, 51.

26. Karl Marx and Fredrick Engels, *Collected Works*, vol. 4 (New York: International Publishers, 1975), 39. [As quoted in PN1, 434n.38, with original italics re-added.]

27. See Benedetto Croce, "La Preistoria di un Paragone," published in *Critica* (1906) and quoted by Gramsci in the reprint in *Conversazioni Critiche: Serie seconda* (Bari: Laterza, 1918) (1950, fourth edition), 292–94. For a detailed indication of the sources provided by Croce, see Antonio Gramsci, *Filosofia e Politica. Antologia dei "Quaderni del carcere"*, ed. Fabio Consiglio and Fabio Frosini (Florence: La Nuova Italia, 1997), 62–65 and footnote.

28. See G. W. F. Hegel, *Lectures on the Philosophy of History*, vol. 3, trans. E. S. Haldane and Frances Simson (London: Routledge and Kegan Paul, 1968), 359–60, and G. W. F. Hegel, *Lectures on the History of Philosophy*, trans. R. F. Brown and J. M. Stewart (Berkeley: University of California Press, 1990).

29. Since France represents intuitive thought, which produces practical overturning, it can be almost perfectly overlapped onto the *Gemeinverstand* conceived as practical intellect. An analogous consideration can be made regarding the couplet Germany-philosophy. Thus, what counts is not the diverse origin of the two couplets of concepts, but rather that Gramsci makes them converge.

30. On this initial tendency in Gramsci, see G. Cospito, "Struttura e sovrastruttura nei 'Quaderni' di Gramsci" [Structure and Superstructure in Gramsci's "Notebooks"], in *Critica Marxista* 3–4 (2000): 98–107.

31. Q1§154, which Gramsci transcribes in Q10II§60 together with Q1§152. Both are entitled *Marx and Hegel.*

32. Q1§150, 133.

33. Q1§150, 133, PN1, 230.

34. Q1§150, PN1, 229. See the previous quoted passage.

35. Q1§151, PN1, 231.

36. Q1§152, PN1, 232. Frederick Engels stated, "It was a time when, as Hegel says, the world stood upon its head" (here Engels put the passage from Hegel's *Philosophy of History* in the footnote) (Engels, "Socialism: Utopian and Scientific," *Marx and Engels: Collected Works*, vol. 24 [London: Lawrence & Wishart, 1989], 285). Gramsci knew this text, even though he didn't have it in the prison in Turi. Another interesting passage is in Engel's *Ludwig Feuerbach and the End of Classical German Philosophy*: "Thereby [i.e., through Marx's dialectic] the dialectic of concepts itself became merely the conscious reflection of the dialectical motion of the real world and thus the Hegelian dialectic was placed upon its head; or rather, turned off its head, on which it was standing, and placed upon its feet." *Marx and Engels: Collected Works*, vol. 26 (London: Lawrence & Wishart, 1990), 383.

37. Q1§151, PN1, 230.

38. Q8§208, PN3, 355.

39. In "Traduzioni e Metafore in Gramsci" (see chapter 10, pages 187–211). Maurizio Lichtner draws a correspondence between the irreducible metaphorical character of language and the impossibility of arguing on the theoretical level in favor of a concept of "truth," unless it immediately refers to "history." Yet in this way the theoretical value of this concept would be annulled. I believe that the basis of Lichtner's assessment is the assumption that the metaphorical nature of language and its ideological character are the same, for Gramsci. But rethinking the concept of truth within metaphor consists of thinking criteria that allow to distinguish between truth effects and ideology effects within this mutable and by definition incomplete terrain. That is not to say that truth refers to history (as something external or other), but rather about the historical production of truth. The fact is that all the interpretation by Lichtner is based on the theses by Biagio de Giovanni, according to whom the truth of praxis consists of its actuality (see pages 88–89 and notes 8, 9, and 10 in this volume). This perspective ends up separating again the terrain of history from that of truth, as can be well seen from Lichtner's conclusions.

10

Translations and Metaphors in Gramsci

*Maurizio Lichtner**

To take an expression in a metaphorical sense means attributing to it a different meaning than the literal one. But is it always possible to trace back and define perfectly the literal meaning to which the expression refers? Isn't it the case that sometimes metaphor is used specifically because the precise meaning of an enunciation cannot be provided? The conceptual content the metaphor refers to might be similar to those indistinct images, which Wittgenstein talks about, that cannot be profitably substituted with sharp images.[1]

In 1988, Badaloni raised the role that the recognition of metaphors has in Gramsci's reading of Marx.[2] Gramsci's *critical* attitude consists precisely in recognizing that certain expressions of Marx are metaphorical, that they indicate something, "an orientation and a line of tendency," but they must not be taken literally—that is, *reified*. Gramsci avoids the "mere reproduction of Marx's formulations." His project, Badaloni says, is to "re-utilize that which, in Marx, has been lowered to 'metaphor' in a context where the 'metaphorical' summarizes conceptual meaning. In sum, to carry out a critical reading of Marx means to 're-attribute' a new conceptual value to the metaphorical meanings."[3]

At the center of his interpretation of Marxism as historicism, or absolute historicism,[4] there is then a particular metaphor, that of *immanence*. Marx uses this expression in a metaphorical sense. He certainly does not mean what the speculative tradition meant (the presence of the divine in the world), but something new. If this is fundamental to understanding historical

* Translation from "Traduzioni e Metafore in Gramsci," *Critica Marxista* 39, 1 (January/February 1991): 107–31. Translated by Rocco Lacorte with assistance by Peter Ives.

187

materialism, then it must be explained and conceptualized. The new concept of immanence—Badaloni says—is to be understood as a "unity of theory and praxis, overcoming of the dichotomy between traditional idealism and traditional materialism."[5] The new concept of immanence means that "it is neither possible to do without reality reducing it to a mere expression of human acts nor is it historically right to exaggerate the duty of reality to the point of re-attributing rationality to it, and putting it in the domain of personified thing-ness."[6]

Certainly, Marx's metaphor of immanence is not accidental. It points out something specific which couldn't be expressed in other words with respect to the theory-praxis relationship and the structure-superstructure relationship. But is Gramsci able to conceptualize it to the point of reinstating a precise meaning to the metaphorical expression? Is Gramsci able to substitute a "theory" for the metaphor? Or does his very critical, anti-dogmatic approach to Marx's text have another result? The conclusion might in effect be that the metaphor, once recognized as such, can no longer be used as a concept and it is not even possible to substitute it with a precise and "clear" conceptual definition. One can only substitute contingent—that is, historically determined—affirmations to the claim of absoluteness which is typical of the metaphorical way of speaking. The thesis of this article is that we cannot retrieve from Gramsci any "theory" of the structure-superstructure relationship or of the theory-practice relationship. Also, for Badaloni the "penetration of structural and superstructural elements" that characterizes Gramsci's concept of the historical bloc has a justification that is purely historical. It is the "decisive historical character of the epoch in which we live" that the "relevance of subjective factors resulting from conscious human will and organization structured in hegemonic relationships are not fixed a priori but are historically displaced." Gramsci's concept has value today because "we live in a period of transition," in which "nothing is irreversibly decided within the articulated 'historical bloc.'" The "new philosophy of immanence" that Gramsci elaborates is adequate to the historical moment, because in it "no result is preconstituted and everything depends on the reaction of the structure and the superstructure, of material agents and of human wills, on the whole."[7]

Every recent and thorough reading of the Notebooks has accomplished a historicization of Gramsci's formulations. For example, De Giovanni, in his 1985 essay, "Il Marx di Gramsci" [The Marx of Gramsci], concentrates his attention on what he calls the "*synolon* philosophy-politics." He doesn't ask himself how the synolon can be conceived, but how "this synolon has become actual" in Gramsci's reflection.[8] The actuality of the identification philosophy-politics, theory-praxis, originates from a determined interpretation of the "modern" by Gramsci: the "form" of modern history, De Giovanni says, appears to him "as revolving around great hegemonic clashes and around the re-organization of all kinds of knowledge in relation to those clashes." The XI Thesis on Feuerbach is, therefore, valid for him, because of the "subjectivization of the masses and of their collective practical agency." The structure-superstructure relationship expresses a history that is more "dense with consciousness,"[9] where what was objective is transferred into the subject. De Giovanni continues, the modern "comes about through the intrusion of praxis, that is, through the dense constitution of praxis as a terrain able to absorb every other element"—that is, the *objective* elements as well as the *abstract* ones.[10] However, beyond the recognized actuality or representative capability of Gramsci's formulations with respect to the "modern," the problem remains: why doesn't Gramsci succeed in his attempt to substitute Marx's metaphor with "a theory"? Why does Gramsci need "to translate" Marx's annunciations and why is this translation never satisfactory, that is, always provisional and relative?

MARX'S METAPHORS

Following the *Prison Notebooks*, let's start by looking at how Gramsci's reflections on the metaphorical quality of Marx's expression come to light and what they lead to.[11] Let's consider, in particular, the three series of the "Appunti di Filosofia" [Notes of Philosophy] in Notebooks 4, 7 and 8, where Gramsci's reasoning is particularly concentrated and coherent with respect to its objectives and its developments, along the leading thread which is common to all three series—that is, *materialism and idealism*. The reference to the subsequent, "special" notebooks, dealing with philosophical topics (Notebooks 10 and 11), can obviously not be left out, but here we limit ourselves to mentioning the "rewritings" of the notes contained in the "Notes on Philosophy," together with the eventual modifications.[12] The idea that some of Marx's fundamental terms are metaphors emerges in correspondence with the critique of Bukharin's *Popular Manual* initiated in Notebook 4. In note 11, "Problemi Fondamentali del Marxismo" [Fundamental Problems of Marxism],[13] Gramsci continues his reflection which tends to liberate Marx from the so-called orthodox traditional interpretation, in a materialist vein.[14] Gramsci, therefore, distinguishes the "philosophical currents" that Marx studied, his "philosophical culture," the "elements" from which "Marx started his philosophizing"[15] from that which is effectively his position.[16] The philosophy of Marx is not reducible to the previous systems, in particular, to materialism. Among the other previous systems, Gramsci says, the most important is Hegelianism, "especially for his attempt to overcome the traditional conception of 'idealism' and 'materialism.'" It is at this point that the term "immanence" comes on stage: "When one says that Marx uses the expression 'immanence' in a metaphorical sense, one says nothing: in reality, Marx provides the term 'immanence' with a proper meaning, that is, he is not 'pantheist' in the traditional metaphorical sense, but he is 'a Marxist' or a 'historical materialist.'"[17] Here Bukharin is not named but it is his statement to which Gramsci refers. Thus, at first, it seems essential to Gramsci to repeat that Marx's term "immanence" is not empty of content but, among other things, it *has* a central meaning that must be defined.[18]

In the subsequent notes, the critique of the *Popular Manual* [*Saggio Populare*][19] starts taking shape, and Gramsci comes back to the question of the term "immanence" in note 17. He accepts the idea that this term is a metaphor; but all of language, he objects, is a metaphor: "When one conception gives way to another, the earlier language persists, but it is used metaphorically. All of language has become metaphor,[20] and the history of semantics is also an aspect of the history of culture: language is a living thing and simultaneously a museum of fossils of the past life."[21] To the extent that there is historical continuity, and, at the same time, there is transcendence, one can speak of metaphorical use of the previous terms: in effect, "Marx continues the philosophy of immanence," and, at the same time, "he rids it of its whole metaphysical apparatus and brings it to the concrete terrain of history."[22] The use of the term is metaphorical, Gramsci continues, "only in the sense that the conception has been overcome, has been developed, etc."[23] However, Gramsci admits that Marx's conception of immanence is not completely new in the history of thought (and he cites Giordano Bruno).

The expression "immanence" in Marx has, in any case, a "precise meaning," Gramsci says, and "this [Bukharin] should have defined." And then he adds, "Such a definition would really have been 'theory.'"[24]

The metaphor seems to refer, therefore, to the definition, namely, to the concept; but shifting to some notes of Notebook 7, one will face more complex reasoning. In note 36, Gramsci goes back to Bukharin's statement that Marx uses the term "immanence" only as metaphor. This statement, Gramsci says, is, "crude and unqualified" and is made as if it were a "self-sufficient explanation." Again it calls to mind the conception of language as metaphor and leads to very important consequences. Gramsci states, "All language is metaphor, and it is metaphorical in two senses: it is a metaphor of the 'thing' or 'material and sensible object' referred to, and it is a metaphor of the ideological meanings attached to words in the preceding periods of civilization."[25] This second aspect is central to Gramsci; this is confirmed by the sentence introduced in the rewriting of this note in Notebook 11:

> If perhaps it cannot quite be said that all discourse [*discorso*] is metaphorical in respect of the thing or material and sensible object referred to (or the abstract concept) so as not to widen the concept of metaphor excessively, it can however be said that present language [*linguaggio*] is metaphorical with respect to

the meanings and the ideological content which the words used had in preceding periods of civilisation.[26]

It is this interest in the stratification of meanings that characterizes Gramsci's historicism.

Yet, consequently, it is not possible to eliminate the metaphors substituting them with rigorous definitions; if one eliminated the metaphor, the historical density and the stratification of the meanings would be lost. Rather, a critical discourse on metaphor should provide an account of these meanings making them explicit. As Gramsci says, the following are erroneous tendencies: both the attempt of creating "fixed or universal languages" and the conception of "language as source of error," which is typical of the "pragmatists,"[27] who would like to substitute common language with a "completely abstract" "mathematical language."[28] According to Gramsci's approach, to rationalize language, taking away its metaphorical character—namely, its "extensive"[29] meanings—would mean annihilating its historicity.

However, we can obtain a more radical consequence. The same conceptual definition of what metaphors point out will, in turn, be affected by historicity, and new metaphors which have different origins will insert themselves in the "theory" that we pretend substitutes for the metaphor. Gramsci, in effect, does nothing other than use new metaphors when he says that Marx, "rids" the philosophy of immanence of its metaphysical apparatus[30] or when he talks about the philosophy of praxis as "absolute earthliness" of thought,[31] not to mention, naturally, the image of the "historical bloc."

Gramsci goes back to the question of the continuity of language with respect to the past in a note in Notebook 8 entitled "Sul *Saggio Popolare*: La Quistione di Nomenclatura e di Contenuto" [On the Popular Manual: The Question of Nomenclature and Content]. Initially, Gramsci's discourse is on the intellectuals: their characteristic, as a "crystallized social category" is that of "reattaching itself, in the ideological sphere, to a prior category of intellectuals, and it does so by means of a common conceptual nomenclature."[32] The intellectuals, insofar as they are an expression of new historical situations, should, on the contrary, be "new," and not posit themselves as "direct continuation of the previous intelligentsia." Gramsci seems to allude to the distinction (which later became canonical) between "organic" intellectuals and "traditional" intellectuals. However, in those notes, we realize this distinction between the old and new fades. Language never completely changes, "at least in its external formal aspect." It would seem that the *form* could be maintained from tradition and express a new "content." But, in reality, the expression would also have an impact on the content; the "content of language" is changed, Gramsci says, but "it is difficult to have a clear

awareness [*coscienza*] of this change instantaneously." It happens that one
accepts "a term together with the content of a concept that belonged to an
intellectual milieu now superseded; on the other hand, rejection of a term
from another intellectual milieu of the past, even though its content has
changed and it has become effective for expressing the new sociocultural
content." The term "materialism" has been accepted "according to its past
content" within Marxism, and the term "immanence" has been "rejected
because in the past it had a particular historical-cultural content." In sum,
the relationship between "literary expression" and "conceptual content" is
complex: Gramsci ends up saying that one must have an "historical sense,"
and be able to grasp "the different moments of a process of cultural development."[33] It is not so simple to free "the new content" from the "old
literary expression," to decide a new expression without resonance, in order
to define it; it is for this reason that metaphors remain with all that this
involves.[34]

Let's look now at some other Marxist concepts that have to do with the
structure-superstructure relationship which Gramsci thinks he can discover
the origin of and the context from which they were extracted. These concepts as used by Marx result, therefore, in a figurative sense; for this reason,
they lose a lot of their certainty.

In Q1§113, Gramsci reflects on a passage of *The Critique of Political Economy*, in which Marx says that "just as one does not judge an individual by
what he thinks about himself," one also can not evaluate the difference between what an epoch is and how it represents it itself.[35] The expression, he
says, "may be connected to the then relatively recent upheavals in criminal
procedure and related theoretical discussions."[36] The "confession" of the
accused individual is no longer essential; what count are only "the material evidence and the testimony." This possible nexus fascinates Gramsci; it
seems "suggestive" to him—as he adds later on.[37]

Then, in Notebook 8, note 207 ("Questioni di Terminologia" [Questions
of Terminology]), Gramsci considers another one of Marx's expressions to
be a metaphor. This expression is also contained in the 1859 Preface when
he says that "the 'anatomy' of civil society is constituted by its 'economy.'"[38]
The term "anatomy" comes from natural sciences; Gramsci asks himself if
the same concept of structure and superstructure should owe something
"linked to the debates stirred up by the classification of animals, a classification that entered its 'scientific' stage precisely when anatomy, rather than
secondary and incidental characteristics, came to be regarded as fundamental." Gramsci says that finding a concept's context of origin is important:
"the origin of the metaphor that was used to refer to a newly discovered
concept helps one to understand better the concept itself by tracing it back
to the particular historical and cultural world from which it sprang."[39] But
what does it mean, "to better understand"? Gramsci's discourse is more

explicit in the rewriting: to trace a metaphor back to its "linguistic-cultural origin . . . is useful to define the limit of the metaphor itself, stopping it in other words from becoming material and mechanical."[40]

Starting from this note in Notebook 8, these two examples are associated with each other[41]; they then come back together in Notebook 10, note 41xii, in which Gramsci asks himself which cultural and scientific context the philosophy of praxis reacts against at "the moment of its foundation." "Anatomy" and Gramsci's juridical reference are among those "images and metaphors the founders of the philosophy of praxis often go back to"; they constitute true and real "clues," because they specifically expose their place of origin.[42] One finds these two "metaphors" again in Notebook 11, in note 50, where Gramsci's discourse is more radical. The statement that the economy is the anatomy of civil society is defined as a "traditional expression," a "simple metaphor" (where the adjectives "traditional" and "simple" have the evident meaning of lowering and taking away conceptual value),[43] and a "scheme easy to understand" which is used in order to be understood by "culturally backward social strata." The impression of Gramsci's strong relativization of the key concepts of historical materialism is also confirmed by an observation on the heterogeneity of the references: "One must distinguish between the two founders of the philosophy of praxis whose language does not have the same cultural origin and whose metaphors reflect different interests."[44]

In sum, to grasp the origin of concepts, bringing them back to the context where they are commonly used is needed in order to not only to "better understand" the concepts themselves, but to relativitize them, to "define the limit" of their figurative and metaphorical use, and to stop the metaphor from becoming "material and mechanical."[45] We might add, again with Wittgenstein, that to bring words back "from their metaphysical to their everyday use," means to make concepts lose their excellence and *sublimity*; if these concepts "have a use, it must be . . . humble." Their sense is provided by the use made of them in some "language game," namely, in those particular contexts where they originate, that is, have their "original home."[46]

THE TRANSLATABILITY OF LANGUAGES

Another aspect, which is connected to the metaphorical nature of languages, is that of the translatability of languages. In the view of Marxism as historicism, the theme of the translatability of language by Gramsci is fundamental: Marxism appears, in fact, as "the translation of Hegel's historicism." Yet Gramsci speaks of translatability in many senses that do not entirely overlap. We need to make these differences of meaning explicit and also to find in which aspects of these differences Gramsci's theoretical engagement is prevalent.

In Notebook 1, the first reference to one of Marx's texts appears within a different discourse, in the long note on Risorgimento. Speaking of Jacobinism and of the Action Party [Partito d'Azione], as is commonly known, Gramsci claims that classic Jacobinism has a progressive and highly positive character (which represents the more consequential political thought of the French Revolution). [47] Jacobins were not "abstract" (Gramsci uses "abstractionists"): "Jacobins' language perfectly *reflected* the needs of the time, according to French traditions and culture." Moreover, to this point, he adds in parentheses: "See Marx's analysis in *The Holy Family* where it turns out that Jacobins' phraseology corresponded perfectly to the formulas of classical German philosophy, which is today acknowledged to have the greater concreteness and which has given rise to modern historicism." [48]

This correspondence between a historico-political and a philosophical language is the first case of *translation* that we encounter. Gramsci goes back to this theme in note 151, in which he deals with the Restoration, or the post-Napoleonic period, in Europe. He hints at the role of the intellectuals in the situation of "political fermentation," and he affirms that "classical German philosophy is the philosophy of this period and it enlivens the national liberal movements of 1848 until 1870." Gramsci then adds, referring again to the passage from *The Holy Family*, "Consider, in this respect, how Marx reduces the French maxim 'liberté, fraternité, egalité' to German philosophical concepts." [49] Gramsci focuses his attention on this "reduction" made by Marx saying that it seems "extremely important theoretically." [50] From what follows, we derive the sense in which Gramsci focuses his attention on this reduction by Marx. Gramsci refers to the shift from "politics" to "rationality" or from concrete historico-economic to philosophico-abstract discourse; a shift that, as it will be seen, does not go in only one, but in both, directions. That in the passage from "politics" to "rationality" one doesn't end up at all in pure appearance is shown in Gramsci's view of historico-materialism. The only thing that Gramsci asks in this text is that "ideological abstraction" wouldn't be isolated by the "economic concreteness" of which the former is a translation. Gramsci asks himself how a Marxist could prefer abstraction. To deem the level of ideological abstraction "superior" is, in fact, what characterizes "modern philosophical idealism." [51]

In note 48 of Notebook 3, we find another passage in which Gramsci clearly assimilates two senses (politics and rationality) to the "reduction" mentioned above. The topic of note 48 is the relationship between "spontaneity and conscious leadership." After having said, on one hand, that pure spontaneity does not exist—rather, spontaneity must be *educated*, that is, led—within political action and, on the other hand, that direction—that is, "theory"—cannot be separated and abstracted. Gramsci arrives at this consideration: between "modern theory" (Marxism) and "'spontaneous' sentiments of the masses there can not be opposition: between them there is a 'quantitative' difference, a difference in degree, not in quality: a reciprocal (so to say) 'reduction,' namely, a shift from spontaneous sentiments to theory and vice versa must be possible." Gramsci's conceptual reference is twofold: on the one hand, he thinks of the philosophy-commonsense relationship and remembers Kant's interest, as well as Croce's, in maintaining this relationship; on the other hand, the concept of "reduction" takes him to Marx's affirmation in *The Holy Family*—discussed above—of the "formulas of the politics of the French Revolution" that "reduced themselves to the principles of classical German philosophy."[52]

In sum, up to this point, translatability has to do with the relationship between the concrete-abstract and the abstract-concrete. Abstract discourse is the translation of a historical reality, and is in turn retranslated into praxis, mainly in historico-political action. Thus, the concept of translation leads us to the nucleus of the philosophy of praxis. However, in other texts, Gramsci explains more simply the translatability between (French) historico-political and (German) philosophico-abstract language in historiographic terms insofar as they are superstructures that reflect the same structure. In note 42 of Notebook 4, he comes back to a passage of *The Holy Family*, in which Marx "shows how the French political language used by Prudhon corresponds to and can be translated into the language of classical German philosophy." Moreover, Gramsci adds, "This statement, it seemed to me, is *very important* for understanding the innermost value of historical materialism, for finding the way to resolve many apparent contradictions in the unfolding of history, and for responding to certain superficial objections to this theory of historiography."[53] In developing the note, Gramsci thematisizes the historiographical question in terms of the relationship between diverse superstructural formations, which are reciprocally translatable because they can be brought back to the same structure.

As two individuals belonging to the same culture may believe they maintain "different things" because "they use a different terminology" but, in reality, they say the same thing,[54] so happens in the relationship between two national cultures. Gramsci says, "In the international sphere, two cultures, expressions of two fundamentally similar civilizations, believe that they are antagonistic, different, each one superior to the other, because they use different ideological, philosophical terms or because one has a more strictly practical, political character (France) while the other is more philosophical, doctrinal, theoretical." In reality, Gramsci continues, "to the historian, they are *interchangeable:* each one is reducible to the other; they are mutually translatable."[55]

With this, the theoretical nexus seems to dissolve, but reemerges in note 56 (in the part entitled "Miscellanea" [Miscellaneous] of Notebook 4). Gramsci's discourse concerns the autonomy of politics and, therefore, Croce's dialectic of the distincts and Gentile's objections. Yet Gramsci says that Croce and Gentile, through their "reformation" of Hegel's philosophy, have made Hegel more "abstract." In fact, "Have they not lopped off his most realistic, most historicist features?"[56] Hegel reflected on the French Revolution and the Napoleonic wars; his philosophy expresses "an extremely intense historical period during which all previous conceptions were peremptorily criticized by the realities of the time"; therefore, his philosophy could be a true "philosophy of history" instead of an "abstract speculation." The relationship between classical German philosophy and the French Revolution is, thus, especially particular, and reflects the specific character of this philosophy of history that, in the development of Gramsci's reasoning, "should lead to the identification of philosophy with history, action with thought, and the 'German proletariat as the sole inheritor of classical German philosophy.'"[57]

The intertwining of Gramsci's two lines of reasoning is very clear in note 208 of Notebook 8 entitled "Traducibilita Reciproca delle Culture Nazionali" [The (Mutual) Translatability of National Cultures], a very dense text. Reading an essay by Croce contained in *Conversazioni Critciche* [Critical Conversations], Gramsci has found the source of the statement by Marx in *The Holy Family* that "French political language is equivalent to German philosophical language."[58] This source concerns two passages contained respectively in Hegel's *Lectures on the Philosophy of History* and in the *Lectures on the History of Philosophy*. Yet for Gramsci there is another aspect which is more interesting than the question of the translatability of the two languages from a historiographical perspective: in one of his texts, Hegel says that the principle of self consciousness, which the Germans interpreted as "tranquil theory," was, on the contrary, interpreted as revolutionary by the French. In Hegel's text, Gramsci sees the "source" of the thought expressed in the *Theses on Feuerbach* that philosophers have only explained the world and now we need to change it—namely, that philosophy must become "politics" (i.e., "practice") to continue to be philosophy: the "source" for the theory of the unity of theory and "practice."[59] This is essential for Gramsci ("it seems to me . . . much more important"), even though the note closes on the theme "subject of the rubric," namely, "that two similar structures have equivalent and mutually translatable superstructures." But then he adds: "Contemporaries of the French Revolution were aware of this, and that this is of the greatest interest"[60]; that is, again, what, above all, strikes Gramsci with regard to this reciprocal translatability is the specific "awareness"—namely, the inauguration of the unity of theory and praxis.

The translation of Hegelianism into Marxism acquires, in the light of what we have seen thus far, a precise meaning: this translation is possible because we already find in Hegel a new conception of philosophy—that is, we find the capability of translating the abstract-concrete that later becomes the identity of theory and praxis. Moreover, we have the key to understand why, at some point, Gramsci denies the possibility of translating traditional philosophies within historical materialism. This key is in the first note of the second series of the "Notes on Philosophy."[61] Gramsci says that the "translation of the terms of one philosophical system into the terms of another" has limits: "such translation is possible within traditional philoso-phy, whereas it is not possible to translate traditional philosophy into the terms of historical materialism." At first sight, one cannot understand why. Moreover, the reason provided by Gramsci proves nothing. Gramsci states that "the principle of reciprocal translatability is a 'critical' element of his-torical materialism, inasmuch as it presupposes or postulates that a given stage of the civilization has a 'basically identical' cultural and philosophical expression, even though the language of the expression varies depending on the particular tradition of each 'nation' or each philosophical system."[62] This is the historiographical principle of historical materialism: if the struc-ture is the same, the superstructures are reciprocally equivalent, and, in this sense, they are translatable. But this consideration is not firm; if we take into account that historical materialism is also a superstructure—namely, it reflects an epoch—and is not necessarily the only way to reflect it. Gramsci affirmed this in Notebook 4 by saying that historical materialism is "provi-sional"—namely, that it "reflects the realm of necessity" with its conflicts—and it will be overcome, whereas idealism could "become 'truth' after the transition from one realm [necessity] to the other [freedom]."[63] Historical materialism shares the nature and the destiny of the superstructures and is subjected, we may add, to the same conditions of translatability.

Yet what limits the translatability between "traditional philosophy" and historical materialism is something more intrinsic: it is the new way of philosophizing, the affirmation of the identity of theory and praxis, and the conception of philosophy as philosophy of praxis, that creates a discon-tinuity. However, in this way, Gramsci confirms the possibility of, at least, translating between Hegel's philosophy of history and Marxism. In addi-tion, the difference in the way of conceiving philosophy will not impede, as we will see, other retrievals—namely, other translations.

Looking now at the relationship between the translatability and the historicity of languages, still in Notebook 7, note 2, in a very brief note on the *translatability of scientific and philosophical languages*, Gramsci recalls that Lenin, in 1921, "said and wrote: 'We have not been able to "translate" our language into the "European" languages.'"[64] Gramsci refers to a resolution of the Third Congress of the Communist International that Lenin argued was "entirely based on Russian conditions," and, therefore, as incomprehensible and inapplicable to "foreigners."[65]

All this might be reduced to the problem of the reception of Leninism in various countries. The need of translating then would be the expression of the necessity of adapting a discourse valid *per se*—that is, "universal" for different conditions. Yet, later, in a subsequent note (note 3, Notebook 7), one can see that the horizon widens, in the sense that Gramsci rejects every language that pretends to be universal. The "tendency to construct an Esperanto or *Volapük* of philosophy and of science" depends on the incomprehension of the "historicity of languages and hence of ideologies and scientific opinions." Whoever rejects the historicity of languages and wants to turn away from the necessity of continuously translating is like the one who believes that logic and epistemology "exist in and for themselves, abstracted from concrete thought and from particular concrete sciences," and that language resides "in the dictionaries and grammar books" and technique "detached from work." A universal language (a *Volapük*) of philosophy would naturally annihilate as "delirium" and "prejudice" everything that has been said in other languages, that is, in the historical languages.[66] A "form of thought" that deems itself as "'true,'" Gramsci adds in Notebook 11, in note 45,[67] can (and must) "combat other forms of thought," but it must do it "critically," and with an historicist attitude.

Immediately afterwards, in Notebook 11, Gramsci begins a group of notes entitled "Translatability of Scientific and Philosophical Languages." After having copied the already-cited note on Lenin (Q11§46), he recapitulates a series of already-posited problems and then says:

> Thus it is to be seen whether one can translate between expressions of different stages of civilisation, in so far as each of these stages is a moment of the development of another, one thus mutually integrating the other, or whether a given expression may be translated using the terms of a previous stage of the same civilisation, a previous stage which however is more comprehensible than the given language etc.[68]

Beyond Marx's historiographic method based on the structure-superstructure relationship, Gramsci fully retrieves, in the name of the historicity of languages, the possibility of diachronic translation and the use of terms (and concepts) of previous epochs without any limitations. He rules out any definitive way of speaking, that is, he rules out being able to do without further revisions and continuous translations.

Marxism, initially, appeared to us as a translation of Hegel's philosophy of history and its fundamental terms turned out to be metaphors insofar as they were derived from previous philosophies and were found in different areas of the culture of the time. But eventually Marxism seems to fully coincide with the historicist view of language. Caught in the continuous transition from old into new meanings, in the inevitable margin between "literary form" and content, Marxism will require a continuous engagement with interpretation that is the continuous work of translation.[69]

THE TRANSLATION OF MARX
INTO GENTILE AND CROCE'S TERMS

It is a matter of fact that Gramsci's approach to Marx's texts is influenced by Gentile and Croce's readings of Marx. Gramsci's many references, in the *Notebooks*, to *Materialismo Storico ed Economia Marxistica*[70] [Historical Materialism and Marxist Economics] and to Croce's subsequent interventions are well known. The relationship between Gramsci and Gentile's *Filosofia di Marx* [Philosophy of Marx] is much less studied.[71] Yet it is enough to carefully read Gentile's text to become aware that many crucial elements of Gramsci's interpretation of historical materialism—from his critique of the concept of materialism to the question of "monism"—come from Gentile himself.[72]

Here, however, we will not deal with the subject of Gramsci's idealism. We only want to show how he feels the need to translate Marx's text into another language—into the language of idealism and actualism—in order to make it understandable for himself.[73] Yet the point I want to demonstrate is that the character of Gramsci's work of translation is preeminently relative and provisional. The terms that Gramsci uses to clarify the pivotal points of historical materialism are just conceptual references, from which he later distances himself. The impression that one gets is that, in his work of translation, Gramsci eludes a true conceptual definition of those theoretical pivots. However, Gramsci's nonconclusiveness cannot be due only to the fragmented nature of the *Notebooks* nor to Gramsci's supposed theoretical limits; Gramsci's reflection leads, instead, to the conclusion that a true conceptual definition of those pivotal points is impossible in the framework of the philosophy of praxis.

First, we must examine how, in Notebook 4, Gramsci interprets the statement contained in Marx's 1859 Preface that humans become aware of conflicts on the level of ideology.[74] Then, we must examine what consequences he derives from his interpretation of the Preface with regard to the structure-superstructure relationship. In note 15, entitled *Croce and Marx*, Gramsci says, "The most interesting point to examine concerns 'ideologies' and their value." The superstructures for Marx are not "appearances and illusions" as Croce claims; they "are an objective and operative reality."[75] According to Gramsci, the proof is the following: "Marx explicitly states that humans become conscious of their tasks on the ideological terrain of the superstructures, which is hardly a minor affirmation of 'reality.'" Yet, so far, Gramsci has not explained how and in what sense Marx's statement allows us to see the structure-superstructure relationship. Gramsci only says that the superstructures have a "concrete value" in Marx and that there is an essential connection between structure and superstructure. This connection is not clarified by the parallel made by Gramsci: "If humans become conscious of their task on the terrain of superstructures, it means that there is a necessary vital connection between structure and superstructures, just as there is between the skin and the skeleton in the human body."[76]

After some considerations, which have a provisional or nondecisive character,[77] in note 37, Gramsci deals with this subject starting from the question on the *objectivity of knowledge*. Gramsci cites again the sentence of Marx's 1859 Preface and asks himself: is the consciousness human beings gain on the terrain of ideology "limited solely to the conflict between material forces of production and the relationships of production—as Marx's text literally states—or does it apply to all consciousness, that is, to all knowledge"?[78] Gramsci's interpretation naturally follows the latter direction from which springs an extremely dense and implicit reasoning that it is worth referring to in its entirety:

> How is "monism" to be understood in this context? It is obviously neither idealistic nor materialistic "monism," neither "Matter" nor "Spirit," but rather *"historical materialism,"* that is to say, concrete human activity (history): namely, activity concerning a certain organized "matter" (material forces of production) and the transformed "nature" of man. Philosophy of the *act* (praxis), not of the "pure act" but rather of the "impure"—that is, the real—act, in the most secular sense of the word.

First of all, Gramsci takes for granted a certain "monism" that in some way emanates from the structure-superstructure relationship because only in this way can he understand the historical process. Gramsci needs this concept (derived from the reading that he is critical of, and which is part of his cultural heritage) to show a particular type of relationship. That is the relationship between consciousness, or human activity, on the one hand, and "matter" or "nature" on the other. But later, in order to clarify this crucial point, Gramsci has recourse to *the philosophy of the act*. If we want to understand the "philosophy of praxis" in depth, we can call it the philosophy of the act (this is what Gramsci means). But this definition immediately turns out to be provisional; it is an indispensable, conceptual point of reference—so it seems—but it is necessary to detach oneself from it. We must not talk about a pure act but, rather, about an "impure"—namely, concrete (i.e., historical)—act.[79]

This line of reasoning ends in the next note, note 38, where he goes back to Marx's statement "that humans become conscious of the fundamental conflicts on the terrain of ideologies." According to Gramsci, Marx's statement has an "organic" value—namely, is an "epistemological" and not a "psychological" and "moral thesis."[80] Gramsci never truly explains this difference. What he might want to say, however, is evidently that subjectivity, namely consciousness, has a nonderived character with respect to the objective conditions. One should be able to start from the subject as well as from the object, that is, from consciousness as well as reality, in explaining (in a unified way) the historical process.

Let us now take up the problem of the unity of process and of its distinctions. In Q7§2, Gramsci says that the theory of structure and superstructure does not reintroduce a "theological dualism," as Croce maintains. The "detachment" between structure and superstructure is dialectical as well as the detachment "between thesis and antithesis." The superstructure "reacts dialectically to the structure."[81] If so, however, Gramsci says, Marx "affirms in 'realistic' terms, a negation of the negation"; this is a movement that warrants "the unity of the process of the real." Hence, Gramsci appeals to Croce's theory of distincts even though he doesn't agree with the expression "dialectic of distincts." The conception structure-superstructure does not lead to the "fragmentation [*disgregazione*] of the process of reality"[82]; therefore, one can speak of "distinction" in the same way that Croce speaks of distinctions between the "activities of the spirit." After all, Croce himself has been accused of the "fragmentation of the process of reality" by "the followers of Gentile."[83]

Yet it seems that a more radical translation is needed: the concept of "historical bloc," through which Gramsci designates the indissoluble unity of structure and superstructure, must be viewed—he says—as "the philosophical equivalent of the 'spirit' of Croce's philosophy." The "spirit" refers precisely to a unified process, within which all the dialectical oppositions and distinctions can be re-embraced. The "philosophical equivalent" allows us to understand that the causations within the historical bloc do not go one way starting from the material conditions. One must speak of a "dialectical activity and a process of distinction" within the historical bloc, and this "does not mean negating its real unity."[84]

Finally, in note 25, which is about the objectivity of reality, Gramsci affirms that what appears to us as "real" is, at the same time, a historical construction, and vice versa. From this, he derives the courageous conclusion that "the rational and the real become one and the same thing."[85] As he adds, "It seems to me that unless one understanding this relationship, it would be impossible to understand historical materialism, its philosophical position vis-à-vis traditional materialism and idealism, and the importance and significance of superstructures." The structure-superstructure relationship and the unity of the process gain clarity when they are connected to Hegel's *Idea*, which, as it is known, is the synthesis of the rational and the real:

> Notwithstanding what Croce says, Marx did not replace the Hegelian "idea" with the "concept" of structure. The Hegelian idea is [resolved] both in the

> structure and in the superstructures, and the whole [traditional (and not just
> Hegelian)] conception of philosophy is "historicized"; it has been made a reality
> by a different linguistic articulation and therefore by a different philosophy—[if]
> philosophy is taken to mean [a system of] "concepts" concerning reality.[86]

This tormented passage is an example of another radical translation; if,
initially, the unity of the process found its ultimate expression in the philosophy of the act, now the Hegelian idea comes into play, and later it will
be the relationship between "nature" and "spirit," as we will see.[87]

In Q8§61, the structure-superstructure relationship is again explained
in terms of "distinction." As Gramsci says, referring to the problem of the
autonomy of politics, "Croce's approach is based on his distinction of
the moments of the spirit and his affirmation of a moment of practice—a
practical spirit that is autonomous and independent, albeit circularly
linked to all of reality through the mediation of the dialectic of distincts."
However, the concept of distinction can be transferred into the philosophy of praxis, "wherein everything is practice, the distinction will not be
between moments of the absolute spirit but between structure and superstructures; it will be a question of establishing the dialectical position of
political activity as distinction within the superstructures. One might say
that political activity is, precisely, the first moment or first level of the
superstructure."[88]

It can be said that "all of life is politics," but "the whole system of superstructures" can be conceived as a system of "political distinctions." However, here we see Gramsci's explicit and wanted "introduction of the concept of distinction in the philosophy of praxis." The concept of "historical
bloc" will mean a "unity of opposites and of distincts." These distincts will
also introduce themselves in the structure ("technique, science, work, class,
etc."). Everything seems clear, in Gramsci's architecture, but it is not; in fact,
in order to justify the unity of the process in definitive terms, Gramsci must
call the historical bloc a "unity between nature and spirit." In this sense,
the structure ceases to appear as a "hidden god"—a "noumenon"—and to
be opposed to the "superstructures as 'appearances.'"[89]

We have already seen how Gramsci translates Engels's statement about
the worker's movement, the "inheritor of classical German philosophy,"
in terms of an "identification of philosophy with history, action with
thought,"[90] and how he derives, from the *XI Thesis* on Feuerbach, the consequence that philosophy must become "politics"—namely, "practice."[91]

In Q7§35, Gramsci translates Engels's statement in more radically actual-
istic terms: Gramsci enunciates the identity (or "equality"), inside historical
materialism, between "philosophy and politics," that is, between "thought
and action"; this is what the expression "philosophy of praxis" means.
"Everything is political, even philosophy or philosophies . . . and the only

'philosophy' is history in action, life itself." As Gramsci adds, "It is in this sense that one can interpret the thesis that the German proletariat was the heir of classical German classical philosophy."[92]

Yet Gramsci must return to this topic and sensitively modify his own position taking into account Croce's thesis about the *Glosse al Feuerbach* [Glosses on Feuerbach],[93] that "one cannot speak of Marx as a philosopher and therefore one cannot speak of a Marxist philosophy since what Marx proposed was, precisely, to turn philosophy upside down—not just Hegel's philosophy but philosophy as a whole—and to replace philosophizing with practical activity, etc."[94] But how to interpret a unity of theory and praxis in which theory continues to survive as theory? How can theory become practice without becoming annihilated in practice? Gramsci finds himself in a difficult situation. He says that one should "research, study, and critique" the various solutions given to the relationship between theory and practice in the history of philosophy.[95] Here, Gramsci is thinking of the scholastic concept (intellect *"extensione fit practicus"* [*by simple extension becomes practice*]—that is, he is thinking of Leibniz, and of the *verum ipsum factum* [the true and the made are the same] by Vico. Gramsci goes back to Croce's text about the *Glosses* [Theses] and develops it to some extent in Q11§54.[96]

In Q10§31, Gramsci again references Croce's reading of the *Glosses on Feuerbach* in a discourse that focuses on Croce's concept of "religion," which understands "a conception of the world (i.e., a philosophy) with a norm of conduct that conforms to it." Yet, Gramsci asks himself, can a philosophy exist "without a moral will that conforms to it"?[97] How is it possible to conceive the "two aspects"—namely, "the philosophy and the norm of conduct" as "separated from each other"? According to Croce, in the *Thesis on Feuerbach*, Marx "did not so much turn Hegelian philosophy upside down as philosophy in general, every sort of philosophy; and supplanted philosophical by practical activity." Gramsci's answer expresses a much less demanding and radical position with respect to the identification of philosophy and history than what we saw above. This claim is "opposed to 'scholastic,' purely theoretical or contemplative, philosophy." It is in favor of "a philosophy that produces an ethic conformant to it, a will capable of becoming reality, and that is in the last analysis identified in it."[98] As one can see, Gramsci admits this identification only in the "last analysis." *Thesis XI* does not express "a gesture repudiating every type of philosophy," but rather the "irritation towards philosophers and their parrot-like utterances." This thesis is only "the vigorous affirmation of a unity between theory and practice." Gramsci then shifts to Engels's phrase about the proletariat heir—an heir that, according to Croce, "'would rather than carrying on the work of its predecessor, undertake another, *different and opposite in nature*.'" The heir, Gramsci says, on the contrary, continues the work of the proletariat, "since it has deduced from mere contemplation an active will capable of transforming the world." It is true that Gramsci adds, "in this practical activity, there is also contained the 'knowledge,'" but only in the sense that it is laid down in practical activity "is it 'real knowledge' and not 'scholasticism.'"[99] Gramsci is not decisive here. But we can certainly notice how Gramsci's expressions, which echo Gentile's actualism—and even if for only a moment a concept is sharply defined—soon afterwards fail to work. Then Gramsci shifts to Croce's "religion" as a model for the theory-practice relationship.

CONCLUSION

In sum, through his critical work on Marx's text, his recognition of the metaphors, his attempt to connect them to concepts, and his effort to make the theoretical connections of historical materialism understandable by translating them into another language, Gramsci does not reach any definitive solution in terms of "theory."

This does not mean that Gramsci's reading undermines Marx, inviting us to turn our backs on Marxism. On the contrary, it might be the only way of dealing with Marx which is still feasible. One can talk about an active and live relationship with Marx's thought only to the extent that one finds more or less defined problematics in Marx's metaphors which have unspecified limits, but which are still meaningful to us, and to the extent that Marx's terms will turn out to be translatable in some way and that we are interested in translating them.

Yet we have to hint at a basic problem contained in this impossibility of theoretically defining the connections of the philosophy of praxis. Gramsci is aware of the classic objection people make to those who negate philosophy: philosophy cannot be denied without, at the same time, philosophizing and, therefore, reaffirming it.[100] Why didn't Croce refute Marx with this same argument after having accused Marx of having substituted philosophy with practical activity? Why, Gramsci asks himself, did Croce not use "the peremptory argument that philosophy cannot be negated except by engaging in it, i.e. by reaffirming what one wished to deny." The consequence inferred by Gramsci is that Marx does not negate philosophy, that is, he does not properly want to "supplant" philosophy with practice but, rather, he wants to construct a philosophy of praxis. Croce recognized this requirement as valid in the case of Antonio Labriola.[101]

Yet the argument can be proposed again: are the affirmations made in the sphere and from the viewpoint of a philosophy of praxis theoretical or theoretico-practical? To what extent can they be assumed and analyzed in their logical-conceptual aspect?

Should not their truth be searched for elsewhere—namely, in the praxis in which they "realize" themselves, in this historical content they express and in the continuous "translation" that they perform between the concrete and the abstract?

In Q10§41,[102] Gramsci asks himself about the difference between the solution of a conceptual connection in theoretical terms and that solution in historical terms. He asks himself this with respect to the distincts and the opposites and to the relationship that must be posited between the "politico-economic moment" and the "other historical activities." How is a relationship "which is not that of 'implication in the unity of the spirit'" to be defined? Gramsci asks himself, will "a speculative solution of these problems" exist, or is only a "historical one" possible?[103] At first, Gramsci seems to look for it, that is, for a theoretical or logical solution through the confrontation of Croce and Gentile's positions. On the contrary, later, he abandons the two philosophers to their quarrels over the opposites and the distincts because they both have "made Hegel more abstract." To come back to Hegel means again finding the historical content ("the vital and immediate experiences of a most intense historical period")[104] that his philosophy expresses. Thus, the conceptual distinctions reveal themselves as unimportant with respect to that diverse *test of truth* constituted by the translation of the abstract into the historically concrete. For this reason, since, in Hegel, the abstract translates the historically concrete, as we have seen, his philosophy is the premise of the philosophy of praxis in which the reciprocal translation of theory into praxis becomes identification. But if the test of truth consists of shifting to praxis, namely, to history, it is evident that we cannot expect anything *conclusive* on the level of "theory."

An analogous consideration can be made with regard to skepticism. Gramsci is aware that arguing in favor of the appearance (i.e., in favor of the nontruth) of the superstructures cannot be a general affirmation. On the contrary, it can concern only the single superstructures (i.e., single ideologies). To affirm, in general (i.e., as philosophical affirmation), the appearance and the nontruth of ideologies would mean affirming the appearance and the nontruth of the people making the argument. This would be self-refuting skepticism. But the assessment of the other ideologies is, for Gramsci, a theoretico-practical one—namely, a rather "practical act," not a "philosophical act," as he says in Q11§50.[105] The same goes for his position: it must be maintained as "true" (in quotes in Gramsci) because, otherwise, one would slip into "skepticism" or agnosticism, "but it can be a specifically *theoretical* affirmation of one's own 'truth'": the "speculativity," Gramsci says, in the philosophy of praxis is brought back "to its correct limits" negating that it is the "essential character of philosophy."[106] However, if the affirmation of a given "truth" is not specifically theoretical, but rather theoretico-practical, that is, inseparable from a will of historical affirmation, one will be unable to clarify any theoretical conceptions as such (keeping their logical form, their essence) unless they are translated almost instantly into different, "concrete," historical-practical problems.

NOTES

1. In paragraph 71, Wittgenstein says, "Is it even always an advantage to replace an indistinct picture by a sharp one?" If we compare the concept to an area, we can't say that it has "vague boundaries." You cannot tell somebody "Stand roughly there" without tracing drawing some sort of "boundary." The sharp image, the neatly defined concept that one, when drawing "a sharp boundary" (§76), cannot substitute for the blurry image, the faded and undetermined concept that occurs in our language games. Ludwig Wittgenstein, *Philosophical Investigations*, trans. G. E. M. Anscombe (New York: Macmillan, 1953), 34, 36.

2. Nicola Badaloni. *Il Problema dell'Immanenza nella Filosofia Politica di Antonio Gramsci* [The Problem of Immanence in Antonio Gramsci's Political Philosophy] (Venice: Arsenale, 1988).

3. Badaloni, *Il Problema*, 36, 38–39.

4. Even though this expression means nothing more than a "synthetic and eliptic formula," as Badaloni already stated in his earlier essay, *Il Marxismo di Gramsci* (Turin: Einaudi, 1975), 134.

5. Badaloni, *Il Problema*, 22–23.

6. Badaloni, *Il Problema*, 7.

7. Badaloni, *Il Problema*, 38.

8. Biagio de Giovanni, "Il Marx di Gramsci" [The Marx of Gramsci], in *Marx oltre Marx*, ed. Biagio de Giovanni and Gianfranco Pasquino (Bologna: Cappelli, 1985), 13.

9. de Giovanni, 14–16.

10. de Giovanni, 20–21.

11. Antonio Gramsci, *Further Selections from the Prison Notebooks*, ed. and trans. Derek Boothman (Minneapolis: University of Minnesota Press, 1995), 318–19, hereafter cited as FSPN. There is a list of abbreviations on pages ix–x. Q10II§60. [To facilitate locating passages in various translations and anthologies, we use the standard method of providing the notebook (*Quaderno*) number—in this case 10, part II—followed by the section number, §. See the introduction, page 12, for discussion. We will indicate the English translation, if used.]

12. We will not deal with the problem of the new function and sense that some notes assume in the new contexts, namely, this sphere concerning Gramsci's engagement with Croce (Notebook 10) and in the thoroughly structured project ordered in sections of an "Introduction to the Study of Philosophy" [*Introduzione allo studio della filosofia*] that constitutes Notebook 11. On the chronology of the three series of "Notes on Philosophy," about the development of the "rubrics" and of the themes, see Gianni Francioni, *L'Officina Gramsciana* (Naples: Bibliopolis, 1984).

13. I refer back to Valentino Gerratana's note about the circumstance regarding Gramsci's previous use and recent (critical) rereading of Bukharin's *Manual* (the

complete title of which is *The Theory of Historical Materialism: A Popular Manual of Sociology*). Antonio Gramsci, *Quaderni del Carcere*, ed. Valentino Gerratana (Turin: Einaudi, 1975), 2539.

14. The direct antecedent is constituted by §3, where the argumentation is particularly broad.

15. In rewriting this note, in Q11§27, Gramsci adds "and whose language [*linguaggio*] he often reproduces." [Gramsci's reference is to the language of the great philosophers whom the young Marx studied.]

16. Gramsci is developing his particular Marxian philology, the setting of which—very significantly—is provided in the initial note of this notebook.

17. Q4§11. Antonio Gramsci, *Prison Notebooks*, vol. 2, ed. and trans. Joseph Buttigieg (New York: Columbia University Press, 1996), 153, hereafter cited as PN2.

18. This passage is repeated later in Q11§27, QC, 1437.

19. See in particular §13, that is the first note explicitly referring in title to Bukharin's *Popular Manual* and that sets the fundamental problem of the relationship between "historical materialism" and "philosophical materialism" (Q4§13, PN2, 154).

20. In Q11§28, Gramsci corrects himself by saying "all of language [*linguaggio*] is a continuous process of metaphor." Antonio Gramsci, *Selections from the Prison Notebooks*, ed. and trans. Quintin Hoare and Geoffrey Nowell Smith (New York: International Publishers, 1971), 450, hereafter cited as SPN.

21. Q4§17, PN2, 159.

22. Q4§17, PN2, 159. As Trincia correctly observes referring to the rewriting of this note, "In this passage, one can see Gramsci's tendency to simplify and diminish his theoretical argumentation, which is perceived as necessary and is typical of his way of arguing" (F. S. Trincia, "Gramsci pensatore del l'immanenza," *Critica Marxista* 5 (1989): 95). I would argue that this "simplification" partly depends on his particular way of writing, in the sense that the notes often express a maximum of theoretical engagement with an element that is at the center of attention whereas what is left out can be routine. Later I will develop my considerations of Gramsci's use of some purely indicative concepts.

23. This concept is clearer in the corresponding C-text from which I have already quoted: "The old immanence was superseded, has been superseded, yet, it is always presupposed as a link within the chain of reasoning from which the new is born." Q11§28, QC, 1438–39.

24. Q4§17, PN2, 159.

25. Q7§36, Antonio Gramsci, *Prison Notebooks*, vol. 3, ed. and trans. Joseph Buttigieg (New York: Columbia University Press, 2007), 187, hereafter cited as PN3.

26. Q11§24, "Il linguaggio e le metafore" (Language and Metaphor), SPN, 450.

27. When he rewrites his first draft, Gramsci adds that they are errors that derive from "the absence of a critical and historicist conception of the phenomenon of language." Q11§24, SPN, 451.

28. Q7§36, PN3, 187.

29. As stated in the rewritten passage, Q11§24, SPN, 452.

30. Q4§17, PN2, 159

31. Q11§27, SPN, 465.

32. Q8§171, PN3, 332. Translation altered.

33. Q8§171, PN3, 332–33.

34. Later in Notebook 11, *Quistinio di nomenclatura e di contenuto* [Questions of Nomenclature and Content], Q11§16. SPN 453–54.

35. The complete sentence in the Preface continues with: "so one cannot judge such a period of transformation by its consciousness." Karl Marx, "Preface" to *A Contribution to the Critique of Political Economy*, trans. S. W. Ryazanskaya (Moscow: Progress Publishers, 1970), 21.

36. Q1§113, PN1, 198.

37. As we will see, Gramsci goes back to this argument many times, and this passage is repeated in Q16§20.

38. Marx says that his research led "to the conclusion . . . that the anatomy of this civil society, however, has to be sought in political economy." Marx, "Preface," 20.

39. PN3, 354. Translation altered.

40. FSPN, 315. Translation altered.

41. Here Gramsci only rapidly says: "Recall the other indication related to the development of the juridical sciences." Q8§207, PN3, 354. Translation altered.

42. Q10II§41xii, FSPN, 397.

43. Q11§50, FSPN, 315.

44. Q11§50, FSPN, 315.

45. Q11§50, FSPN, 315.

46. Wittgenstein, Sections 97 and 116, 44 and 48.

47. Q1§44, PN1, 147.

48. Q1§44, PN1, 147. Translation altered. See Gerratana's footnote in QC, 2486, about Gramsci's recurring reference to this passage by Marx. Gramsci's observations on this passage come back in Notebook 19, QC, 2028. Translation altered.

49. Q1§151, PN1, 231.

50. It must be noticed that the correspondence has become reduction, and that the reduction is a synonym of translation, as it turns out clearly in Q4§42, PN2, 192.

51. Q1§44, PN1, 147.

52. Q3§48, PN1, 51.

53. Q4§42, PN2, 191.

54. Q4§42, PN2, 192. Gramsci is inspired by an article Luigi Einaudi wrote in October 1930. In this article he posed questions of translatability from one language to another, and he maintained against Ugo Spirito and the followers of Gentile that the novelty of a theory is often only a question of terminology.

55. Q4§42, PN2, 192.

56. Q4§56, PN2, 232.

57. Q4§56, PN2, 232. Translation altered. Here Gramsci is quoting Engels's phrase that concludes his *Ludwig Feuerbach and the Outcome of Classical German Philosophy*, trans. Clemens Dutt (New York: International Publishers, 1995), 64.

58. Q8§208, PN3, 355.

59. Here Gramsci's reference is to Marx's Thesis 11 on Feuerbach.

60. Q8§208, PN3, 356.

61. It is Q7§1, entitled "B. Croce e il materialismo storico" [B. Croce and Historical Materialism].

62. Q7§1, PN3, 153.

63. Q4§40, PN2, 188. Gramsci comes back to this concept in Notebook 11, at the end of §62, SPN, 407.

64. Q7§2, PN3, 157.

65. PN3, note 3, 498. Regarding Lenin's passage and the circumstances it is related to, see Gerratana's footnote in QC, 2748. This passage comes back in Notebook 11 (QC, 1468).

66. Q7§2, PN3, 157.

67. It is the section about *Esperanto filosofico e scientifico* [Philosophical and Scientific Esperanto], in Q11§45, FSPN, 304. Regarding the sense of Gramsci's anti-Esperantist position and his earlier engagement with Esperanto, see Franco Lo Piparo, *Lingua Intellettuali Egemonia in Gramsci* (Bari: Laterza, 1979), 83 and 131.

68. Q11§47, FSPN, 307.

69. From what I have said one can understand how much Gramsci's historicism is characterized according to linguistic perspective. It is also to be noticed that, shifting from A- to C-texts, Gramsci explicitly refers to the "linguistic phenomenon" (see Q11§24, SPN, 450). Yet at times he places his reference in the background, whereas, at other times, he stresses it: in Notebook 11, in the section entitled "Storia delle terminologie e delle metafore" [History of Terminologies and Metaphors] (§50), Gramsci goes back to Q8§207 and changes "another indication" into "another 'linguistic' indication" (PN3, 354, and FSPN, 316 [both translations altered]); shifting from Q7§25 (*Oggettività del reale* [The Objectivity of the Real]) to Q11§20 (*Oggettività e realtà del mondo esterno* [Objectivity and the Reality of the External World]), Gramsci's mention of Marxism drops the reference "another linguistic expression" (PN3, 176, and SPN, 448).

70. Benedetto Croce, *Historical Materialism and the Economics of Karl Marx*, trans. Michael Curtis (New Brunswick, N.J.: Transaction Publishers, 1981) (first Italian edition, 1899).

71. Gentile, *La filosofia di Marx* [The Philosophy of Marx] (Florence: Sansoni, 1955 [1899]).

72. As A. Del Noce observes in his section "Gentile e Gramsci" in the entry "Il pensiero di Gentile" [The Thought of Gentile], *Enciclopedia 1976–77*, vol. 1 (Rome: Istituto dell'Enciclopedia Italiana, 1977), Gramsci's interest in the *Theses on Feuerbach* and in interpreting Marx's thought also relies on Gentile's earlier interpretation of Marx.

73. Here I am not going back to the question about Gramsci's confrontation with Croce, which must be viewed as Gramsci's need of self-clarification rather than only as a mere procedure of politics of culture. I want to stress the relationship, which must be searched for in Gramsci, between the problematic of immanence conceived as unity of theory and practice, structure-superstructure, and his more fundamental choice in favor of immanence as a moral condition, which he derived from Croce in his formative years, and to which he repeatedly goes back also in his *Notebooks* (see how Croce's fragment on *Religione e Serenità* [Religion and Serenity] reemerges in Q7§1and then in Q10§5 and §41i). I believe that Garin's line of interpretation concerning Gramsci's "close dialogue with Croce" is still valid. He presented his interpretation at the Gramscian Conference in January 1958 (Eugenio Garin, "Gramsci nella cultura italiana," *Studi Gramsciani* [Rome: Editori Riuniti, 1958]),

and subsequently in Eugenio Garin, "La formazione di Gramsci e Croce," *Critica Marxista* 3 (1967): 119–33.

74. Regarding Gramsci's translation of this passage, see Gerratana's footnote, in QC, 2631–32, and his abstract from Gramsci's *Notebooks* on translation, in QC, 2359.

75. Q4§15, PN2, 157.

76. Q4§15, PN2, 157.

77. Here I refer to Q4§20 and §31, in which, respectively, Gramsci both deals with the problem of the "intrinsic" value of ideologies and distinguishes Marx's conception of ideology from that of the seventeenth century.

78. Q4§37, PN2, 176.

79. Q4§37, PN2, 176. It is evident that the distinction between "pure" and "impure" act does not have any specific theoretical value. Yet, certainly, Gramsci resists an identification between his *philosophy of praxis* and Gentile's *philosophy of the act*. Since, indeed, Gramsci's is a provisional and relative "translation," one cannot conclude with Del Noce in favor of a theoretical identification between these two philosophies, which would imply that "theoretical Marxism" has been "put into a checkmate by actualism," Del Noce, 297.

80. Q4§38, PN2, 186.

81. Here Gramsci refers to the third *Thesis on Feuerbach*, in which Marx talks about the education of the educator. Regarding Gramsci's use of this passage, see Gerratana's footnote, in QC, 2748.

82. Q7§1, PN3, 157. Translation altered.

83. Gramsci's choice of Croce-Gentile is still a matter of debate. His relationship with Gentile appears as stronger but less conscious (see Roberto Finelli, "Gramsci tra Croce e Gentile" [Gramsci between Croce and Gentile], *Critica Marxista* 5 [1989]: 77–92). In his essay, which I mentioned above, Del Noce speaks of Gramsci's true subordination to Gentile's actualism, which was "neither wanted nor conscious." However, one cannot agree with Del Noce's statement that there is nothing of Croce in Gramsci; Del Noce, 286 and 295. In reference to Croce, Trincia has used the expression "theoretical uneasiness" (Trincia, 100), which is certainly in Gramsci; yet I think that since the perennial tentativeness of his "theoretical" formulations depends on his habit of *translating*, none of his formulations can be truly understood in themselves, but they always refer to something else.

84. Q7§1, PN3, 157. This discourse comes back in Q10II§40, SPN, 368.

85. Q7§25, PN3, 176.

86. Q7§25, PN3, 176. Words in square brackets were Gramsci's additions.

87. Later in Q11§20, SPN, 448.

88. Q8§61, PN3, 271. Translation altered.

89. Q8§61, PN3, 271.

90. Q4§56, PN2, 232.

91. Q8§208, PN3, 355.

92. Q7§35, PN3, 187.

93. [The reference is to Marx's *Theses on Feuerbach*; see PN3, 620.]

94. Q8§198, PN3, 348.

95. Q8§199, PN3, 349.

96. Q11§54, SPN, 364.

97. Q10II§31i, FSPN, 383. Translation altered. QC, 1269.
98. Q10II§31i, FSPN, 384.
99. Q10II§31i, FSPN, 384.
100. I refer to the Q8§198 discussed above, PN3, 348.
101. He returns to this idea in Q10§31, FSPN, 384.
102. [The original has §31, but this must have been a typo.]
103. Q10§41, FSPN, 399–400.
104. Q10§41, FSPN, 399–400.
105. Q11§50, FSPN, 315–16.
106. Q11§45, FSPN, 304. Translation altered.

11

Translatability, Language and Freedom in Gramsci's *Prison Notebooks*

*Rocco Lacorte**

This chapter is part of a larger project concerning the connection between Antonio Gramsci's concept of "translatability" and his (new) conception of language. At the core of this larger argument is the centrality of translatability to the whole philosophy of praxis—that is, to all the key concepts he develops in his *Prison Notebooks*. This involves the intimate link between Gramsci's view of language and his theory of politics, history and freedom. Here I will focus on one specific part of this much larger argument dealing with how Gramsci uses the concept of "translatability" to theorize the unity of theory and practice insisting that "superstructures" are "objective and operative reality,"[1] and not "false consciousness" or some nondialectical product that can be read off from economic "structures."[2] Gramsci takes this further, actually overturning the very distinction between structure and superstructure except for didactic purposes.[3]

Indeed, it can be derived from Gramsci's note 208 in Notebook 8 (Q8§208) that translatability concerns both practical power (or effectiveness) of theory and theoretical power of practice.[4] In this sense, translatability constitutes, at the same time, the theoretical ground for Gramsci's concept of praxis and theory of *immanence*,[5] both of which concern the worldly character of thought and of the superstructures which he sees the germs of in Marx.[6] This means that translatability constitutes the theoretical

* This chapter developed out of a research project on "Gramsci, Translatability and Language," presented initially in 1997, as part of a seminar at the School for High Philosophical Formation in Matera (Italy). Here I must thank the Gallo family, my mother, the Italian Institute for Philosophical Studies in Naples and its president, Gerardo Marotta, for their support. Moreover, I thank Bettina Rousos and Peter Ives for their great and necessary help with these translations and carrying out this volume.

acknowledgment that *everything* must be interpreted in terms of *praxis* (or human activity), insofar as it *cannot* transcend it.[7] Thus, language also must be viewed as praxis,[8] that is, as a necessary "moment" that praxis needs and produces to elaborate, shape, empower and express itself. That is to say, to make itself "more practical and real"[9] or historically and politically effective. This is an important element in Gramsci's critique of Idealism as well as vulgar economistic Marxism. The implications of this argument are that Gramsci's ultimate goal was the overturning of current praxis.[10] His use of the concept of "translation" shows, among other things, how he sees this struggle requiring more than intellectual critique in the traditional sense, and thus, his reflections on translation and reconceiving language are both deeply philosophical and prosaically practical and common.

Gramsci recommends that when studying an author, in his case Marx, it is necessary to reconstruct the history of his cultural biography. However, Gramsci stresses the fact that the novelty of the author's thought cannot be reduced to its sources.[11] While discussing Marx's use of "sarcasm" as a positive articulation of new conceptions, he notes that Marx's "historicism" coincides with the creation of "a new 'taste' and a new language."[12] One of the several themes within Gramsci's development of the concept of "translatability" is precisely this notion of how Marxist historicism or historical materialism "seeks to establish a break from the old conceptions while waiting for the new conceptions to gain strength" become dominant and replace the old conceptions. This is one of the key motifs that he addresses with his particular conception of "hegemony."[13] Gramsci sees these ideas already implicit in Marx and Lenin but he clarifies them by developing the concept of translation and his approach to language that he derived from his studies in historical linguistics.[14] This chapter will trace out how in Notebooks 10 and 11 Gramsci incorporates many of the threads that he discusses in the earlier notebooks into this conception of translation. Indeed, in Notebook 10, Gramsci argues that Marx's philosophy of praxis is born out of translation, specifically the translation of the speculative form of the idea of immanence of German classical philosophy into the realistic one of the philosophy of praxis "with the aid of French politics and English classical economics."[15] Marx *explicitly* posits thought and knowledge as necessary to transform the world (i.e., as practical and political).

My argument, supported below, is that translatability is conceived as necessary to *activate* what the previous knowledge and way of conceiving have neutralized—in other words, the idea that knowledge can have a revolutionary function. Translation and translatability are not merely linguistic, or intellectual—in an abstract sense. They must involve praxis, political struggle and a transformation of daily life, ways of thinking and ways of producing. But this is also true of Gramsci's understanding of language as not a purely intellectual and abstract way of merely communicating, and, as has received much more attention within Gramscian scholarship, his conception of "intellectual activity" which includes the important role of "traditional intellectuals" but also that of "organic intellectuals."[16]

It is this theme of the intellectuals that Gramsci raises in Notebook 10, but is central to many of the important passages in Notebook 1, where we can see these dynamics involving translation begin to emerge. Already in Notebook 1§44, analyzing the failures of the Italian Risorgimento as represented in his critique of Giuseppe Ferrari, Gramsci uses the concept of "translation." Ferrari's failure, according to Gramsci, was that he "was not able to translate 'French' into 'Italian'"; thus he remained on the "outside of concrete Italian reality." His acuity "created new sects and factions but it left no mark on the real movement."[17] In the same note, Gramsci raises Marx's comparisons in *The Holy Family* between French politics and German philosophy. These comparisons are at the root of his discussion of "translation" in Notebooks 10 (in which he adds English political economy)[18] and 11. While he does not clearly draw out the distinction in Q1§44, he seems to be contrasting the inability of Ferrari to "translate," and thus his lack of effective impact on concrete reality, with the Jacobins who only now appear to be "abstractionists," but at the time the "Jacobins' language, their ideology reflected perfectly the needs of the time."[19] Here he uses the term "language" connecting it with ideology and relating it to the integration of politics, economics and culture or philosophy. As we shall see, his reconception of language is an integral part of his insistence of a truly dialectical relationship of superstructures to economic structures—rather than any reduction of the former to the latter. In the note just prior to this one, 1§43, in discussing different types of periodicals, he writes, "In reality, every political movement creates a language of its own, that is, it participates in the general development of a distinct language, introducing new terms, enriching existing terms with new content, creating metaphors."[20] It is also here where he famously extends the term "intellectuals" to mean more than what he will later label of "traditional intellectuals" to include "the whole social mass that exercizes an organizational function in the broad sense, whether it be in the field of production, or culture, or political administration."[21] Note that he also utilizes the formulation of production, culture and politics that parallels his formulation of economics, philosophy and politics in Q4§46, and German philosophy and French politics in Q1§44. He later combines all these formulations as English economics, German philosophy and French politics.

If, as noted, the Jacobins are a key source that interests Gramsci in these passages, Lenin and his partial success with the Russian Revolution is clearly another. Lenin's realized hegemony in Russia together with the experience of its translation into the Italian factory councils constitute the implicit theoretical ground for Gramsci's critique of Ferrari. This means that Gramsci thinks of translatability in connection with the Leninist experience, and he states it explicitly by Q7§2.[22] He entitled it "Translatability of Scientific and Philosophical Languages." And it reads, "In 1921: organizational issues. Vilici [Lenin] said and wrote: 'We have not been able to "translate" our language into the "European" languages.'"[23] He repeats this note in Q11§46, but in the notes around it, he develops a rich discussion and conception of "translation" and "translatability" as we will see below. Thus, it may very probably be that it has been his reflection on Lenin's practical-theoretical experience, and on its translation-realization in Turin, that has made him progressively acknowledge[24] or further acknowledge the presence in germ and the value of the principle of translatability in the passage of Marx's *The Holy Family*, which he already refers to in the same note (Q1§44) but without associating it explicitly with translatability. Moreover, here translatability already appears as the implicit ground for thinking the deep interconnections between hegemony (or politics), language, ideology and culture.[25] All this confirms that the historical events contemporary to Gramsci constitute an essential part of his innovative philosophical and revolutionary perspective, which cannot and must not be overlooked. Gramsci sees that he and Lenin are somewhat preceded by Marx regarding the use (not the theorization) of what he will later call translatability.

The crucial passage where Gramsci puts this most explicitly and lays the foundation for his rich development of translation is Q10II§6, entitled "Introduction to the Study of Philosophy."[26] This passage lays out four points, labeled i–iv, all of which have been translated in the English-language anthologies, but scattered in a fashion that makes their significance much more difficult to determine. Point i is included in the *Selections from the Prison Notebooks*. Points ii and iv are included in *Further Selections from the Prison Notebooks* in the section entitled "Science, Logic and Translatability," and point iii, a hundred pages later in "The Philosophy of Benedetto Croce."

Point iv, entitled "Translatability of Scientific Language," is the culmination of his succinct discussion in point i of the term "catharsis,"[27] in point ii of "The Subjective Conception of the Reality and the Philosophy of Praxis,"[28] and in point iii, "The Reality of the External World."[29] These three themes are expanded throughout the other notes, especially in Notebook 10. Gramsci is explicitly about this in point iv:

> The notes written under this heading are in fact to be brought together in the general section on the relationship between speculative philosophies and the philosophy of praxis and their reduction to this latter as the political moment that the philosophy of praxis explains "politically." Reduction of all the speculative philosophies to "politics," to a moment of historico-political life; the philosophy of praxis conceives the reality of human relationships of knowledge as an element of political "hegemony."[30]

Thus, this notion of "translatability" is precisely the ground on which he criticizes speculative philosophies, that is, both the traditional subjective (point ii) and objective (point iii) worldviews.[31] These correspond, respectively, to his critiques of Croce and Bukharin, as well as of the Pragmatists and of philosophical and linguistic Esperantism throughout Notebooks 10 and 11.[32]

In point i, Gramsci writes:

> The term "catharsis" can be employed to indicate the passage from the purely economic (or egoistical-passional) to the ethico-political moment, that is the superior elaboration of the structure into superstructure in the minds of men. This also means the passage from "objective to subjective" and from "necessity to freedom." Structure ceases to be an external force which crushes man, assimilates him to itself and makes him passive; and it is transformed into a means of freedom, an instrument to create a new ethico-political form and a source for new initiatives. To establish the "cathartic" moment becomes therefore, it seems to me, the starting-point for all the philosophy of praxis, and the cathartic process coincides with the chain of syntheses which have resulted from the evolution of the dialectic.[33]

Points ii and iii then posit those positions that the philosophy of praxis is to absorb, but more crucially critique and replace. Point ii is just two sentences ending with "the theory of the superstructures is the translation in terms of realist historicism of the subjective conception of reality."[34] This formulation is strictly connected to the one in Q10II§9, discussed above, concerning the "the unitary 'moment' of synthesis" of the philosophy of praxis created through German philosophy, French politics and English economics. This passage adds to the notion that the philosophy of praxis itself was born from a "translation" carried out by Marx, who therefore already possesses the method Gramsci will later develop and name "translatability," as discussed above. Thus, what emerges from the reading of Q10II§6 is that the philosophy of praxis has its own autonomous way of seeing that is based on translatability, which itself is not a simple *parthenogenesis*,[35] but rather, at the same time, the theory of the impossibility of the parthenogenesis of any idea or language, including Marxism, which conceives its own truth as historical and political.[36]

By affirming the reality of human knowledge relationships, that is, the impossibility that they *transcend* practice, politics or ideology, Gramsci highlights, first of all, the importance of catharsis or of the elaboration of structure into superstructures in humans' consciousness. This elaboration makes sense because thought is organized by "specialized" intellectuals through linguistic activity into complex superstructures. This has real and practical effects. That is to say, this cathartic elaboration makes sense for Gramsci only in the light of translatability or of that specific way of seeing

language and thought as immanent—that is, as an "element of political 'hegemony'"—as it has been concretely demonstrated by the Russian
Revolution, in which Marx's theoretical language was translated into the
political one of Lenin by adapting it to the concrete Russian situation and
as Gramsci's use of the term "hegemony" in Q10II§6iv witnesses.

Point i also contains Gramsci's quotation by heart of a passage of Marx's
Preface to the *Critique of Political Economy*, noting that a structure can and
must be elaborated into superstructures on the grounds of given necessary
and sufficient historical, social, economic and cultural conditions that coincide with David Ricardo's concept of a "determined market." Any theoretical elaboration that does without the ascertainment of these conditions
or pretends it can transcend them results in abstractism and speculativism.
Catharsis (i) is the concept the philosophy of praxis opposes to both sub-
jectivism (ii) and objectivism (iii); insofar as, on the grounds of translatability (iv), on the one hand, it accepts that thought as human activity has
a relatively creative value and function with respect to reality, but it rejects
that it can transcend it (point ii); on the other hand, it allows criticizing the
position of vulgar materialism, positivism, objectivism, and determinism
(point iii), because to have knowledge even given necessary and sufficient
conditions is not enough to transform a given reality. As he summarizes in
Notebook 10, part II, §48, "The existence of objective conditions, of possibilities or of freedom is not yet enough: it is necessary to 'know' them,
and know how to use them. And to want to use them. Man, in this sense,
is concrete will, that is, the effective application of the abstract will or vital
impulse to the concrete means which realise such will."[37]

With respect to deterministic positions, catharsis further conceives the
necessity of the elaboration of the structure on the level of the "superstructures in humans' consciousness" as a necessary "moment" for creating a
political consciousness and hence for politically *determining* the course of
history by means of the organization of thought into a "material" force
(through linguistic activity), which (consciously) becomes part of the historical contradictions and takes them up actively giving them a direction.
Translatability brings to the fore the consciousness that working towards
catharsis makes sense, insofar as it explicates the (political) role of (theoretical) language with respect not only to interpreting but also to transforming the world.

Gramsci's reference to hegemony in point iv of Notebook 10, part II,
§6, again constitutes his link to Lenin. This connection together with
Gramsci's experience in Turin must be stressed, to the extent that it is the
real contemporary historical and "experimental ground" on which the
theories Gramsci embraced and developed find their real confirmation
and are concretely observed in action and practice. Gramsci writes that
"Hegel cannot be thought of without the French Revolution and Napoleon,

with his wars, that is, without the vital and immediate experiences of a very intense historical period full of struggles and miseries, when the external world crushes the individuals and makes them touch the ground."[38] Likewise, it can be said that his philosophy of praxis together with its theoretical nucleus (i.e., translatability), which is also the ground for his theory of language, cannot be thought of without the Russian Revolution and its impact on him and the Western countries. Lenin is not only the symbol of a crucial collective historical-political event in which theoretical language has demonstrated its reality and ideological value in practice through translation, but also the one who poses the question of hegemony in terms of "translation" in Gramsci's time.[39]

Lenin's "political" words recalled by Gramsci in Q7§2 and Q11§46, discussed above, imply he was conscious that communist hegemony could not be simply imposed from above, but should be constructed, at the same time, taking into account the different (both economic and historical, social, cultural, linguistic) conditions of the various countries outside Russia in order to build up a true international collective will. Hegemony and "real equality" presuppose the unity of theory and practice. This unity, however, does not exist before it is constructed (that is why one should talk about unification). At first, only the possibility of unity exists in relation to the rise of given conditions within given historical force-relationships. Thus, in the *Notebooks*, Gramsci *theoretically* develops translatability as the consciousness, which was to be gained on the practical ground, of the fact that theories, theoretical languages or heuristic knowledge models, as well as any other language, cannot be abstractly or mechanically transferred from one to another sphere of knowledge relationships.

The result of all this is that Gramsci's concept of superstructures or ideologies is a development and translation of Marx and Lenin's in Q10II§41xii: "Men become conscious of their social position and therefore of their tasks on the terrain of ideologies,"[40] that is, politics. Therefore, superstructures from the perspective of the philosophy of praxis "are an objective and operative reality (or they become such when they are not pure individual machinations)." That is, they "are a necessary moment of the overturning of praxis . . . in order to destroy one hegemony and create another."[41] Gramsci derives the expression "overturning of praxis" from the third of Marx's *Theses on Feuerbach*, in which, against materialistic or positivistic determinism and mechanicism, human activity or thought is said to react against given conditions. Gramsci reinterprets Marx's concept simultaneously according to Lenin's and his own concept and experience of hegemony. This illustrates both the continuity among the three "authors" and of the fact that contemporary historical events are the ground for Gramsci's rethinking of Marx and Lenin or for his translation of their practical-theoretical positions. This, then, is more than an argument about Gramsci's notion of "translation" but includes also a methodological model for how we need to approach Gramsci's writings in our times. They require a further "translation" into the context of our times, both the economic and technological changes of electronic, global, "late" capitalism and also the very different ideological and cultural currents of the twenty-first century.

Moreover it should be emphasized that Gramsci's new idea of realistic immanence coincides with a "new conception of 'necessity' and freedom, etc." and hence of *praxis, language*, etc.[42] This new way of viewing immanence coincides with a new philosophy (i.e., the philosophy of praxis) developed in connection with David Ricardo's concept of the "'tendency law' which leads to scientific definition of the fundamental economic concepts of *homo oeconomicus* and of the 'determined market,'" as Gramsci writes in Q10II§9.[43]

Thus, at this stage of his *Notebooks*, Gramsci is capable of rethinking the concept of "praxis," which he previously defined in Notebook 7, §18, as "the relationship between human will (superstructure) and the economic structure."[44] With this conception of translation he also rethinks the concept of "freedom," that is, the modalities in which human wills or superstructures actively react against a given structure.[45]

Now, Gramsci comes to conceive "praxis" according to the dynamic of the "determined market," which is identified by the Ricardian "hypothetical" method ("let us suppose that . . .")[46] which is made permanent by political, moral and juridical superstructures.[47] On the one hand, Gramsci notes that "necessity exists when there exists an efficient and active *premise*, consciousness of which in people's minds has become operative,"[48] which Gramsci calls "automatism," and discusses "the collaborative and co-ordinated activity of a social group that, following certain principles accepted (freely) out of conviction, works towards certain goals."[49] On the other hand, a process of liberation starts when the (subaltern) social groups who live those principles as extrinsic impositions attempt to implement the "shifting of the base of the automatism" so to construct a "new order" or automatism and "conformism," which Gramsci also calls "historical bloc."

These social groups must create a new "collective will,"[50] a fundamental stage of which consists in constituting a *"spirit of cleavage,"*[51] that is, they must develop their "instinctive" sense of distinction into the consciousness of "their own historical personality."[52] These groups act on the ground of a new "necessity" or "premise," whose theories and ideologies (i.e., languages) appear at the beginning as a critique of the superstructures of the old premise.[53] Their liberation requires that they work to produce a "catharsis," which enables them to concretely engage a struggle for "hegemony."[54] For Gramsci, if a practical movement does not develop its own practice into its own language-ideology it cannot develop its will and its political consciousness—that is, it will be unable to develop its own meaning, position and the goals it needs to achieve with respect to a given social-historical environment. This implies that, for Gramsci, without the "linguistic" moment, a historical movement cannot become a political force, a real dialectical pole that can participate in or start a given concrete dialectical process, in order to practically demonstrate its historical rationality and necessity and to change the world.

This argument concerning Gramsci's use of "translation" then opens a larger set of considerations that go well beyond this chapter. As I have argued, Gramsci's theory of superstructures is based on translatability, and this, in turn, rests on historical circumstances. In his synthesis, language is clearly and explicitly conceived as both *interpretive* and *transformative*,[55] that is, as both necessary to interpret and to transform world. Here interpretation and transformation are very closely linked to translation. Similarly, for Gramsci, the "linguistic" and the "logical" can never be understood only as linguistic and logical in a strict sense. Politics or practice is also, at the same time, a necessary "moment" of the creation of a language and coincides with the activity through which both the *real* meaning and sense of a literal expression is exhibited and has significance. Gramsci's consciousness that language is historical and political coincides with the idea that meanings are not eternal, but constantly part of the hegemonic struggle. Therefore, *the struggle for hegemony is at once a struggle for meaning and sense*—that is, simultaneously a cultural struggle for bringing new meanings to life and keeping them alive (in the face of those forces defending the old ones). At the same time, linguistic struggles (to the extent that they involve rational languages or that they are meant to "demonstrate" their rationality) are always struggles for hegemony.

NOTES

1. I will cite Gramsci's *Prison Notebooks* by giving the notebook number preceded by a Q (Notebook), and then an § prior to the note (or section) number, following the definitive source. Antonio Gramsci, *Quaderni del Carcere*, four volumes, ed. Valentino Gerratana (Turin: Einaudi, 1975), hereafter cited as QC. Where an English translation is used it is cited; otherwise translation is by the author. In this case, Q10II§41xii, Antonio Gramsci, *Further Selections from the Prison Notebooks*, ed. and trans. Derek Boothman (Minneapolis: University of Minnesota Press, 1995), 394–99, hereafter cited as FSPN. A list of abbreviations can be found on pages ix–x.

2. See Q10II§41, FSPN, 403–15; Q8§208. Antonio Gramsci, *Prison Notebooks*, vol. 3, ed. and trans. Joseph Buttigieg (New York: Columbia University Press, 2007), 255–56, hereafter PN3 (the first two volumes will be cited as PN1 and PN2 and were published in 1992 and 1996 respectively); Q15§10, Antonio Gramsci, *Selections from Prison Notebooks*, ed. and trans. Quintin Hoare and Geoffrey Nowell Smith (New York: International Publishers, 1971), 243–45, hereafter cited as SPN; Q15§22, SPN, 364–66.

3. Q7§1, PN3, 153–57; Q10II§41i, FSPN, 403–15; Q15§10, SPN, 243–45; and Q15§22, SPN, 364–65.

4. In Q8§208, entitled "The [Mutual] Translatability of National Cultures," Gramsci writes, "philosophy must become 'politics' or 'practice,'" meaning that these last two terms cannot be taken only in a strict sense; PN3, 355. He explicitly refers to one *aspect* of translatability—that is, the real effectiveness of theoretical language, whereas in what follows this sentence, by writing "in order to continue to be philosophy," he refers to another aspect of translatability (i.e., the one concerning the knowledge power of practice). This aspect is also the one Gramsci writes in Q10II§12 about Lenin's realized hegemony; SPN, 365–66. See also Q4§46, PN2, 196–97.

5. See also Fabio Frosini, *La Religione dell'Uomo Moderno*, chapter 6 (Rome: Carocci, 2009), which also contains some of his previous essays, including the one in this volume. See also Lichtner in this volume, pages 187–211.

6. See, for example, Q10II§9, SPN, 399–402, and below.

7. In Q7§35, Gramsci writes, "*Everything is political*, even philosophy or philosophies (see the notes on the character of ideologies), and *the only 'philosophy' is history in action, life itself.*" PN3, 187, emphasis added. See also Q11§59, SPN, 345–46.

8. See also Domenico Jervolino, "Croce, Gentile e Gramsci sulla Traduzione," in *Croce Filosofo*, vol. 2, ed. Giuseppe Cacciatore, Girolamo Cotroneo and Renata Viti Cavaliere (Soveria Mannelli: Rubbettino Editore, 2003), 431–41.

9. Q15§22, SPN, 364–65, and see also Q15§10, SPN, 243–45.

10. For example, QII§41xii, FSPN, 405–6.

11. Q11§27, SPN, 463.

12. Q1§29, PN1, 118. In the rewriting of this passage, the C-text, Gramsci adds, as "means of intellectual struggle." Q26§5, QC, 2301. For an explanation of A- and C-texts, see introduction, page 5.

13. Q1§29, PN1, 118.

14. There is a growing literature that supports this point in nuanced ways as evident in many of the chapters of this volume, especially chapters 1–5, but the classic reference is Franco Lo Piparo, *Lingua, Intellettuali, Egemonia in Gramsci* (Bari: Laterza, 1979).

15. Q10II§9, SPN, 399–400.

16. Q4§49, PN2, 199–210, and Q12§1, SPN, 5–14.

17. Q1§44, PN1, 140.

18. In Q4§46 (October–November 1930), Gramsci includes the concept of "economics" together with "politics" and "philosophy." Gramsci adds "English political economics" to French politics and German philosophy only from the beginnings of 1932, in Notebooks 8 and 10, when he formulates the hypothesis that David Ricardo's "tendency law" and "homo oeconomicus" would have a central role in the genesis of the philosophy of praxis.

19. Q1§44, PN1, 147.

20. Q1§43, PN1, 126.

21. Q1§43, PN1, 133.

22. See also Q3§48, PN2, 48–52.

23. PN3, 157.

24. See Q4§42, PN2, 191–92, and, above all, Q5, part 5 (§46–49), FSPN, 306–13.

25. Later on, in Q10II§41x, Gramsci will explicitly write that, in Marx, one can find "contained in a nutshell the ethico-political aspect of politics or theory of hegemony and consent, as well as the aspect of force and of economics." FSPN, 399. All this is already implicit in Gramsci's connection of Marx's passage to his concept of hegemony in Q1§44.

26. Indeed, reading Q10II§6 together with Q8§208, Q10II§9 and part 5 (§46–49) of Notebook 11 allows one to grasp the crucial role of translatability in Gramsci's philosophy.

27. See SPN, 366–67.

28. See FSPN, 306.

29. See FSPN, 402–3.

30. FSPN, 306.

31. In Q10II§9, Gramsci's implicit reference to objectivism and neo-objectivism (i.e., also to Buhkarin) is expressed by the expression "speculative determinism." He writes that the "the necessary laws of regularity"—that is, the "laws of tendency" are "not laws in the naturalistic sense or that of speculative determinism, but in a 'historicist' sense, valid, that is, to the extent that there exists the 'determined market.'" SPN, 401. The philosophy of praxis insists that "[i]n the economy the element of 'interference' is the human will, the collective will, differently oriented according to the general conditions of life of men, i.e. 'tending' or organised differently." Q10II§57, FSPN, 190. Ricardo's laws, which had an impact on Marx, implied organized collective will as the ground of his "determined market." Yet Gramsci sees how Marx extends Ricardo's "to the whole of history" giving birth to a new and original conception of the world. Q10II§9, SPN, 401.

32. See Gramsci's rewriting of some lines of Q7§1, PN3, 153–54, in Q11§47, FSPN, 307.

33. Q10II§6iv, SPN, 366–67.

34. FSPN, 306.

35. Q6§71, Antonio Gramsci, *Selections from Cultural Writings*, ed. David Forgacs and Geoffrey Nowell-Smith, trans. William Boelhower (Cambridge, Mass.: Harvard University Press, 1985), 178, hereafter cited as SCW.

36. See Q11§62, SPN, 404–7.

37. SPN, 360.

38. Q10II§41x, FSPN, 399–401.

39. See Q11§46, FSPN, 306.

40. FSPN, 395. In the same note Gramsci adds, "The philosophy of praxis is itself a superstructure, on the terrain of which specific social groups become conscious of their own social being, their own strength, their owns tasks, their own becoming. In this sense, what Croce asserts is correct. . . . The philosophy of praxis is 'history made or in the making.'"

41. FSPN, 395.

42. The "etc." would seem to mean that for Gramsci, this new philosophy is *also* a new conception of "language"—that is, it contains a new way of conceiving language rooted in its autonomous practical-theoretical principles, which is not simply the one of linguistics.

43. SPN, 401.

44. Q7§18, PN3, 170.

45. See Q7§1, PN3, 153–57, and its C-text, Q10II§41i, FSPN, 403–4 and 406–15.

46. Q8§128, PN3, 309. See also Q10II§8, FSPN, 179–80.

47. Q11§52, SPN, 410.

48. Q11§52, SPN, 412–13.

49. Q10II§8, FSPN, 179.

50. See, for example, Q1§43, PN1, 125–36; and Q8§195, PN3, 346–47.

51. See Q3§49, PN2, 53. The "spirit of cleavage" is a "moment" of the cathartic process, which also coincides with the "passage from necessity to freedom"; see above discussion of Q10II§6i.

52. See, for example, Q3§46, PN2, 44–47; Q3§48, PN2, 48–52; Q3§49, PN2, 52–53; Q11§12, SPN, 323–43, and a consistent thread throughout Notebook 25.

53. See, for example, Q8§195, PN3, 346–47.

54. For example, in Q8§227, PN3, 373: "There is a struggle between two hege-monies—always. Why does one of them triumph? Because of its intrinsic 'logical' qualities?" See also Q7§12, PN3, 165: "Conformism has always existed; today there is a struggle between 'two conformisms,' that is, a struggle for hegemony."

55. For example, in Q29§1, devoted to the study of grammar, Gramsci confirms that this study has a political value as such: "Grammar is 'history' or 'a historical document': it is the 'photograph' of a given phase of a national (collective) language [linguaggio] that has been formed historically and is continuously developing, or the fundamental traits of a photograph. The practical question might be: what is the purpose of such a photograph? To record the history of an aspect of civilisation or to modify an aspect of civilisation?" SCW, 179–80.

III

POLITICS, THEORY
AND METHOD

12

Language and Politics in Gramsci

*Francisco F. Buey**

> The whole of language [*linguaggio*] is a continuous process of metaphor, and the history of semantics is an aspect of the history of culture; language is at the same time a living thing and a museum of fossils of life and civilisations.
>
> Antonio Gramsci, 1932–1933[1]

1

Gramsci's preoccupation with the question of language and linguistic problems has always been constant from his earlier writings until his last notes in the *Prison Notebooks* in 1935 and his last letters. This preoccupation is well enough documented for the period of *L'Ordine Nuovo* as well as in the case of the *Notebooks* and the letters from prison. Some interpreters of his work, such as Franco Lo Piparo and Tullio De Mauro, have stressed at various times the importance that the young Gramsci's education as a linguist and philologist at the University of Turin had for the elaboration of his entire work and for configuring his philosophical and political thought.

* Translation from "Lingua, Linguaggio e Politica in Gramsci," in *Marx e Gramsci: Memoria e Attualità*, ed. Giuseppe Petronio and Marina Paladini Musitelli (Rome: Manifesto Libri, 2001), 197–211. The publication was supported by Istituto Gramsci del Friuli Venezia-Giulia, International Gramsci Society and Istituto Italiano per gli Studi Filosofici. Originally translated from Spanish to Italian by Antonino Firenze. Translated by Rocco Lacorte with assistance by Peter Ives. See introduction concerning the Italian words *lingua* and *linguaggio*, which are conflated in this translation of the title.

Valentino Gerratana has put forth the hypothesis that Gramsci's historical philological reflections, and in particular, his conception of language as a conforming activity—conforming on one hand to common feelings and beliefs and on the other to social fractures—had a decisive importance not only for his elaboration of a theory of culture based on the idea of a moral and intellectual reform but also in the elaboration of the theory of hegemony which is the central nucleus of Gramsci's mature political philosophy.

I believe that today it is particularly interesting to stress again such aspects of Gramsci's work: his will to communicate beyond specialist jargon and beyond the formulas established within the realm of a common and determined tradition of thought.

I think this for two reasons. First, because it seems to me that if Gramsci, among all Marxist theorists, is better known and has more to tell us, this is due not only to what he said and wrote but also to *how he said it and the form in which he said it.*

Second, because the search for an adequate language [*linguaggio*] through which one can establish a dialogue between different generations that share a common emancipatory tradition is perhaps the main *pre*-political task of the left if it is to dignify its name at the end of the twentieth century.

In effect, the fight to give meaning to the words of one's own tradition and the fight to name things is probably the first autonomous act of the fight among ideas during the end of the twentieth century. The Marxist socialist tradition finds itself in a situation similar to the one Girolamo Savonarola alludes to when, at the end of an earlier century, at the origin of European modernity, before the degeneration of official Christianity, he proposed to continue utilizing the key words of the Christian tradition, but to recuperate the concrete meanings that they once had and that they maintained for a small minority of people.

Along these lines of reasoning, one can observe that Gramsci left us a suggestive reflection that could usefully be applied to language [*linguaggio*] and to the metaphors utilized by the founders of the philosophy of praxis. "Language is always metaphorical," Gramsci said in this context (Q11§28); even though it is not convenient to exaggerate the meaning of the term "metaphor" by arguing that every discourse is necessarily metaphorical, one can still say that "the present language is metaphorical with respect to the meanings and the ideological content which the words used had in the previous periods of civilization."[2]

This observation is also valuable in determining the meaning of the terms of the philosophy of praxis, such as "civil society," "ideology" and "hegemony" (not to mention "socialism" or "material democracy"), that are part of the current language of social sciences and of educated citizens in our epoch.

There is no doubt that Gramsci used some of these words (mainly "ideology") with a different meaning than they had in Marx's work. But undoubtedly, shifting to current discourse and to the handbooks of political sociology today, these terms have changed in meaning. The expression "civil society," for example, has acquired so many different connotations in political and sociological language that one cannot escape a feeling of uneasiness hearing or seeing it ambiguously attributed to Gramsci.

Thus, the problem is what to do, that is, how to operate, starting from such observations. Gramsci discards two contemporary and historically pervasive solutions: the utopia of fixed and universal languages, and the tendency of [Vilfredo] Pareto and the Pragmatists to abstractly theorize language as a cause of error. These solutions that looked for a resolution to the problem in question (that is, the ambivalence between daily and diverse language usage, the words of "the simple people,"[3] on one hand, and the language of "educated" intellectuals, on the other) through a specific "dictionary" or through the creation of a pure (formal or mathematical) and universally usable, and used, language.

Regardless of what one thinks of the epistemological integrity of Pareto and Russells's attempt to find languages in which terms are used univocally—and even separately from what one thinks of the (more recent) extension of those attempts to political science—it seems evident that such a pretense escapes the realm of concrete political activity. In fact, in this realm, one has to become acquainted with the impossibility of overcoming ambiguities, equivocations and metaphors. This, at least, is Gramsci's point of view. Gramsci's perspective implies the search for a nonformal or nonformalized, and in some sense metaphorical, language in which intellectuals and people that fight for a new culture can understand each other despite belonging to distinct generations.

To put it a different way, the renewal of the Marxist and socialist tradition, today, lacks any considerable effort being put toward the communication and understanding between generations, of diverse experiences and different views: an effort of linguistic innovation similar to the one made by Gramsci himself, first, in *L'Ordine Nuovo* and, subsequently, in his prison years.

The characteristics of this type of Gramscian effort can be synthesized by specifying, on the one hand, that it is methodologically innovative, on the level of form, in the way it presents one of the traditions of the (Marxist) workers' movement and, therefore, for the way it interprets Marx's work. On the other hand, on a substantial level, this effort is also innovative with respect to the elaboration of socialist thought—a body of thought that comes from the same tradition, but that, in reality, focuses in an unprecedented way on new socioeconomic and cultural problems, which the classics of Marxism neither considered nor foresaw. The form in which

Gramsci shapes his discourse, the language that he invents in order to interpret Marx and to think in continuity with Marx, but at the same time being innovative, is indeed fundamentally dialogic. I would like to stress this here. Gramsci's is neither the tendentiously "architectonic" dialectical form used by Marx in the *Critique of Political Economy* and in *Capital* nor is it the type of "system" drafted by Engels in *Anti-Duhring* and in his reflection on the shift from utopian socialism to scientific socialism; nor is it the type of "tract" favorable to Bukharin; nor the almost always instrumental form adopted by Lenin in the majority of his works; nor the "essay" form that imposes a posterior "theoretical" Marxism. The form of Gramsci's discourse is, above all, a simultaneous or deferred dialogue with three interlocutors: with the classics of the tradition (in order for him to specify their particular innovation), with the contemporaries close to him (in order to decide, if a decision is possible, what the preoccupations and problems of the moment are) and with himself, but without conceit, starting from the reconsideration of the experiences he had since 1917.

2

The importance Gramsci gave to language and speech during his entire life can be detected and studied from different spheres. In this chapter I will mainly refer to three of these spheres, especially focusing on the *Prison Notebooks*. The first that must be taken into account is—naturally—that from which Gramsci draws his special considerations of language and its history, of grammar, of linguistic problems, and of Italian culture and the literature connected to these problems. As is well known, as early as his initial research plan in prison—the one where Gramsci announces, with a certain irony, that he would like to create something *für ewig*—namely, in an disinterested way, appropriating Goethe's conception recuperated from [Giovanni] Pascoli; he intended to reserve a specific section for these reflections. Not only was the second subject of his plan "nothing less" than a study of comparative linguistics, but also the other subjects (the study of the formation of a public spirit in nineteenth-century Italy, the transformation of the theatrical taste starting from the work of Pirandello and the elaboration of popular taste in literature) appear directly connected to interests of a philological nature.

Although Gramsci modified his plan in subsequent years for different reasons and after a certain moment he even declared not to have a plan of systematic study anymore, his desire for "squeezing juice from a dried fig"[4] undoubtedly allowed him to lay out at least one part of his "disinterested" project. His illness, the impossibility of having the appropriate scientific and academic materials available in prison, his political and sentimental problems and the constant effort of introspection of his later years convinced Gramsci that, given his situation, he could really only carryout a *substantially polemical* work. Through his introspective exercise Gramsci shored up the unity between the Socratic "know thyself" and making virtue out of a necessity, being conscious that this was the only thing he could really do under his conditions:

> Perhaps it is because my entire intellectual formation has been of a polemical order; even thinking "disinterestedly" is difficult for me, that is, studying for study's sake. Only occasionally, but rarely, does it happen that I lose myself in a specific order of reflections and find, so to speak, in the things themselves enough interest to devote myself to their analysis. Ordinarily, I need to set out from a dialogical or dialectical standpoint, otherwise I don't sense [*senso*] any intellectual stimulation. . . . I don't like to cast stones in the darkness; I want to feel a concrete interlocutor or adversary; in my family relations too I wish to carry on dialogues.[5]

Yet, from what can be seen in the *Notebooks*, Gramsci's final realization of his project results in something more than a simple polemic. Certainly, it results in something more than a mosaic of fragmentary reflections—as it has been sometimes said, too hastily. Some examples of what is more than a simple polemic in Gramsci's *Notebooks* are the notes on the following: the mobility and stratification of language; the tension between living grammar and normative grammar; the relationships existing between the expressive or stylistic choices and the forms of culture and social life; or those notes on the possibilities of the translatability of languages and cultural formations. In all this, there is a red thread that is tied to the question of the formation of a new culture—which is the culture of subaltern classes—and to the fight for hegemony, a red thread that goes beyond a polemic form and the fragmentation of the Gramsci's notes. In a certain way, one can say that Gramsci's project unfolds itself from a conjunction between his academic knowledge as a philologist and a historian of language [*lingua*], and the experience he acquired as a communist political leader vis-à-vis the study of the history of Italy and of the critique of culture. The result of this is, considering the *Notebooks* on the whole, a draft of political sociology of the present drawn from an explicit viewpoint and with great consciousness of what history is. Gramsci's initial historical-critical considerations of the question of language [*lingua*] and intellectual classes or of the diverse types of grammar are connected back to his consideration of the politics of language,[6] politics of culture and sociology of the present. These reflections focus substantially on the reorganization in the present of a cultural hegemony:

> Every time the question of the language [*lingua*] surfaces, in one way or another, it means that a series of other problems are coming to the fore: the

formation and enlargement of the governing class, the need to establish more intimate and secure relationships between the governing groups and the national-popular mass, in other words to reorganize the cultural hegemony. Today, we have witnessed various phenomena which indicate a rebirth of these questions.[7]

Thus, besides ascertaining that Gramsci's consideration of the [national] language [*lingua*], language usage [*linguaggio*] and literature in relation to hegemony can be found at the beginning (in the first notebook, begun February 8, 1929) and at the end of the *Notebooks* (in the "Notes for an Introduction to the Study of Grammar," written in 1935), one must say that the kind of consideration he makes continues to be of great relevance, particularly in countries such as ours [Italy], where the question of language [*lingua*] (or, better, of languages [*lingue*], of the dialectal and of the cultures that encounter and clash) became, for some time, one of the main themes of public debate. Even with respect to this, Gramsci's main lesson is a methodological one, considering methodology in a wide—philosophical—sense. Avoiding making such a pre-political question into an instrumental political theme (which is precisely what is happening in the controversies on languages and cultures in recent times), Gramsci was able to intuit very well the political and politico-cultural dimensions that are hidden—or that are not always declared—in each project of linguistic normalization (when the question of the language surfaces) starting from the variations of normative grammar. Today, in the epoch of multiculturalism, but also of globalization and of a new onset of nationalisms and of particularisms, we can confirm daily what is at stake in these polemics that seem, at first sight, to be only linguistic, philological, sociolinguistic or culture-anthropological, is, actually, at the same time, the struggle for (cultural, economical and political) hegemony between the distinct fractions of the national bourgeoisies, the distinct bourgeoisies of the multinational and multilinguistic states, and the bourgeoisies and the middle classes of states composed of important dialectal variants.

In this sense, it seems to me that bringing the keen notes of Gramsci on "Americanism" together with his considerations regarding the political-cultural background of the historical projects on linguistic normativity or with his observations on the national popular can greatly help the rational understanding of what is happening in our geographical context—which is not a good sign. It might also be said that the pendulum of history has changed direction: Gramsci evolved from the autonomism of his youth to progressively stressing the importance of the "national-popular" with internationalist intentions, though respecting differences. Whereas, today, partly as a reaction to the globalization and the cultural standardization that it implies, we move toward an identification of the "national-popular" with autonomism (in diverse political versions: the regionalist, nationalist, separatists and so on).

3

The second sphere that is relevant to this chapter is the one concerning the considerations that Gramsci made in his correspondence with Julia and Tania on languages [*lingue*] as a means of communication. From this viewpoint, it can be said that the problem of language and of expressive possibilities becomes almost obsessive for Gramsci in his communication with Julia Schucht.

Gramsci's obsession has two dimensions: a private and sentimental dimension which is tied to the effort of keeping a "true correspondence" and an "authentic dialogue" alive between persons that love each other but do not always understand each other, and a political one. We face the relationship between an Italian man who has difficulties in reading and understanding the Russian language and a Russian woman who expresses herself by writing in Italian with some difficulty. If the communication between two such persons also presents some difficulties in normal circumstances, the difficulties become acute because of the distance (Gramsci in Italy, Julia in Moscow), the mutual physical and psychological illnesses, and the prison (which does not allow open and frank discussions about anything, neither about sentiments nor about politics).

One understands why, in such conditions, Gramsci had insisted many times on the importance of Julia expressing herself with clarity and precision. One also understands why, sometimes, Tania's well-intended mediations would irritate him. And, at least partially, one can understand Gramsci's specific obsession for reading the same letter more than once to grasp all the nuances contained in just one bit of information or one affirmation by Julca.[8]

This obsession for the language [*linguaggio*] of interpersonal communication so evident in Gramsci's correspondence would become, in some moments of his prison life, a true neurosis. It is not possible to maintain a sentimental long-distance relationship between two people who have children together through the philological and, at times, pedantic pickiness that appear in Gramsci's letters. In any case, such pickiness must be considered one of the exemplary elements of the tragedy of the person, Gramsci, in prison and of Julca in Moscow.

Given that this issue is delicate and requires that one deals with it delicately, I will stop here. Not without quickly adding, however, that the banality of the tragedy of Gramsci, the man, in his relationship to Julia Schucht, that we witnessed, in these last years, especially in Italy, produces nausea and takes away the will to continue writing. Before this spectacle that now, as I can see, appears in the pages of the newspapers, there is nothing left to do but repeat the biting and slightly melancholic words written by Valentino Gerratana in 1992: "When only a simulacra of culture exists, as in this case, there can not be a true dialogue, neither with Gramsci, nor with anyone else."

4

Identity or locality in politics which overlap with the sentimental relation-ship complicate the communication between people who base the dignity of culture on its capability of transforming humans and their real relation-ships. In effect, in the years of the Third International, linguistic precision and an appropriate use of words would be doubly important between peo-ple who, though sharing the same objectives, were obliged to take imme-diate decisions with regard to the divisions between friends and acquain-tances. In such conditions, even jokes and irony had to be measured.

One of the negative consequences of the Russianization of the European communist parties—which Lenin already perceived in the Fourth Congress of the Third International and to which Gramsci opportunely refers—is that such a process obliges the understanding of themes and national ques-tions that are sometimes difficult to translate through different categories and words. The division that, in this period, was coming to light between a "Russian Marxism" and a Marxism that was called "Western" has its pre-political origin in a problem of translation. This problem concerned the translation of Marx's view of history and of humanity, which he elaborated in relation to class struggle in Germany, France and England. But it had to be translated into Russian in a manner that the peasants could understand it. This division has its origin also in the fact that Marx's view was later retrans-lated from Russian (in Leninist terms) into German, English or Italian.

For an intellectual, who knew Marx's work fairly well, even for an intel-lectual like Gramsci who greatly appreciated Lenin's work, this double process of translations and retranslations from Russian and into Russian, of relatively known socioeconomic and cultural problems, could have been as-sessed as equivalent to a "betrayal" [of the original]. Since, in a certain way, and even in this case, *il traduttore è traditore* [the translator is a traitor].

In effect, in analyzing the political controversies from 1924 to 1936, not enough attention has been given to the preliminary problem of the defini-tion of the properly political: namely, could the interlocutors for Russian, German, Hungarian, Italian, French, Polish, Spanish and so forth really understand the key words of the discussion in the same sense and accord-ing to the same values? Not to mention, moreover, when, in this context, people start speaking of the Chinese Revolution with terms and concepts of French political language [*linguaggio*] translated from Russian.

I propose that Gramsci—who devoted some very incisive paragraphs of the *Notebooks* to the problem of the translatability of languages,[9] who wanted to devote himself to translation and who had serious problems of communication even with his prisonmates discussing the strategy of the Third International—was obviously sensitive to the question that might be entitled "Babel in the Internationalism of the Third International," namely, how to construct a common language [*linguaggio*] understandable by people speaking many languages [*lingue*] and belonging to different nationalities, knowing that while, theoretically, workers should not have a homeland, as a matter of fact they do have one (as World War I proved).

There is no doubt that when Gramsci proposes to himself the problem of the translatability of scientific and philosophical languages [*linguaggi*], what he has in mind is precisely the problem of the national traditions in the frame of the International. Moreover, this reflection comes precisely from one of Gramsci's citations of Lenin, according to whom they did not know how to "translate our language [*lingua*] into the European languages."[10]

The problem of translating an internationalist strategy shared by workers and intellectuals who speak different languages [*lingue*]—and who belong to different nationalities—into a common language [*linguaggio*] is already present in the first years of the First International. One cannot deal with this question only from the viewpoint of class (spontaneous or conscious) solidarity. Since then, part of the socialist and communist movement acted as if the affirmation that "workers do not have a homeland" were a judgment or a sociological proposition deduced from some inquiry conducted among representative segments of the world's industrial proletariat. Yet, with even a little reflection, one will see that, in reality, this is a normative affirmation—the affirmation of a *desire.*

Marx himself became aware of the importance of this problem. In an interview he granted in 1871 to *The World,* a New York magazine, he said:

> The [International Workers'] Association does not dictate the form of political movements; it only requires a pledge as to their end. It is a network of affiliated societies spreading all over the world of labor. In each part of the world some special aspect of the problem presents itself, and the workmen there address themselves to its consideration in their own way. Combinations among workmen cannot be absolutely identical in detail in Newcastle and Barcelona, in London and Berlin. The Association does not pretend to impose its will on them and does not pretend to give them advice: but to every movement it accords its sympathy and its aid within the limits assigned by its own laws.[11]

Yet Gramsci goes further. He shifts this reflection from the political-organizational level to an anterior one, that of the possibility of translating languages [*linguaggi*] and different cultures, by attempting to simultaneously overcome ethnocentric primitivism and absolute relativism. Criticizing "philosophical Esperantism" as well as the "utopia of fixed and universal

languages [*lingue*]" or the "resistance to a development of a national common language [*lingua*] by the fanatics of the international languages,"
Gramsci succeeds in instituting a relationship and in putting into question
scientific pragmatism of positivistic origin as well as Bukharin's attempt in
his *Popular Manual*, since they are both undermined by a kind of ethnocentrism that does not understand the historicity of languages [*linguaggi*] and
of philosophies and that leads one to believe that everything which is not
expressed in one's own language is delirium, pre-judgement or superstition.[12]

In this context, Gramsci elaborates a couple of theoretical criteria which
are very useful in founding the possibility, though imperfect, of a reciprocal translatability within the realm of the philosophy of praxis between
national languages and cultures which belong to different traditions. These
criteria are:

a) To clarify, in relationship to one's own language [*linguaggio*] and
   one's own worldview, "the doses of criticism and skepticism" that are
   necessary to maintain as an alternative to one's own culture without
   paralyzing (or demoralizing) oneself and without falling into sectarianism;
b) To admit, not only as a possibility, but also as a reality, that there
   are cultures which are superior to others, even though—this is crucial—they are almost never superior for the reasons which their own
   fanatic defenders, primitivist or ethnocentric, believe they are and
   never, above all, are they considered in their entirety and totality.

5

The third sphere to study is that of the repercussion of such a preoccupation
with language [*linguaggio*] and specific languages [*lingue*] within the evolution of the political thought of Gramsci. In this realm, one must say that,
notwithstanding that the reflection on the nexus between language [*linguaggio*] and politics is not always explicit, the originality of Gramsci, and, in particular, of his Marxism, is due mainly to his will of *expressing, in a new form,
a new form of doing politics*. Such a dimension of Gramsci's work has always
been recognized by people from other traditions and cultures: from Piero
Gobetti to Camillo Berneri and from Joaquim Maruin to Bendetto Croce.

Therefore, Gramsci followed the path opened by Marx with his proposal,
making philosophy earthly, conceived as a form of realization-overcoming
of philosophy itself, by developing Marx's considerations about the problems of a humanity that suffers and that thinks. If already in the Marx of the
1840s, and even more in the Marx of the 1850s, we can find a documented

journalism with historical-philosophical notions and viewpoints, we find a journalistic form as original as Marx's in the Gramsci of *L'Ordine Nuovo*: informed, learned, polemical and simultaneously problematic and true. This is not an accident, but is due, instead, to Gramsci's specific reflection on both the alternative culture of the subaltern classes (in a polemic with Tasca and Bordiga) and on the more adequate linguistic form of communication necessary to establish and maintain a living relationship between the intellectuals and the people.

This reflection is like a red thread that runs through Gramsci's entire work from 1918 to 1935, which was elaborated by fundamentally taking into account two factors: on the one hand, the comparison between the new world view and the history of the institutionalization of Christianity and the Church and, on the other, the necessity of opposing the vulgarization of Marxist socialism, which tended to treat workers as "simple people" or "mere troops." Gramsci aims at building a link between leaders and led in the field of the same tradition (he says, "explicit and active worldview"), whose basis is one shared language [*linguaggio*] and not, as in the case of churches, two languages [*linguaggi*] where one is for the clergy, and another for the simple people.

In the framework of this research, Gramsci's proposal of the dialogical form goes together with the proposal of a new type of philosopher, whom he calls the "democratic philosopher," and whose personality is not limited to cultivating individuality but aims, above all, at an "active social relationship which modifies the cultural environment." This is precisely how Gramsci translated Marx's way of making philosophy worldly. Gramsci's adaptation to the epoch of the "fist in the eye"—namely, to the years of fascism and Nazism—is expressed in his recognition of the necessity to shift, with humility, from feeling like a "plowman of history" to considering ourselves the "manure of history." Gramsci says, "Once everybody wanted to be a plowman of history. Nobody wanted to be the 'manure' of history. But is it possible to plow before feeding the soil? Something must have changed because there are people who 'philosophically' adapt themselves to being manure, who know they must be manure and that, therefore, adapt themselves."[13] Politics, above all, in the bad moments, must be, first of all, pedagogy, and its language [*linguaggio*]—the language of politics—must be pedagogical, passionate and sincere, but without being vulgar or primitive.

This reflection leads Gramsci to a consideration on the state of the soul and style, which are more adequate to the new period, namely, to that historical phase in which the old was dying with difficulty, and the new was coming to life with difficulty.

I would like to recall another two passages from the *Notebooks* which are interesting as well because of the consideration of the relationship between language [*linguaggio*] and politics.[14] The first passage refers to the question of young people and to the importance reserved to the intergenerational dialogue in the fight for hegemony. The second, which is also a dialogue between Gramsci and his own tradition, refers to the style, namely, to the more appropriate form through which the "historical bloc" can be elaborated and to the creation of a "center of nexus" between the intellectuals and the people.

Several times, Gramsci has called attention to the importance of the ruptures and the generational crises in the fight for hegemony as well as to the responsibility of the somewhat older people in this fight. The generational crises are directly related to a cultural malaise. It is, therefore, essential to find a common language [*linguaggio*] thanks to which people of different ages, which aim at transforming the world, can understand and communicate their own different life experiences to each other. Gramsci is trying to propose, in positive terms, a delicate theme, to which Turgenev and Dostoevsky had already devoted excellent essays, entitled "Fathers and Sons" and "Liberalism and Nihilism," respectively. Given that this continues to be one of the themes of our times, it will not be useless for this paper to devote a few words to extending Gramsci's preoccupation to the present.

One of the problems we must now cope with is the fact that the dialogue between generations is mediated by the trivialization and manipulation of the history of the twentieth century by historiographic "revisionism." Revisionism is deeply penetrating and already appears as an ideology functioning decisively in the interests of the dominant classes in the epoch of cultural homogenization and standardization. What is called "postmodernism" is, on a cultural level, the latest step of capitalism and, as John Berger wrote, "the historical task of capitalism is to destroy history, to cut every tie with the past and to direct all efforts and the entire imagination toward what is currently happening."

This is how it has been and how it is. Since it is so, we need to provide young people, who were formed in a culture of fragmentary images, with a new reading of history, different from the one given by the great traditional chronological narration of history, in order for them to become interested in who Marx and Gramsci were and what they did—namely, in the Marxist socialist tradition. We have to provide the younger generations with an interpretation of history which substantially restores, through fragmentary images, the continuing centrality of class struggle in our epoch—namely, in between the chiaroscuro of the tragedies of the twentieth century. Gramsci dealt with theater, popular literature, poetry and narrative. Moreover, he understood the importance of the (oral and written) word for the elaboration of worldviews and for the construction of a great historical narration. These reflections ought to be continued. It is probable that, today, the more adequate language [*linguaggio*] to restore the dialogue between generations, in the realm of liberating the tradition of socialist culture, would be an alternative use of the cinematographic and visual techniques—namely, a combination of historical documentation and reasoned passion.

I would like to conclude with a consideration of the style of the new way of doing politics. There is a reflection, contained in a note from 1935, on the "contradictions of historicism and of their literary expressions" which summarizes well, in my opinion, the lesson of style that Gramsci wanted to leave us. Such a reflection deals with irony and sarcasm as stylistic forms and is of surprising relevancy.

Gramsci wrote:

> It is correct to use "irony" to describe the attitude of single intellectuals, individually, that is without immediate responsibility towards the construction of a cultural world or to point out the detachment of an artist from the sentimental content of her own creation (who either can "feel" but not "share," or can share but in more intellectually refined form).

"Irony" can be appropriate either for describing the attitude of single intellectuals, individually, that is, of those who have no immediate responsibility in the construction of a cultural world, or to point out the detachment of an artist from the sentimental content of his creation (which he can "feel," but on which he cannot "agree," or on which he can agree, but in a more refined intellectual form). Yet, in the case of historical action, the element of "irony" would only be literary or intellectualized and would indicate a form of detachment connected to a somewhat amateurish skepticism, caused by disillusion, fatigue, and a "superman" complex. *Instead, in the case of historical-political action the adequate stylistic element, the characteristic attitude of the detachment-understanding, is "sarcasm," though understood in a specific way, that is, as "passionate sarcasm."* In the founders of the philosophy of praxis one can find the highest expression, ethically and aesthetically, of passionate sarcasm. . . . In the face of popular beliefs and illusions . . . there is a passionately "positive," creative and progressive sarcasm: one can understand that what is mocked is not the most intimate feelings of those illusions and beliefs, but their immediate form—which is connected to a given "perishable" world—that is, the stench of a corpse that seeps out through the humanitarian face makeup of those professionals of "immortal principles."[15]

In this passage, Gramsci clearly distinguishes between "impassioned sarcasm" and a sarcasm of the anti-humanistic right that is rarely impassioned and that always presents itself as negative, skeptical, and, hence, destructive, not only of the contingent forms but also of the human content contained in the sentiments and beliefs mentioned above. And so he continues: "One tries to give new form to the live nucleus of the aspirations contained in these beliefs (hence to regenerate and better determine these aspirations) not to destroy them." But, as it always happens, the first and original manifestations of sarcasm often give birth to slavish imitations: even what initially was style risks deteriorating into rhetoric and jargon; but this must be avoided, and, especially, in our epoch.

Historicism cannot be conceived as a discourse that is expressible in an apodictic or sermonizing form. It has to create a new stylistic taste and a new language [*linguaggio*] as a means of intellectual struggle. Sarcasm appears, therefore, as the stylistic-literary component of a series of theoretical and practical exigencies, which can only superficially be presented as irreconcilably contradictory; its essential element is passion which becomes a criterion of the stylistic power of the individuals (of sincerity, of deep conviction as opposed to parroting and being mechanical).

NOTES

1. Antonio Gramsci, *Selections from the Prison Notebooks*, ed. and trans. Quintin Hoare and Geoffrey Nowell Smith (New York: International Publishers, 1971), 450, hereafter cited as SPN. [There is a list of abbreviations on pages ix–x. Q11§28. To facilitate locating passages in various translations and anthologies, we use the standard method of providing the notebook (*Quaderno*) number—in this case 11—followed by the section number, §. See the introduction, page 12, for discussion. We will indicate the English translation, if used.]

2. Q11§28, SPN, 450.

3. [Gramsci uses the term *i simplici*, which has the meaning of "simpletons" but also an opposition like that in English between "the commoners" and the "intellectuals" which we think is best captured by "the simple people." It is in quotations because Gramsci is opposing the notion that they are not intellectuals to some degrees.]

4. [Buey is referring to Gramsci's use of the Italian version of "squeezing water from a stone."]

5. Antonio Gramsci, *Letters from Prison*, two volumes, ed. Frank Rosengarten, trans. Raymond Rosenthal (New York: Columbia University Pres, 1994), volume 1, 369, hereafter cited as LP1 and LP2. This letter is from December 15, 1930.

6. Q29§2, Antonio Gramsci, *Selections from Cultural Writings*, ed. David Forgacs, trans. William Boelhower (Cambridge, Mass.: Harvard University Press, 1985), 180–82, hereafter cited as SCW.

7. Q29§3, SCW, 183–84.

8. [Buey is echoing Gramsci's own alternation between the Italian and Russian diminutive, Gulia and Julca, his wife.]

9. Q11§47–Q11§49, Antonio Gramsci, *Further Selections from the Prison Notebooks*, ed. and trans. Derek Boothman (Minneapolis: University of Minnesota Press, 1995), 307–13, hereafter cited as FSPN; and Q11§65, SPN, 403–4.

10. Q11§46, FSPN, 306.

11. [Karl Marx, "Our Aims Should Be Comprehensive," in Karl Marx and Friedrich Engels, *Collected Works*, vol. 22 (New York: International Publishers, 1975), 600. No citation provided in original.]

12. Q11§45, FSPN, 303–4.

13. Q9§53, QC, 1128.

14. Q1§27, PN1, 212–13, and Q14§58, QC, 1717–18.

15. Q26§5, QC, 2299–2300. Translation made with reference to the A-text, PN1, 117–18.

13

Gramsci's Subversion of the Language of Politics

Anne Showstack Sassoon *

Over the years an extensive literature has built up on Gramsci and language. For the most part it has focused on Gramsci's writings on language. This literature usually refers to his studies in linguistics in Turin, and connects his notes on language to his concept of national-popular, to his criticism of the cosmopolitanism of Italian intellectuals, and to his verification of the significance of popular culture both as a field of study and as a starting point for which, it is agreed, not only elucidates other important concepts such as hegemony or the intellectuals, but is a foundation stone for those concepts.[1] In Italy, of course, where only a tiny minority of the population used Italian as its daily language as late as the beginning of the [twentieth] century, where the very study of cultural anthropology by, for example, Ernesto De Martino, had important political significance, where to this day written Italian is much more distant from the spoken language than is the case, for example, with English, and where "intellectual" and "political" Italian both as language and as discourse can often represent communication between a self-selected few, the political import of language goes without saying.

Beyond Italy, Gramsci's writing on language is recognized as an important contribution to developing a sociology of language or a science of language.[2] Interest has also grown in this aspect of his work, first because of debates about ideology and, more recently, because of the growth in what is rather generically referred to as discourse theory. For at least some writers

* Originally published in *Rethinking Marxism* 3, no. 1 (1990): 14–25. [Material inside square brackets has been added by the editors including translations unavailable when first published and other citation information for consistency with the other chapters.]

who use concepts from discourse analysis, Gramsci is important,[3] and his writing on language appears a natural object of analysis. What I want to do here is different. I have often been struck by how difficult it is to understand Gramsci. Moving beyond what had been the common explanation for this difficulty, which attributes it to the need to fool the prison censor, the harsh conditions of prison life, Gramsci's precarious state of health and the problem of obtaining material, I recently arrived at the conclusion that much of the difficulty stems, in fact, from Gramsci's complex view of the world. This is connected to the form of his work. That is, consciously or unconsciously, he made a choice to write in note form and not a book. Consequently, he produced an archetypal open text that the reader must recreate each time she or he reads it. This is not, by any means, to argue that it says anything or everything to everybody. Indeed, it is all too tempting to read Gramsci for instrumental political reasons while the very difficulty of his language and his discourse means that he tends to be absorbed in preexisting schema.[4]

Despite this difficulty, his work is widely read, or at least his concepts are a frequent reference point. Others may find him fascinating for different reasons. I would, however, suggest that the intrinsic interest lies in the way in which Gramsci, writing in an earlier period of crisis of Marxism and the working-class movement and of epochal change, speaks to us because of the questions he asks and because he seizes on the perplexing, the contradictory, the surprising, those features of society which escape ready classification as the most fertile and productive points to analyze.

The difficulty we face is, to some extent, rooted in his necessarily compacting several concepts into one note (as anyone who has ever tried to put together a sample of his writings will attest) because of the multifaceted, interconnected nature of reality. It is not surprising that he did not write a logical treatise, even though others did in fascist prisons. Further, it is not easy to follow the way in which his discussion grows out of the seeming minutiae of intellectual and political debate in the 1930s fascist Italy. While this provides the reader with a rich culture, his thinking often traces an intuitive path rich in results whose import, however, has to be rearticulated to furnish theoretical indications for a different context. But he is also fascinating precisely for those very aspects which make him difficult. On the one hand, our creative reading of Gramsci holds the danger that we stamp our schema—for example, populist, idealist, functionalist or post-Marxist—on him.[5] But on the other, his intuitive, sensitive use of the confusion of the new, of the fractured interrelatedness of reality, of the historically and nationally specific to try to push forward a theoretical understanding of the trends and patterns and possibilities of the present as the basis for helping to create the future, escape many of the blind alleys of recent debates. More recently it has struck me that Gramsci is also difficult because of his use of language—not because the words are difficult, which they are not, and not only because the concepts they refer to are complex, which they often are, but precisely because he uses ordinary or traditional words to signify something new and, further, he often uses a word both in a traditional way and in a novel and sometimes an almost absurd manner. Pasolini has written a sensitive piece on Gramsci's use of Italian, drawing on his (Pasolini's) interest in dialect.[6] And, of course, at a different level, some of Gramsci's writings are notoriously difficult to translate, although I am not sure that this is not simply a question of Italian political language. Compared to other Italians writing in his time or ours, he is a paragon of lucidity.

What I detect is *his* difficulty with language. What comes through is a *struggle* with language both in terms of the significations carried by individual words, as he attempts to find a way to depict not just new but old phenomena which look different because of a leap in understanding, and above all, because he cannot see, or comprehend, if these phenomena are reduced to one aspect and yet he says, explicitly, that methodological distinctions are necessary.[7] He ranges between these distinctions and the utility of connecting them, insisting that form cannot be divided from content,[8] that theoretical generalization is only given meaning by the historically specific, that (and here he is both using and subverting the metaphor) structure is joined organically to superstructure,[9] that while international trends are the context, national developments must be the point of departure. When he uses a word in two ways, one is normally its usual or commonsense meaning and the other is new, indicating an extended or advanced concept which bursts beyond the bounds of the old.

He is highly aware of this problem of language. The language which is available does not easily accommodate the dual perspective which he insists is necessary in politics. His notes are full of explanation indicating when he is using a word in its "usual" way and when, on the contrary, it is "new." Indeed, the notes are filled with words in inverted commas—a distancing and specifying device. Why is there this trouble with language? In part it is related to the increasing complexity of the phenomena in question and of Gramsci's view of them. And naming complex sociopolitical and historical phenomena is not like naming a new mechanical discovery which can be labeled, perhaps, by going back to a Greek or Latin root. As Gramsci himself notes, language has historical and social roots and a word cannot be created out of the blue, abstractly. In that sense we are often stuck with the old words as developments grow beyond the old significations.

Moreover, as he comments, ideas lag far behind "economic facts"[10] and so does language. But Gramsci's difficulty with language is also related to something else which is indicative of, dare I use the word, Gramsci's very dialectic, that is, his view of the complex tendencies contained within the historical present, representing influence and continuities with the past, the reproduction of the old but in new forms and the problems and possibilities so radical, so revolutionary that their resolution, to the extent that we are able to conceive of it at all, lies in the superseding of a whole historical epoch which spans capitalism and socialism—that is, in a society with a new mode of production, in communism. In addition to the fact that I have put this in sweeping, general brush strokes,[11] what I have painted is hard to visualize because it is much easier to see what has been lost, or what is being reproduced in new forms, than the seeds of the revolutionary contained (and I mean this word in two ways) within current developments.

Because I want to concentrate here on Gramsci's subversion of the words or language of politics (a subversion dictated by historical development), and not undertake a general reading of his problematic, and because of constraints of time and space, what follows are some comments on some examples of what I have been referring to above. Although I will not tackle it here, it would be interesting to compare what Gramsci does with the language of politics with what he has to say about language. And to the extent that there is a difference between the way in which we understand certain words and what Gramsci means, we could well ask what this says to us about the dominant ways of viewing politics today, which influence our commonsense views as specialist intellectuals. The divergences between Gramsci's use of language and ours may well indicate traditional ways of thinking which may prevent us from comprehending the possibilities on the historical agenda.

The most obvious place to start might appear to be with hegemony. In political language, the traditional sense of hegemony is diametrically opposed (or appears to be—we shall return to this) to Gramsci's meaning. In international relations it has traditionally indicated dominance or power over.[12] In traditional Marxist language, hegemony indicated the leadership of a class over allies.[13] Thanks to Gramsci, it is today used not only in these ways but also to indicate consent and moral and intellectual leadership.[14] There is an enormous literature on the concept of hegemony. I do not want to rehearse it here, in part because I want to concentrate on Gramsci's struggle with finding appropriate language, and in part because I would argue that passive revolution is equally or more important as an analytic concept in Gramsci.

But more crucially, it is important to situate hegemony as belonging to a cluster of words (state, civil society, political society, political, intellectual, democratic, discipline, party, democratic centralism, crisis and historical), the reference points of which keep shifting and/or mean more than one thing, partly because of historical changes which have already taken place, and partly because processes are underway, according to Gramsci, which make possible the subversion and transformation of politics or the resolution of what Gramsci calls the fundamental question of political science, the division between leaders and led.[15]

The shifts, for example, in Gramsci's definition of the state manifest the need, first, to connect to a historically and politically defined discourse which restricts its meaning to government, coercion, force; second, to push its meaning to encompass the transformation of political power in the modern period, which was de facto undermining the liberal "night watchman" state; and third, to take account of those questions posed, on the one hand, by the Russian Revolution, which put the construction of a workers' state and a full expansion of democracy on the historical agenda, and on the other, by fascism's challenge, both practical and theoretical, to the liberal concept of state and practice of politics. The state cannot be thought of in a restricted sense because of these historical changes.[16] Thus, while Gramsci insists on the need to distinguish between civil and political society, he argues at the same time that these are methodological or analytical distinctions[17] whose meaning in the real world lies in the form of the articulation between the different dimensions of political power, a form which is not natural or a necessity of a mode of production but historical. Here again we find a word used in two ways by Gramsci—to indicate what is made by human beings in specific circumstances, the parameters of which, above all, are national and determined by political intervention, and long-term trends of an epochal and international character which are "given." Gramsci not only rereads Marx's Preface to *A Contribution to a Critique of Political Economy*,[18] but he also reinterprets Marx's famous statement in *The Eighteenth Brumaire* that men make history but not in conditions of their choosing.

Now I want to switch and consider another example: intellectual. It is well known how Gramsci uses this word to refer to an extended list of categories, to claim that everyone is an intellectual, and generally to confuse us as he breaks with both orthodox liberal and Marxist ideas. If we examine some of the associated words, such as "connective," "organizational," "skills," "specialist/specialization," "function," "division of labor" and "technical," the effect is both demystifying and confounding. We may well ask, why does he hold on to a word which he has extended and subverted in this way? Why, when he is convinced of the importance of ideas and ideology, does the example he gives of everyone's being an intellectual come from daily, practical life? Why does it have nothing to do with ideas or rationality but everything to do with the skills which come from specialization and the division of labor: that while we may all fry an egg or sew on a button from time to time, this does not mean that we are all cooks or tailors?[19] Is our being confounded a warning? That is, to the extent that we fill the word with an outmoded concept, be it the supposed inhabitants of an ivory tower or the science carriers of a class, or mere ideologues, we will not understand reality. We will not be aware that the debate has moved on.

I have analyzed Gramsci's discussion of the intellectuals as specialists elsewhere.[20] Here I would simply reiterate the point that he is by no means a populist, that he is highly critical of much in popular ideas, that he states clearly that, given that the working class needs intellectuals as specialists and as leaders of the highest order, it faces unprecedented difficulties. And yet there is a very important reason that Gramsci insists that everyone is an intellectual: for isolated intellectuals cannot hope to understand reality by force of technique alone. Gramsci continues to use the word "intellectual," rather than, say, "petit-bourgeois" or *"declassé,"* because a sociological or economic class term is not appropriate, while "specialist" is too limited. "Intellectual," in its restricted and extended meanings, can indicate the full range of historical and, ultimately, political possibilities and necessities. This leads us to why Gramsci turns another expression on its head, "democratic centralism." As so often in the *Notebooks,* Gramsci engages in a double-edged polemic, aimed both at Italian fascism and at the working-class movement as he redefines democratic centralism. How distant it is from its usual connotation. In his notes, it concerns the need to understand change, movement, diversity, in order to understand ultimately the general or the universal. As with his discussion of the party, an organizational term relates to a theoretical task and a theoretical problem. Note how it is defined in terms of an exchange between different elements, which is echoed in his definition of democracy.[21] How "flexibility," "elasticity," "practical" and "experimental" are contrasted with "mechanical," "rigidity," "rationalistic," "abstract" and "bureaucratic," and following from this consider what he does with "vanguard," "leadership," "discipline," "spontaneity" or "democratic." They, too, are defined in terms of a function, a problem and a historical task.[22]

Gramsci defines "vanguard" in its connection to a class and a society at large.[23] We can also find this in Lenin, but Gramsci draws from it a different consequence. At the risk of reinforcing a reductive, Hegelian reading of Gramsci, he defines "vanguard" in its becoming, or, more precisely, its meaning cannot be separated from the transformation of the working class and society in the period in which not only the transition from socialism but the "need" for communism is on the historical agenda. From the more immediate perspective of the problem of politics in the here and now, when Gramsci considers the classical question of the relationship between "spontaneity" and "conscious leadership" or "discipline"[24] he puts the terms between inverted commas. This signifies his difficulty with the available language and puts us on our guard.[25] Moreover, while they are analytically distinct, the problem being considered is the nature of the link between them. Their unity becomes conceivable if posed in terms of creating the conditions for mass politics. Neither their meaning nor this unity can derive from the revolutionary claims of an isolated sect.

This question was posed by Lenin, and in different ways, by, on the one hand, Bordiga and, on the other, the syndicalists. This is the political history which informs the reading of these words and which is one reason

Gramsci is forced to distance himself from them as givens. But if he corrupts or subverts them or pushes them to their limits or argues that, as usually understood, they are meaningless (as with the case of spontaneity), it is not simply because of political polemic. It is because he is convinced that, in the era of mass politics, their traditional, historically constructed meanings are being superseded or tendentially so. Yet the old or reduced meaning often still has resonance and is still necessary in specific conditions. Thus, for example, Gramsci defines "discipline"[26] in such a way as to render it almost unrecognizable. He defines it in terms of a historical possibility and therefore of a political task, of overcoming the traditional split between leaders and led. He counterposes it to its traditional meaning, a meaning the roots of which lie in institutions like the Church and the military, and which has to be extended to people's commonsense understanding as the mere execution of orders. This traditional meaning, however, is still appropriate on certain occasions, and thus the word itself has multiple definitions.

When Gramsci discusses the significance of the source of discipline, we find still another, apparently absurd, redefinition. "Democratic" is related to specialization, division of labor and a process of creating the conditions whereby there is an organic exchange between leaders and led.[27] That is, it is defined in terms of what Gramsci calls that central problem of political science, the relationship between rulers and ruled, no longer posed in terms of political obligation, going beyond questions of legitimation or consensus until it is posed in such a way that it encompasses the full possibilities of the current historical epoch—the creation of communism or regulated society.[28] Once again words have no fixed meanings, not only because of the complexity of the past and present which construct their meanings today, whether in the heads of specialized intellectuals or in those of mass woman or man, but also because this present is part and parcel of a transition to an unprecedented historical future. The possibilities inscribed in the present, such as the redefinition of politics which is on the historical agenda not only because of the Russian Revolution but also because of the latest developments of capitalism, make us, according to Gramsci, confront unprecedented problems. Similarly, the awareness of the dialectic of the present and future undermines our traditional way of attempting to capture and ultimately control reality in fixed schema or, I should say, in a particular Enlightenment tradition of doing so which can be conceived as the culmination of a whole history of thought and reason.

Gramsci makes us think of many of the questions posed more recently in debates about postmodernism. And perhaps the manifestation of the difficulties we face today in comprehending reality can be found in our use of language, our relation to traditional discourse, and our very thought processes. This has struck me in various ways as I have thought of my experiences as a practicing specialist intellectual. First, although these are in no particular order, when I lecture on political theory and come across references to universal man, I stumble, I stray, I go off on a tangent which is similar to those inverted commas, those multiple meanings and constant explanations, and redefinitions scattered through Gramsci's notes as he, too, is troubled by language. How disturbing, disrupting, distracting to our traditional language is the moral and intellectual revolution constituted by feminism and the invasion of difference, of gender into our thought processes.

Indeed, here I come to my second point: I have been struck by how difficult it is to write about Gramsci in the logical, rational order for which we have all been trained as part of our professional apprenticeships. His writing, his approach, his language keep escaping and leading us astray. This brings me to another point which I mentioned earlier. Although Gramsci himself was aware and wary of the unfinished nature of his work in prison, he gave himself permission to work on several notebooks at the same time, to consider a wide range of topics, to change and develop his categories and to write in note form.[29]

Whatever he might have done had he been freer, we are at liberty to appreciate the usefulness and not just the problems of his mode of discourse. His explicit critique of abstract, deductive, rationalistic projects unrelated to experience, to the passions, to the feelings of those unspecialized generalist intellectuals who are the mass of the population and who possess a wealth of skills, information and knowledge is, as I have argued elsewhere, not a form of populism.[30] What Gramsci does do, of course, is validate the questions arising from daily life as providing the raw material for advanced, specialist, intellectual labor, and here he coincides with one of the lessons from feminism.[31] And yet, he by no means abandons the attempt to generalize, to theorize, to develop the language of today in an effort to capture process, diversity, particularity. But the meaning, the content, the effective terrain of our knowledge and expertise is always ultimately in reference to the concrete and the historical. I want to finish by illustrating this with a discussion of Gramsci's use of two terms—"passive revolution" and "historical bloc"—and by raising some questions about a third, regulated society. "Passive revolution" and "historical bloc" are both terms which have double but interrelated meanings. Gramsci uses them to refer to two levels of analysis: theoretical problems and historical phenomena. Gramsci himself is explicitly concerned about possible difficulties ensuing from this approach with regard to passive revolution, which, he argues, is useful as a theoretical tool—for example, describing the very dialectic of the reproduction of capitalism in the very period of its organic crisis, as he paraphrases Marx in the Preface to *A Contribution to the Critique of Political Economy*.[32] This long-term, general, international tendency is given meaning by a series of seemingly diverse, nationally specific, historically concrete political and economic developments. And yet, in explaining the capacity of capitalism to survive in the course of change, and thus the possibility both of developing a system of passive consent and the basis for a Crocean, historicist justification of past and present,[33] it can lead to a fatalistic, passive acceptance which ignores the revolutionary implications of transformations. In the few notes in which Gramsci discusses historical bloc[34] he uses it, first, to refer to the relationship between base and superstructure. Here he would have been advised to put these words within inverted commas, because the effect of both the term "historical bloc" and its second usage is to subvert the metaphor. For the second usage is to describe the complex way in which actual, historically and politically formed classes and groups articulate their relations and form the basis, or better, the weave of a society.

The use of the same terms to refer to theoretical and concrete historical phenomena has various implications and consequences. First, it is a manifestation of Gramsci's insistence that theory acquires meaning from its usefulness in analyzing the concrete, a concrete in which he gives great weight to national specificities within the generality of the international, and local differences within the parameters of the national. Thus, there is a message about abstraction, generalization and rational discourse which Gramsci insists must not be confounded with or reduced to schemas or mathematical logic. But second, there is a message about politics which also has an echo for theory. For this double usage of "passive revolution" and "historical bloc" tells us the following: if long-term tendencies of the reproduction of capitalism and of problems—such as division between leaders and led and expressions of it such a bureaucracy, which overarch capitalism and socialism—provide the basis of a theoretical concept abstracted from its specific form, which enables us to comprehend the general and the long term, its meaning is articulated in concrete forms which are not natural, but are historically limited and are thus amenable to change, although nonetheless tenacious and enormously problematic. The terrain of intervention or, effectively, our very subjectivity, our identity is the particular. And one type of knowledge is limited to the fragmented, the immediate, the specific. But there are many different kinds of knowledge, and our effectivity and autonomy, a word much favored by Gramsci, is augmented by an understanding of the long term and the general, not least because it contains within it the seeds of the corruption of the traditional, of the supersession of the past, contained in the present.

Here we end with a puzzle and an invitation. In reference again to Gramsci's language, I have been trying to think about why he uses "regulated society" instead of some other term to refer to communism. Is Gramsci once again engaging in a multiple polemic? After all, the overcoming of conflict is the professed aim of the Hegelian or neo-Hegelian rational state, of a utilitarian synthesis of conflicting interests, of fascist corporatism, of Soviet and other kinds of planning. All of these imply regulation by the state, whereas Gramsci uses it to indicate the expansion of civil society.[35] More could be said. I have some ideas, but for the moment I will leave it here for us all to ponder.

NOTES

1. See, for example, Franco Lo Piparo. *Lingua, Intellettuali, Egemonia in Gramsci* (Rome: Laterza, 1979). Tullio De Mauro and Luigi Rosiello have also written widely in this area [see chapters 2, 3 and 15 in this volume].

2. See Leonardo Salamini, "Gramsci and the Marxist Sociology of Language," *International Journal of Sociology of Language* 32 (1981), or Utz Maas, "Der Sprachwissenschaftler Gramsci" [see this volume, chapter 5].

3. See, for example, Ernesto Laclau and Chantal Mouffe, *Hegemony and Socialist Strategy* (London: Verso, 1985).

4. See the preface to the second edition of Anne Showstack Sassoon, *Gramsci's Politics* (London: Minneapolis: University of Minnesota Press, 1987).

5. See "Postscript, the People, Intellectuals and Specialised Knowledge," in Sassoon, *Gramsci's Politics.*

6. Pier Paolo Pasolini, "Gramsci's Language," in *Approaches to Gramsci*, ed. Anne Showstack Sassoon (London: Writers and Readers Publishing Co-operatives, 1982).

7. Antonio Gramsci, *Selections from the Prison Notebooks* (London: Lawrence and Wishart, 1971), 12, for example, cited hereafter as SPN. [A list of abbreviations is on pages ix–x.]

8. Antonio Gramsci, *Quaderni del Carcere* (Turin: Einaudi, 1975), 1245. [To facilitate locating these passages in various translations and anthologies, we will give the notebook (*Quaderno*) number—in this case 10, part II—followed by the section number, §7. We will indicate the English translation, where available—in this case, Antonio Gramsci, *Further Selections from the Prison Notebooks*, ed. and trans. Derek Boothman (Minneapolis: University of Minnesota Press, 1995), 439, hereafter cited as FSPN.]

9. SPN, 377 [Q7§21].

10. SPN, 168 [Q13§14].

11. The argument is more fully developed in my "postscript."

12. Stephen Gill and David Low, "Global Hegemony and the Structural Power of Capital," *International Studies Quarterly* (Summer 1989), discuss the traditional use and argue that Gramsci's concept has greater explanatory power, as does Robert W. Cox, "Gramsci, Hegemony and International Relations Theory: An Essay in Method," *Millenium* 12 (1983). Edward Said has recently used "hegemony" to indicate American international dominance through cultural means. "Identity, Negation and Violence," *New Left Review* 171 (September–October 1988): 57.

13. See Perry Anderson, "The Antinomies of Antonio Gramsci," *New Left Review* 100 (November 1976–January 1977); Christine Buci-Glucksmann, *Gramsci and the State* (London: Lawrence & Wishart, 1980), 7–8.

14. SPN, 144 [Q15§4] .

15. SPN, 275 or 12 [Q3§34 or Q12§1].

16. SPN, 12 [Q12§1], 258 [Q8§179], 262–63, 275 [Q6§88, Q3§46], and my *Gramsci's Politics*, 109–19.

17. See my entry on civil society in Tom Bottomore, ed., *A Dictionary of Marxist Thought* (Oxford: Blackwell Reference, 1983).

18. In a paraphrase which recurs several times when he discusses passive revolution, Gramsci argues that the "fundamental principles of political science [are]: (1) that no social formation disappears as long as the productive forces which have developed within it still find room for further forward movement; (2) that a society does not set itself tasks for whose solutions the necessary conditions have not already been incubated, etc." SPN, 106 [Q15§17].

19. When Gramsci writes that "all men are intellectuals . . . but not all men have in society the function of intellectuals," he illustrates his point with the following example: "(Thus, because it can happen that everyone at some time fries a couple of eggs or sews up a tear in a jacket, we do not necessarily say that everyone is a cook or a tailor)." SPN, 9 [Q12§1]. In the original this parenthetical comment follows directly.

20. See my "postscript."

21. SPN, 188–90 [Q13§36].

22. For just some of the relevant passages, see QC, 236–37 [Antonio Gramsci, *Prison Notebooks*, vol. 1, ed. and trans. Joseph Buttigieg (New York: Columbia University Press, 1992), 323–24], 1706 [Q14§48]; SPN, 198 [Q3§48], 214 [Q13§23]; and Sassoon, *Gramsci's Politics*, 162–79 and 222–31.

23. QC, 236–37 [Gramsci, *Prison Notebooks*, vol. 1, 323–24].

24. SPN, 214 [Q13§23].

25. For example, SPN, 214 [Q13§23].

26. QC, 1706 [Q14§48].

27. QC, 1706 [Q14§48].

28. SPN, 144 [Q15§4].

29. Luisa Mangoni has an excellent discussion of how Gramsci developed his categories; "La genesi delle categorie storico-politiche nei Quaderni del carcere," in *Studi Storici* 3 (1987). Gianni Francioni provides insights into the order in which the notebooks were written; see *L'officina gramsciana* (Naples: Bibliopolis, 1984).

30. See my "postscript."

31. See "Introduction: The Personal and the Intellectual, Fragments and Order, International Trends and National Specificities," in *Women and the State*, ed. Anne Showstack Sassoon (London: Hutchinson, 1987).

32. See note 18.

33. See Mangoni, "La genesi." We could well apply this approach to patriarchy, for example.

34. SPN, 366 [Q10II§12], 377 [Q7§21], 418 [Q11§67].

35. In today's language, of course, "regulated" still connotes state intervention, or it might make us think of regulation or the reproduction of a society in an expanded complex sense as in regulation theory. This last certainly has points of contact with Gramsci's ideas, in some forms at least. We might well ask what the historical conditions are of this extension of the words "regulate," "regulated" and

254 Anne Showstack Sassoon

"regulation." An excellent recent discussion of changes occurring in the forms of power and control imbedded in the leading edges of post-Fordist development, which suggests forms of decentralized regulation necessitated by the increasing complexity of society, has strong parallels with Gramsci's insights into the implications of long-term developments for concretely posing the question of the withering away of the state. See Geoff Mulgan, "The Power of the Weak," in *Marxism Today* (December 1988).

14

Some Notes on Gramsci the Linguist

*Tullio De Mauro**

In this contribution I am going to deal only tangentially—or almost not at all—with two of the salient aspects regarding the theme "Gramsci and the question of the [Italian] language [*lingua*]." I will say very little about Gramsci as an actor within the Italian linguistic reality of the 1910s, 1920s and 1930s, and as a privileged user, reporter and essayist operating within the linguistic practices of Italian society. I will also say little about and discuss only tangentially Gramsci's dealing with what in the nineteenth century would have been called the question of the language [*lingua*]. Perhaps today, instead of using the word "language" [*lingua*], we should say the "linguistic norm"—that is, that type of language which the various kinds of literary or informative writing conforms to or deviates from. Several of my colleagues—Lo Piparo, Gensini and Rosiello—and other younger scholars have dealt exhaustively with both of these aspects.

I would rather like to take this opportunity to discuss some issues, particularly four that have been only partially treated before now, without pretending at all to be extraordinarily innovative.

The first issue concerns a concise weighing of the studies on Gramsci and language or Gramsci the linguist. If I may still use this playful title, I will try to deal with the question of why the studies on Gramsci the linguist are not popular in Italy, at least among scholars.

The second issue is to try to understand if and in what way language [*linguaggio*] and linguistic realities form the fundamental poles around which

* Translated from "Alcuni Appunti su Gramsci Linguista," in *Gramsci la Modernità: Letteratura e Political tra Ottocento e Novecento*, ed. Valerio Calzolaio (Naples: CUEN, 1991), 135–44. Translated by Rocco Lacorte with assistance by Peter Ives.

Gramsci's reflection revolves. The third regards the innovative way that Gramsci deals with what I am calling the poles of aggregation of his reflection, not only in relation to language [*linguaggio*], but, at the same time, by using methodologies he learned at the school of "the good" Professor Bartoli. Finally, in the last paragraph, I will try to establish if Gramsci has made an original contribution to our current way of looking at language [*linguaggio*] from a theoretical and operative viewpoint with respect to the effective linguistic reality of our times, and, if so, what kind.

THE STATUS OF THE SCHOLARSHIP

Not all Italian dictionaries include the adjective *abarico*. An area or *abarico* field is that zone where the attraction between two celestial bodies is balanced[1]—as the *Garzanti* dictionary says (I truly believe that not many other dictionaries have included this curious adjective, and rightly so). Therefore, objects that find themselves in that area float without knowing precisely where to go, or better, without going anywhere.

This is precisely the impression one gets looking at the studies on Gramsci and language [*linguaggio*]. It seems that they drift in a sort of *abarico* field: They get produced but they remain unnoticed, without getting much attention from anybody. Yet they are very exquisite studies and often accomplished by very authoritative scholars. It seems to me, without trying to offend anyone, that Natalino Sapegno began this line of inquiry in 1952 with "Manzoni fra De Sanctis e Gramsci" [Manzoni between De Sanctis and Gramsci],[2] reflecting promptly on the extraordinary importance linguistic questions have within the entire Gramscian construction. In 1955, two studies by Soriano followed[3] and the very precise volume by B. T. Sozzi on Gramsci in the context of the question of language [*lingua*] in Italy.[4] Then there are three "classics" by Luigi Rosiello on the role of linguistics in the formation of Gramsci's historicism (starting from the one that appeared in 1959 in the edited volume *La Città Futura* [The Future City]),[5] and still a little-known but very exquisite study, often left out of bibliographies, by Amodio, on Gramsci as a reader of Pragmatism and of Vailati's linguistic ideas, of Pareto and the Pragmatists from Piemonte at the beginning of the twentieth century.[6] Regarding the importance these readings have had on Gramsci, Amodio's study has been supported further by Emilia Passaponti's beautiful thesis at the University of Rome, which has come out in bits later on, here and there, including in party publications.[7] Still, I would like to recall, at least, the works by Antonio Carannante and Stefano Gensini, whose contributions appeared in several rounds; and, finally, Franco Lo Piparo's *Lingua, Intellettuali e Egemonia in Gramsci* [Language, Intellectuals, and Hegemony in Gramsci], which is fundamental, very broad, irate and punctilious but full of data and analyses.[8]

I tend to think that some of the theses of these works have been generally accepted. The first is Rosiello's thesis, much before Lo Piparo, that it is not possible to grasp the particular feature, the physiognomy of historicism, of Gramsci's theory of history if, as Rosiello used to say, one does not take into account the linguistic component of his historicism. In other words, one cannot understand his theory of culture, his theory of hegemony or his theory of politics without considering the linguistic component.

The second strong point resulting from these studies is above all the fertility of Gramsci's suggestions with regard to our country's linguistic history. There is a history of Italian linguistics scattered in various parts of Gramsci's work, particularly in the *Notebooks*, which is condensed at some points, mainly in Notebook 29. It is a very suggestive and important history, which anticipates themes that later on Italian linguistic history has succeeded in recovering for the most part, after having provided more documentation and through further effort.

Another interesting element, which also has an historical character, is the analyses and perspectives on the current linguistic situation in Italy and on the consequences it must have on the direction of the politics of culture (in a country like Italy shattered into many linguistic pieces) and of linguistic pedagogy, from the point of view of the organization of cultural centers and schools.

An additional series of important issues clearly relates to Gramsci's theory of language [*linguaggio*]: the theory of translation and the theory of the radical sociality and culturality of every linguistic structure and order. These are not insignificant issues, given that I am talking about a great personality for the culture. Yet one gets the impression that the acknowledged weight of the analyses of these contributions by Gramsci continues to be a patrimony shared by only a few. It does not enter or it hardly enters the reference works on the subject. Gramsci's name does not appear in the first edition of the *Storia della Lingua Italiana*, 1960 [History of Italian Language], by Migliorini; it does not appear in the second edition of the shorter, more accessible and ideologically more attentive *Profilo di Storia Linguistica Italiana* [Outline of History of Italian Linguistics] by Devoto, nor does it appear in the second edition of the *Storia* [History of Italian Language] by Migliorini subsequently re-edited by Baldelli-Migliorini. It is not included in a little-known incisive book by Zarko Muljačic, the *Introduzione allo Studio della Lingua Italiana* [Introduction to the Study of the Italian Language].[9]

It is curious that Gramsci is not included in a very important book that came out in the mid-1970s by two young scholars, Renzi and Cortellazzo, entitled *La Lingua Italiana, un Problema Politico e Scolastico* [The Italian Language: A Political and Scholastic Problem]. It is a beautiful book, but it seems that Gramsci is omitted because he is too much of a genius, as if the authors do not want to group him with other scholars, which in a devious way prevents his contribution to the social and scholastic issues related to the Italian language. It is like when a professor tries to find fault with a student's work because it is too good.

When Alfredo Stussi wrote his account of linguistic studies in Italy, he considered some of these and similar works linguists have done on Gramsci, to say, "Certainly they are exquisite, elegant; Gramsci, though, is altogether something else. Gramsci's greatness resides in something completely different," in having been something else: the secretary of the Communist Party.[10] This is also the result in his other very important book on Italian literature and regional literatures where Alfredo Stussi discusses all these authors in his usual very detailed and penetrating fashion. But he never cites Gramsci.[11] And this is a very curious fact because his book is deeply influenced by Contini, who does not talk much of Gramsci the linguist (according to the judgment of Pasolini). But Contini does deal with Italian linguistic and literary questions after having fully absorbed Gramsci's problems and made them his own. Stussi follows Contini but, on one hand, he does not mention Gramsci. On the other hand, the official scholarship on Gramsci completely ignores all that has to do with grammar when looking for the framework, roots and genesis of Gramsci's position. Franco Lo Piparo has recently made this point polemically, feeling a certain imbalance (including stylistic) and restraint.

In sum, either one deals with language [*linguaggio*] and linguistics, and therefore not with Gramsci, or one deals with Gramsci the politician and, again, not with Gramsci the linguist.

More recently, Gramsci's name does appear in Durante's book, in which, obviously, works by younger people and scholars like [Stefano] Gensini appear.[12] I would also like to mention the recent book by Francesco Bruni.[13] In these two works Gramsci enters triumphantly. This could be the sign of an ongoing change. Still, I believe that, on the whole, we have to register a sort of loss with respect to the work that I and other linguists have produced on Gramsci and language [*linguaggio*]. Some of us feel somewhat frustrated. We feel we are not taken seriously—and we don't understand why—when we assert that Gramsci was seriously considering these problems. Consequently, some have become exasperated. Anyone who is more isolated becomes upset and ends up saying, "A Marxist? Gramsci was not a Marxist at all. Gramsci was not a politician at all. Gramsci was a linguist. Gramsci was an Ascolian. Only by chance has he become the Secretary of the Communist Party." This is an exasperated reaction; and since he who takes such a stance is a cautious and responsible person—even if it is true that not everybody always succeeds in being cautious and responsible—the fact that such an exasperated reaction has occurred is something on which one must reflect.[14]

My contribution is an attempt to let everyone who is not professionally a linguist or an historian of linguistic ideas engage, to a certain degree, with the question: why did Gramsci insistently talk about language?

2

It seems to me that the main part, not to say the totality, of Gramsci's *Notebooks* focuses on four poles that are not there by chance. These four poles interest Gramsci because it is by means of them that he isolates those aspects of individual and collective experience. These aspects mark the detachment of human beings from what is purely natural and the emergence of human beings to history, that is, abstractly speaking, the emergence of historicity.

These schematically dominating and aggregating four poles can be divided as follows: (1) the economic-productive element pole; (2) what I would call following Gramsci, the cultural pole; (3) the pole of politics; and (4) the linguistic and communicative pole.

Gramsci is interested in the connection between these four realities. One has to understand if and in what way these four realities can be and are connected. Gramsci's best and most fundamental reflections revolve around them. It seems to me that this is what Gramsci is interested in on the theoretical, conceptual and philosophical level. He is interested in refining those theoretical and conceptual connections which may be able to link together productivity (in the economic sense), culture (in the anthropological sense), politics and linguistic-communicative realities.

What I am claiming is banal for those who read Gramsci solely from the philosphical-ideological point of view. However, Gramsci is profoundly a "philosopher." He is a philosopher not because he is an ideologue; he is a philosopher because his texts, the authors he engages with, and his references are primarily of European philosophy. One might enjoy doing the following: counting the references made in the *Notebooks*. You will see that certainly key Marxist authors are well represented according to a hierarchy that goes from Trotsky to Lenin, to Engels, and to Marx, the most quoted and represented in every sense, not only crudely quantitative.

Nonetheless, it is interesting to see that each of those authors referenced has a triumphant rival from what used to be called "bourgeois philosophy" (what I tend to call "European philosophy"). Kant defeats Trotsky in the number of quotations. Giovanni Gentile largely defeats Lenin at several points. Hegel overwhelms Engels; Croce surmounts Marx, even if one takes out all the references to Croce strictly conceived as a man of letters. Philosophers who write academic books defeat Marxist political theorists.

I believe that Gramsci is very careful about specific philosophical questions and about the fashion in which Kantian, Hegelian philosophy posits

them and in which they are posited within the debate between Gentile and
Croce. I see the connection among the four poles as interesting to the extent
that it is a connection of purely conceptual possibilities. In my view, this
constitutes his primary interest. Gramsci is then interested in the historical
level, which constitutes the second level of the connections among these
four realities. Gramsci continuously tries to understand in what way the
following four moments—the economic-productive, the expressive-linguis-
tic, the cultural and the political—interweave and behave in various ways,
giving rise to the different national histories and identities diversely present
and acting within history (I have adopted the Crocean term "expressive-
linguistic" provocatively, but I don't think I am betraying Gramsci's text).
This interweaving offers us the keys not only to understand Italian history,
but also to do it in the context of the other national and European concrete
histories that might still occur.

The third level is the one that, in order to avoid confusion, I would call
"operative." Gramsci was the secretary of the Italian Communist Party, was
a leader of the Communist International, and was responsible for the whole
communist policy in Europe and in Italy. Gramsci's research in fact was not
only enriched by this experience: he was not a professor of linguistics who
experiences how to rule in city hall. The outcome of the workers' and democratic movements was the prevailing interest and the point toward which
Gramsci's reflection tended. He was interested in understanding how, on
the historical and philosophical level, the four realities [poles] I mentioned
above are related. He was, in fact, convinced that only control of these possible theoretical connections, and of how they had given rise to the concrete
Italian and international historical reality, can orient the communist movement within the difficult choices related to the problem of the transition
toward socialism. This relates to defeating fascism and the bourgeoisie that
were in crisis though reaffirming their will to control the crisis.

What, in fact, interests Gramsci was complementing the philosophical
and historical with the practical and operative dimension.

3

At this point, I will try to explain some original aspects in Gramsci—not only
in Gramsci the linguist, but also in Gramsci the politician, the theoretician
and the historian, a great, overwhelming intellectual figure within European
and Italian culture in our century. A first original aspect is the materiality
itself, in the narrow, reductive materiality of the four poles around which
Gramsci organizes his reflection sometimes almost obsessively. There certainly have been great economists sensitive to "other" dimensions and great
theoreticians in the field of economics, historians like Schumpeter. There

have been some linguists, some psycholinguists, mainly Soviet, attentive to the economic-productive preludes of linguistic reality. In short, there have been many people who have worked to sew these four poles together. Yet, if one looks for anyone trying again and again to make and remake the path between those four poles from different directions, in one sense or another, I believe that one could find very few scholars like Gramsci within the horizon of contemporary culture. I have already mentioned one group of such scholars above: scholars of Soviet psycho-pedagogy forgotten in the Soviet Union, except by those pedagogues not forgotten in the West: Vygostky, Leont'ev and Luria. These are scholars who were interested in studying the moment in which creative capabilities emerge. These creative capabilities allow both making history according to diverse ways and inventing the diverse historical paths of the human beings in relation to the complex and articulated warp of productive techniques, of economic organization, communicative techniques, techniques and horizons of cultural comprehension of the world, political orders.

I must also recall the contributions of German scholars belonging to the Frankfurt School, whether or not you agree with them on every point. I am afraid that not much can be added to this. Moreover, notwithstanding the very rich landscape of nineteenth-century Europe, I don't believe there is anywhere else where these normally divergent interests that I have mentioned above (the interest in economic reality, linguistic reality, cultural reality considered in the anthropological sense and political reality) are brought together and made complementary.

A second original element regarding Gramsci as a theoretician in general, and not only as a linguist, seems to lie within the proposal of considering and utilizing his philosophical, historical and operative reflections as complementary. There is no doubt that Gramsci took into account both Marx's and Croce's indications, which he was mainly deriving from Marx with respect to the complementary philosophical and historical analysis. It was from Marx that Gramsci derived the idea that the theoretical-historical dimension is fertile for the operative dimension. Still, in our century, nobody equals Gramsci with respect to this theoretical achievement. After all, it seems to me that Gramsci recalls another of his favorite authors, more often than Marx, when addressing the relationship among these three dimensions. The author I am referring to is Machiavelli, who, a long time ago, had elaborated the same viewpoint in the midst of a tormented century.

Gramsci's third original aspect consists in that he utilized the study of the relationships among the four poles mentioned above both on the philosophical level and on the historical level and, thanks to his operative experiences, in order to break the solidity of each of them. Recalling his pages on Fordism and Taylorism, the connections with respect to the economic-productive side with the work habits and with the present and previous economic orders, it seems to me, Gramsci analyzes each of those four poles proposing again and again a procedure exemplified by historians of literature and literati. That is, he compares the high moments—those that are very institutionalized, in which these four poles are incarnated—with the chaotic mixture of experiences dispersed at a basic level. These experiences are contradictory, often marginalized, and with which Gramsci himself often has little sympathy. These experiences contain within them segments of the high, institutionalized moments—for example, Taylorism or Manzoni's language.[15] I believe it is with respect to these issues that Gramsci uses the methodologies he learned at the school of the good professor Bartoli. These methodologies taught him to see, within the construction of the high linguistic styles, the moments of diverse and composite linguistic realities. Gramsci's phrase "the good professor Bartoli" also means taking into account the quite extraordinary book by Antoine Meillet, which Gramsci knew extremely well: *Esquisse d'une Histoire de la Langue Latine* [A Sketch of the History of Latin Language].[16] This book shows how classical Latin, Latinate characteristics, lasted for centuries, stemming from a procedure of selection, from a reduction of the broad potentialities of Latin, which were only partly saved and condensed in Cicero's style of commentaries, orations and letters. His style was then transmitted as a purified and refined moment of the Latinate culture, which lives and can be understood only as rooted within a much more complex, spurious and heterogeneous Latinate culture. It is this purified moment of Latin that has then had the strength to stand for what is known as Latin in the subsequent centuries: in other words, this has been nothing but a procedure of selection and construction of a hegemony of a certain style.

I believe that the dialectic between these high moments and low, chaotic mixtures of reality, discontinuity and continuity is, in fact, one of Gramsci's contributions to the analysis of economic-productive and political realities, which he derives from the linguistic teachings and studies and that he transfers to the other poles, and in particular to the pole of culture. If one reanalyzes Gramsci's texts, what can be inferred is that Gramsci's notion of culture is a very broad anthropological notion, conceived as a vital capability of constructing systems which allow us to control interactions among us and between us and the environment. In other words, Gramsci does not deal only with "culture" conceived as an intellectual notion. Intellectual culture is nothing but a high moment of these cultural potentials. Literary culture, then, the only type of culture that Asor Rosa mentions in his *Storia della Letteratura Italiana* [History of Italian Literature],[17] is only a moment, often a high moment, within the whole of intellectual culture, that is, it is a moment of a moment. This is not the broad conception of culture as a whole that Gramsci and Marx taught us to conceive.

Therefore, what Gramsci is interested in is trying to see how processes of giving and receiving, fracture and continuity, discontinuity and continuity, are possible within the four related poles that I have been elaborating. There is a fourth point that seems important to me with regard to the questions put forward by Franco Lo Piparo, though from a less exasperated perspective. The four realities we have been talking about so far (the economic-productive, the political, the cultural and the linguistic) are four reciprocally autonomous realities, four moments autonomous with respect to each other. They are concretely connected and theoretically connectable. But none of them rules over the others. In other words, Gramsci's analyses appear to tell us, it seems to me, time after time, in every situation one form can partially dominate the others, but it cannot be determined ahead of time which form will dominate. Gramsci's view of these four realities is a very formal and "Kantian" one. They are forms according to which every possible human experience organizes itself, in which human beings detached themselves from purely mechanistic and biological consequentiality and come to history (i.e., to the possibility of tracing ways different from the ones already inscribed in the genetic code).

Finally, therefore, these considerations, viewed from the perspective of the history of ideas, make a crucial point: "the" strong point of Gramsci's thought is a theory of history in relation to natural reality. Thus, I fully agree with the fact that his theory is highly systematic, regardless of the form that the fascist prison forced Gramsci to present his reflections in. Gramsci's *Notebooks* do not favor fragments nor advocate fragmentation.

4

Does anything original and interesting result from all I have been saying so far which allows one to understand languages [*linguaggi*] and linguistic realities better and more thoroughly? I believe so. A *Miscellanea* [an edited collection of essays] celebrating the centenary of Isaia Ascoli's birth was published while Gramsci was in prison. As Gramsci himself says, and as Lo Piparo demonstrated, Ascoli certainly is one of the sources of Gramsci's theoretical elaborations, but, for me, not the only one. So this *Miscellanea* appears, but obviously Gramsci can not participate and contribute to it. He is absent from it. Leo Spitzer reviewed it in 1934 and delivered a speech that has had much influence on us (i.e., on the guild of linguists). He said: "There is something intriguing about the fact that, whereas all the nineteenth century's great linguists"—or Gramscians?—"in all European countries (Michel Bréal, Ferdinand de Saussure, William D. Whitney in the United States) have been followed by an impressive blossoming of studies in our century, Ascoli, by contrast, had no successors."[18] This is so if one looks at the history of Italian academies in the early twentieth century. I find that Sebastiano Timpanaro's attempt to demonstrate that Salvioni—or other skilled dialectology and glottology professors of the early twentieth century—is the real heir of a scholar as eminent as Ascoli to be generous but inane. In the 1930s, Spitzer could not have known the only real successor of Ascoli's legacy—namely, Gramsci. He was not uniquely a follower, but a successor. The only successor of Ascoli is Gramsci. I would like to recall very briefly some strong points of Gramsci's linguistic theory.

First, there is the very important tension within the semantic dimension of the organization of meanings within the languages [*lingue*]. By the way, it would be worth introducing, in the index of Gerratana's edition of the *Prison Notebooks*, the term "semantics," because the references to it are scattered and discontinuous. Gramsci's sources include all the work of historical linguistics, in particular by that minority of historical linguistics that had shown how each language has its own way to semantically organize the same reality, according to ways that differ from one language to another; this posits a problem of *translatability* from one language to another, which is one of Gramsci's issues. Gramsci maintains that it is always possible to translate from one language [*lingua*] to another thanks to an inner force of the language [*lingua*] itself, which is the expanding metaphorical force of meanings. It is through this force that meanings expand until they conquer a wider terrain and succeed in facing the requirements of saying and translating newer and newer things.

Now, all these problems are completely atypical with respect to mid-nineteenth-century linguistics: they have been recovered only recently. So one could affirm: "Linguists are dumb!" Well, this is it. In other words, Gramsci is not a banal theoretician of language [*linguaggio*], one who is repetitive. He is a strong innovator.

The last point of great interest: Gramsci does not agree with the restriction of what Humboldt had called "confrontation [and] comparison among different languages" in order to understand how each language is made and the peculiar historicity of each language. That comparison was reduced solely to phonetics and morphology, to the study and comparison among ending systems and phonetic systems: this was what linguistics and the good professor Bartoli had done. Gramsci, who did not seem to have read Humboldt much, recovers, probably by means of Ascoli and by reading the *Zibaldone*,[19] the more complex dimension regarding comparison as a technique that allows the understanding of, not only on the linguistic terrain, how a particular historical situation is made.

One must really agree with and understand in depth the complex irony and the auto-irony with which Gramsci judges himself in one of his letters. It is the famous letter of 1927: in it Gramsci recalls how the good professor Bartoli assigned him the task to be "archangel destined to put to definitive rout the neogrammarians," and to destroy them once and for all.[20] Gramsci is ironic, here and elsewhere, about his own project because he is aware that the task is more complex. But the task he has given to himself and which he has carried out is more complex; not because it was not worth wiping out the neo-grammarians. It was only possible to carry out that task in a much more complex and broad framework, the one related to the entire liberation of intellectual and moral capabilities, which is the liberation Gramsci has given us as an assignment to carry out.

NOTES

1. [While there is no English translation of *abarico*, the Italian term is sometimes used in English astronomy. It is the phenomenon of a body at the Lagrangian point, as described].

2. Natalino Sapegno, "Manzoni fra De Sanctis e Gramsci," *Società* 1 (1952): 7–19.

3. Marc Soriano, "Problèmes de critique littéraire par Antonio Gramsci," *Les Lettres Nouvelles* 23 (1955): 74–76; and especially "Problèmes scolaires," *Europe* 111 (1955): 81–82.

4. Bartolo Tommasso Sozzi, *Aspetti e Momenti della Questione Linguistica* (Padova: Liviana, 1955).

5. Luigi Rosiello, "La componente linguistica dello storicismo gramsciano," in *La Città Futura. Saggi sulla figura e il pensiero di Antonio Gramsci*, ed. Alberto Caracciolo and Gianni Scalia (Milan: Feltrinelli, 1959), 299–327; "Problemi linguistici negli scritti di Gramsci," in *Gramsci e la Cultura Contemporanea*, ed. Pietro Rossi (Rome: Editori Riuniti–Istituto Gramsci, 1970), 347–67 [and chapter 2 of this volume].

6. Luciano Amodio, "L'interpretazione gramsciana del linguaggio" [Gramsci's Interpretation of Language], *Il Corpo* I, no. 2 (1965): 83–88.

7. Emilia Passaponti, *Temi Linguistici nel Pensiero di A. Gramsci* [Linguistic Themes in Gramsci's Thought], unedited thesis (Rome, 1976–1977).

8. Franco Lo Piparo, *Lingua, Intellettuali e Egemonia in Gramsci* (Bari: Laterza, 1979).

9. Giacomo Devoto, *Profilo di Storia Linguistica Italiana* (Florence: La Nuova Italia, 1953); Bruno Migliorini, *Storia della Lingua Italiana* (Bologna: Sansoni, 1960); Ignazio Baldelli, *Breve Storia della Lingua Italiana* (Florence: Sansoni, 1964); and Zarko Muljačić, *Introduzione allo Studio della Lingua Italiana* (Turin: Einaudi, 1970).

10. Alfredo Stussi, "Storia della Linguistica Italiana," in *Dieci Anni di Linguistica Italiana, 1965–1975*, ed. Daniele Gambarara and Paolo Ramat (Rome: Bolzoni, 1977).

11. Alfredo Stussi, *Studi e Documenti di Storia della Lingua e dei Dialetti Italiani* [Studies and Documents of History of Language and of Dialects] (Bologna: Il Mulino, 1982).

12. Marcello Durante, *Dal Latino all'Italiano Moderno: Saggio di storia linguistica italiana* [From Latin to Modern Italian: Essay on the History of Italian Language] (Bologna: Zanichelli, 1981).

13. Francesco Bruni, *L'italiano: Elementi di storia della lingua e della cultura. Testi e documenti* [Italian: Elements for the History of Language and Culture. Texts and Documents] (Turin: Utet, 1984).

14. See Franco Lo Piparo, "Studio del linguaggio e teoria gramsciana," *Critica Marxista* 2/3 (1987): 167–75 [chapter 1 of this volume].

15. [For a summary of what De Mauro is indicating, see Green and Ives, chapter 16, pages 298–300, in this volume, concerning Manzoni.]

16. Antoine Meillet, *Esquisse d'une Histoire de la Langue Latine* (Paris: Hachette, 1968).

17. Alberto Asor Rosa, *Storia della Letteratura Italiana* (Florence: La Nuova Italia, 1973).

18. [No citation provided.]

19. [Giacomo Leopardi's massive collection of notes; see chapter 6, note 3, in this volume.]

20. Antonio Gramsci, *Letters from Prison*, vol. 1, ed. Frank Rosengarten, trans. Raymond Rosenthal (New York: Columbia University Press), 83.

15

The Lexicon of Gramsci's Philosophy of Praxis

*André Tosel**

In his important book, *L'Officina Gramsciana: Ipotesi sulla Struttura dei "Quaderni del Carcere"* [Gramsci's Workshop: Hypotheses on the Structure of the "Prison Notebooks"], Gianni Francioni verifies the fruitfulness of his methodological suggestions by applying them to the thematic concerning the philosophy of praxis.[1] A diachronic-structural examination of the appearances and elaboration of the term "philosophy of praxis" reveals that Gramsci does not use it to be cautious—that is, to elude the vigilance of the prison censorship.

Initially Gramsci takes the term "philosophy of praxis" as a linguistic equivalent of the expression "historical materialism"—which was common in the cultural-political environment of the Third International—and later in the course of the *Notebooks* he recuperates it as an identity card of a program capable of elaborating Marxism in response to the challenges of the times, and explicitly joined to the path delineated by Antonio Labriola that was later blurred by the different idealistic operations of Benedetto Croce and Giovanni Gentile.

In the three series of "Notes on Philosophy" throughout Notebooks 4, 7 and 8, Gramsci most often uses the term "historical materialism" and even "Marxism." Notebook 8 constitutes the beginning of a change. Moreover, Notebooks 10 and 11 contain a sort of eruption of an autonomous problematic of the "philosophy of praxis." Not only does Gramsci develop the necessity of retranslating the origins of the foundational debate of 1895–1900 into new terms, but he also produces new concepts through which

* Translated from "Il Lessico 'Filosofia della Prassi' di Gramsci," *Marxismo Oggi* 1 (1996): 49–67. Translated from the Italian by Rocco Lacorte with assistance by Peter Ives.

the crisis of socialism and the workers' movement could be thought on a double level: philosophical-conceptual and historical-analytical.

ELEMENTS OF PHILOLOGY

"Philosophy of Praxis" as a Nomenclature and as a Theoretical Question

Valentino Gerratana's subject index of his critical edition of the *Prison Notebooks* allows us to document the texts of the "Notes on Philosophy," series I, II, III, where the term "historical materialism" has been replaced by "philosophy of praxis." The comparison between A-texts and C-texts shows the systematic character of this substitution.[2] The decisive point is that Gramsci himself has in some way theoretized this substitution under the rubric the "Question of Nomenclature" and "General Questions." We can start from the indications Gramsci gives us referring to the term "material-ism" [*materialismo*] (the "Notes on Philosophy" are subtitled "Idealism and Materialism"). For Gramsci, pursuing the pure problematic of materialism is a sign of an old way of thinking that should be replaced by the thematic and concept of immanence. The disappearance of the use of "historical materialism" and "Marxism" coincides with the emergence of this question of nomenclature that is itself parallel to the generalization of the use of the term "philosophy of praxis." Therefore, the question of nomenclature is a conceptual and substantial one.

Gramsci presents the problem in Notebook 8§171. Marxist orthodoxy—Plekhanov, Bukharin and others—confuses lexical and substantial questions. It lacks a historical sense and does not understand that materialism as a general philosophy goes back to a traditional way of positing the question of theory. Marxist orthodoxy remains imprisoned in the abstract schemes of formal logic: it is not capable of intuiting and developing the potential within the modern question of immanence. Notebook 11§16 is the corresponding C-text of Notebook 8§171. It continues this text and makes clear that the inability of finding the right term (nomenclature) is a form of the inability of dealing with the new task—namely, the creation of a new super-structure or of a new intellectuality. "The new social group which organi-cally represents the new historical situation" is not able to perform its func-tion and identifies itself with a conservative residue of a social group that is historically overcome.[3] Linguistic innovations demand conceptual innova-tions: an unprecedented historical situation demands its own concept and language. The formula "historical materialism" is tied to a historical situ-ation that put on the agenda that the forces slated to become hegemonic had to reach compromises with the classes dominated by the ideology of transcendence, and which were tied to the economic-corporative moment of force relationships. On the contrary, the phrase "philosophy of praxis" is tied to a phase in which a more accomplished and perfect system is imposing itself and in which a new philosophy is necessary, one which is capable of "posing and resolving critically the problems that present themselves as an expression of historical development."[4] A contemporary note from the same Notebook 11—§28—is even more clear and specifies the connection between immanence and the philosophy of praxis: "The philosophy of praxis continues the philosophy of immanence but purifies it of all its metaphysical apparatus and brings it onto the concrete terrain of history."[5] An ultimate proof of Gramsci's tendency to systematically replace the terms "historical materialism" and "Marxism" with "philosophy of praxis" is provided (still in the first half of 1932) by the emergence of his reference to Antonio Labriola under the banner "philosophy of praxis." There is no doubt that Notebook 3§31 referred to the general "philosophical views of Labriola," but it did that in the frame of an analysis of the rupture of the so-called Marxism into two currents—that is, a materialist and an agnostic one (Austro-Marxism). Gramsci already posits this problem in relation to the necessity of constructing a "new type of state" and of elaborating a very refined and decisive worldview.[6] Yet, in Notebook 11§70, which is a C-text, this theme erupts: Gramsci insists on the autonomy—namely, on the self-sufficiency—of the philosophy of praxis and makes a direct reference to hegemony: "From the moment in which a subaltern group becomes really autonomous and hegemonic, thus bringing into being a new form of State, we experience the concrete birth of a need to construct a new intellectual and moral order, that is, a new type of society, and hence the need to develop more universal concepts and more refined and decisive ideological weapons."[7] Now the moment has come to deal systematically with the philosophy of praxis as theory and a live form of hegemony. Now it is necessary to go back to the interrupted link with "the only man who has attempted to build up the philosophy of praxis scientifically."[8]

"Philosophy of Praxis" as Genre and Species

The parallel between the "Notes on Philosophy" (I Notebook 4, II Notebook 7, III Notebook 8) and the more elaborated thematic Notebooks allows us to understand that the philosophy of praxis is at once genre and species of the genre. As genre, the philosophy of praxis refers to its "founder" Marx and indicates Marxism—namely, a general form of theory-conception of the world which continues and crowns the movement of intellectual and moral reformation begun in the Renaissance and the Reformation, which is then developed through the Enlightenment and the French Revolution, and finally refined as idealistic German philosophy. As a species of this genre—as worldview—the philosophy of praxis represents the actual phase in which what is at stake is the elaboration of the philosophy of praxis itself: the construction of hegemony demands that "Marxism" is determined as the philosophy of praxis in a strong sense, that is, capable of criticizing and integrating the idealist-revisionist critique of the Second International's Marxisms—that is, the economistic orthodoxy and agnosticism.

We can follow the development of this issue by comparing an A-text and a C-text about the same nexus of problems. The first text, Notebook 4§3, entitled "Two Aspects of Marxism," revives the analysis that Gramsci laid out in the already-quoted Notebook 3§3, but analyzes it at a further level of complexity: the two revisions of Marxism—economistic materialism and agnosticism—now form only one current that is assimilated and overcome by Italian idealism, which knew how to rejuvenate itself by integrating the vital elements of the so-called orthodox Marxism and of its impotent agnostic critique. Gramsci, at this point in the *Notebooks*, does not talk about "philosophy of praxis" but still of "Marxism" and of "historical materialism." He writes:

> Marxism had two tasks: to combat modern ideologies in their more refined form; and to enlighten the minds of the popular masses, whose culture was medieval. This second task, which was fundamental, has absorbed all its energies, not only "quantitatively" but also "qualitatively." For "didactic" reasons, Marxism became mixed with a form of culture that was somewhat superior to the popular mentality but inadequate to combat the other ideologies of the educated classes; yet, at its inception, Marxism actually superseded the highest cultural manifestation of the time, classical German philosophy.[9]

Gramsci formulates the interrupted program as follows: "Historical materialism, in its dialectic of popular culture–high culture, is the crowning point of this entire movement of intellectual and moral reform. It corresponds to Reformation + French Revolution, universality + politics."[10]

The second passage (Q16§9) returns to this entire thematic, enriching it and putting it under the explicit title: "Some Problems for a Study of the Philosophy of Praxis." This time Antonio Labriola is recognized as the only one who "distinguishes himself from both currents [the orthodox Marxists and the agnostics] by his affirmation (not always, admittedly, unequivocal) that the philosophy of praxis is an independent and original philosophy which contains in itself the elements of a further development, so as to become, from an interpretation of history, a general philosophy."[11] Now what is needed is to overcome Croce and to refuse "the reduction of the philosophy of praxis to an empirical canon of historical research."[12] Only in this way can the economic-corporative *impasse* of the Marxism of Bukharin—the best representative of the Third International—be overcome. This is a point of arrival that concludes a starting point based on a "general philosophy"—that is, "a philosophy which is also politics and a politics which is also a kind of philosophy."[13] Thus, Gramsci affirms the link between the formation of a new intellectual group, the transformation of the common sense of the subaltern masses and the emergence of the ethical-political state. The theoretical autonomy and independence of the philosophy of praxis as a hegemonic plan imply its dependence on the "historical-moral development"—dependence that characterizes immanent philosophies—and specifies its theoretical-critical tasks connecting them to a "total liberation from any form of abstract 'ideologism,' the real conquest of the historical world, the beginnings of a new civilization."[14]

Now we can legitimately argue that "the affirmation that the philosophy is a new, independent and original conception, even though it is also a moment of world historical development, is an affirmation of the independence and originality of a new culture in incubation, which will develop with the development of social relations."[15]

Moments of the Appearance and of the Consolidation of the "Philosophy of Praxis": From "Notes on Philosophy" I, II, III to Notebooks 10 and 11

A rapid analysis of the three series of "Notes" shows that they center on the critique of the theoretical-practical form of Bukharin's *Essay*. Yet almost immediately Gramsci makes recourse to Croce, the leader of international revisionism, who developed the capability of criticizing this "deviation" of the philosophy of praxis. The need to return to the philosophical dimension is required by his need to further elaborate the theme of the relationships between structure and superstructure: Notebook 8 marks out the decisive turning point toward the autonomization of the philosophy of praxis.

A

Gramsci does not use the term "philosophy of praxis" in Notebook 4. If in its place, however, one finds the term "historical materialism," the new thematic is present as a critique of the philosophical weakness of Bukharin's historical materialism, divided between a positive sociology of classes and a vulgar materialism. Gramsci's use of the term "philosophy of praxis" is marginal: it tangentially appears in §28 when he makes a reference to the book of Antonino Lovecchio, *Philosophy of Praxis and Philosophy of the Spirit* [*Filosofia della Praxis e Filosofia dello Spirito*], regarding the Labriola-Croce-Gentile debate. The elaboration in Notebook 4 goes beyond problems of lexicon and nomenclature.

In Notebook 4§37, the noun "praxis" appears to denote the integral activity of humanity as the object of so-called historical materialism. But

Gramsci uses the language of the actualist philosophy of Giovanni Gentile, defining praxis as an "impure act." Gramsci does not name Gentile, but his allusion is clear: the path toward Labriola is somewhat mediated by the memory of Gentile. Yet Gramsci amends this memory immediately, in the sense of a concrete determination of the economic and political contents of praxis. The problem concerning the value of the ideological superstructures and the objectivity of knowledge cannot be solved for him by resorting to "monism":

> It is obviously neither idealistic nor materialistic "monism," neither "Matter" nor "Spirit," but rather "historical materialism," that is to say, concrete human activity (history): namely, activity concerning a certain organized "matter" (material forces of production) and the transformed "nature" of man. Philosophy of the act (praxis), not of the "pure act" but rather the "impure"—that is, real—act, in the most secular sense of the word.[16]

Notebook 4 reaches the decisive idea, in terms of content [although not nomenclature], of "a systematic treatment of historical materialism" that implies that it should "deal with the general philosophical part in its entirety, and furthermore it should also be a theory of history, a theory of philosophy, a theory of economics."[17] This point is made within his critique of Bukharin's *Popular Manual*. In this way, however, Gramsci leaves open the question of the lexical adjustment that Notebook 4 itself is positing. In this notebook, we have at least two examples of Gramsci's position of the problem of nomenclature. The first one appears in §17, when Gramsci questions the relevance of the term "immanence" to define the true tradition in which Marx's theory is inserted—a theory that, at the same time, renews that tradition.[18] The second one can be found in §34, which Gramsci entitles "Regarding the Name Historical Materialism." This note quotes the words of the scientist [Alessandro] Volta, who said, "'I believe that, when something new is discovered in the sciences, one must adopt an entirely new term for it. . . .' and that those who specify terms that maintain 'some resemblance or connection between the old idea and the new one [confuse] science and [this] leads to useless controversies.'"[19]

B

Before examining Notebook 7, it is important to point out an isolated text: Notebook 5§127, dedicated to Machiavelli. Gramsci maintains that the author of *The Prince* did not write books about immediate political action or a utopia.[20] On the contrary, Machiavelli "in his treatment, in his critique of the present, he articulated some general concepts that are presented in an aphoristic and nonsystematic form. He also articulated a conception of the world that could also be called"—I need to emphasize this—"'philosophy of praxis' or 'neohumanism,' in that it does not recognize transcendental or immanent (in the metaphysical sense) elements but is based entirely on the concrete action of man, who out of historical necessity works and transforms reality."[21] Machiavelli and Marx therefore had the same theoretical destiny: they are revolutionary theoreticians of practice, who revolutionized even philosophy, but who did not explicitly elaborate their philosophy. The problem of philosophy coincides, therefore, once again with the question of the conquest-foundation of a new type of state. Yet the specific philosophical problem posed by the work of Marx, unlike the one posed by Machiavelli, implies only "a system of principles asserting that the end of the state is its own end, its own disappearance: in other words, the reabsorption of political society into civil society."[22]

C

The term "philosophy of praxis" recurs more often in Notebook 7. This happens above all when Gramsci discusses Croce, whom he acknowledges as a superior theoretician of history and politics than Bukharin, in his schematic *Manual*. Gramsci's recourse to Labriola's philosophy of praxis was mediated by his recollection of Gentile's actualism, which itself was mediated by his engagement with Croce—the only one who was able to utilize the perspective of the methodology of history to determine and make concrete the content of praxis.

In this notebook, Gramsci uses the noun "praxis" more frequently than earlier, which he regards as a unitary concept that allows one to think of the dialectical development of the historical process, and to specify the relations of force between economy, politics, culture, philosophy without the unilinear mechanism of structure-superstructure. Note 18—also a B-text—considers "[t]he unity in the component parts of Marxism" and specifies that in the frame of the general theme of the "unity comes from the dialectical development of the contradictions between man and matter (nature-material forces of production)" is necessary to specify the unity within the domains of economy, philosophy and politics: "In economics, the center of unity is value, that is, the relation between the worker and the industrial forces of production. . . . In politics [it is] the relation between the state and civil society, that is, the intervention of the state (centralized will) to educate the educator, the social milieu in general." The equivalent of value in "philosophy" or in these relations in economics and politics is nothing but "praxis, that is, the relation between human will (superstructure) and the economic structure."[23] Another note from the same notebook, devoted to the examination of the concept of human nature, explicitly identifies historical materialism "with a philosophy of praxis." Note 35 identifies the problem posited by "historical materialism" as philosophical, defining it as the "problem of what man is":

> The problem of what man is, then, is always the so-called problem of "human nature," or of so-called man in general; in other words, it is the attempt to create a science of man (a philosophy) that has for its starting point a "unitary" concept, an abstraction capable of containing everything "human." . . . The correct framing of the problem demands defining "human nature" as "the whole ensemble of human relationships" . . . because it includes the idea of becoming—man becomes, he changes continuously with the changing of social relations—and because it negates "man in general."

The term "philosophy of praxis" is more adequate, as Gramsci writes: "Thus one arrives also at the equality of, or the equation between, 'philosophy and politics,' thought and action, that is, at the philosophy of praxis. Everything is political, even philosophy or the philosophies . . . and the only 'philosophy' is history in action, life itself."[24]

D

In Notebook 8, Gramsci regularizes in ways his tendency to substitute the phrase "the philosophy of praxis," but does not eliminate the use of "historical materialism." This generates a situation of competition between "philosophy of praxis" and "historical materialism." Yet, in this notebook, the sense of Gramsci's tendency to such a substitution becomes clearer because only *the* philosophy of praxis (and not a "philosophy of praxis") can think through and determine the revolutionary process of the "overturning of praxis." Likewise, §182 (a B-text) puts forth the revision of the concept of "historical bloc":

> The structure and the superstructures form a "historical bloc." In other words, the complex and discordant ensemble of the superstructures reflects the ensemble of social relations of production. From this, one can conclude that only a comprehensive system of ideologies rationally reflects the contradiction of the structure and represents the existence of the objective conditions for revolutionizing praxis.[25]

But even more important is §198. It is maybe the first to be entitled "Philosophy of Praxis." In this note, criticizing Croce's critique of Labriola's proposal ("to construct a 'philosophy of praxis' on the basis of Marxism"), Gramsci looks again at Marx's fundamental argument concerning Feuerbach and refuses the absorption of the philosophical dimension inside practical activity alone.[26] Since we cannot retrace the entire path of this truly pivotal notebook—where we must recall that Gramsci explicitly posits the problem of lexicon and nomenclature (§171)—it will be enough to notice three significant texts (§220, §232, and §235). The decisive step forward, which the *Notebooks* consolidate, is then constituted by the elaboration of the connections unifying philosophy–common sense–worldview under the point of view of hegemony.

Notebook 8§220 (which was rewritten in Q11§12) affirms that "[a] philosophy of praxis must initially adopt a polemical stance, as superseding the existing mode of thinking. It must therefore present itself as a critique of 'common sense' . . . [and also] as a critique of the philosophy of intellectuals, out of which the history of philosophy arises." The philosophy of praxis should thus be developed following two axes: on the one hand, as a reformation of common sense by employing the position that all humans are philosophers; on the other hand, as an exposition of the "'problems' that arose in the course of the history of philosophy, in order to criticize them, demonstrate their real value (if they still have any) or their importance as links in a chain, and define the new problems of the present time."[27]

Notebook 8§235 (which was rewritten in Q11§12) makes the plan for an *Anti-Croce*,[28] a task for the new philosophy of praxis, which can constitute itself only as critical heir of the historical series "transcendence, immanence, and speculative historicism." This *Anti-Croce* proceeds on two fronts: the fight against speculative philosophy and the critique of the "deterioration of the philosophy of praxis" (positivism and mechanic theories). The philosophy of praxis still uses Croce's speculative historicism in order to correct its own deviations and to form a new theoretical structure capable of historicizing itself by identifying the tasks of the epochal moment. Notebooks 10 and 11 will produce the outlines of this structure that, insofar as it is the philosophy of praxis, goes beyond the old plan called "historical materialism" that has become antiquated.[29]

ELEMENTS OF THE PHILOSOPHY OF PRAXIS:
NETS, POLES, DIAGONALS

Notebooks 10 and 11 are explicitly devoted to the elaboration of the philosophy of praxis, but from different points of view. As Francioni has made clear it is above all Notebook 11 that constitutes the most organic effort of thematization: Gramsci's critique of Bukharin's crude historical materialism, which is the peak of the Third International's Marxism, implies that the pernicious division between positivist sociology and transcendental metaphysical materialism must be overcome. The philosophy of praxis wins back its position and asserts itself by positing the general question of science, of scientific tools and of the relationships between common sense, worldview and language, opening in this way the perspective of dialectic beyond Engels's speculativism. With specific regard to Notebook 10, one can say that it is not so much a special notebook, but rather a new series of "notes," the plan of which is Gramsci's critical recuperation of Croce's philosophical elaboration to serve the purposes of the new perspective pursued by the philosophy of praxis. The *Anti-Croce* is the obligatory path to start a methodology and a theory of history. It furnishes the key of the "ethico-political" moment—namely, the question regarding both the "historical bloc" and hegemony.

All these themes are intertwined: the continuation of theory poses the question of what philosophy is, specifically concerning historical causality, science and the relationships among science, ideology and the worldview of the masses. Moreover, the problem of science is connected, in turn, to common sense, the historical function of the intellectuals and, therefore, of politics, and the joining of structure and superstructure. The articulation of the two notebooks that were written almost contemporaneously—Notebook 10 was finished after Notebook 11—can be better specified.

Notebook 10 continues by integrating the ethico-political moment into the theory of history; it reveals the place and the function of philosophy as a worldview, as politics and culture. This integration is made in the name of *Anti-Croce* (which means, at the same time, *With-Croce*). This integration also implies a historical-critical axis, to the extent that philosophy, insofar as it formulates itself as philosophy of praxis, thinks its own historicity and goes beyond the representation of itself as eternal opposition between materialism and idealism. Notebook 11 elaborates theoretically the general program of the philosophy of praxis: it starts from the politics-culture nexus, it clarifies the relationship of worldview–common sense and reveals the decisive function of language and its levels (the scientific constitutes the highest linguistic level). The question of philosophy as translatability of scientific languages becomes the nucleus of the general plan, which, instead of turning into an internal limit, closed to the outside, opens anew onto politics as intellectual and moral reform of the subaltern masses as a candidate for hegemony. The axis of Gramsci's research is therefore rather historical-systematic: this is how the movement of Notebooks 10 and 11 can be explained—but one should not crystallize this historical-systematic proposal.

The Philosophy of Praxis as a Methodology of History: Ethical-Political Moment and Worldview (on Notebook 10)

The *Anti-Croce* produces a re-elaboration of the concept of the theory of history by criticizing the economistic-deterministic view of historical causality. Gramsci's retrieval of Croce's ethical-political history allows doing away with a unilinear representation of the relationship of economy (structure)/politics (superstructure) and substituting it with a reticular conception of the "historical bloc." The theoretical center of Notebook 10 is philosophically constituted by the methodology of causality. Thus the philosophy of praxis transforms the strong reduction done by Croce (who had reduced historical materialism to an empirical canon, stressing the importance of the economic factor) and retranslates the methodology of the ethico-political moment, which Croce himself conceived as an anti-Marxist function, into a theory of history as strong (following the line of "catharsis" and of the "historical bloc" where the instances of praxis are thought according to a network with equal poles). It would be useful to reread part one of Notebook 10 ("Reference Points for an Essay on B. Croce"), and above all §7, §8, §11 and §12. This is what Gramsci writes in §7:

> One can say that not only does the philosophy of praxis not exclude ethico-political history, but that, indeed, in its most recent stage of development it consists precisely in asserting the moment of hegemony as essential to its conception of the state and in attaching "full weight" to the cultural factor, to cultural activity, to the necessity for a cultural front alongside the merely economic and merely political ones.[30]

It is, therefore, important to learn Croce's methodological lesson, but then to develop a theory of the "historical bloc." This theory is no longer a simple empirical canon of research, but a conquest of concrete-historical reality. The passage mentioned above is completed by a passage in the second part of the same notebook, 10§41: "The concept of the concrete (historical) value of superstructures in the philosophy of praxis needs to be developed further, by juxtaposing it with Sorel's concept of 'historical bloc.'"[31] Yet perhaps Gramsci had already forced, by means of an unwitting irony, the theme of the empirical canon toward the affirmative sense of a theory of integral history, when in the first part of Notebook 10§12, he specified:

> For the philosophy of praxis the conception of ethico-political history, in that it is independent of any realist conception, may be adopted as an "empirical canon" of historical research which needs constantly to be borne in mind in examining and understanding historical development, if the aim is that of producing integral history and not partial and extrinsic history (history of economic forces as such, etc.).[32]

The answer to the question about a theory nonreductive of historical causality—culminating in a proposal regarding a reticular theory of the historical bloc—imposes, in turn, the retrieval of the problem concerning the link connecting the theoretical and the historical aspect of philosophy by affirming a radical immanence: "The philosophy of praxis certainly derives from the immanentist conception of reality, but only in so far as this latter is stripped of its speculative halo and reduced to pure history or historicity or to pure humanism."[33] Croce must, therefore, be criticized for excessive speculation, that is, for not having understood that the concept of structure indicates:

> the ensemble of social relations in which real people move and act as an ensemble of objective conditions which can and must be studied with the methods of "philology" and not by means of "speculation." It must be studied as something "certain" that may also be "true," but it must be studied first of all in its "certainty" in order for it to be studied as "truth."[34]

This reference to Vico shows the anti-mechanistic value of the concept of cause, which includes human activity. Gramsci rectifies the speculative historicism of Croce and his reading of Vico. The reformulation of causality implies the dependency of theory and philosophy on historical reality and social relations. The independence of the philosophy of praxis establishes itself as independent from the concreteness of human practices and shows the place of philosophy as human activity which culminates in a series that includes common sense and various opposing worldviews.

As has already been noted:

> The philosophy of praxis is bound up not only with immanentism but also with the subjective conception of reality in so far as it turns this latter upside down, explaining it as a historical fact, as the "historical subjectivity of a social group," as a real fact which presents itself as a phenomenon of philosophical "speculation" while it is simply a practical act, the form assumed by a concrete social content and the way that the whole of society is led to fashion a moral unity for itself.[35]

The rediscovery by the philosophy of praxis of the ethico-political moment implies the historicization of the philosophy of praxis itself and the development of the subjective conception of the reality of a new historical group still entangled in a Ptolemaic and roughly objectivist common sense. Philosophy amends—does not negate—common sense, because it is not a pure and a priori theoretical activity, which is closed in itself and in its autonomized categories. If "catharsis," as a shift from the economic-corporative to the ethico-political moment, coincides with "the superior elaboration of the structure into superstructure in humans consciousness," if "the fixation of the 'cathartic' moment becomes, in this way, the starting point for the entire philosophy of praxis,"[36] then philosophy must assign itself its historical-political place and mirror the continuity that connects it to common sense and determines it as religion—as Croce would say.

Thus, philosophy is not something that is very difficult and specialized: certainly it determines new theoretical truths and above all popularizes those already discovered. Philosophy intervenes by leading masses of human beings to think in agreement, producing a new conformism, which is superior to the extent that it is tied to fundamental activities of the masses of workers. The philosophy of praxis presumes that acting and thinking can not, and must not, be separated. One can now understand the extraordinary thesis of Notebook 10, which synthesizes the logical-historical shift: politics-culture-philosophy: "Reduction of all speculative philosophies to 'politics,' to a moment of historico-political life; the philosophy of praxis conceives the reality of human relationships of knowledge as an element of political 'hegemony.'"[37] Croce knew how to formulate this problem, but could not avoid the *impasse* of liberal culture that crystallized the separation between intellectuals and masses. The philosophy of praxis is tied to daily productive activity and does not have the task of forming intellectuals who are isolated and who act "efficaciously" according to a preestablished theory. Rather, it holds the possibility of organic intellectuals emerging from the masses of workers who are capable of confronting the economic, political and cultural exigencies of the historical situation—that is, of conceiving the problem posited by the possible constitution of a new historical bloc and of searching for the "proper" ways of practical transformation. Knowing how to think concretely about situations is an essential element of the unity of praxis. Theory cannot be anything other than the development of the questions posited by praxis. The philosophy of praxis only has the possibility of continuing—criticizing it because of its narrowness—the work begun by the Renaissance, the Reformation, the Enlightenment and the French Revolution. This work consisted and consists of producing an intellectual and moral reformation of the masses that unifies the theory of historical process conceived as a formation of historic blocs and the common sense, which has become—since it has been amended and historicized—good sense, that is, a critical and effective worldview. The philosophy of praxis transforms the "religion of freedom" by Croce into "heresy" that tends to educate one with the other: namely, high theory and popular "religion."[38]

"The nature of the philosophy of praxis is in particular that of being a mass conception, a mass culture, that of a mass which operates in a unitary fashion, i.e., one that has norms of conduct that are not only universal in idea but 'generalised' in social reality."[39] Modern liberal culture is losing contact with the "simple people" because of how it produces and performs politics and how it is disassimilating the subaltern. The philosophy of praxis faces the following challenge: it must weave the threads of its engagement with scientific problems, above all those regarding political science, with the masses. Thus, weaving the connection with the masses becomes, for the philosophy of praxis, an eternally open problem because, to the extent that it is historical knowledge, it has the task of conceiving historical relationships, their transformations, and their hegemonic possibilities. It has to constitute itself as an organic worldview which is assimilated and criticized through the experience of the masses, since the educator must be educated by being in permanent contact with those being educated. The intellectual and moral reformation determines itself as an endless reformation of common sense (as a critique of economistic, mechanistic and vulgar materialistic elements through the phase in which the masses become a state). Philosophy conceived as knowledge is not separated from common sense conceived as pure illusion and prejudice, but rather penetrates the heart of common sense itself in order to give shape to the historical epoch to which it must ask the questions concerning its "proper" daily identity. The elaboration of the philosophy of praxis is established, therefore, as a simultaneous process of transformation of common sense and of itself conceived as a theory of history and political science. The (philological) interpretation and transformation of it as common sense and as technical philosophy go together. Citing a quite long text will make explicit the trajectory of Notebook 10 through politics-culture-philosophy-common sense-politics:

> for the philosophy of praxis the superstructures are an objective and operative reality. . . . It explicitly affirms that human beings become conscious of their social position and therefore of their tasks on the terrain of ideologies . . . the philosophy of praxis is itself a superstructure, the terrain on which specific social groups become conscious of their own social being, their own strength, their own tasks, their own becoming.

But there is more, only the philosophy of praxis

> does not aim at the peaceful resolution of existing contradictions in history and society but is rather the very theory of these contradictions . . . [i]t is the expression of the subaltern classes who want to educate themselves in the art of government and who have an interest in knowing all truths, even the unpleasant ones, and in avoiding the (impossible) deceptions of the upper class and—even more—their own.[40]

The Philosophy of Praxis Conceived as Translatability of Scientific Languages and as Reformation of Common Sense (Concerning Notebook 11)

We know that Notebook 11 primarily criticizes Bukharin's *Popular Manual*, taken as a symptom of the aporias of the superior Marxism of the Third International and as an expression of the Soviet state's lack of hegemony. Yet, besides the critical part, this notebook contains a real constructive element that Leonardo Paggi has rightly called the general theory of the philosophy of praxis. However, this general theory is not limited to a reformation of the position of historical causality alone, nor does it consist only of the capability of elaborating a "political science." The notebook has a higher ambition, even though it does not present a restoration of a "system," but prefers the form of a *work in progress*. Thus, in speaking of the philosophy of praxis, Gramsci defines it as a "theory of the contradictions existing in history and society." Notebook 11 specifies and generalizes Gramsci's programmatic affirmation. Section 26 reads as follows:

> "Theory of the philosophy of praxis" ought to mean a logical and coherent systematic treatment of the philosophical concepts generically known under the title of the philosophy of praxis (many of which are spurious and come from other sources and as such require to be criticised and eliminated). The first chapters should treat the following questions: What is philosophy? In what sense can a conception of the world be called a philosophy? How has philosophy been conceived hitherto? Does the philosophy of praxis renew this conception? What is meant by a "speculative" philosophy? Would the philosophy of praxis ever be able to have a speculative form? What are the relationships between ideologies, conceptions of the world and philosophies? What is or should be the relationship between theory and practice? How do traditional philosophies conceive of this relationship? etc. The answer to these and other questions constitutes the "theory" of the philosophy of praxis.[41]

The thematization of the cultural pole requires raising the problem of the theory of philosophy conceived as linguistic reality—that is, as specific theoretical language [*linguaggio*] tied, on the one hand, to the linguistic dimension of science in general and of particular sciences, and, on the other hand, simultaneously joined with the reality of the language [*linguaggio*] of common sense. Thus, the question of the theory of philosophy is the question of a theory of science and of language.

Notebook 11§33 illuminates the side of this question that concerns science and defines the philosophy of praxis as the "science of dialectics or the theory of knowledge, within the general concepts of history, politics and economics are interwoven in an organic unity."[42] This "systematic treatment of the philosophy of praxis" implies a relationship between the general ("to develop all the general concepts of a methodology of history and politics, and in addition, of art, economics, and ethics" and "to find a place within the overall construction for a theory of the natural sciences") and the particular that would not be a relationship of metaphysical subsumption but, rather, a circular relationship like that of a web. Dialectics is not the science of sciences but, rather, a function of critical connectivity that is internal to the various kinds and levels of knowledge. Dialectics assumes the task of translating scientific languages [*linguaggi*] as "expressions of different stages of civilization, in so far as each of these stages is a moment of the development of another, each thus reciprocally integrating the other." In Notebook 11§47 this frames the question of sciences in linguistic terms as the "translatability of scientific and philosophical languages," one can again find: translatability is "a 'critical' element that belongs (in an organic way) just to the philosophy of praxis, being appropriable only in part by other philosophies."[43] Marx's explicit translation of the political economy of Ricardo is not the constitution of a meta-language [*metalingua*] but a critical operation that provides the critique of political economy itself an addition of life, enabling it to understand the dynamism and the repressed and hidden possibilities of the structure. It should be possible to say the same with respect to the translation of French politics (Jacobinism) and to German classical philosophy, but Marx didn't accomplish the translation of these languages [*linguaggi*]. And perhaps it is the philosophy of praxis that realizes this act producing in the same historical moment the science of politics and the general theory of philosophy of praxis itself.[44] The philosophy of praxis is not an absolute language [*linguaggio*], the language of languages; it remains only a language that is more capable of thinking the historical situation, of identifying new social agents and of adding potentials to the practices of economy and politics. The constitution of a new space of intertranslatability coincides with the constitution of a new social space (the historical bloc). The translating language remains language the same as the other ones and must deal with the challenges of the conjuncture, solving the open problem of new translations, showing in this way its capacity of assimilation and universalization—that is, its availability for the production of a superior culture, which should be richer and able to assimilate the human kind.

Turning to common sense, it is necessary to posit the problem of language in its breadth. Born from the need to communicate, which structures all the moments (the economic and the ethico-political), language is the framework, that is, the concrete *medium*, in which human historicity manifests itself as the activity of the production of the human world. Language, in particular, is always charged with passions, hopes, prejudices and judgments. We can quote a decisive passage from Notebook 10 part II, §44, that shows the importance of the ensemble "language, speech, and common sense" to the general theory of the philosophy of praxis:

> We have established that philosophy is a conception of the world and that philosophical activity . . . above all as a cultural battle to transform the popular "mentality" and to diffuse the philosophical innovations which will demonstrate themselves to be "historically true" to the extent that they become concretely—i.e. historically and socially—universal. Given all this, the question of language in general and of languages in the technical sense must be put in the forefront of our enquiry.[45]

The philosophy of praxis cannot be an intellectual and moral reformation of the common sense of the masses if it does not acknowledge the plural reality of the linguistic strata of common sense and the unifying potentials of each linguistic stratum. The desired reformation is itself based on an approach of translating the strata of common sense into good sense, although without negating the ontological irreducibility of common sense. Translation is the life itself of language and of thought, because it makes new fields of human activity visible and appropriable and allows the creation of a supplement of (even common) sense, of experience, and of history. The function of the philosophy of praxis as ideology is not that of eliminating common sense, but that of transforming or amending it. The task of the philosophy of praxis is to help communication recover from illnesses—caused by the heterogeneity of the more or less retrograde linguistic strata and from socially determined distortions. This forms the language capable of unifying the "collective human" translating into good sense her fundamental experiences. Once again, translation produces a supplement of meaning, of subjectivity and of creativity—that is, a "plus" based on the critique of the disparate languages of common sense.

> From this one can deduce the importance of the "cultural aspect," even in practical (collective) activity. An historical act can only be performed by "collective man," and this presupposes the attainment of a "cultural-social" unity through which a multiplicity of dispersed wills, with heterogeneous aims, are welded together with a single aim, on the basis of an equal and common conception of the world, both general and particular, operating in transitory bursts (in emotional ways) or permanently (where the intellectual base is so well rooted, assimilated and experienced that it becomes passion). Since this is the way things happen, great importance is assumed by the general question of language, that is, the question of collectivity attaining a single cultural "climate."[46]

Since that is the way this happens, it appears that the importance of the general linguistic question is the collective reaching of the same "cultural climate." If this text belongs to Notebook 10II§44, Gramsci develops its topic in Notebook 11, above all in §12, "Notes for an Introduction and a Commencement to the Study of Philosophy. 1. Some Preliminary Points of Reference."[47] Gramsci deals here explicitly with the formation of a unified and critical worldview, linking it to the translatability of languages. A great culture implies both the capability of its national language to translate other languages and cultures and the formation of a collective will linguistically unified, capable of "speaking" the economic-corporative condition of the new producers and the possibilities of ethico-political catharsis.

> If it is true that every language contains elements of a conception of the world and of a culture, it could also be true that from anyone's language one can assess the greater or lesser complexity of her conception of the world. Someone who only speaks dialect, or understands the standard language incompletely, necessarily has an intuition of the world which is more or less limited and

provincial, which is fossilised and anachronistic in relation to the major currents of thought which dominate world history. . . . A great culture can be translated into the language of another great culture, that is to say a great national language with historic richness and complexity, and it can translate any other great culture and can be a world-wide means of expression. But a dialect cannot do this.[48]

The philosophy of praxis implies, therefore, the shift from the cultural pole to the pole of [national] language [*lingua*] and language [*linguaggio*], which is connected to the thematic of the historical bloc—that is, to the economy and to politics. The philosophy of praxis does not substitute the knowledge of each of these four poles [the cultural, linguistic, economic and political] and does not confuse itself with the critique of political economy, with political science, with grammar and linguistic sciences or with the disciplines that deal with culture and hegemonic apparatuses, but intervenes between the various kinds and levels of knowledge in order to formulate theoretical problems at the level of the categories and in order to determine their place and practical orientation. The same goes for the category of historical causality of determinism or of collective will-subjectivity or for the concepts of historical bloc, common sense and worldview, linguistic-cultural conformism and translatability. This effort of critical-systematic conceptual elaboration facilitates the right formulation of the problems and the locating of new theoretical tools. The philosophy of praxis contributes to weaving the threads between the four poles—economics-politics-culture-language—and to specify the network and the diagonals of the so-constituted quadrangle. The philosophy of praxis is not autonomous from this work of permanent mediation, but must explicitly formulate the problem of its originality and its systematic elaboration that concretizes itself along a twofold line: (a) the categorical effort of being specific with concepts necessary for the analysis of the diverse moments of praxis (the poles of economics, politics, of culture and of language [*linguaggio*]); (b) the effort of determining philosophy considered with respect to its entire range of specialized theory, of technical language, of mass worldview, of common sense, and of an ensemble of different languages, which are different from one another. These two efforts are immanent within each other because they are immanent to praxis itself: they are the condition of each other and are immersed in the same historicity. Translation is the common means, and the practical form of this constitutive operation of translation is the transition—the infinite two-way transition from being passive to being active, from labor to politics, from politics to culture and from culture to communication. This is a transition that for the modern subaltern masses represents the shift from feeling to understanding. For the democratic state and its intellectuals this represents the shift from understanding to feeling. The philosophy of praxis always poses the same the question:

Is it better to "think," without having a critical awareness, in a disjointed and episodic way? In other words, is it better to take part in a conception of the world mechanically imposed by the external environment, i.e. by one of the many social groups in which everyone is automatically involved from the moment of her entry into the conscious world. . . ? Or, on the other hand, is it better to work out consciously and critically one's own conception of the world and thus, in connection with the labours of one's own brain, choose one's sphere of activity, take an active part in the creation of the history of the world, be one's own guide, refusing to accept passively and supinely from outside the moulding of one's personality?[49]

One can, therefore, talk about an internal troublesome problem of the *Prison Notebooks* directed toward a system of the philosophy of praxis for which Notebooks 10 and 11 are decisive. They draw the quadrangle where the reticular dialectic among the poles of practice is constituted and where the diagonals of the elaboration of categories are formed, categorization always being immanent to the question of the practices, including the theoretical practices, of the specialized philosophy for which Gramsci proposes the consecrated name of dialectics. One understands why Gramsci talks about a circle: not because he wants to repropose Hegel's speculation, but to stress the nature of the philosophy of praxis as circulation that translates and that is productive of ideas and perspectives within the problems imposed by history under the irreducible viewpoint that consists of the subaltern masses' hegemonic possibility. What is at stake here is in reality a new idea of theorizing itself and, even more, a new practice of such a theory. This is what the project of a philosophy of praxis demands.[50]

NOTES

1. Gianni Francioni, *L'Officia Gramsciana: Ipotesi sulla struttura dei "Quaderni del carcere"* (Naples: Bibliopolis, 1984).

2. [See the introduction for an explanation of the A-texts (original versions), B-texts (only versions) and C-texts (rewritten sections), page 5.]

3. Antonio Gramsci, *Quaderni del Carcere*, ed. V. Gerratana (Einaudi: Turin, 1974), 1407, hereafter cited as QC. [A list of abbreviations is on pages ix–x. To facilitate locating these passages in various translations and anthologies, we will give the notebook (*Quaderno*) number—in this case 11—followed by the section number, §, here 16. For further discussion, see introduction, page 12. We will indicate the English translation, where used. In this case, Antonio Gramsci, *Selections from Prison Notebooks*, ed. and trans. Quintin Hoare and Geoffrey Nowell Smith (New York: International Publishers, 1971), 453, hereafter SPN. Here we altered the location of the quotation marks to be consistent with Gramsci's text.]

4. Q11§16, SPN, 455.

5. Q11§28, SPN, 450.

6. Q3§31, Antonio Gramsci, *Prison Notebooks*, vol. 2, ed. and trans. Joseph Butti-gieg (New York: Columbia University Press, 1996), 30–31, hereafter cited as PN2.

7. Q11§70, SPN, 388.

8. Q11§70, SPN, 387.

9. Q4§3, PN2, 141.

10. Q4§3, 424; PN2, 142.

11. Q16§9, SPN, 390.

12. Q16§9, SPN, 391.

13. Q16§9, SPN, 395.

14. Q16§9, SPN, 399.

15. Q16§9, SPN, 398.

16. Q4§37, 455; PN2, 177.

17. Q4§39, 465; PN2, 188.

18. Q4§17, PN2, 159; see also the considerations on the metaphorical nature of language.

19. Q4§34, 452–53; PN2, 174.

20. [Gramsci actually stated that "Machiavelli wrote books of 'immediate politi-cal action'; he did not write a utopia"—thus Tosel is presumably highlighting the implication of Gramsci placing the phrase in quotation marks.]

21. Q5§127, PN2, 378.

22. Q5§127, PN2, 382. This is a B-text—that is, Gramsci never rewrote it.

23. Q7§18, Antonio Gramsci, *Prison Notebooks*, vol. 3, ed. and trans. Joseph But-tigieg (New York: Columbia University Press, 2007), 170, hereafter cited as PN3.

24. Q7§35, PN3, 186–87.

25. Q8§182, PN3, 340.

26. Q8§198, PN3, 348.

27. Q8§220, PN3, 369.

28. [Like Marx's *Anti-Duhring*.]

29. Q8§235, 378. N.B. I had finished my analysis before seeing the fine work of Maria Rosaria Romagnuolo presented at the conference in Pavia. My reading is validated by Romagnuolo's exhausting and very precise reconstruction; see Maria Rosaria Romagnuolo, "Quistioni di nomenclature: Materialismo storico e Filo-sofia della prassi nei Quaderni gramscini," *Studi Filosofici* 10–11 (1987–1988): 123–66.

30. Q10I§7; Antonio Gramsci, *Further Selections from the Prison Notebooks*, ed. and trans. Derek Boothman (Minneapolis: University of Minnesota Press, 1995), 345, hereafter cited as FSPN.

31. Q10II§41xii, FSPN, 396–97.

32. Q10I§12, FSPN, 357–58.

33. Q10I§8, FSPN, 347.

34. Q10I§8, FSPN, 347.

35. Q10I§8, FSPN, 347–48.

36. Q10II§6, SPN, 366–67. Translation altered; see QC, 1244.

37. Q10II§6, FSPN, 306.

38. Q10I§13, FSPN, 361.

39. Q10II§31, FSPN, 385.

40. Q10II§41, FSPN, 395–96.

41. Q11§26, SPN, 425. Translation altered so that *filosofia della praxis* is translated as "philosophy of praxis" rather than "historical materialism"; see QC, 1431.

42. Q11§33, SPN, 431.

43. Q11§47, FSPN, 307. [Gramsci's text has quotations around "critical," which were left off by Tosel.]

44. See Q11§48, FSPN, 308.

45. Q10II§44, SPN, 348.

46. Q10II§44, SPN, 349.

47. Q11§12, SPN, 323–43.

48. Q11§12, SPN, 325. Translation altered slightly; see QC, 1377.

49. Q11§12, SPN, 323–24. Tranlsation altered slightly; see QC, 1375–76.

50. The first who understood the systematic structure of Gramsci's Notebooks is the great linguist Tullio De Mauro. I have simply attempted to augment this incisive point of De Mauro [see chapters 3 and 14, especially pages 259–63].

16

Subalternity and Language: Overcoming the Fragmentation of Common Sense

Marcus E. Green and Peter Ives *

Within Gramsci's legacy, the concept of "subalternity" and his attention to language politics often take secondary and merely supportive roles to the more influential themes such as hegemony, passive revolution, organic intellectuals and war of position. Not only are "subalternity" and "language" cast as second fiddles, especially in the English-language literature, but also many meticulous scholars will note that Gramsci writes specifically about subaltern groups and language quite late in his prison notes. Indeed, when considering the chronological composition of the *Prison Notebooks*, the two thematically organized "special notebooks" that Gramsci devoted to subaltern groups and language appear toward the end. Notebook 25 ("On the Margins of History. History of Subaltern Groups") dates to the period of 1934, and Notebook 29 ("Notes for an Introduction to the Study of Grammar"), which is Gramsci's last notebook, dates to the period of 1935. However, the themes of subalternity and language appear throughout the *Prison Notebooks*.[1]

Elsewhere, the individual authors of this chapter have tried to show the profound centrality subalternity and language, separately, to Gramsci's overall project.[2] In different ways, we have argued that the examination of subalternity and language in the *Prison Notebooks* illuminates Gramsci's entire social and cultural theory. This chapter brings these two perspectives together and discusses the interrelationships between Gramsci's lifelong concern with the themes of subalternity (if not the actual term) and language from

* A slightly longer version of this chapter was originally published in *Historical Materialism* 17, no. 1 (2009): 3–30. We would like to thank Brill for allowing us to republish it here.

childhood in Sardinia, through his university studies and pre-prison political activity to his prison writings.

Focusing on the relationships between Gramsci's analysis of subalternity
and his discussion of language reveals a central dynamic in his approach to
politics, what might be called the *differentia specifica* of his Marxism, or at
least one of the major themes within it. Where various strains of Marxism
have seen it as an analytic or "scientific discovery" that needs to brought
from the outside (whether by Marxist experts or party leaders) to enlighten
the exploited, Gramsci emphasized the need of intellectual activity to be
immersed in the lives and experiences of the masses. Much of Gramsci's
critiques of both positivism and idealism rest on the very general position
that they both separate the lived experiences of capitalism from the analysis
and understanding of it purported to be necessary to overcome it. Gramsci
raises this point in his critique of Benedetto Croce's liberal idealism, as well
as that of Nikolai Bukharin's positivistic Marxist materialism.[3] Of course,
Gramsci's well-known and influential detailed analyses of the role of intellectuals not solely within socialism but also in maintaining bourgeois
hegemony leads him to the focus on the role of "organic intellectuals" who
do not bring political consciousness and organization from "without" but
work through the experiences, worldviews, fragmented common sense,
folklore and languages of subaltern social groups.

As Kate Crehan has explored, while Gramsci had respect for "peasant
culture" and "subaltern common sense," as she puts it, "he was never sentimental about it, seeing it both as narrow and parochial, and needing to be
transcended."[4] Crehan elaborates that it is "the inability of subaltern people
to produce coherent accounts of the world they live in that have the potential to challenge existing hegemonic accounts . . . in any *effective* way."[5]
However, she correctly emphasizes that one of Gramsci's major criticisms
of Bukharin was that he did not start from an engagement with the fragmentary nature of subaltern common sense. He was thus unable to grasp
what for Gramsci was essential, the distinction between what Crehan calls
"explicit" and "implicit conceptions of the world,"[6] what Gramsci discussed
as the contrast between thought and action, between a conception of the
world "borrowed from another group" that is affirmed verbally, and that of
action, though it may only manifest itself "occasionally and in flashes" and
is perhaps only "embryonic."[7]

Crehan goes a substantial way in showing how the "common sense"
of subaltern groups becomes fragmented and incoherent, according to
Gramsci, and why this is a political problem and a detriment to political
organization and action.[8] But she only begins to touch on the notion of
how that incoherence and fragmentation can be overcome, that is, what it
means to begin from the position of "common sense" and why it is that the
process cannot, for Gramsci, be directed from a position outside of com-

mon sense or why order and coherence cannot just be imposed through rational analysis.

Similarly, as Fabio Frosini has emphasized, Gramsci explicitly distinguished his own notion of "common sense" in relation to his philosophy of praxis from those of both Kant and Croce, both of whom sought an agreement between philosophy and "common sense." Thus, Frosini notes how Gramsci's discussion of "common sense" is a critical response to the debates between Croce and Giovanni Gentile in the 1920s and 1930s.[9] Although Croce maintained that he abandoned "the traditional distinction between plain thinking and philosophical thinking," he claimed that "the distinguishing feature of philosophy is consistency" and that "non-philosophers are those who are not troubled by inconsistency or incoherence and do not trouble to escape it."[10] Thus, for Croce, the distinction between philosophical and nonphilosophical thinking is not "a logical difference in the quality of the thought" but "a purely psychological difference of interest and attitude."[11] Frosini makes an incredibly insightful argument about how Gramsci's development of the concept of "translation" repositions the relationship between "common sense" and philosophy. We take a different, though not contradictory, path of highlighting and describing the process whereby "common sense" and language change are integral to the process of transforming the fragmented conditions of subalternity.[12]

As André Tosel has argued, for Gramsci, "The philosophy of praxis should thus be developed following two axes: On the one hand, as a reformation of common sense by employing the position that all humans are philosophers; on the other hand, as an exposition"—Tosel quotes Gramsci here—of the "'problems' that arose in the course of the history of philosophy, in order to criticize them, demonstrate their real value (if they still have any) or their importance as links in a chain, and define the new problems of the present time."[13] Most of the scholarship, including Frosini and Tosel, follows the second of these axes focusing on Gramsci's engagement with the traditional intellectual activity of various philosophers and philosophical systems. While these axes are obviously closely related and not separable projects precisely because of the complex relation between common sense and philosophy, our point here is to focus on the first axis, the reformation of common sense, the difficulties that "everyone" (i.e., those in subaltern social groups) faces in philosophizing and how Gramsci's writings on language and subalternity together are the best indication of what Gramsci means by this.

Thus, we offer a very different interpretation than that of Andrew Robinson, who emphasizes Gramsci's notion of transforming common sense, but focusing on Gramsci's negative assessment of "common sense" as indicating the need to "break" with it and resist the "tendency to pander to existing beliefs."[14] We are proposing a different and more dialectical overcoming of the fragmentation of subaltern "common sense." As Guido Liguori has shown, for Gramsci, common sense cannot be eliminated but is "what is at stake in the struggle for hegemony."[15] The transformation of the condition of subalternity requires not the elimination of common sense but the critique and transformation of it. Gramsci emphasizes this point in his critique of Bukharin, for Bukharin's attempt at producing a "popular manual" failed because it did not begin from a critique of common sense, but rather it reinforced elements of common sense uncritically. In the struggle for hegemony, as Gramsci emphasizes, the formation of a homogenous social group must be accompanied by the formation of a systematic philosophy that provides a basis for the criticism of common sense.[16] Thus, the critique of common sense functions as an elementary phase in the struggle for hegemony. In Liguori's words: "Revolutionary theory is born *against* existing common sense."[17]

Our point is not to reduce Gramsci's political analysis to questions of unification or differing conceptions of the world, but to show how they are intimately tied to questions of political organization and struggle. As Tullio De Mauro has argued, "For Gramsci, the economic-productive element is interwoven with the element of invention and cultural elaboration, and both cannot subsist without being woven into the capability of linguistic elaboration and communication and with the construction of life in common in both the ethnic and national dimensions of life."[18]

These questions become all the more important with the advent of debates around postmodernism, ideologies of multiculturalism, the "culture wars," discussions of "the multitude" a la Hardt and Negri, and the complex of economic, social, political and cultural transformations unsatisfactorily described with the term "globalization." Our current contexts provide particular resonances for questions of "common sense" and fragmentation. It is within these contexts that Gramsci's ideas are so critical for us today and which focus our attention on how Gramsci understands the fragmentation of "common sense" as shown in his writings on the subaltern and language.

THE SUBALTERN CONDITION: "COMMON SENSE" AND FRAGMENTATION

In the *Prison Notebooks*, Gramsci develops a critical interpretation of the condition of subaltern groups, in which he surveys the factors that contribute to their subordination, in addition—but not unrelated—to their economic exploitation, such as their modes of thought, worldviews, levels of political organization and culture. In his analysis, Gramsci attempts to identify what prevents subaltern groups from acting as effective political agents and from overcoming their subordination. Subaltern groups in modern Italian history, in his view, are characterized by ineffectual political activity. Although the history of their spontaneous political activity, such as peasant revolts and insurgencies, illustrates their discontent and their will to generate political change, the political activity of subaltern groups rarely goes beyond certain limits, and the groups appear to be incapable of achieving permanent victory or maintaining a level of political power. In this sense, Gramsci is grappling with what Frantz Fanon describes as the positive and negative attributes of "spontaneity."[19] One of the major impediments preventing subaltern groups from overcoming their subordination—economic and cultural—is the lack of conscious leadership and organization to provide the groups with coherence and direction. Gramsci attributes this lack of coherence and direction to the composition of subaltern groups' culture and consciousness. In Gramsci's view, the common sense and worldview of subaltern groups in Italy tended to lack the critical elements required to provide conscious and organized leadership. In Notebook 3§48, Gramsci observes that within spontaneous political movements "there exist a 'multiplicity' of elements of 'conscious leadership,' but none of them predominates or goes beyond the level of the 'popular science'—the 'common sense,' that is, the [traditional] conception of the world—of a given social stratum."[20] Because of this, Gramsci contends that common sense provides inadequate foundations for establishing an effective political movement capable of producing political change. Thus, in Gramsci's view, common sense is one of the factors that hinders the ability of subaltern groups to assert political autonomy and to overcome their subordination. However, his conclusion is not that "common sense" needs to be or can be rejected in its entirety or that there exists some "philosophy" outside of "common sense" by which "common sense" can be judged and corrected. Rather, Gramsci suggests common sense needs to become critical. As Liguori points out, common sense is constituted by a "Janus-faced" contra-position of fragmentary elements on the one hand and the potential to become critical on the other.[21] We want to go further along the direction indicated by Liguori, Frosini and Crehan's recognition of the nuances of Gramsci's positive and negative assessments of "common sense" by showing how he relates it to the fragmented conditions of subalternity and subaltern languages and how he sees the movement from there to nonfragmented consciousness and truly popular common language.

In other words, the Gramscian notion of "common sense" can be understood as popular social thought or as the common beliefs and opinions held by ordinary people. In some ways, common sense can be understood as the mentality or psychology of the masses.[22] Gramsci uses language to develop his notion of "common sense" both metaphorically and literally. Gramsci also sees languages as an important element of "common sense."

At times he goes as far as stating that "language also means culture and philosophy (if only at the level of common sense)."[23]

In his attack on elitist notions of "philosophy," he argues that it is "essential to destroy the widespread prejudice that philosophy is a strange and difficult thing just because it is the specific intellectual activity of a particular category of specialists or of professional and systematic philosophers."[24] He then defines "spontaneous philosophy" (i.e., the intellectual activity of "everybody") as such:

> This philosophy is contained in: 1. language itself, which is a totality of determined notions and concepts and not just words grammatically devoid of content; 2. "common sense" and "good sense"; 3. popular religion and therefore, also in the entire systems of beliefs, superstitions, opinions, ways of seeing things and of acting, which are collectively bundled together under the name "folklore."[25]

He continues by referring to "language" again as an indication of intellectual activity, even if unconscious, in which "there is contained a specific conception of the world," and then poses the question whether it is "better to take part in a conception of the world mechanically imposed by the external environment" or "to work out consciously and critically one's own conception of the world and thus, in connection with the labours of one's own brain, choose one's sphere of activity, take an active part in the creation of the history of the world."[26] Thus, Gramsci's analysis of the fragmentary nature of subaltern common sense is intimately tied to his notions of language and its role in conceiving the world. As Frosini argues, "Language [*linguaggio*] is not an instrument that can serve us arbitrarily, but it is a concrete real form that thought assumes; indeed, it is the specific historical structure of thought."[27]

In using language and linguistics in political and cultural analysis of subaltern common sense, Gramsci is drawing on his studies in linguistics at the University of Turin with Matteo Bartoli. Bartoli was engaged in debates with the neo-grammarian school from which Ferdinand de Saussure emerged and "structuralist" linguistics was created.[28] In addition to, but not disconnected from, his more technical training in linguistics, the context of language politics in Italian society is very important. As a Sardinian born in 1891, Gramsci grew up in the midst of the Italian government's attempt to "standardize" Italian—that is, create a national Italian language used by its citizens.

Language was a central feature in the process described by Massimo d'Azeglio's famous proclamation shortly after the Risorgimento: "Italy is a fact, now we need to make Italians." Italian historical linguists estimate that at the time, somewhere between 2.5 and 12 percent of the population spoke anything that could be considered "standard" Italian.[29] The many dialects were not mutually understandable from north to south. While literary Italian had existed for centuries as a written language, a *truly* common, national language for most Italians did not exist. Moreover, about 75 percent of Italians were illiterate, with regions like Sardinia having illiteracy rates as high as 90 percent.[30]

This lack of a "standard" language especially in comparison to the powerful nation-states of France and England, if not Germany, was of major political concern for the new nation. In 1868, one of Italy's most renowned authors, Alessandro Manzoni, was appointed to head a government commission on linguistic unification. Having rewritten his classic novel, *I Promessi Sposi* (The Betrothed), in an Italian closely modelled on spoken, bourgeois Florentine "Italian," Manzoni's solution was to take Florentine as the "standard" Italian, fund dictionaries and grammar books based on Florentine, and recruit school teachers for all of Italy from the Tuscan region. Gramsci was very critical of Manzoni's "solution" well before he was imprisoned. In 1918 in the pages *Il Grido del Popolo* he launched an attack on it, comparing it to Esperanto.[31]

With these linguistic realities and debates consistently in mind, in his prison writings, Gramsci considered common sense among Italian subaltern groups to be uncritical, unreflective, unsystematic, and operating with an incoherent conception of life and the world. In his view, these characteristics contributed to the subordination of subaltern groups and inhibited them from developing long-term political strategies. The point of his analysis is to understand the ways in which the masses think, conceive the world and perceive their activity, in order to ascertain what elements prevent them from effectively organizing and acting. Ultimately, Gramsci is interested in transforming common sense and developing a "new common sense" and by extension a truly transformed language founded upon a critical awareness that will provide the masses with a foundation to transform their conditions. Gramsci suggests that critical awareness develops through a process of critical self-reflection, in which one understands one's history, position and activity in relation to dominant and prevailing structures of power. But this critical construction cannot take place without engaging with current "common sense" and its various and contradictory elements. Gramsci stresses that it is necessary for subaltern groups to understand the historical and political origins of their conditions, instead of assuming their circumstances are the result of some sort of natural or spiritual determination or inferiority, which the Catholic Church's worldview tended to reinforce.

Gramsci describes common sense as a "fragmentary collection of ideas and opinions" drawn from differing philosophies, ideologies, religion, folklore, experience, superstition and from "scientific notions and philosophical opinions which have entered into common usage."[32] Common sense is composed of a variety of perspectives that often contain elements of truth but also tend to be disjointed, incoherent and contradictory. In the words of Marcia Landy, common sense assumes "pastiche-like qualities";[33] it contains "fragmentary ideas, a collage of opinions and beliefs, giving the illusion of a coherent world view and of acting which is not at all coherent and certainly not critical."[34] Gramsci's discussions of common sense often appear alongside his discussions of folklore, and although the two categories often appear synonymous, folklore represents only one of the elements that comprise common sense. To understand common sense, in Gramsci's view, it is also necessary to understand folklore and its influence in the composition of the masses' worldview. Although both common sense and folklore contain heterogeneous and contradictory elements, Gramsci contends that they should be studied as one would study a coherent philosophical worldview, since they inform the worldview of the masses. "Folklore," he writes, "must not be considered an eccentricity, an oddity or a picturesque element, but as something which is very serious and is to be taken seriously."[35] As Crehan emphasizes, for Gramsci folklore is not primordial or premodern, but is always in flux, always being modernized and is tied in some ways to the dominant classes, but "the instability of folklore and its readiness to absorb elements from the dominant culture are important in that they give folklore a potentially progressive quality."[36] In this sense, Gramsci analyzes common sense and its composition of multifarious elements as a sociohistorical phenomenon, *as if* common sense were a coherent ideology or philosophy, and he attempts to identify and isolate the elements of common sense in relation to their historical and cultural context. His purpose is to ascertain the content and meaning of common sense, to understand how the masses conceive life, the world and politics, with the point of radicalizing common sense and providing subaltern groups with the intellectual tools necessary to confront dominant hegemony, philosophy and power.

Gramsci often refers to common sense as the philosophy of the people, in that it represents the "philosophy of non-philosophers,"[37] "the philosophy of the man in the street"[38] or "spontaneous philosophy,"[39] which implies that common sense represents the conceptions of the world and modes of thought practiced by nonprofessional philosophers, namely the masses. Gramsci defines "philosophy" as a coherent worldview, whereas "common sense" refers to the popular ways of thinking and speaking among the people.[40] Gramsci compares common sense to philosophy, because common sense operates similarly to a coherent worldview in that it provides a point of reference for thought and action, even though it is incoherent.

However, Gramsci is not taking coherency of a philosophy or worldview as the gold standard or even the sole element of the analytic distinction between "common sense" and philosophy. Along with his critique of elitist notions of philosophy as a specialized and difficult activity, he argues: "Philosophy in general does not in fact exist. Various philosophies or conceptions of the world exist, and one always makes a choice between them. How is this choice made? . . . [I]s it not frequently the case that there is a contradiction between one's intellectual choice and one's mode of conduct?"[41] This leads Gramsci to contrast "thought" and "action" as displaying "two conceptions of the world, one affirmed in words and the other displayed in effective action," which is why "philosophy cannot be divorced from politics."

Whereas philosophy constitutes a coherent conception of the world and mode of thought, common sense actually represents "a chaotic aggregate of disparate conceptions, and one can find there anything that one likes."[42] Unlike philosophy, common sense does not follow a uniform conception of life and the world, and it does not exist in a homogenous form. [43] In Gramsci's words: "Common sense is not a single unique conception, identical in time and space. It is the 'folklore' of philosophy, and, like folklore, it takes countless different forms. Its most fundamental characteristic is that it is a conception which, even in the brain of one individual, is fragmentary, incoherent and inconsequential, in conformity with the social and cultural position of those masses whose philosophy it is."[44]

One might assume that Gramsci is accepting a general presumption of rationalism and the Enlightenment in favoring coherence and consistency in any worldview or philosophy, whether spontaneous or more systematic. Thus, fragmentation, incoherency and a sort of eclectic amassing of various ideas, values, morals and understandings of the world are problematic and unfavorable in and of themselves.[45] But on closer examination, one of Gramsci's most useful contributions to questions of ideology critique is precisely the notion of why and how such fragmentation is problematic. He does not merely assume that fragmentary common sense is detrimental and coherency and consistency are preferable. Rather, he tries to show how "common sense" and folklore together with incommunicable dialects are practical impediments to effective political organization, political action and the transformation of society. This is perhaps one place where Gramsci still has much to contribute to debates concerning postmodernism and multiculturalism. The key is to understand how, for Gramsci, fragmentation and incoherency should be addressed. This point is evident in Gramsci's critique of Esperanto and Alessandro Manzoni's strategy for creating a "standard" Italian language. It provides one example of how, for Gramsci, achieving a systematic and coherent language, or worldview, can be even more detrimental than holding a fragmented worldview.

ESPERANTISM AND MANZONI—
IMPOSING LANGUAGE AND CULTURE FROM ABOVE

As we have been describing, one of the crucial questions that runs through much of Gramsci's wide-ranging prison research project is how to transform this fragmentary "common sense" that is debilitating for subaltern social groups. One of Gramsci's major contributions that has made him so influential across a range of academic disciplines and diverse political struggles is his insistence that transforming "common sense" cannot take the form of the *imposition* of a superior worldview or understanding of the world originating outside of the previously accepted "common sense." Such responses characterize many so-called progressive attempts, Marxism and non-Marxism alike, to create a more just world by coming up with the "correct position" or a blueprint that oppressed people should follow. Such approaches exacerbate one of the key elements of the conditions of subalternity—the dissonance between the imposed worldview and the conditions and understandings of those who are supposed to accept it. This reinforces passivity and does not create critical engagement or, as Gramsci quotes Socrates, knowledge of oneself, but takes the meaning of this process for political organization and collective struggle far beyond anything implied in any of Plato's dialogues.[46]

But Gramsci is no anarchist and has little faith in the effectiveness of purely spontaneous uprisings specifically because the fragmentary and inadequate understanding made possible by subaltern "common sense." He agrees to some degree with Lenin, that the mere conditions of capitalism do not *automatically* lead to political consciousness capable of effective and organized resistance. Given, as we have seen, that Gramsci connects "common sense" to language, it is possible to see him addressing this question of the fragmentation of subaltern common sense in his analysis of the so-called standardization of the Italian language.

Just as Gramsci argued that there is a choice, a political choice, to be made among different philosophies or ways of seeing the world (or the elements that make them up), so, too, he argued that the establishment of a "written normative grammar" connected to a common language is a "political act," "an act of national-cultural politics." In this context, his argument about language, dialects and the question of a "standardized" national Italian language parallels his analysis of the effects of fragmentation of "common sense." In the last notebook that he started in prison, Notebook 29, Gramsci writes:

> It is rational to collaborate practically and willingly to welcome everything that may serve to create a common national language, the non-existence of which creates friction particularly in the popular masses among whom local

particularisms and phenomena of a narrow and provincial mentality are more tenacious than is believed.[47]

On one hand, this statement in favor of a national Italian language might not seem surprising and could tend to reinforce the view that Gramsci posed a harsh critique of the "backwards" and particularistic parochial worlds of "common sense," folklore and dialect—and that he simplistically wanted to replace them with a coherent Marxist worldview. On the other hand, this passage contains some enigmas that are productive in illuminating his more nuanced position that emphasizes the need to work through "common sense" and warns of the pitfalls of any imposition of a external worldview however coherent and logical. This passage implies that a common national Italian language, in 1935, does not exist and must be created. It *seems* anachronistic. This description of the nonexistence of an Italian common national language is perhaps accurate for 1861 as described above. But by 1931, the overall level of illiteracy in Italy had fallen to 21.6 percent and in the "south" was about 38.8 percent, with these gains from the previous levels of 75 percent and 90 percent, respectively, being made in some language that could be called a "standard" Italian.[48] If we are to take Gramsci literally, then, this declaration of the "nonexistence" of a "common national language" must mean that he does not consider this "Italian" to be a truly "common national popular language." To explain what he must mean, we can look to his pre-prison writings mentioned above.

In 1918, Gramsci published an article in *Il Grido del Popolo*, "A Single Language and Esperanto," in which he criticizes the proposal that the Italian Socialist Party adopt Esperanto.[49] In mounting his argument he equates the notion of adopting an artificial language with that of Manzoni in "standardizing" Italian. Manzoni would likely have been appalled by the comparison.[50] Gramsci's response to Manzoni was that

> not even a national language can be created artificially, by order of the state; that the Italian language was being formed by itself and would be formed only in so far as the shared life of the nation gave rise to numerous and stable contact between the various parts of the nation; that the spread of a particular language is due to the productive activity of the writings, trade and commerce of the people who speak that language. . . . If a single language [i.e., Manzoni's "standard Italian" based on the dialect of Florence], one that is also spoken in an given region and has a living source to which it can refer, cannot be imposed on the limited field of the nation, how then could an international language [Esperanto] take root when it is completely artificial and mechanical, completely ahistorical, not fed by great writers, lacking expressive richness which comes from the variety of dialects, from the variety of forms assumed in different times?[51]

At first blush, it seems that in 1918 Gramsci was against the formation of a "common national language," or certainly any active strategy to create one. Whereas by 1935, so it seems, he welcomed it and argued, as quoted above, "It is rational to collaborate practically and willingly to welcome everything that may serve to create a common national language." However, this would be to miss the point of both arguments, which go to the heart of the issues of fragmentation of common sense under the conditions of subalternity.

On one hand, Gramsci is utilizing the arguments of G. I. Ascoli, a prominent Italian linguist at the end of the nineteenth century and one of the main opponents of Manzoni, who argued that dialects and previous languages of speakers exert "pressure" on new languages being learned and, thus, there's continual pressure that changes the "standard" language being imposed.[52] On the other hand, Gramsci is not just making a technical linguistic point about the degree of success of this strategy. He points out that while, from Manzoni's position, Florentine is a "living" language enabling its speakers to be creative, expressive and productive, for most of Italy it is more like an "artificial" language imposed from the outside that enables little more than mechanical repetition and acceptance of a foreign conception of the world, and ultimately the subordination to a culture and philosophy that is not understood as belonging to the speaker herself.

This view is confirmed by what Gramsci wrote to his family members when in prison. On March 26, 1927, Gramsci sent a letter to his sister, Teresina, concerning her son, Franco:

> I hope that you will let [Franco] speak Sardinian and will not make any trouble for him on that score. It was a mistake, in my opinion, not to allow Edmea [Gramsci's niece] to speak freely in Sardinian as a little girl. It harmed her intellectual development and put her imagination in a straitjacket. . . . I beg you, from my heart, not to make this mistake and to allow your children to absorb all the Sardinian spirit they wish and to develop spontaneously in the natural environment in which they were born.[53]

While Gramsci favors children speaking their local languages, he encourages them to learn other languages and is fully aware of the prestige and cultural politics involved in these questions of which languages children learn to speak. In a letter to his son, Giuliano, Gramsci reflects on his own childhood, noting how his classmates had great difficulty with speaking Italian, giving him a position of superiority over them.[54] He writes that sometimes better knowledge of Italian makes a student "seem to be more intelligent and quick, whereas sometimes this is not so."[55]

It is in Notebook 29 that Gramsci begins to develop the clearest set of concepts that help him theorize the political elements of concern about vernacular languages or dialects and their relations to a common language.

The central concepts that he employs are "spontaneous" or "immanent grammar" and "normative grammar." Gramsci uses the phrase "subaltern classes" in a very telling sense when redefining the traditional concept of "normative grammar" as being made up of "reciprocal monitoring, reciprocal teaching and reciprocal 'censorship' expressed in such questions as 'What did you mean to say?,' 'What do you mean?,' 'Make yourself clearer' etc." Here Gramsci describes a key element in the condition of "subalternity" rather than a method for trying to overcome the power relations between the elite and the subaltern. He writes parenthetically:

> A peasant who moves to the city ends up conforming to urban speech through the pressure of the city environment. In the country, people try to imitate urban speech; *the subaltern classes* try to speak like the dominant classes and the intellectuals, etc.[56]

While only in its provisional and unfinished form, Gramsci is contrasting the "grammatical conformism" of those in a new situation—here the peasant who has moved to the city—with those whose situation has not changed—the peasant who is still in the country—but also *tries* to *imitate* the dominant classes and intellectuals under very different circumstances. Where the peasant who has immigrated to the city seems to succeed in "conforming" to the new environment and speakers, the subaltern classes are not said to "conform" but to "try" to conform and "imitate"—such attempts, he implies, are likely not to be successful, or if they are successful at an individual level, it will result in the creation of a "traditional intellectual" cut off from her "organic" roots.

While Gramsci is not simply advocating the "spontaneous" or "immanent" grammar of a dialect, which is akin to his notion of "common sense" in that it is fragmented, accepted uncritically and unconscious or seems "natural," he is also not advocating any sort of "normative grammar" where the rules are coherently set out, consistent and noncontradictory. Rather, he is making an argument for a specific method of transforming "spontaneous grammar" into "normative grammar" through a conscious and critical interaction among the existing "spontaneous grammars."

As we saw above with Gramsci's critique of the fragmentary nature of common sense, here too we have his assessment of how fragmentation in language impedes effective political action. But this cannot be rectified through the imposition of a logically coherent, unfragmented language. The result of such an external imposition actually reinforces parochialism and narrow thinking but also prevents various subaltern social groups—specifically the southern peasantry and the northern working class—from communicating with each other, developing solidarity with their conditions which are different in many ways but ultimately tied to their mutual subordination by the dominant classes and the uneven development of capitalism. Gramsci's solution for fragmentation and the incoherent and contradictory characteristics of language usage in Italy is not a simple adoption of Esperanto or some pragmatic language (such as the dialect of Florence) in which communication can occur. The creation of a truly common language requires the interaction and creative engagement among those who speak the diverse dialects, the elements of which will be transformed into a new language and worldview.

TRANSFORMING SUBALTERN COMMON SENSE AND LANGUAGE FROM THE BOTTOM UP

Thus, in Gramsci's writings specifically on Italian language, we find a clear example of his more general argument about fragmentation within common sense and the conditions of subalternity. He is critical of the lack of coherence and the historical process of sedimentation that renders both the common sense of various and diverse subaltern social groups and the vernacular languages they use an impediment to effective political organization. But this fragmentation cannot be dealt with through the imposition of a coherency based on purely technical logic, abstract reason or Esperanto. Rather, it must be actively grappled with, sifted through, understood and sorted out by the very users of language and holders of "common sense." And these processes are not purely linguistic or in the realm of ideas and consciousness, but are always related to human labor and changing lived experiences. This is why it is so crucial that in Gramsci's view, common sense, folklore and languages are not homogeneous or static, just as "the people themselves are not a homogeneous cultural collectivity but they present numerous and variously combined cultural layers."[57] "One must keep in mind," as he writes, "that in every region, especially in Italy, given the very rich variety of local traditions, there exist groups or small groups characterized by their own ideological or psychological impulses: 'every village has or has had its local saint, hence its own cult and its own chapel.'"[58] In other words, in the Italian context, the heterogeneity of common sense is distinguished by the heterogeneity of Italian culture and the lack of national unity. Thus, common sense assumes specific qualities among various regions and social groups. In addition, common sense changes and adapts to new elements that are absorbed into common practice. As Gramsci writes in Notebook 1, §65, and later rewrites in Notebook 24, §4:

> Every social stratum has its own "common sense" which is ultimately the most widespread conception of life and morals. Every philosophical current leaves a sedimentation of "common sense": this is the document of its historical reality. Common sense is not something rigid and static; rather, it changes contin-

uously, enriched by scientific notions and philosophical opinions which have entered into common usage. "Common sense" is the folklore of "philosophy" and stands midway between real "folklore" (that is, as it is understood) and the philosophy, the science, the economics of the scholars. "Common sense" creates the folklore of the future, that is a more or less rigidified phase of a certain time and place.[59]

Here Gramsci conceptualizes what Tosel frames as two axes, mentioned above, the reformation of "common sense" and critique of traditional philosophy, as a continuum. But our point remains the same, where so much of Gramscian scholarship has detailed the relation between "common sense" (as the "folklore of philosophy") and science, economics and philosophy of scholars, our focus is directed toward the other end of the spectrum, between "real folklore" and "common sense." The crucial point here is that although common sense continually changes, it tends not to be progressive, because it uncritically absorbs new elements from the scholarly end of the spectrum. They enter into common practice, rather than consciously and selectively incorporating specific elements.[60]

Agreeing in part with Marx and Engels's famous argument that "the ideas of the ruling class are in every epoch the ruling ideas,"[61] Gramsci emphasizes that languages and common sense often contain elements of truth but in seemingly contradictory forms with respect to the actual experiences and conditions of the masses. These "ruling ideas," as Marx and Engels note, have "material force" but were formed from the perspective of the dominant groups, and often the dominant groups of previous periods in history.[62] Where Marx and Engels do not specify any timeline for the "ideas of the ruling class," Gramsci notes that, for example, "previous religions have also had an influence and remain components of common sense to this day, and the same is true of previous forms of present Catholicism."[63] Similarly, Gramsci suggests that elements of modern thought and science enter into folklore, but in this process they are "torn from their context, fall into the popular domain and 'arranged' within the mosaic of tradition."[64] Thus, although the elements of folklore may change, new elements are incorporated within a traditional worldview.

Gramsci suggests that critical consciousness—established through the process of forming historical consciousness—should provide the foundation for a "new common sense" (or what he also calls "good sense"), but the process of developing historical consciousness presents a difficult task for subaltern groups. Due to the contradictory nature of the ensemble of social relations and conditions of exploitation and poverty, subaltern groups are not only prohibited an active voice in dominant discourse; they are also excluded from actively participating in dominant institutions, culture and politics, and because of their exclusion they are placed in a difficult position to develop a critical understanding of the nature of the power relations that form their subalternity. Without participation in dominant institutions, culture, politics, and language, subaltern groups achieve a partial understanding of their position in relation to dominant social and political relations. The stress here is on active participation that not only enables subaltern groups to use the language and institutions and to consume or absorb culture, but also allows subaltern groups to use them creatively, to add to them, alter them in relation to their experiences. In this sense, Gramsci is worried about the outcome of institutions, culture, politics and language being "imposed" from "above" or "outside" in a manner that reinforces feelings of inferiority and passivity in subaltern groups.

Gramsci understands this not as an overall condition in the sense of Theodor Adorno's "administered society" but as a matter of degree depending on different conditions of various subaltern groups. The least "advanced" subaltern groups, who have been deprived of institutional political participation, face a more difficult task in developing critical consciousness than a more politically organized subaltern group. Thus, the contradictory nature of common sense is not the product of some sort of intellectual or psychological deficiency on the part of the masses. Rather, the contradictory nature of common sense is largely defined by the contradictory nature of the ensemble of social relations, economic exploitation and the various exclusions they produce and reproduce. But Gramsci does not draw the deterministic conclusion from this logic that common sense can only follow and become critical once economic exploitation has ended or social relations have been transformed. Quite the contrary, his point is that such changes require a critical perspective to be elaborated from within common sense. The development of critical consciousness requires the articulation of a "historical consciousness" that is developed autonomously from imposed principles and dominant cultural values. As Gramsci explains:

> Since the ensemble of social relations is contradictory, human historical consciousness is contradictory; having said that, the question arises of how this contradictoriness manifests itself. It manifests itself all across the body of society through the existence of the different historical consciousness of various groups; and it manifests itself in individuals as a reflection of these group antinomies. Among subaltern groups, given the lack of historical initiative, the fragmentation is greater; they face a harder struggle to liberate themselves from imposed (rather than freely propounded) principles in order to arrive at an autonomous historical consciousness.[65]

Gramsci suggests that in the Italian context the contradictory nature of common sense along with the lack of a truly popular national language is a reflection of the contradictory nature of the ensemble of social relations, which were largely produced by the incompleteness of the Risorgimento, the non-national popular aspects of Italian intellectuals, and the cultural influence of the Catholic Church. The nature of the Risorgimento, Catholicism, and the function of Italian intellectuals contributed to a passive culture and fragmented dialects that developed among the people, particularly peasants, who were encouraged to accept their subordinated position as natural. The hierarchical authority of the Church and state—through the mediation of intellectuals—politically and ideologically contributed to the subordination of workers and peasants.

This is one of the central elements of Gramsci's analysis of the Risorgimento as a "revolution without revolution" or a "passive revolution" in that the dominant classes consolidated their power and unified the state without a mass base, without exercising active hegemony among the masses, without promoting a national culture, and without fundamentally altering the previous social relations.[66]

Because the Risorgimento and "standard Italian" were not popular movements—but in the end actually the juridical suppression of a potential mass movement—they reinforced the non-national popular aspects of Italian culture that actively excluded subaltern social groups from participating in dominant political institutions. For this reason, Gramsci writes that "in Italy the liberal-bourgeois always neglected the popular masses."[67] Related to this issue, as Gramsci began to address in his final essay prior to his arrest, "Some Aspects of the Southern Question," the peasantry lacked and continued to lack its own category of organic intellectuals to provide it with coherence and political direction. Ironically, however, as Gramsci points out in the *Prison Notebooks*, "It is from the peasantry that other social groups draw many of their intellectuals and a high proportion of traditional intellectuals are of peasant origin," but such intellectuals do not remain organically linked with the peasantry, such as priests, lawyers, and state functionaries.[68] The Italian peasantry not only lacked its own category of intellectuals to provide homogeneity and direction; the non-national popular character of Italian culture reinforced the separation of the intellectuals from the masses at large. As Gramsci points out in the "special notebook" on the "Problems of Italian National Culture": "In Italy the term 'national' has an ideologically very restricted meaning, and does not in any case coincide with 'popular' because in Italy the intellectuals are distant from the people, i.e., from the 'nation.'"[69] As we have seen in linguistic terms, "national Italian" was also restricted and was unsuccessful in becoming truly "national." Gramsci recounts different phases in Italian history when "once again, Italian is a written not a spoken language, a language of scholars, not of the nation" and this is a central aspect of the increasing "split between the people and the intellectuals, between the people and culture."[70]

In turn, the popular masses function within a social and political environment they did not create, in a language that they may learn but one that is not their own and is "mastered" only through submission to the

authority of the elite. Because of the cultural tradition of Italian intellectuals, the popular masses lack their own category of intellectuals and their
own languages to provide coherence and political direction to their activity.
Thus, because of the practical separation of intellectuals from the masses,
common sense or the philosophy of the masses gravitates around folklore
and traditional conceptions of the world.

In Gramsci's view, it is necessary for subaltern groups to produce their
own category of organic intellectuals and linguistic innovations, as effectively as dominant social groups create their organic intellectuals, in that
the intellectuals remain in contact with, or organic to, the social groups' life
experiences so as to provide organization, direction and leadership in the
movement to achieve political power and hegemony. The necessity of the
subaltern to develop their own category of organic intellectuals resolves one
of the central issues contributing to the condition of subalternity—that is,
that the non-national popular character of traditional Italian intellectuals
creates a practical disconnect between intellectuals and the people. Gramsci's well-known discussion of traditional intellectuals includes the crucial
linguistic component of this disconnection. Gramsci describes his analysis
of "the relation between the intellectuals and the people-nation" as being
studied "in terms of the language written by the intellectuals and used
among them." He notes parenthetically that "the use of Latin as a learned
language is bound up with Catholic cosmopolitanism." Then in tracing the
history of this relationship, he sets out one version of his famous distinction between organic intellectuals (of the fourteenth-century ruling class)
and traditional intellectuals: "It is not a stratum of the population which
creates its intellectuals on coming to power (this occurred in the fourteenth
century), but a traditionally selected body which assimilates single individuals into its cadres."[71]

It is largely due to this lack of intellectual connection for subaltern social
groups that the level of conscious leadership with the subaltern's spontaneous political activity does not move beyond common sense.[72] In Gramsci's
words:

> Creating a group of independent intellectuals is not an easy thing; it requires
> a long process, with actions and reactions, coming together and drifting apart
> and the growth of very numerous and complex new formations. It is the con-
> ception of a subaltern social group, deprived of historical initiative, in continu-
> ous but disorganic expansion, unable to go beyond a certain qualitative level,
> which still remains below the level of the possession of the State and of the real
> exercise of hegemony over the whole of society which alone permits a certain
> organic equilibrium in the development of the intellectual group.[73]

Here Gramsci's suggestion that the "disorganic expansion" of subaltern
groups permits "a certain organic equilibrium in the development of the

intellectual group" directly connects to his view of the political party as the "collective intellectual" or "modern prince" that facilitates the rearticulation and unification of subaltern worldviews in a "common language."[74] For Gramsci, the party is not a tool to impose an external or transcendental worldview but functions as a practical link between social multiplicity and political unity in which the articulation of a "collective consciousness" is created that has the potential to challenge dominant hegemony. As Gramsci metaphorically explains:

> A collective consciousness, that is a living organism, cannot be formed until after the multiplicity is unified through the friction of individuals: neither can one say that "silence" is not multiplicity. When an orchestra is preparing for a performance, with each instrument tuning up individually, it gives the impression of the most horrible cacophony; yet, it is such preparations that bring the orchestra to life as a single "instrument."[75]

In Gramsci's methodological criteria of subaltern analysis, the development of the political party signifies an initial first step in political transformation.[76] The party provides a vehicle for subaltern groups to represent their views and aspirations, yet the crucial moment in the political activity of subaltern groups occurs when they become aware of the fact that their political goals cannot be fulfilled within the present state and that the state must be transformed.[77] Posing the question of the state in turn brings the issue of hegemony to the forefront of political struggle.

When the subaltern emerge from their subordinate position and achieve a level of political power, they move from a position of resistance to effective agency. This stage marks the pivotal point in the development of the subaltern in achieving "integral autonomy." In Gramsci's words, "If yesterday the subaltern element was a thing, today it is no longer a thing but an historical person, a protagonist; if yesterday it was not responsible, because 'resisting' a will external to itself, now it feels itself to be responsible because it is no longer resisting but an agent, necessarily active and taking the initiative."[78] In other words, at this point the subaltern has achieved "integral autonomy" and is no longer subordinate, adopting the language of its rulers, but is active, speaking and leading.

CONCLUSION

We have attempted to bring into relief the direct connections between subalternity and language by showing how the concepts overlap with respect to Gramsci's analyses of common sense, intellectuals, philosophy, folklore and hegemony. Moreover, we have argued that for Gramsci fragmentation of any social group's "common sense," worldview and language is a political detriment. However, it cannot be overcome by the imposition of a "rational" or "logical" worldview. Instead, what is required is a deep engagement with the fragments that make up subaltern historical, social, economic and political conditions. We have thus attempted to show how Gramsci provides an alternative to both the celebration of fragmentation fashionable in liberal multiculturalism and uncritical postmodernism as well as other attempts of overcoming it through recourse to some external, transcendental or imposed worldview. In this sense we hope to have enriched the understanding of Gramsci's analysis of the Italian situation and the complex process required in contemporary contexts for subaltern groups to overcome their subordination.

NOTES

1. We will cite Gramsci's *Prison Notebooks* by giving the notebook number preceded by a Q (*Quaderno*—notebook), and then an § prior to the note (or section) number, following the definitive source; Antonio Gramsci, *Quaderni del Carcere*, four vols., ed. Valentino Gerratana (Turin: Einaudi, 1975), hereafter cited as QC. There is a list of abbreviations on pages ix–x. The English translation of this critical edition is under way; Antonio Gramsci, *Prison Notebooks*, vols. 1, 2, 3 (New York: Columbia University Press, 1992, 1996 and 2007), hereafter cited as PN1, PN2 and PN3, respectively. We will cite the English translations used.

2. See Marcus E. Green, "Gramsci Cannot Speak: Representations and Interpretations of Gramsci's Concept of the Subaltern," *Rethinking Marxism*, 14, no. 3 (2002): 1–24, and "Gramsci's Concept of Subaltern Social Groups," PhD dissertation, political science, York University, Toronto, 2006; and Peter Ives, *Gramsci's Politics of Language: Engaging the Bakhtin Circle and the Frankfurt School* (Toronto: University of Toronto Press, 2004), and *Language and Hegemony in Gramsci* (London: Pluto Press, 2004).

3. The first two "special notebooks" in Gramsci's prison *opus* deal directly with idealism and materialism. Notebook 10 ("The Philosophy of Benedetto Croce") contains Gramsci's critique of Croce's idealism, and in Notebook 11 ("Introduction to the Study of Philosophy"), Gramsci critiques Nikolai Bukharin's positivist conception of Marxism.

4. Kate Crehan, *Culture and Anthropology* (London: Pluto Press, 2002), 98.

5. Crehan, 104.

6. Crehan, 115–19.

7. Q11§12; Antonio Gramcsi, *Selections from the Prison Notebooks*, ed. and trans. Quintin Hoare and Geoffrey Nowell-Smith (New York: International Publishers 1971), 326–27, hereafter cited as SPN.

8. In contrast to the familiar notion of "common sense" in contemporary Anglo-American usage, as sound and uncomplicated judgment, the Gramscian notion of "common sense" draws on the Italian spectrum going from *senso comune* (common sense) to *buon senso* (good sense). In this context, "common sense" refers more literally to beliefs that are common, modes of thought, opinions and conceptions of the

world held by the masses, and "good sense" has more of the English resonance of "common sense" as good practical judgment. See editor's note in SPN, 323n1.

9. Fabio Frosini, *Gramsci e la Filosofia: Saggio sui Quaderni del Carcere* (Rome: Carocci, 2003), 170–76, and chapter 10 of this volume. See also Q3§48, PN2, 51; Q4§18, PN2, 159–60; Q8§173 and §175, PN3, 333–34 and 335–36.

10. Benedetto Croce, "The Identity of Philosophy and the Moral Life," in *My Philosophy and Other Essays on the Moral and Political Problems of Our Time*, trans. E. F. Carritt (London: George Allen & Unwin, 1949 [1928]), 226.

11. Croce, 226.

12. Frosini, chapter 9 of this volume, pages 171–86. Frosini explores Gramsci's concept of "translatability" in this context, which is obviously related to Gramsci's approach to language. Here we wish to add to Frosini's focus (also in Frosini, *Gramsci e la filosofia*) on Gramsci's engagement with philosophy—what he astutely sees as the translatability between theory and practice—with our focus on the fragmentation of common sense from the perspective not of philosophers like Croce or Gentile, but the subaltern classes. Derek Boothman's discussison of translation is also important here, but well beyond the scope of this essay. See chapter 8 in this volume and Derek Boothman, *Traducibilità e Processi Traduttivi* (Perugia: Guerra Edizioni, 2004).

13. See André Tosel, chapter 16 of this volume, page 275; Q8§220, PN3, 369.

14. Andrew Robinson, "Towards an Intellectual Reformation: The Critique of Common Sense and the Forgotten Revolutionary Project of Gramscian Theory," in *Images of Gramsci: Connections and Contentions in Political Theory and International Relations*, ed. Andreas Bieler and Adam David Morton (New York: Routledge, 2006), 76, 83.

15. Guido Liguori, *Sentieri Gramsciani* (Rome: Carocci, 2006), 79.

16. Q8§175, PN3, 333–34.

17. Liguori, 78. While it is well beyond the scope of this chapter, our position is to insist on the importance of Gramsci's discussion of "immanence" in the process of transforming common sense to good sense and the philosophy of praxis; see, for example, Peter Thomas, "Immanence," *Historical Materialism* 16 (2008): 239–43; Ives, *Language and Hegemony*, 84–90; Frosini, *Gramsci e la Filosofia*, 143–49. This theme is also connected to Gramsci's use of "immanent grammar" as synonymous with "spontaneous grammar" discussed below.

18. De Mauro, chapter 3 of this volume, page 59. See also Frosini, *Gramsci e la Filosofia*, especially 30–33 and 168–82.

19. Frantz Fanon, *The Wretched of the Earth*, trans. Richard Philcox (New York: Grove Press 2004), 63–96.

20. Q3§48, PN2, 48. The bracketed insertions are Gramsci's.

21. Liguori, 74–75.

22. Francesco Paolo Colucci, "The Relevance to Psychology of Antonio Gramsci's Ideas on Activity and Common Sense," in *Perspectives on Activity Theory*, ed. Yrjö Engeström, Reijo Miettinen and Raija-Leena Punamäki-Gitai (New York: Cambridge University Press, 1999).

23. Q10II§44, SPN, 349.

24. Q11§12, SPN, 323.

25. Q11§12, SPN, 323.

26. Q11§12, SPN, 323.

27. Frosini, *Gramsci e la Filosofia*, 99.

28. See Boothman, *Traducibilità*, 27–50; Ives, *Gramsci's Politics of Language*, 20–37; Ives, *Language and Hegemony*, 43–53; and Frosini, *Gramsci e la Filosofia*, 38–41.

29. Tullio De Mauro, *Storia Linguistica Dell'Italia Unità* (Bari: Editori Laterza 1986), 43; and Howard Moss, "Language and Italian National Identity," in *Politics of Italian National Identity*, ed. Bruce Haddock and Gino Bedani (Cardiff: University of Wales Press, 2000), 98–123, 200.

30. De Mauro, *Storia Linguistica*, 95.

31. Antonio Gramsci, "La Lingua Unica e l'Esperanto," *Il Grido del Popolo* (February 16, 1918), translation in Antonio Gramsci, *Selections from Cultural Writings*, ed. David Forgacs, trans. William Boelhower (Cambridge, Mass.: Harvard University Press, 1985), 26–31, hereafter cited as SCW.

32. Q11§12, SPN, 328; Q1§65, PN1, 173. Also see Q1§89; Q4§3; and Q24§4.

33. Marcia Landy, *The Folklore of Consensus: Theatricality in the Italian Cinema, 1930–1943* (Albany: State University of New York Press, 1998), 4.

34. Marcia Landy, "Culture and Politics in the Work of Antonio Gramsci," *Boundary 2*, 14, 3 (1986): 49–70, 57.

35. Q27§1, SCW, 191.

36. Crehan, 108, and Q9§15, SCW, 194.

37. Q8§173, PN3, 333; Q11§13, SPN, 419.

38. Q4§18, PN2, 160; Q11§44; Antonio Gramsci, *Further Selections from the Prison Notebooks*, ed. and trans. Derek Boothman (Minneapolis: University of Minnesota Press, 1995), 301.

39. Q8§204, PN3, 351–52; Q1§12 and §13, SPN, 323, 421.

40. Q8§213III, PN3, 360.

41. Q11§12, SPN, 326.

42. Q11§13, SPN, 422. See also Q8§173 and Robert Dombroski, *Antonio Gramsci* (Boston: Twayne Publishers, 1989), 12–13.

43. Frosini argues, as do we, that Gramsci's redefinition of "common sense" highlights that it is not unitary and static but continually being transformed and redefined, that its role in unifying a social group depends on the way that the common sense comes about and that it must be actively utilized so that it becomes "ours." Frosini, *Gramsci e la Filosofia*, 170–76.

44. Q11§13, SPN, 419.

45. This argument can be taken as a defense of Gramsci in the face of José Nun's critique that he is overly critical of common sense in contrast to philosophy and postulates a "radical asepsis of common sense, defined as the opposite of philosophy." José Nun, "Elements for a Theory of Democracy: Gramsci and Common Sense," *Boundary 2*, 14, 3 (1986): 197–229, 222.

46. On Gramsci's Socratic conception of culture, see Gramsci, "Socialism and Culture" (January 29, 1916), in Antonio Gramsci, *Selections from Political Writings, 1910–1920*, trans. John Mathews, ed. Quintin Hoare (Minneapolis: University of Minnesota Press, 1977), 10–13; "Philanthropy, Good Will and Organization" (December 24, 1917), in SCW, 23–26; and Q11§12.

47. Q29§2, SCW, 182.

48. De Mauro, *Storia Linguistica*, 58–59.

49. The entire exchange is available online at www.andreamontagner.it/?p=43.

50. Manzoni was a Romanticist who rejected the classicists' attraction to the "purity" of literary Italian. Instead, very influenced by German Romanticism, Manzoni upheld actual spoken languages as being "living" languages, as expressive, beautiful, creative and productive. As Bruce Haddock notes, Italian Romanticism was not associated with conservative and reactionary views as it was in Germany; Bruce Haddock, "State, Nation and Rigorgimento," in *Politics of Italian National Identity*, ed. Bruce Haddock and Gino Bedani (Cardiff: University of Wales Press, 2000), 23.

51. SCW, 28–29.

52. See Ives, *Gramsci's Politics of Language*, 24–30; Franco Lo Piparo, *Lingua, intellettuali, egemonia in Gramsci* (Rome: Laterza, 1979), 67–102; and Sebastiano Timpanaro, "Graziadio Ascoli" *Belfagor* 27, no. 2 (1972): 149–76. This argument has interesting parallels with much of the work being done by sociolinguists concerning "varieties of English," such as Braj Kachru and others. See Braj B. Kachru, *Asian Englishes Beyond the Canon* (Hong Kong: Hong Kong University Press, 2005).

53. Antonio Gramsci, *Letters from Prison*, two volumes, trans. Ray Rosenthal, ed. Frank Rosengarten (New York: Columbia University Press), volume 1, 89, hereafter cited as LP1 and LP2. While we may want to reject his distinction here between "dialect" and "language" (e.g., Jonathan Steinberg, "The Historian and the *Questione della Lingua*," in *The Social History of Language*, ed. Peter Burke and Roy Porter [Cambridge: Cambridge University Press, 1987], 199; Robert Phillipson, *Linguistic Imperialism* [Oxford: Oxford University Press, 1992], 38–40), Gramsci may also be thinking of the argument made by his professor, Bartoli, that the role of the Sardinian language had been underappreciated in the history of Italian vernaculars. Moreover, Franco Lo Piparo contends persuasively that Gramsci posits an isomorphic relation between national language and dialect and those of city/country and official culture/folklore (Lo Piparo, 179–89).

54. LP2, 356.

55. LP1, 240.

56. Q29§2, SCW, 180–81, emphasis added.

57. Q5§156, SCW, 195.

58. Q1§43, PN1, 128.

59. Q1§65, PN1, 173. Gramsci rewrites this section in Q24§4—the "special notebook" on "Journalism"—adding "good sense" to "common sense" in the first line. This has clear resonances with his 1918 critique of Esperanto, which concludes: "Each new social stratum that emerges in history, that organizes itself for the good fight, introduces new currents and new uses into the language and explodes the fixed schemes established by the grammarians for the fortuitous convenience of teaching. . . . New moral and intellectual curiosities goad the spirit and compel it to renew itself, to improve itself, to change the linguistic forms of expression by taking them from foreign languages, by reviving dead forms and by changing meanings and grammatical functions." SCW, 31.

60. Q8, §173, PN3, 333–34.

61. Karl Marx and Friedrich Engels, *The German Ideology* (New York: International Publishers, 1970), 64.

62. Q11§13, SPN, 419–25. See also Crehan, 108–10.

63. Q11§13, SPN, 420.

64. Q1§89, PN1, 186; Q27§1, SCW, 188–91.
65. Q8§153, PN3, 321.
66. Q1§44, PN2 1992, 136–37; Q19§24, SPN, 59.
67. Q19§3, QC, 1973.
68. Q12§1, SPN, 6.
69. Q21§5, SCW, 208.
70. Q3§76, SCW, 169, 168.
71. Q3§76, SCW, 167–68, 169.
72. Q3§48, PN2, 48–52.
73. Q16§9, SPN, 395–96.
74. Q11§55, QC, 1482–83; Q13§1, SPN, 125–33.
75. Q15§13, QC, 1771.
76. Q25§5, SPN, 52. See Green, "Gramsci Cannot Speak," 9–10.
77. Q13§17, SPN, 177–85.
78. Q11§12, SPN, 337.

Index

Adorno, Theodor, 304
Albanian, 85
Alberti, Leon Battista, 121
Alighieri, Dante, 59, 85, 94
alphabetization, 57–58, 91
Ambrosoli, Luigi, 3
Americanism, 97n37, 232
Amodio, Luciano, 256
anarchism, 298
Anderson, Perry, 38
Asor Rosa, Alberto, 262
Ascoli, Graziadio Isaia, 19, 25, 32–34, 37–38, 45, 47n17, 53–56, 71–74, 84–85, 98n39, 103, 258, 263–64, 300
Austin, J. L., 67
Austro-Marxism, 269
automatism, 220

Bachelard, Gaston, 66
Badaloni, Nicola, 72, 184n7, 187–88
Bakhtin, Mikhail, 6
Bakunin, Mikhail, 95n2
Baldelli, Ignazio, 257
Balibar, Etienne, 101
Balibar, Renée, 41
Baratta, Giorgio, 101

Bartoli, Matteo, 2, 19, 22–25, 29–31, 34–38, 48n25, 53–55, 71, 73, 85, 139, 144, 164n16, 256, 262, 264, 294, 311n53
base (economic). *See* superstructure and (economic) structure or base
Bassnet, Susan, 11
Bellamy, Richard, 7
Berger, John, 238
Berneri, Camillo, 236
Bernstein, Basil, 70
Bertoni, Giulio, 34–36, 48n28, 144
Bettelheim, Bruno, 149, 156
Betti, Emilio, 128
bilingualism, 58. *See also* multilingualism
Bloomfield, Leonard, 68
Bobbio, Norberto, 167n62
Bochmann, Klaus, 94n1
Bonaparte, Napoleon, 173, 181, 194, 196, 218
Boothman, Derek, 10, 11, 135
Bordiga, Amadeo, 237, 248
Borghese, Lucia, 7, 8, 9–10, 15n37
Bourdieu, Pierre, 6
Bréal, Michel, 53, 54, 59, 60, 263
Brecht, Bertolt, 3, 160, 162

Brothers Grimm, 9, 137, 139–42, 146, 148–58, 161, 167n66
Bruni, Francesco, 258
Bruno, Giordano, 190
Brunot, Ferdinand, 41
Buci-Glucksmann, Christine, 38, 72
Buck-Morss, Susan, 7
Buey, Francisco F., 5, 6, 7, 8
Bühler, Karl, 58
Bukharin, Nikolai, 111, 146, 147, 173, 189–90, 206n13, 207n19, 217, 230, 236, 270–73, 275, 280, 290, 292, 308n3
Buttigieg, Joseph, 12

Calvino, Italo, 61
Cameron, Deborah, 6
capitalism, 72, 90, 220, 238, 246, 249, 250–51, 290, 298; global, 72, 220
Carannante, Antonio, 51, 256
Carlucci, Alessandro, 4
Cassirer, Ernst, 117
catharsis, 172–75, 184n7, 216–18, 220, 277–78, 283
Catholic Church, 295, 305; and culture/ideology, 41, 43, 92, 303, 306
causality, 184n10, 201, 276–78, 280, 284
China, 42–43, 145
Chinese (language), 144–45, 166n48
Chinese Revolution, 234
Chomsky, Noam, 6, 64–69
Cicero, Marcus Tullius, 262
cinema, 11, 44, 53, 239
civil society, 8, 11, 21, 24, 46, 72–73, 143, 167n62, 192–93, 208n38, 228–29, 246, 252, 273
class, 9, 21, 27, 31, 33–34, 37–46, 57, 61, 70, 75, 101–2, 112, 118, 119, 130, 147, 181, 182, 202, 231–32, 234–35, 237–38, 246, 247–48, 251, 268, 270–71, 280, 296, 303, 305, 309n12; ruling/governing, 37, 43, 45, 303, 306; working, 73, 92, 145, 244, 248, 301. *See also* subalternity
code, restricted and elaborated, 70

coercion, 7, 25, 158, 247
collective will, 24, 26–27, 219–20, 223n31, 283–84. *See also* national-popular
Comintern. *See* Third International
common sense, 6, 9, 26, 39, 70, 76, 83, 89, 92, 151, 158, 162, 172, 175, 178–80, 271, 275–76, 278, 280–84, 289–312
Communist Party (Italian), 20, 23, 57, 71, 79, 147, 258, 260
competence, linguistic, 46, 64, 66, 68
conformism (linguistic), 27, 44, 59, 64, 73, 74, 220, 224n54, 278, 284, 301
consensus, 25, 33, 79, 91, 93, 249
consent, 7, 25, 143, 223n25, 246, 251
Contini, Gianfranco, 258
Cortellazzo, Michele, 257
cosmopolitanism, 10, 21–22, 24–25, 32, 41–43, 85, 87, 243, 306
Cox, Robert, 8
Crehan, Kate, 290, 293, 296
critical linguistics, 52
Croce, Benedetto, 9, 24, 34–36, 43, 45–46, 48n28, 53–56, 58–59, 85, 92–94, 96n11, 108–9, 111, 117–21, 130, 137, 145, 162, 166n49, 172, 174, 176–77, 179–80, 195–96, 199, 201–6, 209n73, 210n83, 216–17, 223n40, 236, 251, 259–61, 267, 270–71, 273–79, 290–91
Cronin, Michael, 10, 11
culture/cultural, 3, 6, 8, 10, 11, 20, 23, 25–27, 37–43, 53, 57–61, 65, 73–76, 79, 82, 87–88, 90, 95n3, 97n28, 99n46, 104, 109, 113–14, 119, 123–25, 135–36, 139, 144–46, 158, 162, 171–72, 175–81, 183, 189–90, 194–96, 198, 209n73, 215–16, 227–39, 244, 257, 259, 261–62, 270, 303–5; bourgeois, 146; difference/diversity, 4, 35–39, 102; hegemony, 27, 45, 61, 231–32; high, 121, 270; Italian, 20–21, 35, 42, 46n3, 260, 302, 305; popular, 93–94, 121, 145, 243, 270, 273, 276, 279–80, 283–84, 290, 292–94,

296, 298, 300; sociology of, 19; studies, 1, 2; subaltern, 34, 231

Cuoco, Vincenzo, 130

Dante. *See* Alighieri, Dante

d'Azeglio, Massimo, 294

De Giovanni, Biagio, 186n39, 188–89

Del Noce, Augusto, 209n72, 210n79, 210n83

De Martino, Ernesto, 243

De Mauro, Tullio, 3, 49n52, 69, 70, 75, 79n35, 79n40, 128, 143, 227, 287n50, 292

democracy, 4, 24–25, 56, 57, 65, 73–74, 79, 228, 237, 246–48, 260, 284

democratic centralism, 246, 248, 249

Derrida, Jacques, 8

Derwing, Bruce, 66–68

De Sanctis, Francesco, 73, 159, 256

Devoto, Giacomo, 257

dialect, 6, 21, 27, 30–31, 33, 35–38, 40–42, 45, 52–54, 56–57, 64, 68–70, 73–76, 82, 84–89, 93, 144, 149, 168n72, 232, 245, 249, 264, 281, 283–84, 295, 297–302, 305; of society, 42, 307–8

dialectic, 6, 21, 36, 39, 54, 64, 88, 160, 162, 172, 186n36, 196, 201–2, 213, 215, 217, 221, 230–31, 245, 249–50, 262, 270, 273, 275, 281, 285, 291

dialogic, 230–31, 237

discourse, 108, 110–13, 115, 118, 120–22, 125–30, 177, 190, 194–95, 198, 228–30, 240, 243–44, 247, 303; analysis, 2

Dittmar, Norbert, 70

Dostoevsky, Fyodor, 238

Doyal, Len, 116

Eckermann, Johann Peter, 137, 140–41, 145

education, 2, 34, 45, 65, 74–76, 79n39, 83–84, 87–89, 92, 94, 139, 142, 157–62, 178, 227

Egerman, E. Ja., 48n25

Einaudi, Luigi, 113, 115, 137, 208n54

Elia, Annibale, 68–69

Engels, Friedrich, 33, 58, 82, 95, 107, 114–15, 120, 158, 178, 182, 184n10, 186n36, 202–3, 230, 259, 275, 303

Engler, Rudolf, 75

English (language), 21, 125, 140, 143, 234, 243, 311n52

Enlightenment, 32, 65, 88, 249, 269, 279, 297

Esperanto, 32, 43, 86–87, 144, 198, 295, 297, 299, 302

ethnocentrism, 236

evolution, in linguistics, 144, 172, 217

faith, 118, 145, 162

false consciousness, 10, 102, 213

falsification, 66

Fanon, Frantz, 293

Farinelli, Arturo, 139, 145, 159, 163n15, 167n66

fascism, 57–59, 85, 92–94, 96n11, 99n46, 163n15, 237, 247–48, 260

feminism, 2, 6, 250

Ferrari, Giuseppe, 110, 215

Feuerbach, Ludwig, 120, 162, 173, 183, 189, 196, 202–3, 219, 274

Finck, Franz Nikolaus, 48n25, 137–44

First International, 82, 86, 235

Firth, J. Raymond, 69, 128

folklore, 24, 34, 40, 74, 143, 158, 290, 294–97, 299, 302–3, 306–7

Fontana, Benedetto, 4

Fordism, 73, 75, 97n37, 254n35, 261. *See also* Americanism; Taylorism

Foucault, Michel, 6

fragmentation: of common sense and philosophy, 201, 263, 290, 292, 297–98, 300–302, 304, 307–8; of language, 42, 144, 301–2, 307–8. *See also* dialect

Francioni, Gianni, 112, 267, 253n29, 267, 275

Frankfurt School, 261

freedom, 42, 125, 137, 173, 197, 213, 217–18, 220, 224n51, 279

Frege, Gottlob, 67

French Revolution, 41, 86, 110, 130, 179–80, 182–83, 194–96, 218, 269, 270

Frosini, Fabio, 7, 10, 11, 132n51, 291, 293–94, 310n43

Fubini, Elsa, 156

Gadda, Carlo Emilio, 61

Gandhi, Mahatma, 7

Garin, Eugenio, 209n73

gender, 119, 250. *See also* feminism

generational difference, 5, 22, 45, 160, 228–29, 238

Gensini, Stefano, 3, 6, 255, 256, 258

Gentile, Giovanni, 9, 45–46, 58, 85, 117, 158, 174, 196, 199, 201, 204–5, 208n54, 209n72, 210n79, 210n83, 259–60, 267, 271–73, 291, 301n12

Gentzler, Edwin, 9, 11, 14n17

Gerratana, Valentino, 5, 9, 12, 43, 48n25, 52, 72, 132n51, 137, 139–40, 142, 156, 164nn19–21, 165n30, 166n48, 166n56, 167n62, 206n13

Gestalt psychology, 58

Giarrizzo, Giuseppe, 57

Gill, Stephen, 8

Gilliéron, Jules, 25, 31, 37–38, 71

Gioberti, Vincenzo, 117–18

global civil society, 11. *See also* civil society

globalization, 4, 8, 10–11, 220, 232, 292

Gobetti, Piero, 52, 104n1, 130, 236

Godel, Robert, 69, 75

Godelier, Maurice, 98n45

Goethe, Johann Wolfgang von, 137, 140–41, 143, 145–46, 166n50, 230

Goldmann, Lucien, 103, 130

grammar, 4, 23–24, 27, 32, 34, 43–46, 57, 59–60, 66, 82, 140, 198, 224n55, 230–31, 258, 284, 295, 298, 301; historical, 43–44, 230; immanent, 44–45, 60, 75, 301, 309n17; normative, 27, 44–46, 59, 75, 231–32, 298, 301; spontaneous, 27, 44, 301, 309n17; transformational, 66

Gramsci, Carlo, 142, 156, 164n21

Gramsci, Delio, 86, 149, 157, 159

Gramsci, Giuliano, 85, 149, 300

Gramsci Paulesu, Teresina, 30, 74, 86, 142, 148, 156, 159, 300

Greek, 4, 76, 85, 118, 161, 180, 245

Green, Marcus, 12

Grimm, Wilhelm and Jakob. *See* Brothers Grimm

Gruppi, Luciano, 38

Guha, Ranajit, 7

Habermas, Jürgen, 6

Haddock, Bruce, 311n50

Hall, Stuart, 1, 5, 13n7

Halliday, Michael, 66

Hardt, Michael, 292

Harris, Roger, 116–17

Haug, Wolfgang Fritz, 3, 107–8

Hegel, Georg Wilhelm Friedrich, 58–59, 110, 114–15, 117–20, 159, 163n15, 165n45, 179–80, 182–83, 186n36, 189, 193, 196–98, 201–3, 205, 218, 248, 251, 259, 285

hegemony, 2, 4, 7–8, 13n7, 23–27, 38–41, 45–46, 61, 70–73, 76, 103, 143, 172, 174, 182, 183, 184n2, 214–16, 218–21, 228, 231–32, 238, 243, 246, 257, 262, 269, 270, 275–77, 279–80, 289–90, 292, 296, 305–7; sources of the concept, 4, 23, 26, 38, 71–74, 103, 219, 231

Heidegger, Martin, 130

Helsloot, Niels, 52

historical bloc, 188, 191, 201–2, 220, 238, 250–51, 274, 276–77, 279, 282, 284

historicism, 3, 11, 36–37, 71, 114, 119, 136, 160, 162, 187, 191, 193–94, 198, 207n27, 209n69, 214, 217, 223n31, 239–40, 251, 256–57, 275, 278

Holborow, Marnie, 6

homology, 70, 103, 127

Houdebine, Jean Louis, 6

humanism, 145, 163n15, 273, 277

human nature, 87, 158, 273–74

Humboldt, Wilhelm von, 117, 144, 165n45, 264

identity politics, 2, 10, 234
ideology, 6, 10, 32, 40, 70, 102, 120, 157, 178, 182, 186n39, 199–200, 215–17, 220, 228–29, 238, 243, 247, 268, 276, 286, 296, 297; critique, 10, 70, 175, 182, 297
illiteracy. *See* literacy
India, 7
individuality/individualism, 27, 237
intellectuals, 20–26, 27, 29–35, 38, 41–44, 53–54, 56–57, 61, 64–65, 71–72, 75, 85, 89–93, 104, 114, 119, 130, 143, 145, 162, 175, 178, 180–81, 191–92, 194, 215, 217, 229, 231, 235, 237–40, 243, 246–50, 256, 268–71, 275–76, 279–80, 284, 289–91, 294, 301, 304–7; and irony, 239; organic, 91–93, 215, 306; traditional, 91–93, 215, 291, 305–6
International. *See* First International; Second International; Third International
International Encyclopedia of Linguistics, 52
internationalism, 57, 235
international language, 32, 86–87, 236, 299. *See also* Esperanto
international political economy, 1, 8
irony, 154, 159–62, 239, 264, 277

Jablonka, Frank, 3
Jacobinism, 24, 84, 86, 88, 107, 110–13, 117–18, 181–82, 194, 215, 282
Jakobson, Roman, 66, 77n11, 78n19
jargon, 37, 75, 113, 228, 240
Jervolino, Domenico, 9, 183n2
journalism, 53, 237, 311n59

Kachru, Braj, 311n52
Kant, Immanuel, 58, 113, 117, 179–80, 195, 259, 263, 291
Kautsky, Karl, 57
Klein, Gabriella, 96n11

Klemperer, Victor, 98n37
Kristeva, Julia, 6
Kuhn, Thomas, 110, 128, 130

labor, 89–90, 94, 117, 235, 247, 249–50, 284
Labov, William, 6, 65, 69–70
Labriola, Antonio, 165n45, 177, 204, 267, 269–74
Laclau, Ernesto, 1, 3, 6
Ladin (language), 85
Landy, Marcia, 296
language: games, 4, 67, 193; imprecision of, 121; national, standardized, 1, 40, 87, 283, 294–95, 297–300, 305; unified, 32, 44–45, 60–61, 102, 178, 295. *See also* Wittgenstein, Ludwig
Laporte, Dominique, 41
Latin, 21, 30, 37, 41, 43, 46n3, 55, 118, 123, 127, 161, 180, 245, 262, 306
Lecercle, Jacques, 6
Lefevere, André, 8, 11
Leibniz, Gottfried, 203
Lenin, Vladimir, 2, 21, 23, 26, 38, 57–58, 73, 82–83, 95n3, 97n34, 103, 109, 114, 129–30, 136, 197–98, 214–16, 218–19, 230, 234–35, 248, 259, 298
Leont'ev, Aleksei N., 261
Leopardi, Giacomo, 102, 104, 264
Lexicon Grammaticorum, 52
Lexis, Wilhelm, 115
liberalism, 6, 19, 45, 71–72, 113, 130, 181, 194, 238, 247, 279, 290, 305, 308
Lichtner, Maurizio, 3, 10–11, 186n39
Liguori, Guido, 292–93
linguistic diversity, 4, 6, 38, 232, 250
literacy, 79n41, 84–85, 87, 96n25, 295, 299
Lombardo Radice, Guiseppe, 59–60, 89, 96n11
Lo Piparo, Franco, 2–6, 29, 35, 37–38, 46, 52, 59, 70–74, 95n4, 103, 143, 227, 255, 256–58, 263

Lovecchio, Antonino, 271
Low, David, 252n12
Lukács, Georg, 130, 166n53
Lunacharsky, Anatoly, 121
Luria, Alexander, 78n16, 261
Luxemburg, Rosa, 95n5
Lyons, John, 67

Maas, Utz, 3, 7, 8
Machiavelli, Niccolò, 21, 27, 53, 103,
    111–13, 129, 161, 272–73
Malinowski, Bronislaw, 69, 124
Mangoni, Luisa, 253n29
Manzoni, Alessandro, 21–22, 27, 32,
    34, 46n3, 54, 56–57, 60, 71–72, 84,
    256, 262, 295, 297–300
Marcuse, Herbert, 130
Maruin, Joaquim, 236
Marx, Karl, 2, 21, 54, 58, 82, 91,
    102, 107, 110–11, 114, 120, 122,
    129, 137, 141, 147, 171–72, 174,
    179–83, 187–92, 194–96, 199–201,
    203–4, 213–14, 216–17, 219, 230,
    235–36, 238, 250, 259, 261–62,
    269, 273, 282, 303
Marxism, 3, 10, 19–20, 23–24, 26, 29,
    38, 108, 111, 130, 146–47, 171–72,
    187, 189, 192–93, 195, 197–99,
    204, 214, 217, 229–30, 234, 236,
    244, 267–70, 273–75, 280, 290,
    298
Marzani, Carl, 108, 109, 130
mathematics, 11, 58, 64, 66, 102, 113,
    115, 121, 127, 136, 182, 191, 229,
    251
Mazzini, Giuseppe, 95n2
McKey, William, 58
Meillet, Antoine, 25, 37–38, 71, 262
metaphor, 8–11, 52, 63, 65, 73, 75,
    109, 114, 123, 125, 127, 129, 136,
    146, 159, 160–61, 186n39, 187–93,
    198, 204, 215, 227–29, 245, 251,
    264, 293, 307; Marx's use of, 123–
    29, 188–93, 204
Migliorini, Bruno, 257
Milani, Don Lorenzo, 61
Milton, John, 164n25

mimesis, 143
modernism, 127
morphology, 53, 166n48, 264
Morton, Adam David, 8
Mouffe, Chantal, 1, 3, 6
multiculturalism, 2, 10, 232, 292, 297,
    308
multilingualism, 53, 57, 59, 74,
    97n28
Muscetta, Carlo, 156

Napoleon. *See* Bonaparte, Napoleon
nation, 24, 7–8, 19, 24, 26–27, 33,
    37, 41, 43–44, 53–54, 57, 59, 61,
    74–75, 82, 84–85, 93, 101, 109–11,
    113–14, 116–17, 122, 124–27,
    135–36, 144, 175, 177–82, 194–97,
    232, 234–35, 247, 251, 260, 292,
    295, 298–99, 305–6
nationalism, 8, 82, 95n2, 232
national-popular, 24, 27, 33, 45, 61,
    72, 101, 143, 232, 243, 299. *See also*
    people-nation
nation-state, 7, 19, 72, 295
Negri, Antonio, 292
neo-grammarians, 2, 22, 29, 31, 34–37,
    59, 63, 71, 84, 264–65, 294
neo-linguistics, 22, 25, 29, 31, 34–37,
    71. *See also* Bartoli, Matteo
Nida, Eugene A., 123–24
normative grammar. *See* grammar
Nun, José, 310n45

objectivity, 58, 200–201, 272
October Revolution. *See* Russian
    Revolution
ordinary language philosophy, 4, 67
organic intellectuals. *See* intellectuals

Paggi, Leonardo, 72, 147, 163, 280
Pagliaro, Antonino, 58
Pareto, Vilfredo, 229, 256
parthenogenesis, 217
Pascoli, Giovanni, 230
Pasolini, Pier Paolo, 3, 61, 94, 99n49,
    245, 258
Passaponti, Emilia, 3, 256

passive revolution, 73, 182–83, 246, 250–51, 289, 305
Paul, Hermann, 36
Paulesu, Mimma, 156
people-nation, 24, 27, 45, 181, 306
Perrault, Charles, 149
phonetics, 41, 264
Piaget, Jean, 58
Pirandello, Luigi, 22, 230
Plekhanov, Georgi, 268
polyvocality, 160
Popper, Karl, 66
post-Marxism, 2, 244
postmodernism, 127, 238, 249, 292, 297, 308
poststructuralism, 1–2
pragmatism, 53, 59, 113, 129, 174, 178, 191, 217, 229, 236, 256
Prague structuralism (the Prague School), 58, 68
prediction, 173, 184n7
prestige, 7, 25–26, 38, 44, 53, 71–72, 84–85, 300. *See also* hegemony
Prestipino, Giuseppe, 10
Prieto, Luis, 69, 75
Proletkult, 90, 97n37
Prometheus, 145–46
Proudhon, Pierre-Joseph, 110, 183

Quine, W. V. O., 116
Quinet, Edgar, 130

race, 8, 142
Reformation, 119, 269–70, 279–80
regulated society, 130, 249–51, 253n35
reification, 187
relativism, 39, 175, 193, 235
Renaissance, 21, 269, 279
Renzi, Lorenzo, 257
Restoration, 181, 194
revolution, 11, 24–25, 70–71, 73, 75, 82–83, 92–93, 102, 146, 160, 179, 181–82, 196, 214, 216, 246, 248, 250–51, 273–74, 292. *See also* Chinese Revolution; French Revolution; passive revolution; Russian Revolution

Ricardo, David, 114–15, 125, 129, 218, 220, 282
Richter, Julius, 166n58
Risorgimento, 24, 27, 42, 71, 75, 84, 117, 181, 194, 215, 294, 304–5
Robespierre, Maximilien, 115
Robinson, Andrew, 291
Romagnuolo, Maria Rosaria, 286n29
Roman Empire, 21, 27, 46n3, 87
Romanticism, 33, 40–41, 82, 88, 139, 144, 163n15, 167n66, 311n50
Rosiello, Luigi, 3, 12, 51, 78n29, 255–57
Rossi, Teofilo, 148
Rossi-Landi, Ferruccio, 127
Russell, Bertrand, 229
Russian (language), 58, 136, 142–43, 233–34
Russian Revolution, 97n34, 109, 146, 198, 215, 218–19, 234, 247, 249

Said, Edward, 252n12
Salvioni, Carlo, 263
Sanguineti, Edoardo, 11
Sanguineti, Federico, 103
Sapegno, Natalino, 256
Sapir, Edward, 69
sarcasm, 93, 214, 239–40
Saussure, Ferdinand de, 2, 6, 12, 39, 60, 63–65, 67–69, 75, 96n22, 122, 163, 294
Savonarola, Girolamo, 228
Schiaffini, Alfredo, 56–57
Schirru, Giancarlo, 4, 57
Schmidt, Carl, 7
Schrödinger, Erwin, 115
Schucht, Julca (Julia), 11, 135, 139, 155, 157, 159, 164n22, 166n48, 233
Schucht, Tania (Tatiana), 21–22, 31, 71, 112, 114, 119, 121, 129, 141–42, 148, 164nn21–22, 233
Schumpeter, Joseph, 260
science, 9, 32, 36, 53, 63, 102, 108–10, 119, 127–28, 130, 144, 161, 175, 192, 198, 202, 247, 272, 274–76, 281, 293, 303

Searle, John, 67
Second International, 48n25, 82, 84, 95n2, 270
secularism, 151, 154–55, 157–58, 161–62, 200, 272
Selenu, Stefano, 4
semantics, 30, 52–53, 59, 64, 67–68, 75, 190, 227, 264
semiotics, 43, 63, 67
Sen, Amartya, 4
Serra, Renato, 159
Showstack Sassoon, Anne, 5
Siguan, Miguel, 58
Socialist Party (Italian), 25, 32, 166n50, 299
Socrates, 102, 162, 231, 298
Sorel, Georges, 277
Soriano, Marc, 256
Soviet Marxism, 23–24, 38, 58, 72, 121, 127, 280
Soviet Union, 57, 130, 152, 161, 280
Sozzi, Bartolo Tommasso, 51, 256
Spaventa, Silvio, 117
speech, 7, 12, 25, 30, 36–37, 39–41, 45, 53–54, 57, 60, 64, 90, 118, 128, 230, 243, 263, 282, 295, 299, 301, 305
Spender, Dale, 6
Spirito, Ugo, 208n54, 271
Spitzer, Leo, 263–64
Spivak, Gayatri, 1, 7
spoken language. *See* speech
spontaneity, 25–27, 31, 44, 46, 73, 84, 86, 88–89, 145, 155, 158, 161–62, 177–78, 194–95, 235, 248–49, 293–94, 296–98, 300–301, 306
spontaneous grammar. *See* grammar
Spriano, Paolo, 53
Sraffa, Piero, 4, 114, 125, 164n21
Stalin, Joseph, 57, 60, 95n3
state, 7–8, 20, 25, 27, 46, 54, 71–75, 82–84, 87, 90, 93, 112, 180–82, 232, 246–47, 252, 253n35, 269, 271, 273, 277, 280, 284, 295, 299, 305–7
Steinthal, Heymann, 34, 144, 165n45
Stowe, Harriet Beecher, 157–58

structuralism, 2, 58, 66, 68–69, 104, 294
Stussi, Alfredo, 258
subalternity, 7, 34, 40, 44, 159, 220, 231, 237, 269, 271, 276, 279–80, 284–85, 292–308
subaltern studies, 6
"superman" complex, 239
superstition, 103, 120, 145, 151, 162, 177, 236, 294–95
superstructure and (economic) structure or base, 10, 117, 123, 129, 135–36, 188–89, 192, 195–202, 205, 213, 215, 217–21, 245, 251, 268, 271–74, 276–78, 280
supplement of meaning, 283
syndicalists, 248
syntax, 21, 41, 64

Taber, C. R., 123–24
Tasca, Angelo, 237
Taylorism, 73, 90, 97n37, 261–62. *See also* Americanism; Fordism
Third International, 38, 82, 109, 234–35, 267, 270, 280
Timpanaro, Sebastiano, 263
Togliatti, Palmiro, 20, 23–24, 73
Tosel, André, 184n2, 184n7, 291, 303
Trincia, Francesco Saverio, 207n22, 210n83
Trotsky, Leon, 58, 259
Trubetzkoy, N. S., 68
Turgenev, Ivan, 238

Uncle Tom's Cabin, 157

Vailati, Giovanni, 113, 115, 129, 176, 256
value, economic, 273; linguistic, 63
Venuti, Lawrence, 8
Verfremdung-Effekt, 160
vernacular, 41, 300, 302. *See also* dialect
Vidossi, Giuseppe, 36
Vigotskij, Lev, 58, 75, 78n16, 261
Vincenti, Leonello, 146, 166n58
vocabulary, 41, 55

Voloshinov, V. N., 96n25
Volta, Alessandro, 272
Vossler, Karl, 36

war of position, 289
Weinreich, Uriel, 69
Whitney, William D., 263
Wittgenstein, Ludwig, 4, 6, 58, 67, 75,
  116, 121, 187, 193, 206n1

Wolin, Richard, 130
Woodfin, Fabiana, 13n7
world history, 8, 40, 59, 87, 284
written language, 21, 41–43, 46n3,
  47n17, 53–55, 56, 58, 60, 87, 89,
  91, 94, 144, 233, 255, 295, 299

Žižek, Slavoj, 10
Zola, Emile, 140

About the Contributors

Giorgio Baratta taught moral philosophy at the University of Urbino (Carlo Bo) before his untimely death just as this volume was going to press. He was one of the founders of the International Gramsci Society (IGS) and the president of the IGS-Italia. He published several books on Gramsci, including *Le Rose e i Quaderni: Il Pensiero Dialogico di Antonio Gramsci* (2003) and *Antonio Gramsci in Contrappunto* (2007). He made two films about Gramsci—*Gramsci l'ho Visto Così*, with Gianni Amico, and *New York e il Mistero di Napoli: Viaggio nel Mondo di Gramsci Raccontato da Dario Fo*—and a theatrical piece, *Dialogo di Gramsci con la Sua Ombra*. He is also the author of a book on Husserl and essays on Hölderlin, Marx and Sartre.

Derek Boothman teaches translation at the University of Bologna's faculty for interpreters and translators (SSLMIT). He edited and translated the anthology of Gramsci's writings *Further Selections from the Prison Notebooks* (1995). He has written extensively on Gramsci, including *Traducibilità e Processi Traduttivi: Un Caso: A. Gramsci Linguista* (2004). He is a member of Rome's Seminario gramsciano.

Lucia Borghese teaches German philology in the Deperment of Comparative Languages, Literatures, and Culture at the University of Florence. She has written several essays on Gramsci, edited Italian translations of Kafka and a volume on Heinrich Böll. She also coordinates the international doctorate course in German Philology Florence-Bonn.

Francisco F. Buey is professor of political philosophy at the University Pompeu Fabra, Barcelona, Spain, and Coordinator of the Center for the Study of Social Movements (CEMS). He was one of the founders of the Sindicato Democrático de la Universidad de Barcelona in 1966, and has been active in creating the Comisiones Obreras de la Enseñanza and the Consejo de Coordinación Universitaria. He has written many books and articles on Lenin, Gramsci, Marx and Einstein, including *Leyendo a Gramsci* (2001), *Ideas para una Globalización Alternativa* (2004) and *Utopías e Ilusiones Naturales* (2007).

Tullio De Mauro is one of Italy's most prominent linguists, the author of many books and essays, including *Storia Linguistica dell'Italia Unita* (originally 1963, with ten editions), *Introduzione alla Semantica* (1965), an introduction, translation and commentary to Ferdinand de Saussure's *Corso di Linguistica Generale* (1967) and, more recently, *La Fabbrica delle Parole* (2005). He has written extensively on Wittgenstein, semiotics and the philosophy of language and is the general editor of a major eight-volume Italian dictionary. He is also the director of the Department of Linguistic Science at the University of Rome La Sapienza. He has also been an active public intellectual and an elected politician, including as the minister of public education (2000–2001). He wrote the preface to Franco Lo Piparo's 1979 book, *Lingua, Intellettuali, Egemonia in Gramsci*.

Fabio Frosini is a research fellow in the Department of Philosophy, University of Urbino (Carlo Bo), Italy. He is author of many articles and books, including *Contingenza e Verità della Politica: Due Studi su Machiavelli* (2001), *Gramsci e la Filosofia: Saggio sui "Quaderni del Carcere"* (2003) and, most recently, *Da Gramsci a Marx: Ideologia, Verità, Politica* (2009). With Guido Liguori, from 2000 to 2006 Frosini coordinated the International Gramsci Society–Italy seminar on the vocabulary of Gramsci's *Prison Notebooks*.

Stefano Gensini teaches philosophy of language at the University of Rome "La Sapienza." He has written several essays and books on the history of the philosophy of language, linguistics and semiotics, including works on Condillac, Leibniz, Vico, Leopardi and Gramsci.

Marcus E. Green is assistant professor of political science at Otterbein College. He is secretary of the International Gramsci Society and author of "Gramsci Cannot Speak: Representations and Interpretations of Gramsci's Concept of the Subaltern" in *Rethinking Marxism* (2002).

Peter Ives teaches political theory in the politics department at the University of Winnipeg, Canada. He is author of *Gramsci's Politics of Language:*

Engaging the Bakhtin Circle and the Frankfurt School (2004) and *Language and Hegemony in Gramsci* (2004), and numerous articles on Gramsci, language politics, "global English," cosmopolitanism and global capitalism.

Rocco Lacorte is a PhD candidate at the University of Chicago completing a dissertation on Gramsci and Pasolini. He participates in the activities of the International Gramsci Society, Rome's Seminario gramsciano, and has written ten entries in the *Dizionario Gramsciano*, edited by G. Liguori and P. Voza (2009).

Maurizio Lichtner teaches general pedagogy at the University of Rome "La Sapienza." He studies learning processes and social and pedagogical research methodologies. He has published extensively on these topics, particularly on adult education and lifelong learning, including *Soggetti, percorsi, complessità sociale* (1990), *La Qualità delle Azioni Formative* (1999), *Valutare L'Apprendimento: Teorie e Metodi* (2004), *Esperienze Vissute e Costruzione del Sapere* (2008) and *Le Prime Parole: Diario di una Bambina* (1999).

Franco Lo Piparo is a full professor in the philosophy of language at the University of Palermo where he directs the Institute of the Theory and History of Ideas. He is author of one of the most important books on Gramsci and language, *Lingua, Intellettuali, Egemonia in Gramsci* (1979), and many other works, including *Linguaggi Macchine Formalizzazione* (1974), *Aristotele e il Linguaggio: Cosa fa di una Lingua una Lingua* (2003), *Filosofia, Lingua, Politica* (2004) and, most recently, *Comunista? La Chiave Linguistica dell'Originalità di Gramsci* (2008).

Utz Maas is professor of general and German linguistics at the University of Osnabrück, Germany. His work ranges from German phonetics and grammar to sociolinguistics, including Arabic and issues of migration and politics. He is author of *Sprachpolitik und Politische Sprachwissenschaft: Sieben Studien* (1989), *Sprache und Sprachen in der Migrationsgesellschaft: Die Schriftkulturelle Dimension* (2008) and *Phonologie: Einführung in die Funktionale Phonetik des Deutschen* (2006).

Luigi Rosiello taught linguistics at the University of Bologna before his death in 1993. He studied the philosophy of language and history of linguistic ideas, particularly those of the French philosophers of the Enlightenment, and wrote extensively on linguistics and structuralism and on linguistics and Marxism. Some of his most famous books include *Struttura, Uso e Funzioni della Lingua* (1965), *Linguistica e Marxismo* (1974) and *Letteratura e Strutturalismo* (1983).

Edoardo Sanguineti is a well-known Italian writer, poet, artist, translator and founder of the avant-garde movement *Gruppo 63*. From 1979 to 1983, he was a member of the Italian Parliament for the Partito Communista Italiano. He has translated Shakespeare, Joyce, Goethe and many others into Italian.

Anne Showstack Sassoon is emeritus professor in politics at Kingston University and visiting professor at Birkbeck, University of London. She has published many books and articles on the work of Antonio Gramsci, on civil society, citizenship and globalization, on the changing socioeconomic roles of women and the welfare state and on the politics of New Labor.

André Tosel is professor of philosophy at the University of Nice, France. He is the author of many volumes on Marxism, Spinoza and the political philosophy of liberalism and democracy. These include *Kant Révolutionnaire: Droit et Politique* (1988); *Marx et sa Critique de la Politique*, in collaboration with Cesare Luporini and Etienne Balibar (1979); *L'esprit de Scission: Études sur Marx, Gramsci, Lukács* (1991) and *Etudes sur Marx (et Engels)* (1998).